Islamic Political Thought

Islamic Political Thought

AN INTRODUCTION

◇◇◇

Gerhard Bowering, Editor

PRINCETON UNIVERSITY PRESS
PRINCETON AND OXFORD

Copyright © 2015 by Princeton University Press
Published by Princeton University Press, 41 William Street, Princeton,
New Jersey 08540
In the United Kingdom: Princeton University Press, 6 Oxford Street,
Woodstock, Oxfordshire OX20 1TW

press.princeton.edu

Jacket photograph © Cardaf/Shutterstock.

Library of Congress Cataloging-in-Publication Data

Islamic political thought : an introduction / Gerhard Bowering, editor.
    pages cm
  Includes bibliographical references and index.
  ISBN 978-0-691-16482-3 (pbk. : alk. paper) 1. Political science—Islamic
countries. 2. Political science—Philosophy. 3. Islam and state. 4. Islam and
politics. I. Böwering, Gerhard, 1939–
  JA84.I78I85 2015
  320.55'7—dc23   2014023882

British Library Cataloging-in-Publication Data is available

This book has been composed in Garamond Premier Pro and Gill Sans

Printed on acid-free paper. ∞

Printed in the United States of America

10 9 8 7 6 5 4 3 2 1

Contents ◇◇

Islamic Political Thought

Introduction ∞∞∞∞∞∞∞∞∞∞∞∞∞∞∞∞∞∞∞∞∞∞∞

Gerhard Bowering

Islamic Political Thought: An Introduction contains 16 chapters adapted from articles in *The Princeton Encyclopedia of Islamic Political Thought*, a reference work published in 2013. This volume, shorter and more streamlined than the parent work, presents broad, comprehensive discussions of central themes and core concepts. These chapters were designed to integrate and contextualize the contemporary political and cultural situation of Islam while also examining in depth the historical roots of that situation.

The Islamic World in Historical Perspective

In 2014, the year 1435 of the Muslim calendar, the Islamic world was estimated to account for a population of approximately a billion and a half, representing about one-fifth of humanity. In geographical terms, Islam occupies the center of the world, stretching like a big belt across the globe from east to west. From Morocco to Mindanao, it encompasses countries of both the consumer North and the disadvantaged South. It sits at the crossroads of America, Europe, and Russia on one side and black Africa, India, and China on the other. Historically, Islam is also at a crossroads, destined to play a world role in politics and to become the most prominent world religion during the 21st century. Islam is thus not contained in any national culture; it is a universal force.

The cultural reach of Islam may be divided into five geographical blocks: West and East Africa, the Arab world (including North Africa), the Turco-Iranian lands (including Central Asia, northwestern China, the Caucasus, the Balkans, and parts of Russia), South Asia (including Pakistan, Bangladesh, and many regions in India), and Southeast Asia (Indonesia, Malaysia, Singapore, and minorities in Thailand, the Philippines, and, by extension, Australia). Particularly in the past century, Islam has created the core of a sixth block: a diaspora of small but vigorous communities living on both sides of the Atlantic, in Europe (especially in France, Germany, Great Britain, the Netherlands, and Spain), and North America (especially in Canada, the United States, and the Caribbean).

Islam has grown consistently throughout history, expanding into new neighboring territories without ever retreating (except on the margins, as in Sicily and Spain, where it was expelled by force). It began in the seventh century as a small community in Mecca and Medina in the Arabian Peninsula, led by its messenger the Prophet Muhammad (d. 632), who was eventually to unite all the Arab tribes under the banner of Islam. Within the first two centuries of its existence, Islam came into global prominence through its conquests of the Middle East, North Africa, the Iberian Peninsula, the Iranian lands, Central Asia, and the Indus valley. In the process and aftermath of these conquests, Islam inherited the legacy of the ancient Egyptian and Mesopotamian civilizations, embraced and transformed the heritage of Hellenistic philosophy and science, assimilated the subtleties of Persian statecraft, incorporated the reasoning of Jewish law and the methods of Christian theology, absorbed cultural patterns of Zoroastrian dualism and Manichean speculation, and acquired wisdom from Mahayana Buddhism and Indian philosophy and science. Its great cosmopolitan centers—Baghdad, Cairo, Córdoba, Damascus, and Samarqand—became the furnace in which the energy of these cultural traditions was converted into a new religion and polity. These major cities, as well as provincial capitals of the newly founded Islamic empire, such as Basra, Kufa, Aleppo, Qayrawan, Fez, Rayy (Tehran), Nishapur, and Sanaa merged the legacy of the Arab tribal tradition with newly incorporated cultural trends. By religious conversion, whether fervent, formal, or forced, Islam integrated heterodox and orthodox Christians of Greek, Syriac, and Latin rites, and included large numbers of Jews, Zoroastrians, Gnostics, and Manicheans. By ethnic assimilation, it absorbed a great variety of nations, whether through compacts, clientage and marriage, persuasion, threat, or through religious indifference, social climbing, and self-interest of newly conquered peoples. It embraced Aramaic-, Persian-, and Berber-speaking peoples, accommodated the disruptive incursions of Turks and the devastating invasion of Mongols into its territories, and sent out its emissaries, traders, immigrants, and colonists into the lands beyond the Indus valley, the semiarid plains south of the Sahara, and the distant shores of the Southeast Asian islands.

By transforming the world during the ascendancy of the Abbasid Empire (750–1258), Islam created a splendid cosmopolitan civilization built on the Arabic language; the message of its scripture, tradition, and law (Qur'an, hadith, and shari'a); and the wisdom and science of the cultures newly incorporated during its expansion over three continents. The practice of philosophy, medicine, and the sciences within the Islamic empire was at a level of sophistication unmatched by any other civilization; it secured pride of place in such diverse fields as architecture, philosophy, maritime navigation and trade, and commerce by land and sea, and saw the founding of the world's first universities. Recuperating from two centuries of relative political decentralization, it coalesced about the year 1500 in three great empires, the Ottomans in the West with Istanbul as their center, the Safavids in Iran with Isfahan as their hub, and the Mughals in the Indian subcontinent with Agra and Delhi as their axis.

As the Islamic world witnessed the emergence of these three empires, European powers began to expand their influence over the world during the age of global discoveries, westward across the Atlantic into the Americas, and eastward by charting a navigational route around Africa into the Indian Ocean, there entering into fierce competition with regional powers along the long-established network of trade routes between China on the one hand and the Mediterranean and East Africa on the other. The European exploration of the East and the growing ability to exploit an existing vast trade network, together with the inadvertent but eventually lucrative "discovery" of the New World, were to result in Europe's economic and political hegemony over the Islamic world, with which it had rubbed military and mercantile shoulders since the early Muslim conquests. The early modern Islamic world (and much of the rest of the world) fell definitively behind the West economically and politically with the advent of the Enlightenment in the 18th century and the Industrial Revolution in the 19th century.

By about 1800, small European nations (e.g., England, France, and Holland) had established rule over large regions of the Islamic world. Their trading companies and imperial outposts in distant Muslim lands were transformed into colonies of European supremacy that were eager to benefit from Western industrialization. It took until the end of World War II for the global geopolitical map to become reorganized into an array of discrete nation-states on the European model. Muslim nations perceived Islam not only as the way of life led by the majority of the population but also as the source of normative principles for social order.

In the 19th century two diametrically opposed trends would preoccupy the Muslim intelligentsia in their effort to effect social and religious renewal. Modernism proposed adapting Islam to Western ideals, while revivalism advocated restoring the vigor of the original dynamics of Islam; neither approach would lead to the utopia of a Pan-Islamic caliphate. Islam was now challenged to express itself within the framework of independent nations, with their focus on ethnicity, territoriality, and culture.

At the beginning of the 20th century, the Islamic world witnessed the explosion of Turkish secularism; in its middle period, it sought sovereignty and honor in Arab, Iranian, Pakistani, and Indonesian nationalism; at the end of the 20th century, it became increasingly dominated by militant trends. "Islamism," a fundamentalist reaction to Western ascendancy, calls for an Islamic state rigorously based on Islamic law; its public image is dominated by marginal yet high-profile extremists advocating the use of terrorist attacks and suicide martyr missions to achieve this end. Both Sunni and Shiʻi expressions of Islamism—in Algeria, Sudan, Iran, or Afghanistan—were inspired by their belief that if only Muslims were to return to their religious roots, God would grant them success in this world and bliss in the next. The past glory of the Islamic world would be restored, and the West would again study at its feet.

At the beginning of the 21st century, the world has drawn closer together through the power of advanced technology, the speed of global communication, and ubiquitous access to mobile phones and the Internet, including social network-ing services. Those advances enabled the annihilation of the Twin Towers in New York City on September 11, 2001, and other acts of terror that have occurred since that date. Yet they also may be nurturing a different response of Islam to the modern world, as rumblings of freedom, cries for liberation from corrupt regimes, and calls for democratic forms of government echo from Muslim lands through cyberspace.

The Evolution of Islamic Political Thought

The development of Islamic political thought tracks the differing positions Islam has occupied during its political expansion over the course of 14 centuries. Just as Islamic history both preserved its tradition and reshaped its internal culture con-sistently over this period of expansion, so did Islamic political thought maintain certain principal foundations while undergoing successive stages of evolution. The foundations of Islam neither allow for distinctions between spiritual and temporal, ecclesiastical and civil, or religious and secular categories, nor envisage the same duality of authority accepted in Western political thought as standard, such as God and Caesar, church and state, and clergy and laity. Over the centuries, Islamic forms of state and government, power and authority, and rule and loyalty have exhibited great diversity. Although they were all based on the premise of a unity of religion and state, it has nonetheless been impossible for Islam to formulate a norm of political thought that would stand above and apart from its various cul-tural permutations.

In contrast to the West, the respective realms of religion and state are intimately intertwined in Islam and subject to a process of fluid negotiation; the concepts of authority and duty overshadow those of freedom and the rights of the individual. Islamic political thought deals not only with matters of government, politics, and the state, but also addresses questions of acceptable behavior and ethics of both the ruler and the ruled before God. Islamic political thought cannot be measured by Western criteria and standards of political theory. It must be understood from within its own tradition, characterized by a vibrant integration of the secular and sacred in obedience to God and His Prophet. In its very nature, Islam is dynamic, not static, both as a way of life and a way of monotheistic worship. It is a living real-ity rather than a frozen system.

Rudimentary but enduring foundations for Islamic political thought were laid beginning with the Prophet's career in Medina. Significant divisions, however, came to the fore under the Umayyad caliphs (658–750), the first Arab dynasty ruling from Damascus. Arabic, the language of Muhammad and his early succes-sors (632–61), was propagated by the conquests of Islam and became established as the language of high Islamic culture and political thought during the caliphate of 'Abd al-Malik (685–705). On the criterion of its scripture (*kitāb*), Islamic political thought enforced the basic principle of obedience to God and His Prophet. That principle was articulated in the nucleus of its creed, the *shahāda*, and extrapolated in oral tradition by the early practice of the community, modeled after the Prophet, known as its sunna.

The Umayyad rulers belonging to the Quraysh, Muhammad's tribe, claimed to be the rightful caliphs as heirs to the Prophet but saw their leadership challenged by both the Shiʿis, who reserved legitimate leadership for Muhammad's family, and the Kharijis, who advocated that the most meritorious Muslim be the ideal caliph. By the end of the Umayyad caliphate in 750, the stage had been set for Islamic political thought to evolve through five successive periods, the trajectory of which may be summarized as follows.

750–1055: The early medieval formulations of Islamic political thought during the ascendancy of the Abbasid caliphate at Baghdad developed in three directions: those of the clerical class of administrators (*kuttāb*), the schools of legal scholars (ʿulama, *fuqahāʾ*) and theologians (*mutakallimūn*), and the circles of philosophers (*falāsifa*). Over a period of five centuries, Islamic thinkers integrated the thought patterns of a great variety of peoples, absorbing the intellectual systems brought into its fold by the converted populations of the Iranian empire and the Byzantine provinces. It appropriated the legacy of their learning and the acumen of their political experience with the help of comprehensive translation movements from Greek and Pahlavi into Arabic.

1055–1258: During this stage, Islamic political thought had to address the upheaval caused by Sunni Turkic nomads from Central Asia. Turkic sultans gained effective military control and cut into the economic and administrative strata of an Iran-based society nominally ruled by the Abbasid caliphs. The Turkic Seljuqs neither intended nor attempted to impose their language, culture, and seminomadic social order on the fabric of the Islamic polity; instead they wholeheartedly adopted Islam as their religion and promoted Persian next to Arabic as a language of higher learning.

1258–1500: After the demise of the attenuated Abbasid caliphate of Baghdad in 1258 during the Mongol invasions, Muslim political thinkers were forced to come to terms with three new political powers in the east: (1) Ilkhanid and then Timurid rule in Iran and Iraq; (2) khanate rule of the Golden Horde from Siberia to the Caucasus and from the Urals to the Danube River; and (3) Delhi-based sultanates in India. Farther to the west it saw military control passed into the hands of Mamluk Turks and Circassians who, uprooted from their homelands as military slaves, were sold into the households of their patrons and emancipated as converts to Islam to serve as soldiers in the Mamluk armies in Egypt and Syria. Control of the polity was thus usurped by a medley of foreign khanates and slave sultanates, each attempting to claim legitimacy through the manipulation of Islamic symbols of just rule and institutional affiliation with Sufi shaykhs. Faced with this fragmentation, Islamic political thinkers sought to find new paradigms that reflected the effort to overcome the tumultuous breakdown of order and managed to integrate the foreign conquerors into their community's religion and polity.

1500–1800: From about 1500 onward, the division of the Islamic world into sultanates was succeeded by the rise of three separate and flourishing monarchic empires, none of which used Arabic as their official language of discourse and administration. The Turkish-speaking Ottomans, who had conquered Constantinople in 1453 (now named Istanbul as their seat of government), added Syria and Egypt to their empire in 1517 and eventually adopted the title and legacy of Sunni caliphs. Adopting the Persian idiom, the Safavids established themselves in Iran in 1501 and transformed it into a theocratic Imami Shi'i monarchy. The Mughals, developing a Persian-speaking culture, established their predominantly Sunni rule over India with their victory at Panipat in 1526. In this new threefold constellation, political theory was made to serve the particular vision of rule of each empire rather than that of a universal caliphal culture, and thus Islamic political thought was shaped according to three different modes.

From 1800 onward: The multifarious search for rationales of Islamic political thought from 1800 onward struggled with a situation the world of Islam had never encountered before in its history. It was challenged by a Western culture that had entered its ascendancy. For the first time, Islam neither had the power to conquer nor the capacity to absorb the opposing culture. In response to this anxious and often desperate situation, there gradually emerged revival movements and nationalisms in the Islamic world, whose ideologies covered the spectrum from puritanism, reformism, modernism, secularism, nationalism, and socialism to the extremes of fundamentalism, often termed Islamism. Its apogees are represented on the one hand by the Iranian Revolution of 1979 and on the other hand by the terrorist attack of September 11, 2001, against the United States.

Foundations of Islamic Political Thought (from Muhammad to 750)

Both Islamic history and Islamic political thought began in the twilight of Late Antiquity with the hijra, the emigration of the Prophet from Mecca to Medina in 622. During his prophetic career in Mecca, Muhammad preached with the expectation of apocalyptic end times, focusing his listeners on their future in the hereafter and reminding them of their individual accountability before God. In Medina, he changed course, dominated by the urge to establish the collective religious unity of a community that would enter history here and now, and shape a polity in this world. Once the proclamation of the Qur'an came to an end with the death of the Prophet, eschatological concerns faded; Muslims focused on the victories of the Arab conquest and the resulting exigencies of empire-building and the shaping of polity. The caliphs took charge in their succession to the Prophet as leaders of the community. The crisis (*fitna*) of fraternal wars of succession within the ranks of the believers pitted insiders against outsiders, early Arab Muslims against new client converts, orthodox against heterodox, tribes against tribes, regions against regions, and dynasties against dynasties. It gave rise to sects and parties but, ultimately, did not dismantle the body politic, even though, from the ninth century onward, it allowed for the separation of political functions between caliphs, military amirs, and viziers administering the state. Neither the bifurcation of the caliphate in the middle of the tenth century into the Muslim East under the Buyid amirs in Baghdad and the Muslim West of the Fatimid caliphs in Cairo (and the Umayyad caliphs in Córdoba) nor the influx of Turks and Mongols, respectively, in the middle of the 11th and 13th centuries destroyed the cohesive but highly flexible structure of the Islamic polity.

Early medieval Islamic political thought proved masterfully able to build on the rudimentary foundations of the earliest phase of Islam. Although the Qur'an was not designed to be a book of political thought, it included language that Muslim political thinkers adopted in their formulation of essential concepts. In addition, Muhammad's organization of Medinan society, through a document known as the Constitution of Medina, offered a model of applied political thought and a glimpse into the Prophet's pragmatic approach toward the creation of a new polity. The first four caliphs conquered and quickly established themselves as administrators of the core lands of the future empire and encapsulated their political vision in short directives and instructions. In Umayyad times, the caliphs defended Muslim interests, regarding the state as their family's benefice. The people, most of whom were non-Muslim, were regarded as clients under the caliph's patronage, providing the tax revenue needed by the state. As deputy (*khalīfa*) of the Prophet, the ruler oversaw the rule of law and demanded unconditional obedience on the part of his subjects. Differing views about government and society were put down decisively as manifested by the neutralization of the Shi'is and the suppression of the Kharijis.

Islamic Political Thought in the Early Middle Ages (750–1055)

Upon the accession of the Abbasids as rulers of the empire in 750, the caliph acted as the protector of religion and state (*dīn wa-dawla*). His government was God's shadow on Earth, under whose sheltering protection everyone could find refuge. The clerical class (*kuttāb*) undertook impressive Arabic translations of Persian treatises on Iranian political institutions, a movement spearheaded by its principal proponent, Ibn al-Muqaffaʻ (d. 756), the champion of the courtly ideal of government (*adab*). The *Book of the Land-tax*, written by the chief judge Abu Yusuf (d. 798) at the behest of caliph Harun al-Rashid, set a precedent for treatises on government and fiscal matters written by ʻulamaʼ. In it he covered not only the rules of taxation but also legal and ethical principles as applied to social groups. He defined the role of the caliph as the shepherd of his flock and stressed his obligation to establish divine order among the small and the great. The caliph Ma'mun's (r. 813–33) attempt to establish a high imperial ideal with the primacy of the caliph over the clerical class and the learned elite produced a flourishing high culture infused with the Hellenistic heritage. Neoplatonism, in particular, entered into Islamic political thought through a translation movement of Greek (via Syriac) into Arabic. After the failure of the *miḥna* (trial), the inquisition enforced by an edict of the caliph to impose the theological doctrines of the Muʿtazilis as state creed, however, the clerical and learned classes found a way to resist caliphal authority in matters of religious doctrine and law.

The seat of the caliphs in the center of the circular capital city of Baghdad, conceived as an ideal city, did not become a throne for a pope-like authority; rather, the caliphate had to acknowledge that the ʿulamaʾ, inspired by Shafiʿi (d. 820) and Ibn Hanbal (d. 855), held the allegiance of the masses and would exclusively and collectively represent the teaching authority in Sunni Islam on a consensual basis. The situation was very different with the Shiʿis, who emphasized the teaching authority of their ideal leader. They advocated a theory in which overriding authority was vested in the infallible imam, the gate (*bāb*) through whom God is approached and the guarantee (*ḥujja*) without whom the world would collapse. The Shiʿis, a minority weakened by internal dissensions and schisms, were unable to establish their own political theology as normative and readied themselves to endure the injustice of Sunni ruling institutions by embracing the principle of cautious dissimulation (*taqiyya*). They were sustained by their belief in the hidden presence of the imam and their projection into the future of the Mahdi's apocalyptic return.

The articulate political thought developed by the Muslim philosophers argued for a political society (*madīna*) that evoked the Greek ideal city (*polis*), whence derived the name of *madīnat al-salām* (City of Peace) that the Abbasids adopted for Baghdad, their capital. Farabi (870–950) and Ibn Sina (980–1037), both hailing from Transoxiana, focused on the center of the empire and supported the ideal of the philosopher-king, an ethically perfect individual, as head of a virtuous polity. Farabi's ideal of "the virtuous city" (*al-madīna al-fāḍila*) offered a systematic thesis on the state as the perfect society, in which rational integrity and right conduct are the means for achieving supreme felicity (*saʿāda*). Just as the human body has different parts doing different work in a harmonious manner, so too does the body politic require an efficient division of labor. Just as the body has a head to rule it, so too society has a chief to rule it, guiding society toward becoming an ideal community of the virtuous. Ibn Sina's chapter on governance (*siyāsa*) in his encyclopedic work, *The Healing of the Soul* (*al-Shifaʾ*), stressed the principle of human interdependence and promoted the ideal of the lawgiver who is both philosopher and prophet. Responding to the need for human government in a religious polity and reminding believers of God and the afterlife, the ruler guarantees the observance of the civil (*nāmūs*) and religious (shariʿa) law.

Anchored in reason (*ʿaql*) as its ultimate principle and worked out across boundaries of religious affiliations between Muslims and Christians, the political theory of the Islamic philosophers charted an intellectual trajectory that the majority of the Sunni population was unprepared or unwilling to follow. Unlike the philosophical elite, the Sunni masses needed a political thought system established on the platform of tradition, not abstract reason. Islamic philosophy lacked the institutional basis that an academy would have provided and did not manage to attract the popularly important scholars of law and religion with their deep roots in the literature of the traditions of the Prophet and his Companions (hadith) and their codices of jurisprudence detailing the stipulations of shari'a and amassing a myriad of opinions on legal points (fatwa).

Islamic Political Thought in the High Middle Ages (1055–1258)

The political vision of Sunni Islam can be traced in two classical works on public law: the Arabic treatise on *The Principles of Power* (*al-Ahkam al-Sultaniyya*) by Mawardi (974–1058), the honorary chief judge of the Abbasid caliphs, who defined the standard theory of the Sunni caliphate and its institutions from the perspective of the 'ulama'; and the *Siyasatnama*, the famous Persian work on statecraft by Nizam al-Mulk (1018–92), chief vizier of the Seljuqs, that gives expression to the views of the clerical class. Nizam al-Mulk also created the foundations of a network of educational institutions (madrasas) that offered scholars of law and religion lecterns and listeners for the dissemination of their works for many centuries. The *Siyasatnama*, together with the *Qabusnama*, written in 1082 by Kay Ka'us, represents the apogee of the literary genre of *naṣīḥat al-mulūk* (Advice for Rulers), that is, Mirrors for Princes literature that counseled political leaders on statecraft and diplomacy. Thriving for more than a millennium, the genre continued with treatises of Sufis and courtiers on ethical conduct in political life, and reached its final flourishing during the Mughal and Ottoman empires.

The impact of medieval Islamic political thought is best exemplified by the classical work of Ghazali (1058–1111), presented with great didactic clarity in his encyclopedic *Revival of the Religious Sciences* (*Ihya' 'Ulum al-Din*), which relied on the legal tradition of the Shafi'i school of law and the theological tradition of Baqillani (d. 1013) and Juwayni (1028–85). The major achievement of Ghazali's magisterial work, however, was the theological and ethical platform he laid for Islamic political institutions, a platform that enabled the moral and religious renewal of Islamic society. Offering a Sunni theological interpretation of political thought, Fakhr al-Din al-Razi (1149–1209) tried to combine dialectical theology with a modified version of Ibn Sina's philosophy in order to support the doctrine that the existence of the king-emperor, namely, the caliph, is necessary to maintain the order of the world.

On the far western periphery of the Islamic world in the Iberian Peninsula, Ghazali's books were burned in public by order of the ruling dynasty, bowing to the agitation of Maliki legal scholars. Significant contributions to Islamic political thought, however, were made in Spain through the insightful analysis of state and society by Ibn Rushd (1126–98), one of the most original minds in all of Islam.

According to Ibn Rushd, philosophers were best qualified to interpret scripture, tradition, and law because they possessed the highest form of knowledge. Following Aristotle, he held that right and wrong were determined by nature rather than by divine command and that effective legislation required both theoretical and empirical knowledge.

In the last century of Abbasid rule in Baghdad, Sufism emerged as an organized movement of fraternities, building up the infrastructure of Muslim society and shaping the Islamic identity of the polity for centuries to come; in fact, Sufism made a powerful impact on the fabric of Islamic polity, which contemporary scholarship has widely overlooked. Sufism began in the eighth and ninth centuries in Egypt, Syria, Iraq, and Iran, with groups of men of piety leading an ascetic life and seeking mystic experience of union with God. Led by teaching masters called shaykhs (or *pīr*s in Persian), it developed its ideal of poverty (*faqr*) and trust in God (*tawakkul*) and spread its practice of meditative recollection (*dhikr*). Its radical spiritual and social patterns provoked the scholars of law and theology, stirred up urban populations, and challenged public order. After being eclipsed by the Shi'i renaissance of the tenth century, Sufism reframed its path to God as a branch of the Muslim sciences during the Sunni revival under the Seljuq Turks. Leading into the caliphate of the Abbasid Nasir (1180–1225), Sufism organized itself into a large number of fraternities (*ṭarīqa*) based on a strict order of master and disciples, and marked by initiation rites and common prayer ceremonies. Networks of Sufi centers, called "lodges" (Ar. *ribāṭ*, or Pers. *khānaqāh*), paralleled the educational institution of the madrasa and were favored by sultanate governments. The sultans sought sacred legitimization for the secular leadership they had acquired through usurpation by securing the endorsement of Sufi shaykhs, whom they often honored with the title of shaykh al-Islam.

Sufism was profoundly undergirded by the monist philosophy of Ibn al-'Arabi (1165–1240), whose pivotal concept of the "Perfect Man" (*al-insān al-kāmil*) supplied both an ontological and ethical ideal. Yet Sufism engaged the emotions as well as the intellect, tolerating unruly wandering dervishes (*qalandar*) and growing widely popular through its provocative use of Persian love poetry, especially that of Jalal al-Din al-Rumi (1207–73). Drawing upon an image familiar to steppe populations, the Sufis advocated a "tent" of spiritual rule (*wilāya*) over the entire society. The hierarchy of saints (*awliyā'*) would be anchored in a spiritual pole (*quṭb*), who would in turn be supported by his substitutes, the "stakes" (*abdāl*) and "pegs" (*awtād*).

Sufi institutions, often built at the outskirts of urban centers around the tombs of their founders, produced widely used manuals that disseminated the ethical and spiritual ideal of the Sufi way of life and contributed much to the Islamic identity of populations in India, Southeast Asia, and sub-Saharan Africa. Sufism made its principal impact on Islamic political thought and social practice during the turbulent transition from the fragmentation of the Abbasid Empire and the emergence of its three successors. During the sultanate period of Ilkhanids, Timurids, Mamluks, and

Delhi Sultans, Sufi influence was spread by many orders, among them the Kubrawis in Central Asia, the Shadhilis in Egypt and North Africa, and the Suhrawardis and Chishtis in the Indus and Ganges plains. The three great empires would draw religious and political strength from Sufi resources, the Ottomans from the Mevlevis and Bektashis, the Shi'i Safavids from their Sunni Sufi roots, and the Mughals from the Qadiris and Naqshbandis.

Islamic Political Thought in the Late Middle Ages (1258–1500)

Two writers on Islamic political thought stand out in the late Middle Ages during the period of fragmentation and before the establishment of the three empires: Ibn Taymiyya (1263–1328) and Ibn Khaldun (1332–1406). Ibn Taymiyya, a Hanbali scholar of law and theology, who was active in Damascus and Cairo, engaged in bitter controversies with rationalism, Sufism, Shi'ism, and Christianity. He championed the legal method of individual reasoning (*ijtihād*) to discern the consensus of the believers and chose the middle ground between reason and tradition, as well as between violence and piety. He proclaimed that religion and state need one another because perfect spiritual and temporal prosperity is achieved only when religion is put into practice by religious law that is enforced by a leader who accepts the duty of commanding good and forbidding evil. Ibn Taymiyya maintained that the principles of the state's power ought to be applied rigorously through the use of the shari'a enforced by the ruler—an ideal that the Wahhabi movement adopted in the 18th century.

Ibn Khaldun was active in North Africa, Spain, and Egypt during periods of dynastic declines. Although he studied broadly in philosophy, law, and theology, he presented an empirical analysis gleaned from the history of the Berbers and Arabs in North Africa. His study of the history of civilization revealed a cyclical pattern: the rule of nomadic chieftains would gradually evolve into kingship in a civilized society that, in turn, would be overthrown by another nomadic group. In order to break the cycle, authority of leadership had to emerge from natural dominion, pass through the stage of government by men of intelligence and insight, and stabilize itself in a polity based on the principles of religion laid down by God, as exemplified ideally by the rule of the Prophet and his successors, the caliphs.

Little research has been done on the considerable role women played in the medieval Islamic polity. According to the Qur'an, women are equal to men before God and have similar religious obligations. Though subordinate to men in the public sphere and unequal in many sectors of Islamic law, many women played significant roles in the transmission of hadith, beginning with Muhammad's wives 'A'isha and Umm Salama, and in the organization of court life, the education of scholars, and the welfare of Islamic families and children in medieval times. Muslim biographical works quote hundreds of women involved in teaching Islam and transmitting its tradition, while Sufi women had an impact on Islamic ethics and religious practice. There has been a tendency in secular feminist scholarship to depict premodern women in the Islamic world as utterly backward. Against this backdrop, however, Muslim women now writing on Islam in the contemporary world have begun their own active line of feminist inquiry, which promises to open new vistas on Islamic political thought from a previously neglected sector of Islamic culture.

Since the end of Late Antiquity and through most of the millennium of the early and late Middle Ages, the Islamic world was the leading culture on the globe. It excelled in philosophy and the natural sciences, logic and metaphysics, mathematics, astronomy, optics, alchemy, geography, medicine, and architecture. Its transition from vellum to paper in the eighth century propelled it onto a great curve of literary production in both religious and nonreligious literature. This enormous cultural achievement was accomplished in medieval Islam because the Muslim scholars of medicine and science, the philosophers, and the historians avidly inquired into the roots of world cultures anteceding or surrounding them in India, ancient Iran, and the Hellenistic world. Islamic political thought drew on the classics of Greco-Roman and Irano-Indian antiquity. It also antedated and influenced the appearance of works of political thought in medieval Europe, building a bridge between antiquity and modernity. Islamic political thought developed in a cosmopolitan medieval environment of wide-ranging information about other cultures, with all their riches and restrictions. A significant disruption in this development, however, came about from the 15th to the 16th century, when the Western world of Europe entered upon a course of profound changes in its vision of the world, religion, society, and politics.

Islamic Political Thought in the Early Modern Period (1500–1800)

The Ottomans, a group of Turkic tribesmen, established a small principality in northwestern Anatolia, crossed into Europe in 1357, and took control of the Balkans, moving their capital from Bursa to Edirne in 1366. Although defeated by Timur (known to the West as Tamerlane) at Ankara in 1402, they conquered Constantinople in 1453, making it their new capital of Istanbul. With the conquest of Egypt and Syria in 1517, the Ottomans established a large Sunni empire over Anatolia, the Balkans, and the regions of the eastern and southern Mediterranean. Constantly engaged in warfare with European powers, they suffered a decisive defeat at Lepanto in 1571 and failed to take Vienna in 1683. Increasingly weakened during the 18th and 19th centuries, they acceded to the rule of Muhammad 'Ali (r. 1805–48) as governor of Egypt in 1805. The Ottoman Empire officially disappeared from the geopolitical map when Mustafa Kemal Atatürk abolished the sultanate in 1922 and founded modern Turkey in 1923.

Ruled by pragmatic sultans, the Ottomans created a strong and loyal military force in the Janissaries, who were recruited as children from the Christian subject populations and raised as Muslims. Organizing themselves around the sultan, the Ottomans integrated the military, the learned, and the bureaucracy into their patrimonial state and gave room to the influences of Sufi orders and folk Islam. Seeing the implementation of justice as their right and duty, the sultans conferred upon judges (qadi) the authority to administer both shari'a and their innovative and parallel civil law (*qānūn*).

Ottoman rule excelled in practical politics; its range of political theories, however, was modest. Abu al-Su'ud (1490–1574), a famous commentator of the Qur'an appointed as shaykh al-Islam, worked to strengthen the absolute rule of the sultan as the ultimate religious and civil authority. His fatwas brought the *qānūn* into agreement with the shari'a and established the principle that the qadis derived their competence from the appointment of the sultan and were obliged to go along with his directives in legal matters. In contrast, Kinalizade (1510–72) followed the philosophical tradition of ethics advocating the ideal of the philosopher-king who ruled the Virtuous City. His delineation of four status groups—men of the pen, men of the sword, traders, and craftsmen—became the foundation of an ideal social order known as the "right world order" (*niẓām al-ʿālam*). In practice, however, Ottoman society was organized according to a rougher bipartite order. The ruling class of *ʿaskarīs* (warriors) encompassed the military, the learned, and the bureaucrats; its members were supported by taxes levied on the *riʿāya* (flock), the class of ruled subjects composed of tradesmen, laborers, and minorities. Katib Çelebi (1609–57), the most productive scholar of the Ottoman Empire, advocated the rule of a strong and just sultan and analyzed the financial state of the sultanate. He formulated his thought in medical terms, analogizing the body politic to the human body and its stages of growth and decline. In addition to arguing for a balanced budget, an increase in agricultural production, and a reduction of the armed forces, he also exposed rampant corruption and exploitation of the peasants.

The Safavids, of Kurdish origin and Turkic-speaking, arose from the Sunni Sufi fraternity of the Safawis organized in Azerbaijan by Safi al-Din (d. 1334). There, and in the neighboring regions of eastern Anatolia, the movement became militantly Shi'i under their leader Junayd (1446–60). Led by Shah Isma'il (1487–1524), they brought the whole of Iran under their control after overpowering the regional rule of the Timurid Qara Quyunlu and Aq Quyunlu in 1501. In these military endeavors, they relied on the support of Turkic tribesmen called "Redheads" (Qizilbash) for their distinctive red headgear. Adopting Persian as the language of their monarchy, the Safavid shahs set themselves in opposition to the Sunni Ottomans based at the western flank of their territory. Claiming to be living emanations of the godhead and representatives on Earth of the Mahdi, the Twelfth Imam of Shi'ism, they combined supreme secular and spiritual authority into the office of a single omnipotent ruler. The Safavids imposed Shi'ism as the state religion upon all of Iran and moved their capital to Isfahan where Shi'i Safavid power reached its apex in the reign of Shah 'Abbas (r. 1587–1629). The Safavid dynasty came to an end with the rise of Nadir Shah (r. 1729–47), a chieftain of Turkic tribesmen, who consolidated his rule over all of Iran, and the subsequent Qajar dynasty (1779–1925), a clan that had served in the Qizilbash army under the Safavids.

In the 16th century, the Safavids imposed Imami Shiʻi beliefs on a largely Sunni population, although the distinction between the two groups was marked by significant ambiguity at the time. Shiʻi political thought came vigorously alive in the work of Karaki (1466–1534), a Lebanese scholar who made the provocative claim to be speaking as the general representative (al-nāʾib al-ʻāmm) of the absent imam. Karaki's theory of authority has been accepted and extended from his own time until the present by those scholars known as *uṣūlī*s, that is, those who held that religious authority is derived from the study of jurisprudence (uṣūl al-fiqh). In accordance with this view, the scholars of the Safavid realm recognized the leading jurist as *mujtahid al-zamān* (the independent jurist of the age), and treated his authority as absolute.

The *uṣūlī*s were challenged in the 17th century by Muhammad Amin al-Astarabadi (d. 1626–27), whose work inaugurated what came to be known as the *akhbārī* or traditionist school of thought. The *uṣūlī*s favored rational elaboration of the law (ijtihād) and the acquiescence of lay Shiʻis to the opinions of qualified jurists (taqlīd). The *akhbārī*s saw in revelation the sole source of the law and furthermore claimed that it was most reliably preserved in the *akhbār*, the reports of the imams' words and deeds recorded in the Four Books of Traditions accepted by the Shiʻis. Even the Qur'an, in their view, should properly be understood through the commentary of the imams preserved in these reports. In the later 17th century, the main spokesman for the *akhbārī*s was Muhsin Fayz Kashani (1598–1680), who popularized the political thought of his period by integrating Sufi ideas. The *uṣūlī*s, on the other hand, found their most illustrious proponent in Majlisi (1627–1700), who developed orthodox Imami Shiʻism and brought the state under the direction of the legal scholars, launching attacks against Sufis and philosophers. In the view of Majlisi and similar theorists, the king (shāh) was but the instrument of the clerical class and dependent on the leading *mujtahid*.

During three centuries (1200–1500), Muslim rule in India was organized by Afghan and Turkic sultanates ruling mainly from Delhi. The control of the Mughal emperors over the entire subcontinent began with Babur (1483–1530), a descendant of both Chingiz Khan and Timur, who invaded India from the northwest. After Babur's victory at Panipat in 1526, the Sunni Mughal monarchy was extended over almost all of India during the long rule of Akbar the Great (r. 1556–1605). Akbar, a superb though illiterate administrator, abolished the poll tax levied on Hindus, favored a syncretistic religion, called *dīn-i ilāhī* (divine religion), and created a ruling class of appointees (manṣabdārīs) consisting of Turks, Afghans, Persians, and Hindus. Dara Shikuh (1615–59), inclined toward the Qadiri Sufi order, inspired the translation of the Upanishads into Persian and championed religious assimilation with Hinduism. His program of religious openness was not to last long, as he was executed on the orders of Aurangzeb (r. 1658–1707), his brother and rival. Aurangzeb stood up against the eclectic traditions of his predecessors, breaking the renewed vigor of Hinduism with a reform centered on Islamic values and supported by the Naqshbandi Sufi order. The Mughal Empire lost its glory after Delhi was sacked by Nadir Shah in 1739 and gradually lost all its power under the rule of British colonialism.

The open-minded innovations of the Mughal emperor Akbar broke with traditional patterns of Islamic political thought in an attempt to build a single political community that granted India's majority Hindu population religious toleration and equal status with their Sunni and Shi'i Muslim neighbors. He also tried to reconcile Muslim sectarian groups with one another. Claiming infallible monarchical authority and according himself supreme power as the "perfect man" (*insān al-kāmil*, originally a Sufi concept), Akbar combined the role of king with that of spiritual teacher. Proclaiming himself the highest authority in matters of religious law as well as secular law, he set aside key stipulations of the shari'a and embraced religious tolerance and political equality.

Akbar's vision did not survive in India. Ahmad Sirhindi (1564–1624), who stood in the spiritual line of the Naqshbandis, perceived Akbar's ideology as destructive to Islamic law and religion. He came to be called the "renewer" (*mujaddid*) as Islam entered its second millennium because he wished to restore Islamic values in public and political life, albeit in a form inspired by Sufi piety rather than legalistic rigidity. 'Abd al-Haqq Dihlawi (1551–1642) went a step further and stressed the precedence of religious law over the Sufi path and limited the king's function to upholding the shari'a. Emperor Aurangzeb (1650–1707) repudiated Akbar's tolerance toward Hinduism; he reintroduced a unified legal system of Sunni orthodoxy based on Hanafi law and reimposed the poll tax on non-Muslims. Shah Waliullah (1703–62), a man of encyclopedic learning with roots in the Naqshbandi Sufi affiliation, strove to establish a polity based on the shari'a in India.

Islamic Political Thought in the Later Modern Period (from 1800 to the Present)

During the 19th century, half of the Islamic world passed under the formal colonial rule of European states—geographically tiny but militarily and economically mighty countries in comparison to the vast Muslim territories they ruled and controlled. The reaction of the Islamic intelligentsia to this overpowering control from without was one of reform and revival from within, spearheaded by social and political reformers, some of whom were journalists rather than scholars steeped in Islamic law and religion. Perhaps the most outstanding figure among them was Jamal al-Din al-Afghani (1839–97), an austere man of Shi'i Persian origin and a charismatic lecturer with only a small number of published works. Active in Istanbul, Cairo, Paris, London, India, Russia, and Iran, he devoted his life to the reviving of Muslim intellectual and social life in pamphlets and political articles, commented on current affairs, and, in travels and speeches, agitated for the resurrection of a reformed and purified Islamic identity in the face of European encroachment. Teaching orthodox religion to the masses and natural-law rationalism to the elite, he attacked Darwin in his refutation of materialism and asserted that only religion ensures stability of society, whereas materialism causes decay and debasement. Longing to recreate the glory of Islam in a Pan-Islamic state, Afghani argued that Islam's ultimate orientation toward God enabled it to organize the finest possible political community.

Afghani's chief disciple was Muhammad 'Abduh (1849–1905), often seen as the founder of Egyptian modernism. 'Abduh, who had received a traditional education and attended Azhar University, was attracted to mysticism and considered Afghani to be his spiritual guide. He wrote several theological treatises, among them a defense of Islam against Christianity, and promulgated his program of reform in *al-Manar* (The lighthouse), a Qur'an commentary that he published in installments and that was later continued as a monthly by his highly educated collaborator Rashid Rida (1865–1935), a man of Syrian descent. 'Abduh's political thought had the overriding goal of returning Islam to its pristine condition, emphasizing the Qur'an and sunna and restoring the role of *ijtihād*. Although the exercise of reason and the adoption of modern natural science were of paramount importance, reason must defer to the dogmas of religion, while prophecy focused on the moral education of the masses. Rida, a very prolific writer, refined some of 'Abduh's points and distinguished between the religious duties (*'ibādāt*), unchangeable because based on the Qur'an and sunna, and duties toward other Muslims (*mu'āmalāt*), to be reinterpreted by the exercise of reason so as to serve the welfare (*maṣlaḥa*) of the community.

With roots in the political thought of Ibn Hanbal and Ibn Taymiyya, the modern reform movement of the Salafis began with Afghani, 'Abduh, and Rida, and continued to identify the causes of disintegration of the Muslim community in the infiltration of foreign ideas and practices. The movement taught that Islamic honor and self-respect would only be reestablished if Islam as both a religion and a way of life was redeemed from cultural submission to Western powers and revitalized with its own internal resources. Salafi thinkers called for sweeping reforms to be introduced into Muslim education, combining the values of traditional pedagogy with the creativity of modern education. They advocated resurrecting the ideal of Islamic law and updating the Arabic language to address the realities of modern life. The Salafis had an impact on Algeria with Ibn Badis (1889–1940), on Morocco with Muhammad 'Allal al-Fasi (1910–74), and on Tunisia with Muhammad al-Tahir b. 'Ashur (1879–1973).

The puritan movement of the Wahhabis began in the heart of the Arabian Peninsula with Muhammad b. 'Abd al-Wahhab (1703–92). Also inspired by the thought of Ahmad b. Hanbal and Ibn Taymiyya, he insisted on a single core idea: uncompromising monotheism (*tawḥīd*). God had to be professed as one in word and served in action. Islam had to be purified from all devotion to anything else (*shirk*), in thought and practice. There was no room for saint worship, legal reasoning beyond the Qur'an and sunna, or any innovation (*bid'a*). He allied himself with

'Abd al-'Aziz (1765–1803), the leader of the tribal group of Al-Su'ud, becoming shaykh and qadi in the service of the amir and imam. The Saudi-Wahhabi alliance continued with their sons and extended rule over the Hijaz and the key cities of Mecca and Medina. Eradicating anything they believed would undermine the purity of their beliefs, they destroyed tombs of saints and books of intellectual adversaries, interdicted devotional prayers, and pillaged Shi'i shrines in Iraq. Muhammad 'Ali, the powerful governor of Egypt under the Ottomans, pushed them back, but the Saudi-Wahhabi state, with Riyadh as its capital, was eventually restored in 1902. Over this long history the Wahhabis expressed the staunchest spirit of politically strategic fundamentalism, which inspired many similar movements in other parts of the Islamic world.

Traders brought Islam to West Africa on camelback from the north through the Sahara and to East Africa from the shores of South Arabia, Iran, and India by boat across the Indian Ocean. In West Africa, Sunni Islam of the Maliki legal school became dominant; since the 12th century, Timbuktu has developed into a famous seat of commerce and Islamic learning on the Niger River. Dongola on the upper Nile River was taken under Muslim rule in the 14th century after the collapse of Christian Nubia. The vast independent state (often called the "Sokoto caliphate") established at Sokoto by Muhammad Bello after the death of his father, Usuman Dan Fodio (1754–1817), who had led a successful four-year jihad against neighboring principalities, became the largest autonomous state in 19th-century sub-Saharan Africa.

It was charismatic leadership that transformed sub-Saharan Islamic societies into fundamentalist-inspired states, as can be shown by two examples, one centered on the idea of "the seal of the saints" (*khātam al-awliyā'*) and the other on the messianic idea of the Mahdi, the apocalyptic leader of the end times. In West Africa, the Tijani Sufi affiliation was founded in an oasis of Algeria by Ahmad al-Tijani (1737–1815), who later settled in Fez in Morocco and whose teachings were recorded by a close companion and thereafter elaborated by 'Umar b. Sa'id al-Futi (1796–1864). Ahmad al-Tijani claimed that the Prophet had appeared to him in a waking vision, appointing him to the spiritual rank of the seal of sainthood (*khātam al-awliyā'*, *quṭb al-aqṭāb*), a rank that gave him domination over the age (*ṣāḥib al-waqt*), exclusive knowledge of the supreme name of God (*ism Allāh al-a'zam*), and the power of a vicegerent (*khalīfa*) who alone mediates between God and his creatures. In the middle of the 19th century, 'Umar b. Sa'id al-Futi, a Fulbe of Senegal, assumed the leadership of the Tijanis and the role of a *mujāhid*, launching a militant anticolonial jihad movement across West Africa from Senegal to Ghana and into Nilotic Sudan. By the middle of the 20th century, the Tijanis were transformed into a revivalist movement among the black Africans as Ibrahim Niasse (1900–1975) extended it among the urban Muslims of Nigeria and Sudan.

In (Nilotic) Sudan, Muhammad Ahmad (1844–85), a Sunni with roots in the Sammani Sufi affiliation, proclaimed himself to be the expected Mahdi in 1881. He learned of his divine election in a colloquy with the Prophet himself. Ahmad advocated a reformist brand of Islam; he aimed to restore the primitive *umma* (community of believers), governed by the Qur'an and sunna, through his activity in supreme succession to the Prophet (*al-khilāfa al-kubrā*) and with the assistance of his chief disciples in the role of successors to the Rightly Guided Caliphs. Retreating (hijra) into the Nuba Mountains together with his followers, named Ansar after the helpers of Muhammad in Medina, he called people to arms in a jihad against Turkish, Egyptian, and British overlords. Ahmad died shortly after conquering Khartoum in 1885. He was succeeded by his son 'Abdallah b. Muhammad (1885–99) as his deputy (*khalīfa*), who established a Mahdist state that was overthrown by the British in 1898. The revivalist movement of the Ansar, however, continued under the leadership of 'Abd al-Rahman (1885–1959) and played a decisive role in the Sudan's declaration of independence in 1955. Under the influence of the Muslim Brotherhood, Hasan al-Turabi (b. 1932) worked toward the formation of an Islamic state and the promotion of a fundamentalist regime in Sudan.

Beginning in the ninth century, Islam reached East Africa through traders and seafarers who came from Southern Arabia and Iran and established trading posts on the East African coast. By the 13th century, the Indian Ocean had become a Muslim sea, and Muslims controlled the trade from India and Iran to South Arabia and East Africa. Sunni Islam of the Shafi'i legal school laid the religious foundations for the emergence of the Swahili civilization of the Muslim "coastalists" (*sawāḥila*) in East Africa. Swahili culture remained a coastal phenomenon with only sporadic Islamic inroads into the East African hinterland; in the area of Lake Nyasa, for example, Islam spread among the Yao. In the 16th century, the Portuguese took control of the spice trade away from the Muslims and secured a sea route linking Europe to India. By the end of the 17th century, however, the sultans of Oman reestablished effective rule in East Africa when they exerted dominance over the island of Zanzibar in 1698 and expelled the Portuguese from the Tanzanian coasts in 1730. In 1832, the sultans of Oman moved their capital to Zanzibar, which had by that time become the center of the Arab slave trade. In the late 19th and early 20th centuries, imperialist European powers (Portugal, France, Germany, Great Britain, and Italy) scrambled among themselves for control of East Africa. Islam, however, began to play a significant political role in the region only in the 20th century, as East African states that included large Muslim minorities gained their independence. These states included Tanzania, Mozambique, Kenya, Uganda, and Malawi. Although the Muslims of South Africa, who trace their ancestry to immigrants from South Asia and slaves imported from Southeast Asia, remained a small minority, they attracted worldwide attention in their struggle against the injustice of apartheid.

Islam in India saw its own developments of Islamic political thought in the 19th century. Ahmad Khan (1817–98), known as Sir Sayyid and knighted by the British in 1888, had only a traditional education but became the founder of Muslim modernism and the principal force of Islamic revival in India. An advocate of modern education for India's Muslims, he wrote commentaries on the Bible and the first half of the Qur'an. After the Sepoy Mutiny in 1857, Ahmad Khan worked toward the reconciliation of the British and Muslims in India, and founded the Muhammadan Anglo-Oriental College at Aligarh in 1875. Reinterpreting Islam according to his maxim, "the work of God—that is, nature and its fixed laws—is identical to the word of God," he emphasized a rational approach to Islam and to social reforms in Muslim culture.

The mutiny in 1857 that led to the formal colonization of India by the British also had an effect on the emergence of two Sunni reform movements among the Urdu-speaking Muslims, the Barelwis and the Deobandis. Both movements maintain considerable influence among Muslims in India and Pakistan today. Muhammad Iqbal (1877–1938), an outstanding poet beloved for his commitment to the creation of Pakistan, accused both the West of cheating humanity of its values through the power of its technology and the Muslim society of his day of subsisting in a state of somnolence. He called the whole world to join the dynamism of the "true Islam" of the Qur'an and Muhammad, a dynamism that he believed would harness the forces of history for the moral renewal of all humanity.

Islam came to Southeast Asia (Indonesia, Malaysia, Singapore, and Brunei, as well as territories in Thailand and Mindanao) discreetly over the sea. From about the 13th century onward, Muslim traders in noticeable numbers sailed to the ports of this island world and its adjacent coasts, forming viable and enduring communities. Sultanates, based in the port cities of Malacca on the Malaysian peninsula (1400–1511) and Demak on Java (1475–1588), constituted little-known early Muslim powers. The 16th and 17th centuries saw the formation of four great Islamic empires with their centers in port cities, formed at (1) Aceh, in northern Sumatra and central Malaysia (1500–1650); (2) Bantam, on western Java and southern Sumatra (1527–1682); (3) Mataram, on central Java, southern Borneo (Kalimantan), and eastern Sumatra (1588–1682); and (4) Macassar, on Celebes and Sumbawa (1605–69). As Sunni Islam of the Shafi'i legal tradition spread in Southeast Asia, its law, practice, and essential doctrines set down firm roots. In addition, Sufis coming from India to the Malay Peninsula, and from the Arabian Peninsula to the archipelago, had a significant impact on the formation of the Southeast Asian Muslim polity.

In the 18th and 19th centuries, the Muslims of Southeast Asia were challenged by increasing Dutch colonial supremacy throughout Sumatra, Java, and Borneo, as well as by British colonial administration in Malaysia. At the same time, the fervent practice of the pilgrimage to Mecca kept Southeast Asian Muslims in contact with the world of Islam and facilitated the influence of the Wahhabis and the reformism of 'Abduh and Rashid Rida on Southeast Asian Islam. The development of the *pesantren*, Muslim boarding schools led by groups of religious teachers, created an infrastructure of traditional Muslim education that propelled the spread of Islam, especially in Java. The most influential puritan movement of the Muhammadiyya, founded in Yogyakarta in 1912, adopted Dutch institutional and Christian missionary approaches and opposed Sufi forms of education. It organized a comprehensive educational system that ranged from primary schools to teacher training colleges and expanded social services to the needy. Indonesia achieved independence in

1945 and adopted the five principles (*pancasila*: monotheism, nationalism, humanism, democracy, and social justice) as the philosophical basis for its order of society; Sukarno became the first president (1945–67), followed by Suharto (1967–98). Malaysia gained its independence from the British in 1957; its political system was a mixture of parliamentarianism and authoritarianism. The Malaysian constitution both guaranteed freedom of religion and made Islam the state religion. Ethnic Malays, who are mainly Muslim, dominated politics, and non-Muslim Malays of Chinese or Indian descent ran the economic and financial sectors.

In the 20th century, Europe lost its global leadership during the period of the two world wars, when it experienced the eclipse of fascist nationalism, the downfall of colonial imperialism, and the emergence of the Soviet Union and the United States as the primary shapers of the world order. The Russian revolution and the emergence of the communist systems in the Soviet Union and China left only tangential imprints on Islamic political thought. The forceful entry of the United States into world politics in the aftermath of World War II, however, particularly its projection of military and cultural dominance into Muslim societies, provoked a range of vehement and enduring Islamic reactions. The extremist fringe is characterized by destructive militancy and terrorist movements, such as al-Qaeda, originally a group of American-backed jihadists fighting against the Soviet Union in Afghanistan.

For Islam, the 20th century began with forceful secularist movements and ended with a rising tide of fundamentalist movements seeking to expunge the Western presence from Muslim lands.

In 1924, Atatürk (1881–1938) abolished polygamy, shari'a courts, and Qur'an schools; he also created national banks, reformed the Turkish alphabet, prohibited the wearing of fez and veil, empowered women to vote and obtain a divorce and offered them equality in education and employment, and required citizens to use family names rather than simply first names. Atatürk suppressed the dervish orders and introduced new civil, criminal, and commercial codes, secularizing what was at the time the strongest Muslim empire on the globe. Turkey became the central case of a cultural and political revolution imposed from the top by an authoritarian regime with the result that the country was divided into urban elites (which acceded to secularization) and rural masses (which resisted it). As it opens the back door for Islamic culture and practice to squeeze in again, Turkey is gradually restoring balance to its society. Not all efforts to reappropriate the riches of the Islamic tradition are violent. The Nurculuk movement, founded by Bediüzzaman Said Nursi (1876–1960), with millions of followers forming two major branches today (one led by Fethullah Gülen, b. 1941), is a peaceful revivalist phenomenon manifesting the re-Islamizing trend in Turkey.

On the other side of the spectrum, in the late 20th century the Islamic world became dominated by fundamentalist movements: the Muslim Brotherhood founded by Hasan al-Banna (1906–49) in Egypt and spearheaded by Sayyid Qutb (1906–66); the Islamic Group, established by Mawlana Mawdudi (1903–79) in India and Pakistan; and the movement of clerics and mujahidin led by Ayatollah

Ruhollah Khomeini (1903–89) that culminated in the Iranian Revolution in 1979. These three movements transformed Islam into a political ideology and were not hesitant to use force to secure their political objectives.

Banna, a schoolteacher from Isma'iliyya on the Suez Canal, formed the Muslim Brotherhood in order to combat the influence of a corrupt society by bringing the Egyptian youth back to religion. He gave his movement a militant character with a strict chain of command that consisted of a general guide presiding over the membership, members organized as families and battalions, and a trusted core of its elite defined as a "secret apparatus." His promulgation of the movement's "fundamental law" transformed it publicly into a social and political organization with antiforeign, anti-Zionist, anticommunist, and antisectarian attitudes. After the Free Officers seized power in 1952 and exiled Faruq, Egypt's last king of Albanian descent, President Nasser cracked down on the Muslim Brotherhood, driving the movement underground. Sayyid Qutb, a journalist who had experienced culture shock during a visit to America, returned to Egypt in 1951, proclaimed himself to have been reborn a true Muslim, and joined the Muslim Brotherhood. Imprisoned by Nasser for ten years, he wrote a manifesto for political revolution through personal discipline and violent jihad, which decried Nasser's Egypt as *jāhiliyya*, a land of ignorance and unbelief. He argued that to resurrect the Muslim polity as a collectivity (*jamā'a*) based on Islamic ethics, a vanguard had to be mobilized by an all-inclusive jihad with the aim of establishing a truly Islamic society.

The Muslim Brotherhood achieved a strong popular appeal through its social programs, which assisted the large lower strata of Muslim society in its neighborhoods. It was unable, however, to offer an agenda that would pull Egypt out of lethargy and overcome corruption. It also contributed to social instability by organizing riots that targeted the minority Coptic populations. Later, small spin-offs of the Muslim Brotherhood had recourse to more extreme forms of violence. In 1977, al-Takfir wa-l-Hijra resorted to kidnapping, and in 1981, Al-Jihad assassinated President Sadat (d. 1981). Not unlike his predecessors, President Mubarak curbed the influence of the Muslim Brotherhood by arresting its leadership. When he was removed from power by peaceful mass demonstrations in 2011, however, the Muslim Brotherhood was taken by surprise and began immediately to reorganize its structure to resonate with the new spirit of freedom. The Arab Spring, beginning with mass demonstrations in Tunisia and Egypt early in 2011, created enthusiasm but risks devolving into a leaderless revolution. The key challenge facing Muslim advocates for reform will be to identify and empower balanced leadership in the hitherto unfamiliar environment of human rights and democratic freedom.

In India and Pakistan, Mawlana Mawdudi, an Urdu journalist by profession, became one of the leading interpreters of Islam in the 20th century. Educated as a Hanafi Sunni, he was insulated from Western ideas and the English language but acquired a fluent knowledge of Arabic. Stung by Hindu assertions of Islam having been spread by the sword, he emphasized the spiritual and ethical dimensions of the doctrine of jihad, presenting it as a testimony to his profound conversion to the

Muslim faith. For the rest of his life, Mawdudi published his ideas in a monthly, making it the vehicle for his intense anti-Western feelings and his relentless desire to demonstrate the superiority of Islamic culture. For thirty years Mawdudi worked on his Qur'an commentary, in which he developed his political thought on the Islamic state. In 1941, he founded the Jama'at-i Islami, a carefully selected group that would disseminate his ideas and implement his plan for an ideal Islamic state that was not confined within national boundaries. Mawdudi was initially opposed to the creation of Pakistan as a separate state, out of fear that the Muslims in India would lose their religious identity. Nevertheless, when the subcontinent was divided in 1947, he opted to move to Pakistan, becoming the decisive force that directed the new nation away from the ideal of a secular state toward that of an Islamic state and infusing his ideas into the constitution of Pakistan.

Khomeini came from a family of strict Shi'i religious leaders in Iran; his father was killed on the orders of Reza Shah (r. 1925–41). Having been educated in Islamic schools, and having written extensively on Islamic law and philosophy, Khomeini was proclaimed an ayatollah in the 1950s in Qum, where he received the more exalted title of a *marja'* (grand ayatollah) after the death of Ayatollah Boroujerdi in 1960. Because he spoke out against Muhammad Reza Shah (r. 1941–79) and against Westernization, he was exiled to Najaf in Iraq in 1964. Asked to leave Iraq in 1978, Khomeini settled in a suburb of Paris and agitated from there for the overthrow of the shah and the establishment of an Islamic Republic in Iran. After the ouster of the shah, he returned to his homeland on February 1, 1979, and was acclaimed as the religious leader of the revolution. Khomeini came to power with the help of a network of mosques, the support of the bazaar, and the lower ranks of the military, together with a wide spectrum of leftist, secularist, and conservative traditionalist thinkers.

A new constitution created the Islamic Republic of Iran with Khomeini as its religious leader and legal guardian (*wilāyat al-faqīh*). More generally, a new theocratic political system gave the clerics ultimate control of the state. Although an elected president headed the executive branch, his authority was superseded by that of the legal guardian, who was supported by an advisory council of Shi'i jurists. Under Khomeini's direction, fundamentalist Muslim codes designed to suppress Western influence and restore shari'a were enacted. Women were required to wear the veil, alcohol and Western music were banned, and punishments prescribed by Islamic law were reinstated. Opposition figures were killed, imprisoned, or exiled. The fledging republic managed to survive war with Iraq (1980–88) but was unable to export its Shi'i brand of fundamentalism to other Muslim countries.

Perhaps the thorniest issue for Islamic political thought in the 20th century was the establishment of Israel on native Arab lands in 1948. To make room for Ashkenazi Jewish refugees from Central Europe and Sephardic Jewish immigrants from North Africa and the Middle East after World War II, Palestinian Arabs were driven from their homes without receiving any remuneration and forced to live in refugee camps. Wars in 1967 and 1973 between Israel and its neighbors, as well as

Israeli bombardments of Beirut in 1982 and cluster bombings of Southern Lebanon in July 2006, only deepened Arab resentment. Ongoing construction of new Israeli settlements on the high ground of Palestinian soil west of the Jordan River and dividing walls cutting through Palestinian villages further antagonized the Palestinians, who were promised a two-part quasi state—the Gaza Strip and the West Bank—without territorial, economic, or military sovereignty. While advocates for peace and reconciliation can be found within both liberal Israeli and Palestinian factions, the policies of far-right Israeli leaders have resisted reconciliation and reparation as dangerous weakness. American support of Israel created a deep dislike for American policy in the greater Middle East, which reverberated throughout the entire Muslim world.

In contemporary times, Pan-Islamism has remained a distant dream, secularism severed the bonds with a long and venerable Islamic heritage while fundamentalist movements forced Islam into a puritanical straitjacket, and militancy brought murder and destruction. Islam has not created a comprehensive system of political thought able to integrate the disparate elements informing its current stage of development. Emerging currents in political Islam are attempting to articulate ideologies and organize movements that aspire to inner purity, ethical strength, personal freedom, and collective dignity. Burdened with political and cultural fragmentation and labeled by the West as a violent religion, Islam thirsts for a new paradigm of political thought that will enable it to construct its future as a peaceful order in a pluralistic world.

Authority ⬦⬦⬦⬦⬦⬦⬦⬦⬦⬦⬦⬦⬦⬦⬦⬦⬦⬦⬦⬦⬦⬦⬦⬦

Roy Jackson

From the *laylat al-qadr*, the "night of power" in which the Qur'an symbolically "came down" from God, to the death of the Prophet, Muslim affairs were governed by the special authority of that prophetic-revelatory event, and it remains the primary paradigm of political authority in Islam. Muhammad was a religious, political, and military leader who founded a new form of community, an *umma*, that was both spiritual and worldly in nature. The development of this new community, which defined itself in terms of faith rather than national or tribal boundaries, marked a transition from polytheism to monotheism, and was ultimately shaped by both Arab tribal bonds and Persian monarchic systems.

The Arab Bedouin were not anarchic. Their society was governed by what the 14th-century North African philosopher of history Ibn Khaldun referred to as solidarity (*ʿaṣabiyya*). *Aṣabiyya* signifies internal cohesion, often brought about by the unity of blood or faith. Islam universalized this sense of belonging by replacing local, tribal customs with the sunna (the normative conduct of the Prophet) of the universal tribe called the *umma*, made concrete through the hadith (reports of the Prophet's sunna) and shariʿa (sacred law). In understanding political authority in the Islamic world, this "posttribal" element is essential, as authority does not rely necessarily on formal state structures. First and foremost, Muslims adhere to God and to the expression of God's commands through the medium of prophethood.

The Qur'an is composed in a rhythmic style that makes considerable use of symbolic and allegorical imagery. Its allusions and indirect explanations allow for a multitude of interpretations. Consequently, it is difficult to determine any firm principles of government within the text. The Qur'an provides examples of the proper use of authority, such as Muhammad's consultation with his Companions (3:159) or the imperative to abide by the principles of justice and kindness (e.g., 4:58, 65, 105, 135, and 16:90), but it is concerned more with general principles such as fairness, equity, and discipline than with specific details of government. Political theory in the Qur'an focuses on the status of Muhammad as Prophet and the authority he wielded as long as he was alive, although the Qur'an does suggest that his authority could be questioned and that his role was often one of arbiter among a federation of tribes rather than the possessor of absolute, unquestioned authority.

According to Sunni tradition, Muhammad did not specify a successor, while Shi'is believed that Muhammad had chosen his cousin and son-in-law 'Ali b. Abi Talib to succeed him. As a result of this conflict, a *fitna*, or civil war, divided the *umma* between 656 and 661. The title *khātam al-nabiyyīn* (usually translated as "seal of the prophets"), given to Muhammad in the Qur'an (33:40), has traditionally been interpreted to mean that there were to be no prophets after Muhammad, and so an important symbol of religious and political authority was lost after his death. Abu Bakr was selected as caliph (deputy) partly because he came from a relatively insignificant clan with no pretensions to power; it was a *falta*, an affair concluded with haste and without much reflection, to preserve the unity of the *umma* and avoid the very real danger of tribal conflict. In fact, Abu Bakr's status of successor to the messenger of God (*khalīfat rasūl Allāh*) did not come with great power. At the beginning of his reign he was only a part-time caliph, spending the rest of his time as a merchant. In his short reign of only two years, however, he maintained the Medinan regime, bringing the breakaway tribes back into the fold of the *umma* through the policy of wars of apostasy (*al-ridda*). Abu Bakr and the three caliphs that followed are known as the *Rāshidūn*, or the "Rightly Guided Caliphs," because they knew the Prophet personally and, it is believed, assimilated some of his charisma and values. As such, Muslims looked to the actions and words of the *Rāshidūn* as a source of authority.

Divisions within this new community nonetheless continued. The third caliph, 'Uthman b. 'Affan, was assassinated, and the *umma* was divided between those who supported and those who opposed 'Ali as the fourth caliph. 'Ali was subsequently assassinated by a puritan "seceder" (*khārijī*), and the majority of Muslims accepted his opponent, Mu'awiya b. Abi Sufyan (602–80), as the leader of the fledgling *umma*, thus beginning the reign of the Umayyads. The Sunnis eventually took the *Rāshidūn* as their model, stating that the leader should be elected by a council from within the Quraysh (the dominant tribe in Mecca), whereas Shi'is developed the notion of the imamate, in which leadership belonged to Muhammad's direct biological descendents.

The Umayyads and Abbasids

The period between 661 and 750 marks the era of two great Islamic dynasties: the Umayyad followed by the Abbasid. With the rapid spread of Islam, the *umma* came to include not only Arabs but also many other races and traditions, which affected its political makeup. As the religion spread, it encountered a patrimonial bureaucracy, prevalent in Iran. This absolutist notion of authority placed power in the hands of the monarch and his family, who ruled on behalf of the people. This model was in many respects adopted by both the Umayyad and Abbasid caliphs as the most efficient system to preserve order. Rule of law and stability trumped piety. A shift in title accompanied the shift in style of government: Umayyad and Abbasid caliphs preferred to be known as God's deputy (*khalīfat Allāh*) instead of successor or vicegerent of God's messenger (*khalīfat rasūl Allāh*). This claim to absolute authority was opposed not only by Shi'is but also by some Sunnis.

The Abbasids came to power following the Third Fitna (744–50) and claimed to represent justice, opposing themselves to the monarchical Umayyad regime and thus garnering support from Shi'is. Yet before long, they too became patrimonial, incorporating Iranian practices of government to an even greater extent than their predecessors. An early work on political thought was the *Risala fi al-Sahaba* (Epistle on the caliph's entourage, written 754–56) by Ibn al-Muqaffa', who served as secretary to Umayyad and Abbasid caliphs. In response, one suspects, to the views expressed by the Kharijis, he stated that all men are not, in fact, equal before God. Second, he stated that it was erroneous to obey a leader unconditionally, which seemed to reflect a Shi'i view. Ibn al-Muqaffa' argued for obedience to the caliph only so long as he acted according to the shari'a. This may at first suggest that the ultimate authority is Islamic law, with its basis in the Qur'an and the sunna of Muhammad especially, but Ibn al-Muqaffa' states that while shari'a is dominant, it is the role of the caliph to not only administer the law but also *interpret* it. This effectively takes power out of the hands of the 'ulama' (the religious body) and places it firmly in those of the caliph as God's deputy. This conflict of authority between the 'ulama' and the political body, symbolized by the caliph, has been a concern throughout much of Islamic history, with the 'ulama', on the whole, remaining silent on political matters, especially in the Sunni tradition. The political theory of Ibn al-Muqaffa', though simply presented, was best reflected in the career of the Abbasid caliph Ma'mun (r. 813–33), who put into practice Ibn al-Muqaffa''s view that leadership must have a strong ideological basis. Ma'mun associated himself closely with the Shi'i view of the imam and encouraged the translation of Greek philosophical texts by founding the House of Wisdom (Bayt al-Hikma) in Baghdad. These respected Greek works helped to portray monarchical leadership as more enlightened and therefore legitimized the caliphate, although many within the 'ulama' were suspicious of appealing to a philosophy that they considered "un-Islamic." This presents another conflict that has existed throughout Islamic history: the authority of theological "Islamic" sources as opposed to philosophical "non-Islamic" sources or, put another way, faith versus reason. Ma'mun argued for leadership on rational rather than religious grounds and promoted Mu'tazili teachings on the subject. This led to a Platonic conception of authority with a pessimistic view of human nature, which called for the masses to be ruled by a rational and enlightened caliphate. These views are perhaps best expressed by the Mu'tazili philosopher Jahiz (d. 869).

Although the Abbasids continued to hold the office of caliph, real power was eventually exercised by the Shi'i Buyids (932–1075), followed by the Sunni Seljuqs (1075–1258). From this point, what had been understood as "caliphate authority" transferred to the 'ulama', who also came to be known as imams. In Sunni Islam, the head of state no longer had religious authority. In 1258, the Abbasid capital of Baghdad fell to Mongol rule and the Abbasid caliphate became extinct. Consequently, authority became more communal or neotribal in nature with the development of jurisprudence (*fiqh*). In time the four legal schools (*madhhab*) were recognized and the influence of the legal scholar Shafi'i (d. 820) redefined authority. Shafi'i effectively put religious authority back into the hands of the 'ulama' rather than the caliphate.

Shi'i Leadership

The Zaydi Shi'i Qasim b. Ibrahim (785–860) also argued for a largely Platonic conception of political authority: obedience to the leader is a necessity due to the imperfections of human nature. In Sunni Islam, this meant that the caliphs had to legitimize their power by proclaiming themselves to be less susceptible to desires and emotions than other human beings, while not going so far as to declare themselves prophets. For Shi'is, this claim to legitimacy was made somewhat easier due to the semidivine status accorded to their imams. In Twelver Shi'ism, the imams are considered essential to the existence of the universe, especially the twelfth, Hidden Imam. This doctrine of leadership was developed under the Buyids by such notable figures as Mufid (d. 1022), Murtada (d. 1044), and Tusi (d. 1067). It is the belief of the "Twelver," or Imami, Shi'is that the Twelfth Imam, Muhammad al-Mahdi, went into occultation (*ghayba*, a period of concealment) in 873. While the Mahdi is in occultation, guidance must be provided by the religious scholars who are essentially the Mahdi's representatives. Only when the Twelfth Imam returns are Shi'is obliged to take over the political reins. Until then, they remain politically quiet under illegitimate rulers. In contemporary times, this doctrine led many to believe that Ayatollah Khomeini (1902–89) was the Mahdi.

Imami quietism was countered by a much more politically active Isma'ili doctrine that consisted of a hierarchy of seven emanations of God, with the seventh being the human world, and seven major historical epochs, each having its own prophet and seven imams. Their political hierarchy corresponds with this metaphysical pattern. In 909, the Fatimids declared 'Ubaydallah al-Mahdi (d. 934) to be the Mahdi; he went on to conquer Sicily, North Africa, and Egypt and took control of Mecca and Medina. No longer in hiding, the Fatimid imams could claim much greater political and religious authority than the Sunni caliphs.

The Seljuqs and a New Doctrine of the Caliphate

The creation of the Isma'ili Fatimid caliphate in Cairo, together with the existence of the Umayyad caliphate now residing in Andalusia, raised the question of who was the legitimate caliph and whether more than one caliph could exist at the same time. In addition, a military dynasty called the Buyids had effectively seized power within Baghdad, retaining the Sunni Abbasid caliphate as a symbol of unity, despite the fact that the Buyids were Shi'i sympathizers. Further, another force was on the horizon: the Seljuq Turks, who conquered Baghdad in 1055.

With the rise of the Seljuqs from the 11th century, a new Sunni polity emerged that, to a great extent, rejected rational, philosophical speculation in favor of legalism and literalism. One key figure of this period was Mawardi (972–1058), whose main political work, *On the Principles of Power* (also often translated as *On the Ordinances of Government*, *Kitab al-Ahkam al-Sultaniyya*), was written between 1045 and 1058, during the Seljuq Turks' rise to power in Baghdad. In this treatise, he expresses his preference for a strong caliphate based on revelation. Mawardi criticized the view of philosophers that reason alone was sufficient for an understanding of how to rule a state. For Mawardi, reason—a human construct—has its limitations, whereas revelation is God's word. Like the Christian thinker St. Thomas Aquinas, Mawardi saw a direct link between divinely revealed order and political order.

Another important figure during the Seljuq ascendancy was the theologian, jurist, philosopher, and mystic Ghazali (ca. 1058–1111), universally known as the "proof of Islam" (*ḥujjat al-islām*) and the great "renewer" (*mujtahid*) of the faith. He attempted to synthesize the three main strands of Islamic rationality: theoretical and philosophical enquiry, juridical legislation, and mystical practice. His writings redirected and reinvigorated Sunni religious thought in the aftermath of the Shi'i intellectual dominance of the previous century. In 1085, Ghazali went to Baghdad and joined the court of the celebrated Nizam al-Mulk (d. 1092), who, though merely a vizier, was effectively monarch in all but name and was at the height of his power. Ghazali's best-known work is *The Revival of the Religious Sciences* (*Ihya' 'Ulum al-Din*), in which he argues that the essence of the human being is the soul (*nafs*), which, in its original state—that is, before being attached to the body—is a pure, angelic, and eternal substance. Through reason, the soul has the potential to know the essence of things and acquire knowledge of God, but to achieve this potential it must attach itself to a body, for the body is the vehicle that carries the soul on its journey to God. The body, however, is a corrupting influence that succumbs to anger, desire, and evil. Consequently, the soul, though still possessing its divine elements, also has "animal" elements. To perfect the soul, the person must subordinate the animal qualities and pursue the virtues of temperance, courage, wisdom, and justice. This can be achieved through Sufi practices, which shut the gate to worldly desires. Ghazali points out, however, that it also is important to engage in the rituals associated with Islam, such as pilgrimage, prayer, ablutions, alms, fasting, reading the Qur'an, following the shari'a, and so on. Ghazali's views on religion and mysticism have political implications that are also Platonist in character, for only the few can truly manage to come close to perfecting their soul, and their knowledge of Islam gives them greater political authority. This was Ghazali's attempt to "revive" Islam by making knowledge of religion synonymous with political knowledge, for the religious and the worldly are interdependent.

Andalusian Politics

In the 11th and 12th centuries especially, efforts were made to determine a Sunni religious polity in opposition to the Christian Reconquista (the Spanish and Portuguese word for "reconquest," referring to the retaking of Andalus from the Muslims). Whereas the first major movement led by the Almoravid dynasty emphasized Hanbali literalism and even burned Ghazali's books, the second movement under the Almohads championed Islamic philosophy. This policy was supported by the Aristotelian philosopher Ibn Rushd (also known by the Latin name Averroes, 1126–98). For Ibn Rushd, the truth achieved through the study of philosophy does not differ from the truths of revelation as contained in the Qur'an. What may appear as difference is a matter of interpretation. Ibn Rushd argues that just as reason, through philosophy, can be used to reach truth, so can reason be used to interpret the Qur'anic text. The Qur'an contains many symbols, allegories, and analogies that can be instructive to the less learned, but, Ibn Rushd argues, those possessed of suitable intellect should determine their real meaning rather than treat them literally. It follows from this that the best qualified to interpret shari'a are philosophers, not the theologians. Ibn Rushd wrote commentaries on both Plato's and Aristotle's works, and the influence of these two Greek philosophers is evident in his political views, particularly his view that the leader should be a philosopher-king possessed of a rational intellect.

The Reign of the Mamluks

During the Mamluk regime (1250–1517), there were two great figures of Sunni Islamic political thought: Ibn Taymiyya (1263–1328) and Ibn Khaldun (1332–1406). Ibn Taymiyya was a jurist of the Hanbali school of law, a strict traditionalist who railed against what he saw as the "innovations" (bid'a) of such authorities in Islam as Ghazali, Ibn al-'Arabi, and the Sufis. He emphasized the need to return to what he perceived as the pristine ideals and practices of Islam at the time of the Prophet Muhammad. In his main political work, *Treatise on the Government of the Religious Law*, he argues that under the *Rāshidūn* the Islamic state achieved moral and political purity and that this should be the main aim of Islamic law. In Ibn Taymiyya's view, rulers since the *Rāshidūn* have failed to achieve such perfection. The ruler should follow rigorously the tenets of the shari'a, applying it firmly but fairly and relying on it for all legal opinions and rulings. Those who are ruled should obey the authority of the caliph provided he, in turn, obeys the shari'a. Ibn Taymiyya was dogmatic in his view that religion cannot be practiced without state power. The religious duty of "commanding right and forbidding wrong" (ḥisba), he argues, cannot be achieved without a central power and authority, and so there is a necessary link between state and

religion. Controversial in his own lifetime, he had few followers and little influence until long after his death. A small number of Ottoman scholars studied
him in the 16th century, but in the 18th century, Muhammad b. 'Abd al-Wahhab
(d. 1792) drew on Ibn Taymiyya's ideas to create Wahhabism, which, together
with his military endeavors, led to the creation of the first Saudi state in 1744.
Since that time, Ibn Taymiyya has been seen as the champion of revivalism and
the founder of many reform movements that look to the time of Muhammad and
the principles inculcated in the Qur'an to counter what is perceived as the threat
of modernism.

Ibn Taymiyya's idea that religion and government need each other was explored empirically by the great Muslim philosopher of history, Ibn Khaldun. His
major work on history (*Kitab al-'Ibar*) is divided into three books. The famous first
book, the *Prolegomena*, outlines his methodology and outlook on history as well
as the dynamics of human society. The second book concerns the history of the
Arabs, and the third deals with the history of the Berbers. Although the emphasis
of the work is political and focuses on the rise and fall of dynasties, it also explores
what politics tells us about human nature. Having studied philosophy, theology,
and history, Ibn Khaldun noted that philosophical concepts and reasoning had
been applied to theology but not to history. The central theme in the *Prolegomena*
is the sociology of human society, which he called the science of civilization (*'ilm
al-'umrān*). Studying *'ilm al-'umrān* would reveal the dynamics of human society,
which in turn would enable the historian to sift through historical records and
separate fact from fiction. Hence, historical facts are those that correspond to the
logic of societies' dynamics and their rules of evolution. To Ibn Khaldun, the power
base of each state depends on its *'aṣabiyya*, or group solidarity based on family ties
and lineage, which is to be found mostly among nomadic people and savage nations. Ibn Khaldun argues that the power of each *'aṣabiyya* extends basically to four
generations. The first generation, driven by tribal expansionism or religious mission, would conquer the settled nations and establish a powerful state. The second
generation would consolidate and expand the state, build its institutions, and still
enjoy strong solidarity due to its close connection with a tribal ethos. The third
generation would enjoy the prosperity of the state and provide support for arts, sciences, and culture but would have less solidarity as a result of its urban upbringing.
The fourth generation would waste the achievements of its ancestors. Confined to
a life of palace machinations and the pursuit of material gratification, members of
this generation would concern themselves mostly with raising money to spend on
their own welfare and the preservation of their thrones, which would lead to an
intensified tax burden on the populace. The resulting injustices would lead to the
dissolution of the state and the annihilation of its civilization, making it vulnerable to invasions from other nomadic or savage groups. The cycle then starts anew.
Despite the originality of his thought, however, it seems that his principles were
neither applied nor studied by his Muslim successors.

Muslim Rulers as "Masters of the Age"

Although little new political theory was produced during the period of the Otto-man dynasty, the ruler Süleiman "the Lawgiver" (*al-Qānūnī*, d. 1566), known in the West as "the Magnificent" due largely to his military conquests, oversaw the most detailed codification of Qur'anic and sultanic law that any Islamic state had ever experienced. Süleiman's update of the law codes that had been largely produced by the Ottoman sultan Mehmed II (d. 1481) later became known as "Süleiman's law-code." What came into existence was nonreligious law, known as *kanun*, which was the law of the sultan or Ottoman law (*kanuni osmani*). *Kanun* dealt with criminal infractions and was intended to supplement shari'a by specifying penalties, although the punishments actually tended to be harsher than those under shari'a. It also dealt with the collection of taxes, land tenure, and other matters. Finally, it was concerned with the form of government and the relationships between the various spheres of authority. Because of the integration of *kanun* and shari'a, the judges implemented secular as well as religious law in Islamic law courts. The justification for *kanun* was that shari'a simply could not cover everything required to maintain social order in such a huge empire with a diversity of cultures and beliefs, so, as shari'a law only applied to Muslims, another law was needed. Both systems of law, it was argued, were after the same thing, which was public order and justice. The problem was that *kanun* often conflicted with shari'a, although this raised less concern during Süleiman's reign than it did later, when the Ottoman Empire was in its decline. Süleiman, especially in his early years, considered himself the *ṣāḥib-qirān* (Lord of the Auspicious Conjunction), the very embodiment of human perfection, and thus a reflection of God Himself. The Mughal emperor Akbar (1542–1605) had like-wise given himself such a title, for it also meant that the ruler saw himself as the *universal* ruler of Islam who was responsible for guiding Muslims along the right path. Süleiman also called himself "caliph of the whole world." The Ottomans had claimed the title of caliph for some time, especially when Sultan Selim I (d. 1520) brought Mecca and Medina into his realm. It was believed that the sultan-caliph had not only the responsibility to execute shari'a in all parts of the world but also the power to interpret the law, hence the creation of *kanun*, the product of a ruler guided by divine inspiration.

Responses to Modernity

Sir Sayyid Ahmad Khan (1817–98) was an influential modernist thinker who, rather than shun Western influence, adopted it wholeheartedly. His importance rests in his realization that Islam needed to reform if it was to survive, although he remained a controversial figure due to his collaboration with the British, who occupied India at the time. Khan was a great believer in the need for Islam to modernize, and he saw in Western thought, especially in the realm of science, a force that he did not regard as antithetical to Islam. Like his counterparts in the Middle East, he believed that the survival of Islam required the abandonment of blind imitation (*taqlīd*). He undertook the reinterpretation of the Qur'an, believing the more obscure passages had to be interpreted symbolically, allegorically, or analytically in order to reveal their true meaning. He believed that reason played an important part in this process and that the main principles in the Qur'an were in tune with scientific progress and reason in accordance with nature. Like Ibn Rushd, Khan believed Islam was the religion of reason and nature. Heavily influenced by 19th-century European rationalism and natural philosophy, he also drew heavily on both the reformism of Shah Waliullah as well as the rationalism of Muʿtazilis and the Ikhwan al-Safaʾ (the Ismaʿili-influenced "Brothers of Purity").

Khan's fellow Indian Sir Muhammad Iqbal (1873–1938) remains an important influence not only in South Asia but also in the Middle East. He is renowned and admired for his passionate poetry, but he was also a philosopher, political thinker, and the spiritual father of Pakistan. He was aware of the problems faced by Islam when confronted with so-called modernity, in particular the failure to respond to Western encroachment not only in the political and social spheres but also in the technological and scientific arenas. His more philosophical works culminated in his *Secrets of the Self* (*Asrar-i-Khudi*), which speaks of the need for Muslims to reawaken their souls and act. His rejection of territorial nationalism was based on his belief in the *umma*: a community of like-minded individuals that existed beyond national boundaries. He saw in the Prophet Muhammad the exemplar of the Muslim community: a prophet-statesman who founded a society based on freedom, equality, and brotherhood reflected in the central tenet of "unity" (*tawḥīd*). In the practical sense, Iqbal believed that a requisite of being a good Muslim was to live under Islamic law, which acts as the blueprint for the perfect Islamic society as envisioned by the Prophet Muhammad. In 1937, Iqbal sent a letter to Muhammad ʿAli Jinnah, the leader of the Muslim League and future founder of Pakistan, in which he emphasized the importance of Islamic law if Islam was to remain a force in the region. Aside from the need for shariʿa to exist in any Islamic state, Iqbal also stressed the importance of absolute equality. He believed that democracy was the best form of government, whereas aristocracy suppressed human individuality. When Iqbal talked of democracy, however, he was not referring to Western forms of democracy, which give the franchise to any individual over a certain age regardless of educational level. In this sense, Iqbal shared a view of democracy not dissimilar from his compatriot Mawdudi (1903–79): democracy is only for those who are sufficiently learned to know what they are voting for.

Mawdudi was head and founder of the political movement Jamaʿat-i Islami, the Indo-Pakistan equivalent of the Muslim Brotherhood in Egypt, and was the most controversial and significant Islamic thinker and activist in the region until his death. In many respects, his views echo those of the modernist movement known as the Salafis. Mawdudi's writings and activities contributed greatly to the founding of Pakistan in 1947. His concentration on leaders rather than on the common man is reflected in his doctrine of *al-Jihad fi al-Islam*, in which the social order flows from the top down. This necessarily implies a form of authoritarianism: he believed that practical social change was impossible unless the views of the leadership changed first. On this point, he frequently makes reference to the authority of the Prophet, the caliphs, and the great jurists as prime examples of forces for change. Mawdudi considered an Islamic form of government to be a moral imperative: the system by which the laws of God are given form. Many Islamists, Mawdudi among them, make reference to a "golden era" of Islam, a period that is portrayed as a pure Islamic state, an age of unity between the religious and the secular with Muhammad as its head. In appealing to traditional hadith and histories, the Islamist sees ultimate authority resting with the *Rāshidūn*. Mawdudi does not detail exactly how much authority the rulings of past great jurists would have in his Islamic state, nor does he specify which rulings. In Mawdudi's Islamic state, authority—the power to make and enforce laws—would rest with a small number of individuals, acting as representatives of God. This conception of authority, which he calls "theo-democracy," is reminiscent of medieval European societies rather than any modern democratic system.

Together with his friend and colleague Afghani (1838–97), Muhammad 'Abduh (1849–1905) is the founder of the Salafis. Although considered modernist, this movement looks back to the time of Muhammad and his Companions as a guide to the right way to live. Together, these two figures were the most influential spokesmen for Egyptian Islamic modernism in the 19th century. 'Abduh's writings have had an immense and lasting influence on the Muslim world. His most distinguished follower was the Syrian Rashid Rida (1865–1935). 'Abduh and Rida are considered the great synthesizers of modern Islam. The general policy of the Salafis was to look to the "pious ancestors" (*al-salaf al-ṣāliḥ*, the Prophet Muhammad and his Companions primarily) for guidance but also to appeal to man's rational capacity. While those laws that governed worship, such as prayer, fasting, and pilgrimage, were unchangeable, the majority of legislation, such as regulation on family law and the penal codes, were open to change according to the social and cultural traditions of the time. In theory, then, a Salafi approach to Islam should allow for independent reasoning, although there is always the danger that interpreters would be unwilling to adopt anything other than a literal approach to the "pious ancestors" and the Qur'an, in the same way some Muslim scholars have been reluctant to contradict the rulings of traditional legal scholars.

The Tunisian Rachid al-Gannouchi (b. 1941) is a controversial political and social activist who represents the generation following that of the Salafis. While maintaining essential Islamic values, he sees no contradiction between a multiparty system, pluralism, or women's rights, for example, and Islam. Gannouchi argues that what is at fault with Islam, at least in his own society, is its failure to identify itself with the impoverished working classes and with women. In his view, Islam should be seen as a liberating force, not an oppressive one. In fact, he argues that democracy originates in Islam and that the Western concept was inherited from Islamic civilization during the Middle Ages. For Gannouchi, a state that upholds such values as human rights, the rule of law, a multiparty system, and freedom of speech is in effect a Muslim state, regardless of its secular credentials. He argues that he would rather live in a free secular state than any state that imposes an oppressive version of Islam. As his paradigm, he cites Andalusia (Muslim Spain) as a time when Islam embraced diversity and pluralism and thrived from it.

Recent Shi'i Political Thought

'Ali Shari'ati (1933–77) is regarded as the ideological father of the 1979 Iranian Revolution. His writings were certainly revolutionary, modern in style, and radical in approach, targeting the oppression and alienation experienced by Muslims under the Pahlavi regime in Iran. Shari'ati combined Islamic concepts with Western political philosophy. While acknowledging the popular appeal of Marxist ideology, he criticized it for treating people as mere units of production. Islam, he argued, was always inherently a mass movement but also possessed humanistic values that Marxism lacked. Shari'ati placed great emphasis on the role of man as God's vicegerent on Earth. In other words, God had given man the responsibility of ruling the Earth: "man" did not mean, for Shari'ati, a small minority or a caliph, but all people. Therefore, God's vicegerency was synonymous with the power of the masses, of *al-nās* (the people). To Shari'ati, the *umma* is a classless society over which only God's will can reign. While Shari'ati's ideas owe much to the revolutionary values of Karl Marx and the existential values of Jean-Paul Sartre, he also takes a great deal from the works of mystical Muslims such as Ibn Sina (commonly known by his Latinized name, Avicenna, 980–1037) and Sadr ad-Din Muhammad Shirazi (also called Mulla Sadra, 1571–1641). In his well-known work *The Sociology of Islam*, Shari'ati writes of the "theomorphic man": a "Perfect Man" who possesses the qualities of truth, goodness, and beauty, a rebellious spirit who combines the virtues of Jesus, Caesar, and Socrates. This vision of a "theomorphic being" owes much to the concept of the Perfect Man (*insān-i kāmil*) as promulgated by Ibn al-'Arabi and the Sufis, which was also developed by the Indian poet and reformer Iqbal. In fact, Shari'ati's writings on science and nature are highly reminiscent of Iqbal, for he also regarded the Qur'anic view of nature as close to the scientific view of the world, and perhaps surprisingly, Shari'ati sees Iqbal, a Sunni Muslim, as typical of the Perfect Man.

If Shari'ati was the ideological father of the revolution, Khomeini was its living symbol and guide. In his writings and lectures, Khomeini argued that if Islam was to be rejuvenated, it needed to look toward the Perfect Man for guidance, and he sets out the qualities required. He argued that monarchy is incompatible with Islam and rejects Iranian nationalism in favor of an Islamic universalism, albeit of the Shi'i variety. By the 1970s, Khomeini was arguing that in the absence of the imam, the clergy should do more than simply advise the government; instead, the clergy should rule directly. This doctrine of "rule by the jurists" (*wilāyat al-faqīh*) had little Qur'anic support and was rejected by virtually all the Shi'i clergy. For Khomeini, however, the concept of rule by jurists was a logical conclusion to the much more widely held view that an Islamic state, if it were to be truly Islamic, must be governed by shari'a. It was believed that shari'a amounted to a complete social system, providing regulations for all aspects of life: if this was indeed the case, then all legislation has been provided for by God. The problem rests, however, in interpreting divine law so that it may adapt to changing circumstances. Shi'ism has a long tradition of *ijtihād* (independent reasoning), and Khomeini argued that those best qualified for *ijtihād* are the jurists. Khomeini presents a view of his Republic of Iran not unlike Plato's hypothetical *Republic*: a state governed by philosopher-kings who should rule because they have access to moral truths.

Counter to Khomeini is Abdolkarim Soroush (b. 1945), who has offended the traditional clergy by questioning the validity of the concept of *wilāyat al-faqīh*. Soroush argues that, as the knowledge of the jurists is human rather than sacred, they should not be allowed to claim infallible authority. Instead of obeying the dictates of the ayatollahs, or any person claiming a monopoly in religious knowledge, Soroush argues that the student of religion should struggle to determine his own understanding of the body of religious knowledge through dialogue and questioning. Soroush's democratic approach to knowledge encourages people not to imitate or obey previous rulings but to search for themselves; otherwise, jurists will become power hungry and hypocritical. He has championed the cause of democracy on the basis that Islam cannot thrive unless such a political system exists: people must be free to believe or not, and Islam, or any religion, cannot be imposed upon a people from above.

Further Reading

Aziz Ahmad, *An Intellectual History of Islam in India*, 1969; Hamid Algar, *Religion and State in Iran 1785–1906: The Role of the Ulema in the Qajar Period*, 1969; Joel Beinin and Joe Stork, eds., *Political Islam: Essays from Middle Eastern Reports*, 1997; Patricia Crone and Martin Hinds, *God's Caliph: Religious Authority in the First Centuries of Islam*, 1986; Hamid Enayat, *Modern Islamic Political Thought*, 1982; John Esposito, ed., *Voices of Resurgent Islam*, 1983; Marshall G. S. Hodgson, *The Venture of Islam: Conscience and History in a World Civilization*, 3 vols., 1974; Albert Hourani, *Arabic Thought in the Liberal Age, 1798–1939*, 1983; Roy Jackson, *Fifty Key Figures in Islam*, 2006; Idem, *Mawlana Mawdudi and Political Islam: Authority and the Islamic State*, 2011; Ira M. Lapidus, *A History of Islamic Societies*, 1988; W. Montgomery Watt, *Islamic Political Thought*, 1968.

Caliphate ⌗⌗⌗⌗⌗⌗⌗⌗⌗⌗⌗⌗⌗⌗⌗⌗⌗⌗⌗⌗⌗⌗⌗⌗⌗⌗⌗⌗⌗⌗⌗⌗⌗⌗⌗

Wadad Kadi and Aram A. Shahin

The caliphate (*al-khilāfa*) is the term denoting the form of government that came into existence in Islamic lands after the death of the Prophet Muhammad and is considered to have survived until the first decades of the 20th century. It derives from the title caliph (*khalīfa*, pl. *khulafā'* or *khalā'if*), referring to Muslim sovereigns who claimed authority over all Muslims. The caliphate refers not only to the office of the caliph but also to the period of his reign and to his dominion—in other words, the territory and peoples over which he ruled. The office itself soon developed into a form of hereditary monarchy, although it lacked fixed rules on the order of succession and based its legitimacy on claims of political succession to Muhammad. The caliphate was constrained by neither any fixed geographical location or boundaries nor particular institutions; rather, it was coterminous with the reign of a monarch or a dynasty.

This chapter discusses the political, historical, and institutional aspects of the caliphate but not the theological or judicial. Despite frequent overlap between the terms caliph/imam and caliphate/imamate, this chapter also does not deal with topics that are only relevant to imam/imamate, as in Shi'ism, for example.

The term "caliphate" is most commonly restricted to five periods or dynasties: the Rightly Guided Caliphate (632–61), the Umayyad caliphate (661–750), the Abbasid caliphate (750–1258 and 1261–1517), the Fatimid caliphate (909–1171), and the Umayyad caliphate of Córdoba (928–1031). Throughout the centuries, however, various other rulers have made claims to the caliphate or adopted the caliphal titulature—that is, one or more titles usually associated with caliphs. The first four successors of the Prophet Muhammad are usually called the Rightly Guided Caliphs (*al-khulafā' al-rāshidūn*). But those Muslims who do not accept the legitimacy of some of these rulers refrain from applying this expression to them.

Despite the ubiquitous use of the terms "caliphate" and "caliph" in modern scholarship, they were not the principal or exclusive terms used in official documents or in the writings of Muslim authors, nor were they adopted immediately following Muhammad's death. Many Muslim writers eschewed these two terms in favor of alternatives, especially imam and *imāma*, or (religious) leader and leadership. The two terms, "caliph" and "caliphate," were almost always employed in conjunction with other terms and expressions. They also hardly appear in official or unofficial documentary sources (papyri, coins, rock inscriptions, textiles, weights, and seals), and non-Muslim sources do not use them when referring to Muslim sovereigns or to Islamic political institutions, especially for the first Islamic centuries. The institution of the caliphate developed gradually with time and crystallized only at the beginning of the Abbasid period in the second half of the eighth century. Also, despite their claims to universal rule over all Muslims, few Muslim sovereigns actually did so; many provinces and regions controlled by Muslims did not acknowledge the suzerainty of any caliph. Furthermore, the caliphs possessed actual power for a relatively short period, as they became mostly puppets in the hands of military commanders and high-ranking officials.

The history of the development of the institution of the caliphate can be divided as follows:

632–945. This timespan covers three periods. The foundational period, beginning with the election of Abu Bakr as leader of the Muslim community after the Prophet's death in 632, continued until the end of the second *fitna* (civil war) in the second half of the seventh century. It was followed by the formative period and period of strength, from the reign of 'Abd al-Malik (r. 685–705) to about the middle of the ninth century. The subsequent period saw the decline of central caliphal authority and growth of independent and autonomous regions in the ninth and tenth centuries, when an increasing number of provinces were ruled by semi-autonomous or autonomous dynasties. The gradual loss of power by the Abbasid caliphs culminated with the Buyids gaining control of Baghdad in 945.

945–1517. Two periods are included in this time frame. A period of multiple caliphates, which extended from the 10th to the 12th centuries, began with the establishment of the Fatimid caliphate in 909 in Ifriqiya, followed by that of the Umayyads in Córdoba in 928. The latter, a Sunni caliphate, lasted a century, while the former, a Shi'i Isma'ili one, extended its rule to Egypt and Syria and lasted until 1171. The period of the shadow caliphate ensued as the Muslim world became independent of any caliphal control between the 12th century and 1517. This period saw the demise of the Abbasid caliphate after the Mongols' sack of Baghdad in 1258 and the transfer to Cairo, then under Mamluk rule, of a scion of the dynasty in 1261. This caliphate, which had neither power nor symbols thereof, ended in 1517 with the Ottoman conquest of Egypt. Other dynasties, like the Hafsids (1229–1574) and the Marinids (1269–1465), appropriated the caliphal titulature, although they lacked the universalist ambitions of the original caliphates.

1517–1924. With the fall of the Abbasid caliphate, there arrived a period of multiple pretenders and competition for supremacy in the Muslim world. A greater number of Muslim rulers added the title *khalīfa* to their titulature, although for most rulers that did not correspond to any higher claims of authority over all Muslim lands, as was the case of the Mughal rulers from Akbar (r. 1556–1605) to Shah 'Alam II (r. 1759–1806). The title caliph was also given to Ottoman sultans, first unofficially from the end of the 14th century, and then officially in the 18th and 19th centuries. The end of the caliphate came about in February 1924, when the Grand National Assembly of Ankara deposed the Ottoman sultan 'Abd al-Majid II and abolished the caliphate. Some Muslim rulers attempted but failed to restore the institution, notably the Sharif of Mecca, al-Husayn b. 'Ali, in 1924, and King Farouk of Egypt in 1939.

Not all Muslims considered their rulers primarily as caliphs, nor did all Muslims interpret the title of *khalīfa* in the same way. Not only did the institution of the caliphate itself develop over time, but so did the terminology associated with it and the way that Muslims throughout the world viewed it.

Titulature of Pre-Islamic Arabian Monarchs

For centuries prior to the rise of Islam, sovereigns in the Arabian Peninsula adopted a titulature based on the title *m.l.k* (king, monarch). This is attested in documents written in the various North and South Arabian languages that were in use in the Arabian Peninsula and dating from approximately the seventh century BCE to the mid-sixth century CE. The title was also employed by Arabian dynasties at the northern limits of the Arabian Peninsula (like the Nabataeans and the Palmyrenes) that used non-Arabian languages (Aramaic and Greek) in their documents. The use of the title *m.l.k* occurs in rare pre-Islamic inscriptions in Arabic as well.

That *malik* was the title in Arabic given to the holder of the highest political office is further verified in subsequent literature in Arabic. In the Qur'an, the title appears 13 times in the singular and twice in the plural (*mulūk*) to denote a sovereign, with 5 of the 13 occurrences in the singular actually referring to God, who is described as the ultimate possessor of all sovereignty. In pre-Islamic Arabic poetry, an independent monarch's title is also *malik*. This is also the title given to sovereigns, both Arabian (from the pre-Islamic period) and non-Arabian (of all periods), in Islamic Arabic literary sources from the eighth century onward (e.g., *mulūk Kinda*, or kings of Kinda, and *mulūk al-Rūm*, or kings of the Romans).

The predominance of the title *malik* in the Arabian Peninsula over a 1,000-year period was broken when Muslim sovereigns did not adopt a titulature based on it. The reason for that may be the Qur'anic notion that God is the one and only king of all (creation). Indeed, kingship came to be considered synonymous with worldly rule from early Abbasid times, when a hadith (a Prophetic tradition) was circulated attributing to the Prophet Muhammad the statement, "*Khilāfa* after me will be thirty years; after that it will be kingship." Since the Rightly Guided Caliphs ruled for 30 years, they were given an especially elevated position by Sunni religious scholars, who called their rule the "vicarage of prophecy" (*khilāfat al-nubuwwa*), mostly considering the caliphs' order in succession as their order in merit.

Titulature of Early Muslim Sovereigns up to 750

According to Islamic literary sources, Abu Bakr, the first leader of the Muslim community after Muhammad's death, adopted the title of *khalīfat rasūl Allāh*, "the successor of the messenger of God." It is, however, unlikely that Abu Bakr held any official title, since the literary sources make this assertion for polemical reasons, to argue that the title *khalīfa*, which came into official use much later, is in reality short for *khalīfat rasūl Allāh*, not *khalīfat Allāh*. This debate over the meaning of the term *khalīfa* probably emerged during the early Abbasid period.

The literary sources also assert that 'Umar b. al-Khattab, Abu Bakr's successor, coined for himself the title of *amīr al-mu'minīn*, "Commander of the Faithful," in part because the conquests gave him a military standing. Some reports state that this title was held before him by 'Abdallah b. Jahsh during the Prophet's lifetime. Nonetheless, there is reason to accept that 'Umar was the first sovereign to adopt the title of *amīr al-mu'minīn*, since there is evidence that his successor, 'Uthman b. 'Affan, used it in diplomatic exchanges with foreign rulers. The first documentary attestations of this title to date come from the reign of Mu'awiya (r. 661–80). His full title in Arabic documents reads, "*'abd Allāh Mu'āwiya amīr al-mu'minīn*," or "God's servant, Mu'awiya, Commander of the Faithful"; in Greek documents, it is fully transliterated, and on a silver coin (*dirham*) the titulature is partially transliterated and partially translated into Pahlavi.

In fact, the official full titulature of the earliest Muslim sovereigns up to the end of the Umayyad period was the formula *'abd Allāh* (name of sovereign) *amīr al-mu'minīn*, which means "God's servant (name), Commander of the Faithful." This is found on a variety of official and unofficial documents (most commonly inscriptions, papyri, coins, seals, and weights) and in several languages. The sovereign is normally identified by his first name only, although sometimes the father's name is also included.

The only deviation from this titulature was the addition, on some coins from the reign of 'Abd al-Malik, of the title *khalīfat Allāh*, although the first word of the title had a peculiar orthography *(kh.l.f.t)* that has been read differently by various scholars. The title *khalīfat Allāh* was, however, removed from coins during the reign of 'Abd al-Malik himself, and it does not reappear in the surviving documents until the Abbasid period. Could this have been in response to early objections to the use of this title by the Muslim sovereign? The Umayyad caliphs, including 'Abd al-Malik, did not object to being addressed by such a title by poets in panegyrics.

The term *khilāfa*—not *khalīfa*—appears even later in documentary sources, the earliest being an unofficial inscription dated 737–38 from the reign of Hisham (r. 724–43). It then appears officially near the end of the Umayyad dynasty in a lead seal and two lead bullae of Marwan b. Muhammad (r. 744–50). Such attestations indicate that the office or institution of the caliphate was indeed officially identified by a term derived from *khalīfa* by the end of Umayyad times, although the predominant title of Umayyad sovereigns until the end of their dynasty in 750 remained *amīr al-mu'minīn*.

Although the titulature of Muslim sovereigns in documentary sources presents a clear break with the titulature of pre-Islamic monarchs, the break was not as pronounced in Arabic poetry, where the vocabulary used to refer to politics and political institutions evolved gradually with time. In the poetry allegedly contemporaneous with the Prophet and his first successors, rulers are still mostly referred to with pre-Islamic terms and concepts interspersed with some new Islamic terms. The latter grow steadily in importance and become more prevalent so that by the end of the Umayyad period, they dominate the political vocabulary of the poetry. Beginning with poetry from 'Umar's reign, the titles imam and *amīr al-mu'minīn* are applied to Muslim sovereigns, while *khalīfat Allāh* is first attested from the reign of Mu'awiya. Some scholars have mistakenly assumed that the latter title was already in use during the reign of 'Uthman because it is applied to him in several verses. However, all these verses come from elegies, which means that they were posthumous to 'Uthman's reign. In addition, Mu'awiya and the later Umayyads built their legitimacy partly on their association with 'Uthman, and, therefore, a poet lamenting 'Uthman's death was not only expressing his sorrow for the slain sovereign but also presenting his allegiance to the Umayyads. This in turn means that such verses could have been composed any time during the Umayyad period. Poets with different political allegiances opted for different political vocabulary. Those who favored 'Ali b. Abi Talib and his descendants avoided using the title *khalīfa* for their political leaders, preferring to use imam or *amīr al-mu'minīn*. The latter term eventually became the sole prerogative of 'Ali in Shi'i literature.

In the Islamic literary sources, the titulature applied to Muslim sovereigns varies from source to source. Most sovereigns are referred to just by their first names or by their full names when it is necessary to avoid ambiguity. If a titulature is given to the sovereign, then the choice of titles usually depends on the author himself, although there are trends depending on the religious affiliation of the author and/or the type of literature that is being composed. An author could favor the title *amīr al-mu'minīn*, or imam, or *khalīfa*, or might use all three interchangeably. However, in works of hadith or *fiqh*, the title of imam takes precedence over the others. Imam is also the title preferred by non-Sunni authors, such as the Zaydis, the Ibadis, and the Imami Shi'is. On the other hand, Christian authors writing in Arabic apply the title *malik* to all sovereigns, whether Muslim or non-Muslim.

Non-Muslim authors writing in a language other than Arabic chose one of three ways to refer to Muslim sovereigns in their literary compositions: (1) through their given names only; (2) through a title in their native language that was commonly used to refer to other sovereigns; and (3) by applying the title *amīr al-mu'minīn* to them, in either a transliterated or translated form.

The Meaning of the Title *Khalīfat Allāh*

Most modern scholars have understood the title *khalīfat Allāh* to mean "vicegerent of God" or "deputy of God." However, this was not the original meaning of the expression.

The title itself appears rarely in pre-Abbasid documentary sources and never in papyri. But the term *khalīfa* itself does appear several times in papyri dated from the eighth to the tenth century, beginning with a bilingual, Arabic-Greek receipt dated 643. In most of these examples, the individuals referred to as *khalīfa*s are involved in some financial transaction, usually the collection of, or receipt for, a payment, without any associated political connotation.

For a better understanding of the meaning of the title, we must study pre-Islamic documents from Arabia. In South Arabian languages, words from the root *kh.l.f* have several meanings (e.g., "gate of a town" and "violating an oath"). But one meaning has a political/administrative connotation and occurs in two inscriptions by Abraha, the sixth-century South Arabian monarch of Abyssinian origin. The usage of the verb *s.t.kh.l.f* in these two texts is similar to the Arabic *istakhlafa*, which is a Qur'anic word and is often found in *Sīra* literature to describe the Prophet's appointment of individuals as overseers of Medina with limited authority during his absence from the town. The spelling of the term *kh.l.f.t*, which appears twice in one of these texts, is also identical with that of *khalīfa* as found on the coins of 'Abd al-Malik. The exact meaning of these words remains unclear. Scholars have translated *kh.l.f.t* as "governor" and as "viceroy," but they have been influenced in this interpretation by later Arabic usage.

The most common occurrence of words from the root *kh.l.f* in pre-Islamic documents is in personal names found in North and South Arabian; in Nabataean and Palmyrene, the names are based on the root *h.l.p*. Transliterated forms of these names are found in Greek documents as well. Scholars agree that the names based on the root *kh.l.f* are originally compound names, part of which is the name of a deity, although the latter is often omitted. In all instances where the name of the deity appears in full, the name is *l.h* or *'.l.h*. These compound names have equivalents in Arabic based on the root *kh.l.f* added to the name Allah. Understanding the meaning of these names can provide us with an insight on the meaning of the title *khalīfat Allāh*.

In bilingual inscriptions, names from the Semitic root *kh.l.f/h.l.p* are equated with the Greek Antipatros and less frequently Antigonos. These names were given to newborns considered as replacements for a relative, most commonly the father, who had died. A number of scholars have argued that the belief was that a god had replaced the deceased person with the newborn baby. Equivalent names in Arabic from the root *kh.l.f* carry the same meaning and are attested from the earliest surviving documents in Arabic to the present day.

Scholars thus agree that the meaning of the names based on the root *kh.l.f* is "replacement or substitute (of a deceased person) *by* a god." It is the god that makes (*ja'ala*)—selects, assigns, designates, creates, places—the *khalīfa*. This is exactly the meaning and usage that we find in the Qur'an. It is also the same meaning that late Umayyad ideology used in order to legitimate Umayyad rule, making prophethood and the caliphate parallel institutions, both initiated and implemented by God.

Words derived from the root *kh.l.f* have various meanings in Arabic. But if we focus on the meaning "to substitute" or "to replace," we notice that in the Qur'an, these actions are always associated with God: it is God that is replacing or bringing forth substitutes for individuals or peoples. In other words, the making—selecting, assigning, designating, creating, placing—of *khalīfa*s in the Qur'an is the exclusive prerogative of God. The word *khalīfa* appears in the Qur'an twice (2:30 and 38:26), where God is explicitly said to make or have made a *khalīfa*. The two plural forms *khalā'if* and *khulafā'* occur in similar situations seven times. In all these instances, the verb used is *ja'ala*. However, none of these Qur'anic terms possesses a specifically political connotation, nor did early Muslim scholars in the Umayyad period equate the Qur'anic *khalīfa* with the head of the Islamic community; this had to wait until the tenth century, well into Abbasid rule.

This clearly indicates that the original meaning of the expression *khalīfat Allāh* was "replacement or successor placed by (the agency of) God," and not "vicegerent or deputy *of* God." The title indicated God's approval of the sovereign and God's support of his legitimacy.

Succession to Rule after Muhammad

Soon after the Prophet Muhammad's death in 632, leading Medinan Muslims met to discuss the leadership of the community. Some Meccan Muslims rushed to the meeting and ended any attempts to divide rule over the Muslims. In the spur of the moment, Abu Bakr was given a pledge of allegiance (*bay'a*) as the leader of the Muslim community. His election was formalized at the mosque of Medina, where he received the general allegiance of all present Muslims.

Before his death in 634, Abu Bakr designated 'Umar b. al-Khattab as his successor. The Muslim community did not in this case select their ruler but only endorsed the choice of Abu Bakr by making a pledge of allegiance to 'Umar. After he was critically stabbed in 644, 'Umar appointed a consultative council (*shūrā*) of six members that was to select one of its own as his successor. They chose 'Uthman b. 'Affan. After 12 years of rule, 'Uthman was killed in 656 by a group of Muslims after he refused their demands to abdicate or to accept deposition.

Medinan Muslims subsequently selected 'Ali as 'Uthman's successor. 'Ali was immediately cast in an impossible situation, between arresting or protecting some of his supporters who were implicated in the killing of 'Uthman. He moved his base from Medina to Kufa in Iraq and faced continuous civil strife. 'Ali was victorious at the Battle of the Camel; however, the Battle of Siffin against the governor of Syria, Mu'awiya, ended with an arbitration that led to a stalemate. As a result, a group splintered from 'Ali's camp, the Kharijis, whom 'Ali was forced to fight. He was eventually killed by one of them in 661.

The Kufans immediately elected 'Ali's son, Hasan, to succeed his father. This was the first time that a son succeeded a father as head of the Muslim community. But the Syrians had already elected Mu'awiya as sovereign, and Hasan relinquished his position to Mu'awiya in 661. Then, for the first time in the history of the Muslim community, a sovereign, Mu'awiya, designated a successor, his son Yazid, as his heir apparent during his lifetime. This designation was controversial, but its limited success, followed by Yazid's accession to the caliphate in 680, laid the foundation for hereditary rule. A few years later, Marwan b. al-Hakam (r. 683–85) was able to set up his family as the first Islamic dynasty.

Overall, there were two main methods of succession in the caliphates: by designation, which was the most common method, or by election, when a successor had not been designated. Designation was normally done by a testament (ʿahd), when the heir apparent, normally of the age of majority, was called walī al-ʿahd ("one in charge of safeguarding the testament," equivalent to crown prince); his appointment was binding on him and on the community and could not, in principle, be repealed. In the case of the Marwanids, all their rulers were nominated by their predecessors, with the exception of Marwan, the founder, Yazid b. al-Walid (r. 744), and Marwan b. Muhammad. On some occasions during the Abbasid period, the caliph was elected by a group of dignitaries when the previous monarch died without having designated a successor. But in the case of the Fatimids, succession was accepted solely through an explicit designation (naṣṣ) from the previous caliph/imam.

Several times during the Marwanid and Abbasid periods, the ruling monarch designated two successors simultaneously. This usually caused tensions within the ruling family that occasionally escalated into full warfare. Succession in the various caliphates was agnatic (i.e., restricted to males in the male line) and did not follow rules of primogeniture. In fact, there were no fixed regulations for the succession as any member of the ruling family had a theoretical claim to the throne. Although sons were favored, succession could pass on to a brother, a cousin, an uncle, or a nephew.

Once selected, the new caliph was procedurally given the bayʿa, or oath of allegiance of the community. This was done through a handshake by the dignitaries of the town or province in which the caliph resided. Those in distant lands gave their allegiance through the governors of their respective districts.

The caliph was considered the leader of the Muslim community, just like the Prophet without the function of prophecy. As such, he was the judge and temporal authority in the realm, who appointed the members of his government, maintained order in society, defended the community against its enemies, and collected and distributed its wealth. But above all, he was the Muslims' religious leader who ensured the obedience of the community to the divine law. Thus he led the Friday communal prayer, the Friday sermon was held in his name, he led the Muslim armies in jihad, and he led the annual pilgrimage to Mecca. Under the Abbasids, he protected religion from innovations that departed from established practice; wore in public the Prophet's insignia, his cloak (burda) and scepter (qaḍīb); took up titles that emphasized his relation to God, like al-manṣūr ("one made victorious by God"); and identified himself as "God's power (sulṭān) on His Earth." Whatever religious duty he could not fulfill, he delegated to others to fulfill in his name. Whether he was an interpreter of the law is a more complicated question. Certainly the early caliphs, including the Rightly Guided Caliphs and the early Umayyads, played an active role in shaping and adding to the corpus of Islamic law. In early Abbasid times, the intellectual Ibn al-Muqaffa' proposed to the caliph Mansur (r. 754–75) that the caliph start, supervise, and play an active part in the construction of a unified code of Islamic law. Mansur, however, did not implement his proposal, and the development of the law remained the domain of religious scholars. This situation was confirmed further after Ma'mun's (r. 813–33) and his two successors' failure to impose their theological ideas on those scholars in the famous *mihna*, or inquisition. The interpretation of the law since then remained outside the functions of the caliph.

Once a caliph acceded to power, there were no regulations in place that specified how he could be deposed. The issue is old, raised by the opponents of 'Uthman, as we have seen; both the Umayyads (except Yazid b. al-Walid) and the Abbasid caliphs implicitly believed that only God could remove them from power since it was He who placed them in power. But by the tenth century, it was legally stipulated that if the monarch lost his mental health or certain aspects of his physical fitness after his accession to power, then he should be deposed and replaced. Blindness in particular made one ineligible to accede to the throne. This rule existed already in the Roman and Sasanian empires as well as in the Latin-speaking kingdoms, and it led some political rivals to blind their opponents in order to make them ineligible to rule. Among Muslim caliphs, the first instances of this practice occurred in the tenth century, when several Abbasid monarchs were blinded by high-ranking officials in order to have them replaced: Qahir in 934, Muttaqi in 944, and Mustakfi in 946.

Theoretical Works on the Caliphate

Prior to the decline of the caliphal system in the tenth century, theoretical works on the caliphate were scarce, short, and almost accidental. During late Umayyad times, for example, the distinguished secretary 'Abd al-Hamid (d. 750), in defense of the Umayyads, expressed his vision of the caliphate as an institution parallel to, and succeeding, prophethood, with both institutions created by God and with the obligation of all Muslims to obey "God's caliphs" as they obey God and the Prophet. Under the Abbasids, the Hanafi jurist Abu Yusuf (d. 798) believed God to be the source of power but the imam is His vicegerent on Earth who must have sufficient resources to rule. And the Mu'tazili litterateur Jahiz (d. 869) believed the imamate was necessary due to the predatory nature of humans, but an impious ruler may be removed from power if the circumstances permitted that.

From the 11th century onward, theoretical works intensified among Sunnis with the resurgence of Sunnism under the Seljuqs and their successors. The most influential and authoritative of those works is Mawardi's (d. 1058) *al-Ahkam al-Sultaniyya* (The ordinances of government). There the author considers the caliphate necessary on the basis of divine law, not of reason, giving the caliph alone the mandate to rule from God; it is his prerogative to delegate authority and lend legitimacy to the other members of his government (the vizier, the judge, etc.). The author discusses the requirements for being caliph, vizier, or judge and considers, due to the de facto deterioration of caliphal power, allowing more than one caliph under specific circumstances, validating the rule of usurpers, limiting caliphal power, and even—albeit unclearly—removing him from office. Ghazali (d. 1111) goes further. Although he asserts that the caliph was the supreme symbol of the divine law, he considers the rule of whoever holds actual political power as valid provided he received nominal recognition by the caliph. Writing after the Mongol invasion and the de facto end of the classical caliphal system, Ibn Taymiyya (d. 1348) reaffirmed the legitimacy of those who have actual power and did not even believe that they required legitimation from the caliph.

In the modern era, debates about the political and social meanings of the term "caliph" turned into a platform for Muslim intellectuals to debate the ideas of reform, constitutionalism, and the need to rethink Islamic political theory according to the needs of the modern age. Shah Waliullah (1703–62) separated the social from the political and believed in the existence of two types of caliphate: an outward caliphate (*khilāfat al-ẓāhir*), the political authority in charge of the superficial order, and an inward caliphate (*khilāfat al-bāṭin*), guarded by religious scholars and responsible for the social order. Usman dan Fodio (1754–1817), championing a program for political and social change, declared a jihad that led to the establishment of the Sokoto caliphate (in modern Nigeria) in 1806. The reformist Rashid Rida, in his *al-Khilafa aw al-Imama al-'Uzma* (The caliphate or the supreme leadership, 1922) called for a renewed Arab caliphate, in which the caliph needed to adapt Islamic law to the needs of modern life. In 1925, 'Ali 'Abd al-Raziq, in his *al-Islam wa-Usul al-Hukm* (Islam and the principles of governance), caused great commotion with his call for the separation between temporal and religious power and his characterizing the Prophet's rule in Medina as being independent of his prophetic mission. The interest in the caliphate became a matter of urgent debate with its abolition under the secular regime established by Atatürk in Turkey in 1924, which resulted in the famous Caliphate Conference in Cairo in 1926 that attempted unsuccessfully to revive the caliphate.

In more recent times, some Muslim rulers took up the title *amīr al-mu'minīn*, not *khalīfa*, particularly the kings of Morocco and even the leader of the Taliban in Afghanistan. The use of the term *khalīfa* is nowadays rare, even among groups seeking the reunification of the Islamic community.

Further Reading

Khalil 'Athamina, "The Tribal Kings in Pre-Islamic Arabia: A Study of the Epithet *Malik* or *Dhu al-Taj* in Early Arabic Traditions," *al-Qanṭara* 19 (1998): 19–37; Aziz al-Azmeh, *Muslim Kingship: Power and the Sacred in Muslim, Christian, and Pagan Polities*, 1997; Patricia Crone and Martin Hinds, *God's Caliph: Religious Authority in the First Centuries of Islam*, 1986; Fred M. Donner, "The Formation of the Islamic State," *Journal of the*

American Oriental Society 106, no. 2 (1986): 283–96; Hamilton A. R. Gibb, "The Evolution of Government in Early Islam," *Studia Islamica* 4 (1955): 5–17; Ignaz Goldziher, "Du sens propre des expressions Ombre de Dieu, Khalife de Dieu pour désigner les chefs dans l'Islam," *Revue de l'histoire des religions* 35 (1897): 331–38; Ann K. S. Lambton, *State and Government in Medieval Islam*, 1981; Bernard Lewis, *Political Words and Ideas in Islam*, 2008; Wilferd Madelung, *The Succession to Muḥammad: A Study of the Early Caliphate*, 1997; Carlo Alfonso Nallino, *Appunti sulla natura del "califfato" in genere e sul presunto "califf ato ottomano,"* 1917; Rudi Paret, "Signification coranique de *halīfa* et d'autres dérivés de la racine *halafa*," *Studia Islamica* 31 (1970): 211–17; Wadād al-Qāḍī, "The Term 'Khalīfa' in Early Exegetical Literature," *Die Welt des Islams* 28 (1988): 392–411; Émile Tyan, *Institutions du droit public musulman*, 1957; W. Montgomery Watt, *Islamic Political Thought: The Basic Concepts*, 1968.

Fundamentalism ⊗⊗⊗⊗⊗⊗⊗⊗⊗⊗⊗⊗⊗⊗⊗⊗⊗⊗⊗⊗⊗⊗⊗⊗⊗⊗⊗⊗⊗⊗

Roxanne Euben

Fundamentalism refers to contemporary religiopolitical movements that aim to establish the primacy of scriptural authority as a defense against the moral, political, and social decay that supposedly define the modern world. It is also often used in everyday language to designate inflexible and dogmatic beliefs of any kind, religious or otherwise. Such common connotations tend to obscure the specific cultural and historical circumstances that produced both the term and the movement it originally described. The term "fundamentalism" was coined in 1920 by Protestant Evangelicals eager to rescue American Christianity and culture from what they characterized as the degeneration inaugurated by "modernism in theology," "rationalism in philosophy," and "materialism in life." Committed to "do battle royal for the Fundamentals," such warriors for God launched an offensive against liberalism, Darwinism, and secularism in particular, declaring the Bible the authoritative moral compass for American life, infallible not only in regard to theological issues but also in regard to matters of historical, geographical, and scientific fact.

The broadened understanding of fundamentalism presumes that there is sufficient commonality and overlap among Christian, Muslim, Jewish, Hindu, Buddhist, and other kinds of religious revivalism to warrant a single rubric despite significant cultural, historical, and linguistic differences. There are some good reasons for this assumption. In general, these are historically contemporaneous, distinctively religious movements that assert the authority of transcendent truths and timeless traditions in response to a perceived crisis precipitated by rapid cultural, social, and economic transformations. As urbanization, industrialization, and the crises they are said to engender are distinctive to the contemporary epoch, fundamentalism has, as Bruce Lawrence writes in *Defenders of God*, "historical antecedents, but no ideological precursors." Fundamentalists may well see themselves as custodians of continuity, yet it is precisely this self-description that distinguishes them from believers for whom tradition was simply lived rather than justified. Tradition becomes a conscious commitment in need of systematic justification when longtime rituals, beliefs, and practices can no longer be taken for granted. Paradoxically, then, defenders of tradition are actually reconstructing it in response to challenge and change.

Fundamentalism and Modernity

This means that efforts to restore the primacy of supposedly timeless truths and traditions inadvertently reveal how thoroughly intertwined contemporary religio-political movements are with the conditions, ideas, and processes fundamentalists oppose. This is evident in fundamentalist depictions of modernity as a condition of decay or disease evinced by pervasive corruption, disorder, relativism, and immorality. Fundamentalists contend that such ills are the wages of human hubris, by-products of the misguided assumption that the ever-enlarging scope of human mastery evinced by rapid scientific and technological advances demonstrates the irrelevance of metaphysical sources of knowledge about the world. Such an assumption transfigures sins into natural urges, recasts selfishness as the wellspring of collective life, and reduces the divine plan for the universe and all things in it to a system of physical causality just waiting to be mastered by human ingenuity. Stripped of the moral compass only faith in God provides and bereft of the religious scaffolding that endows life with meaning and purpose, humans are portrayed as lurching toward an abyss we no longer have the ability to recognize, let alone navigate. At this critical juncture, we are told, only the righteous attuned to God's will are capable of charting the path to redemption. Like the prophesies of Cassandra, however, their warnings and guidance are largely destined to fall upon deaf ears.

To the degree that this perspective characterizes a wide range of contemporary religiopolitical movements, fundamentalists can be said to share an ambivalence toward modernity and the rationalist epistemology, or human-centered theory of knowledge, that in part constitutes it. Scholars have interpreted this ambivalence in quite different ways, however. Some portray fundamentalism as the last gasp of atavistic impulses and archaic commitments, the residue of premodern beliefs and practices rendered obsolete by scientific advances, technological innovations, and the globalization of capital. Others argue that fundamentalists' restorative aspirations are less exhortations to re-create the past than rhetorical techniques designed to indict the present. In this view, fundamentalists are antimodern rather than premodern, committed to fighting modern pluralism, secularism, relativism, and rationalism in the name of divinely ordained truth and the sociomoral order it authorizes.

Still other scholars contend that fundamentalism is simultaneously a reaction to and an expression of modernity, its existence and purpose predicated on the socioeconomic processes, philosophical arguments, and political arrangements fundamentalists vociferously oppose and with which they are deeply engaged. This argument in particular has much to recommend it. These religious revivalists are not, for example, Luddites who object to technology on principle. On the contrary, fundamentalists from Jerry Falwell to Osama bin Laden have proven themselves quite fluent in the visual rhetoric made possible by modern techniques of communication and propaganda, deftly deploying various media to lambaste many of the epistemological premises and methods that made such technology possible in the first place.

In addition, comparisons among contemporary religiopolitical movements reveal some striking patterns in education and social class that belie characterizations of fundamentalists as predominantly rural, impoverished, uneducated, or too backward to heed the call of reason and the authority of science. Many Christian fundamentalists are middle-class, college-educated, urban children of rural parents. Similarly, Muslim fundamentalists are frequently the progeny of rural migrants to the city, beneficiaries of an expanded higher education system initiated by modernizing elites, and recipients of advanced training in the natural and applied sciences. Unlike the largely impoverished and uneducated Afghan Taliban, for example, a significant contingent of al-Qaeda is composed of middle-class, somewhat cosmopolitan young men with university educations in engineering, architecture, medicine, agricultural science, technical military science, or pharmacy. One case in point is Muhammad 'Ata, the alleged ringleader of the 9/11 attack on the United States, who was a student at the Technical University of Hamburg-Harburg and had a degree in architectural engineering. Khalid Shaikh Muhammad, said to be crucial to planning both the 9/11 attacks and the murder of the journalist Daniel Pearl, is an engineer, and Ayman al-Zawahiri, Bin Laden's second-in-command, is a doctor.

Conceptualizing fundamentalists as simultaneously children of modernity and among its fiercest critics suggests that they are, among other things, interlocutors in a debate not only about the state of the modern world but also about what modernity itself means. This conclusion does little, however, to differentiate fundamentalism from a succession of movements, thinkers, and arguments, religious and otherwise, that have criticized the processes and presuppositions associated with modernity from its inception. Moreover, given scholarly disagreements about when, precisely, the modern period begins, if or when it ended, and what it consists of, predicating definitions of fundamentalism on modernity may seem a bit like building on quicksand. Finally, inasmuch as fundamentalists themselves seek to challenge prevailing assumptions about what it does or should mean to live in the contemporary world, such arguments beg questions both about what modernity is and whether fundamentalism is usefully understood in terms of it.

These questions are posed sharply by shifting the theoretical perspective from the Euro-American "center" to the "periphery" inhabited by what are often called postcolonial peoples. Many scholars suggest that, at the other end of the colonial project, modernity registers less as an objective index of historical and intellectual maturation than a deracinated account of the ways Europe has ordered its past in relation to its present. Indeed, the content and contours of modernity are rooted in a persistent—albeit contested—narrative in which the rise of capitalism, the consolidation of the nation-state, the discoveries of the scientific revolution, and the development of Enlightenment philosophy are depicted as both cause and consequence of Europe's emergence from the Middle Ages in which "a Great Chain of Being" issuing from God was thought to hold sway.

This vision of civilizational maturation is double edged. On the one hand, it implicitly positions the West as (in Marx's words) the beacon that "shows to the less developed the image of its own future" by deriving modernity tout court from the universalization of historically and culturally specific experiences, assumptions, and standards. On the other hand, it explicitly offers to all peoples the promise of mastery, of control not only over recalcitrant facts and things but also over human suffering through the application of increasingly effective scientific and technical solutions. As the European colonial enterprise gathered scope and speed, this double-edged vision of modernity would spread to other shores by way of territorial incursions, cultural domination, and noblesse oblige. For many colonized peoples, then, modernity and the mastery it promised came to be understood as a prerogative of conquest rather than an index of freedom.

Fundamentalism, Islamism, and the Politics of Terminology

Does the terminology of fundamentalism, like the category of modernity with which it is so closely intertwined, obscure rather than illuminate critical differences among the specific political contexts, cultural idioms, and historical experiences informing contemporary religiopolitical movements? Many scholars of colonial and postcolonial societies explicitly reject fundamentalism on precisely these grounds. In this view, fundamentalism says too little by encompassing too much. For how can a single term derived from a specific moment in American Christianity say anything of substance about the assassins of Egyptian president Anwar Sadat, Hindus who attacked the mosque at Ayodhya, Christian militants who bomb abortion clinics, and Israeli settlers who justify violence in the occupied territories as sanctioned by God?

Many contend that if fundamentalism is empty at best, at worst it deepens long-standing prejudices and generates new distortions by remaking what is unfamiliar in familiar terms. This problem is particularly acute in the case of the contemporary Islamic religiopolitical movement, not least because Islam itself has so often been obscured by a haze of ignorance, prejudice, and polemic, both in the past and in the present. As a result, the term "Islamic fundamentalism" is nearly as controversial as the phenomenon it purports to describe.

At first glance, many objections to it appear to hinge on its origins: fundamentalism was born in a time and place equally distant from the seventh-century Arabia of the Prophet Muhammad and the maelstrom of contemporary Muslim politics. Yet terms originating in one place and language frequently become part of a transcultural political lexicon used widely, if not always consistently, to capture recognizably common phenomena. Both nationalism and socialism are often cited as two cases in point. Another such example is "the West," a category of relatively recent provenance through which Euro-American history and geography have been retroactively organized. Scholars from diverse disciplines routinely argue that what is called the West is an amalgamation of multiple traditions—including Greek, Roman, Judaic, and Christian—and owes myriad debts to diverse civilizations past and present.

They further argue that while it has always been difficult to pinpoint exactly where the West begins and ends, this is particularly true now that peoples, information, and material goods crisscross cultural and national borders at will, creating hybrid and multiple identities that shift and reconstitute themselves in unpredictable ways. Such scholarly arguments nothwithstanding, "the West" continues to be invoked by people throughout the globe, evoking powerful allegiances and enmities.

What is ultimately at stake in most objections to Islamic fundamentalism, however, is power rather than etymology or geography. As philosophers, linguists, and translators have demonstrated, language not only reflects but produces our understandings of the world. Disputes about terminology often raise critical questions about who is using what words to describe whom and for what purposes. In a postcolonial world characterized by rapid globalization, any discussion of Islam operates within a web of social relations in which power—both actual and perceived—has already been apportioned unequally among various peoples, classes, regions, genders, and cultures. Given this context, many argue that the universalization of terms and categories derived from specifically European and American experiences reflects and reinforces the cultural hegemony of West over non-West, center over periphery. Scholarship organized around such categories and background assumptions may thus reveal less about Muslim practices and cultures than about the ability of those who already have power to produce, disseminate, and control a series of descriptions and images about themselves and the rest of the world.

Given this politics of terminology, it is instructive that there was no equivalent for fundamentalism in Arabic, the language of the Qur'an, until the need to approximate the English term called for one. *Usūliyya*, derived from the word for fundamentals or roots (*usūlī*), has emerged as an Arabic name for Islamic fundamentalism, but its currency is due to the way it approximates the English fundamentalism rather than any correspondence with aspects of the Islamic tradition. (On the contrary, *usūlī* is associated with scholarship on the roots and genesis of Islamic jurisprudence, and experts in this discipline are often referred to as *al-usūliyyūn*.) In a 1995 interview, the spiritual leader of Hizbullah in Lebanon, Shaykh Muhammad Husayn Fadlallah, rejected the terminology of fundamentalism as more revealing of Western projections than Muslim revivalism:

> We Islamists are not fundamentalists in the way the Westerners see us. We refuse to be called fundamentalists. We are Islamic activists. As for the etymological sense of *usūliyya*, meaning returning to one's roots and origins [*usūl*], our roots are the Qur'an and the true *sunna* or way of the Prophet, not the historical period in which the Prophet lived or the periods that followed—we are not fundamentalists [*usūliyyīn*] in the sense of wanting to live like people at the time of the Prophet or the first Caliphs or the time of the Umayyads.

Some scholars regard the debate about appropriate terminology as concluded, yet alternatives to the term "Islamic fundamentalism" in use range from "radical Islam" to "Islamic extremism" and "Islamic terrorism" to "political Islam." Indeed, new names for the phenomenon continually arise. A case in point is "jihadism," a neologism derived from the Arabic "jihad" (to struggle or strive) that is frequently used in the press to denote the most violent strands of Islamism, and those associated with what are alternatively called "suicide bombings" or "martyrdom operations" in particular. Older terms put to new uses occasionally gain wide currency as well. Such is the case with "Salafism," which refers to contemporary Muslims who generally eschew the interpretive methods and norms of the classical Islamic schools and take as a guide for proper behavior only the word of God, the teachings of the Prophet Muhammad, and the example set by the *salaf*, the earliest and most pious of Muslims. Perhaps the most widely used term among scholars of Muslim societies is "Islamism," although it is not universally accepted and is frequently invoked with caution and caveats. As some observers argue, for example, Islamism wrongly implies that those who claim the name have captured the essence of Islam; thus it is no more appropriate than calling the former Branch Davidian leader David Koresh a Christianist.

Scholars' apparent preference for the term "Islamism" has not, however, yielded agreement about how to best define or identify it, let alone understand or explain it. Some emphasize the socioeconomic characteristics of the Islamist movement; others identify certain patterns in recruitment, organization, and mobilization; still others foreground the theological and philosophical tendencies of Islamist thought; and some home in on the regional and sectarian dynamics of various Islamist groups. Such disunity is, in part, a function of the disciplinary and methodological differences among historians, anthropologists, political scientists, and scholars of religion, all of whom regard Islamism as within their academic jurisdiction. The best scholarship on Islamism is substantively interdisciplinary and methodologically plural, attending closely to the complex interplay among Islamist ideas and objectives, the specific public spheres in which they operate, and the material conditions that inform and are in turn transformed by them. Yet ultimately, even the most careful scholarship suggests that the kaleidoscopic literature on the subject is less a reflection of academic balkanization than the irreducible diversity of contexts and concerns animating a powerful yet rapidly changing Islamist movement.

Islamism: Origins and General Characteristics

In contrast to the confusion swirling around matters of terminology and definition, the advent of Islamism is almost universally traced to 1928, the year Hasan al-Banna (1906–49) founded the Egyptian Society of Muslim Brothers (al-Ikhwan al-Muslimun). By all reports, Banna was gifted with great personal charisma, rhetorical skill, and organizational acumen; by the time of his assassination in 1949, he had already built a formidable organization with deep roots in Egyptian society and a broad base of membership, ranging from civil servants to soldiers, urban laborers to rural peasants, and village elders to university students. As Banna was more activist than theologian, however, the task of developing an Islamist theoretical framework would largely fall to thinkers who came to prominence in the decades after his death. The most important among them include Sayyid Qutb from Egypt (1906–66), Abul al-A'la Mawdudi from Pakistan (1903–79), and Ruhollah Khomeini from Iran (1902–89). Under the tutelage of these and other Islamist thinkers and activists, the organization Banna founded would inspire a movement that now stretches throughout the Middle East, North Africa, South Asia, and beyond, continuously adapting and transforming itself to divergent political exigencies and changing historical circumstances.

While the Muslim Brotherhood continues to be a formidable presence in places like Egypt and Jordan, its profile and political purchase in contemporary Muslim-majority societies have frequently been eclipsed by what are often dubbed "radical" Islamist groups. Such groups include Egypt's al-Gama'a al-Islamiyya, the Pakistan-based Lashkar-e-Taiba (Army of the Pure), the Islamic Salvation Front in Algeria, and al-Qaeda, the fluid Islamist network linked to violent operations from the Philippines to Kashmir, including the assault on the U.S. embassies in Kenya and Tanzania in 1998, the attack on the World Trade Center and Pentagon in 2001, and the bombings of a Bali nightclub in 2002 and Madrid commuter trains in 2004. Whereas Banna had largely sought to coax action out of quiescence without acceding to the demands of those he described as "overzealous and hasty," these organizations tend to eschew the gradualist path of grassroots sociomoral transformation in favor of immediate, direct, and often violent challenges to the legitimacy of Muslim governments and the power of "infidel" regimes.

This distinction must not be overdrawn, however. Despite significant differences in emphasis and strategy, there is also a fair amount of continuity and overlap between the Muslim Brotherhood and such "radical" groups. Hamas, for example, was founded in 1987 to serve as the "strong arm" of the Muslim Brotherhood by several members convinced that the organization's strategy of "Islamization without confrontation" had been outpaced by events in the Israeli-occupied territories. Conversely, many radical groups share the commitment to charitable endeavors that had been central to Banna's strategy of recruitment and sociomoral transformation. Islamists from Morocco to Pakistan are well known for building schools, mosques, and health clinics, as well as for raising funds to support impoverished Muslims who have been abandoned by ineffective or corrupt state bureaucracies.

Islamism is thus a 20th- and 21st-century phenomenon, its history deeply intertwined with the local, regional, and geopolitical dynamics of the contemporary world. As the present always builds on the past, however, Islamism must also be located within a long and complex tradition of religious reform, revivalism, and even insurrectionism in the history of Muslim-majority societies. The activism and intransigence of many contemporary Islamists, for example, has been likened to the Kharijis, a seventh-century group of Muslims known for an uncompromising emphasis on righteous deeds and the unadulterated authority of the Qur'an. While Islamists often object to such a comparison, they do depict themselves as disciples of

Ibn Taymiyya (1263–1328), the 14th-century jurist who argued that Mongol rulers who mixed Islamic prescriptions with tribal law (the Yasa) had contravened shari'a and could therefore be forcibly removed from power.

Finally, Islamist ideas and preoccupations must be understood as a continuation of 19th-century Muslim political thought rather than a radical break from the concerns and dilemmas that characterized it. For example, Banna's insistence on Islam as a comprehensive way of life and a set of religiopolitical imperatives distorted by corruption, sectarianism, and indifference is, in many ways, an extension of the work of such Muslim reformists as Jamal al-Din al-Afghani (1839–97), Rifa'a Rafi' al-Tahtawi (1801–73), and Muhammad 'Abduh (1849–1905). Like Banna, these thinkers had sought, in different ways, to revive and reinterpret the foundations of Islam as a bulwark against the rise of European power and the internal weakening of the Ottoman Empire.

The preceding discussion only hints at the scope and depth of persistent disagreements about how to best name, define, and delimit this complex and diverse movement. Given such disagreement, it is particularly useful to approach Islamism as an interpretive framework rather than a set of propositions and strategies to which every Islamist subscribes in the same way or to the same degree. Understood as an interpretive framework, Islamism does not simply reflect or obscure a set of material conditions and socioeconomic grievances but instead constitutes a lens on the world that determines how and in what terms such conditions and constraints are understood. Such an approach enables observers to attend to the differences and diversity of what travels under the rubric of "Islamism" without losing sight of it as a complex system of representation that articulates and defines a range of identities, categories, and norms; organizes human experience into narratives that assemble past, present, and future into a compelling interpretive frame; and specifies the range and meaning of acceptable and desirable practices. In short, this approach makes it possible to define Islamism without essentializing or instrumentalizing it.

Islamism refers to those 20th- and 21st-century Muslim groups and thinkers that seek to recuperate the scriptural foundations of the Islamic community, excavating and reinterpreting them for application to the contemporary social and political world. Such foundations consist of the Qur'an and the normative example of the Prophet Muhammad (sunna, hadith), which constitute the sources of God's guidance, in matters pertaining to both worship and human relations. In general, Islamists aim at restoring the primacy of the norms derived from these foundational texts in collective life, regarding them not only as an expression of God's will but also as an antidote to the moral bankruptcy inaugurated by Western cultural dominance from abroad, aided and abetted by corrupt Muslim rulers from within the *umma* (the Islamic community).

Against this backdrop, Islamists conceptualize their work in terms of diagnosis and cure. Muslims must first recognize that the modern world is diseased, its inhabitants corrupted by a condition that Qutb, borrowing from the South Asian Islamist scholar Abul Hasan Nadwi (d. 1999), calls *jāhiliyya*. *Jāhiliyya* derives from

the Arabic verb meaning "to be ignorant" and, in Muslim tradition, refers specifically to the epoch in Arabia before Islam had been revealed to the Prophet Muhammad. As used by contemporary Islamists, however, *jāhiliyya* signals a pathology
into which a society descends when it willfully turns away from the truths Allah
has already made manifest. The new *jāhiliyya* is thus distinguished from the old
by sheer human arrogance. More specifically, it is defined by an unwarranted confidence in human beings' ability to know, govern, and master the world without
divine guidance along with the presumption that human beings have the right and
wisdom to legislate rules for collective behavior. Within an Islamist framework, this
presumption is not only a symptom of human hubris but a transgression against
Allah's sovereignty (*ḥākimiyya*), the scope of which encompasses both public and
private domains of human affairs as well as both visible and unseen dimensions of
the universe. For many Islamists, such transgression is at the root of all human sovereignty in the modern epoch—nationalist, democratic, communist, and monarchical
alike. It is equally evident in a long history of Euro-American aggression against
Islam in which the Christian Crusades, European colonialism, Israeli treatment of
Palestinians, ethnic cleansing in Bosnia, German anti-Turkish violence, the American invasion of Iraq, and Dutch cartoons of Muhammad are but a few examples.

While the roots of the new *jāhiliyya* are usually traced to the West, Islamists also
contend that it is no longer an exclusively foreign pathology. In their view, Muslim
rulers who claim for themselves the legislative authority that belongs only to Allah
represent a metastasizing cancer within the *umma*, inaugurating an internal crisis
of unprecedented scope and scale. Given such a diagnosis, the cure is clear and its
implementation urgent: divine sovereignty must be restored over all domains of collective life, an imperative that entails establishing the primacy of Islamic law through
the agency of the state. This in turn requires righteous action, for while shariʿa is an
expression of divine wisdom and will, it is only realized on Earth by human struggle
in the path of God (*jihād fī sabīl Allāh*). Actualization of *ḥākimiyya* thus requires a
vanguard of Muslims who have penetrated the miasma of *jāhiliyya* and its false gods
of materialism, science, and rationalism. These are the true believers who are capable
of not only recognizing the scope of Islam as a way of life but also cultivating the
discipline, faith, and courage to reshape the world in its image.

As the following discussion makes clear, there is a great deal of disagreement
among Islamists about what, precisely, the establishment of Islamic law entails and
what practices are appropriate or justifiable in pursuit of it. Yet even this preliminary
sketch makes visible several common features that are, again, better understood as
broad tendencies rather than fixed attributes—that is, characteristics of an Islamist
framework that not every Islamist endorses in the same way all the time. In contrast
to those Muslims who primarily seek to cultivate a mystical understanding of the
divine through study or ascetic contemplation, for example, Islamist aspirations may
be characterized as explicitly and intentionally political. Using German sociologist
Max Weber's terminology from *The Sociology of Religion*, Islamism is not defined by
an "other-worldly" orientation in which salvation requires withdrawal from worldly

affairs. It is, rather, a movement in which salvation is possible only through participation in the world, or more precisely "within the institutions of the world, but in opposition to them." As Islamist exhortations to change collective life require words and deeds, they may be further defined not only as political but also as activist, thus distinguishing them from the quietism characteristic of some Saudi Salafis, whose acquiescence to established power is no less political than Islamist intransigence.

Islamism and the Politics of Authenticity

Islamist aspirations to restore foundations located in a mythical past are far from unique. Nor are Islamists alone in their conviction that scriptural authority is guaranteed by its divine author—for in that all Muslims agree. Rather, what distinguishes Islamists from many other Muslims is the claim to recuperate an "authentic Islam" composed of self-evident truths purged of alien and corrupting influences, along with an insistence on remaking the foundations of the state in accordance with such purified prescriptions. Islamists depict such fidelity to the unadulterated word of God as the ultimate expression of deference to divine omniscience. Indeed, humility is not only a proper expression of faith but also a constitutive feature of the human condition, in contradistinction to the nature of Allah. From this vantage point, aspirations to fully know and master the natural and social worlds reflect a human hubris deaf to the Qur'anic admonition that "Allah knows, but/and you do not know" (Q. 3:66).

The Islamist emphasis on the limits of human knowledge, however, requires humility only in relation to Allah. What it rarely yields is humility in regard to their own claims to speak in His name or forbearance toward Muslims who disagree with Islamist claims about what the divine Will requires. This suggests that while Islamist challenges to state power are obviously political, the Islamist claim to authenticity is also political in the coercive power it routinely enacts and justifies, most notably by way of the silences it imposes and the debates it forecloses. As Aziz al-Azmeh points out in *Islams and Modernities*, "The notion of authenticity is not so much a determinate concept as it is a node of associations and interpellations, a trope by means of which the historical world is reduced to a particular order, and a token which marks off social and political groups and forges and reconstitutes historical identities." Whether in the service of Arab nationalism, Christian fundamentalism, European romanticism, or 19th-century Muslim modernism, the claim of authenticity is an act of power that functions not just to reflect the world but to construct it by determining who is included and excluded, who may and may not speak authoritatively, what is the proper realm of debate, and what is beyond contestation.

It is certainly the case that a single "Islam" captures and organizes the perspectives of millions who self-identify as Muslim (among other things), yet what travels under the name "Islam" is inescapably diverse, multiethnic, and defined as much by disagreement as by consensus. Just as the Torah and Bible sometimes lend themselves to radically divergent interpretations of what it means to be Jewish or Christian, the Qur'an and hadith are complex and susceptible to many different, and at times contradictory, enactments. This means that Islam is not a fixed essence but rather, as Talal Asad points out in "The Idea of an Anthropology of Islam," a discursive tradition that captures what is imagined as continuous and unitary in dialectical relationship to those concrete articulations and practices by which it is transformed and adapted in different contexts for plural purposes. It is precisely this understanding of religion that is anathema to Islamists who seek to fix the parameters of Islamic authenticity once and for all. Doing so enables them to arrogate for themselves the right to determine who qualifies as a good Muslim; discredit those 'ulama' (Muslim scholars) unable or unwilling to purge Islam of purported impieties; declare nominally Muslim rulers apostates unfit to govern; and characterize all who disagree as corrupt, heretical, guilty of unbelief, or victims of false consciousness.

In Sunni Islamism, such arguments frequently entail the claim that ordinary, untrained Muslims have the right and obligation to engage the sacred texts directly, without the mediation of those religious scholars who have traditionally served as gatekeepers of the Islamic tradition. Given this claim, it is unsurprising that many prominent Sunni Islamists—from Banna to Zaynab al-Ghazali and from Qutb to Bin Laden—are autodidacts rather than formally trained or credentialed 'ulama'. As the sacred texts contain the rules and regulations meant to govern both public and private affairs, this insistence on unmediated access to the texts can be understood as the grounds on which such self-taught Islamists claim for themselves the stature of religious experts who have penetrated the moral bankruptcy of *jāhiliyya* to clearly see what others cannot. Indeed, despite Islamists' tendency to characterize the "real Islam" as self-evident, many actually assume that only a small vanguard of believers will have the ability to recognize it and act decisively to remake the world in its image. In this way, Islamists position themselves as purveyors of God's will who, like Plato's philosopher-king in *The Republic*, are no longer enthralled by dark shadows cast on cave walls but capable of beholding the truth in direct light.

On the one hand, then, Islamists are committed to establishing a religiopolitical order that simultaneously presumes the supremacy of the few capable of true knowledge and promises a world in which dissent itself will become both unnecessary and illegitimate. On the other hand, this emphasis on the potential wisdom of untrained believers entails a kind of democratization of access to the authority conferred by knowledge of the sacred texts. This claim that religious knowledge depends on commitment rather than training or expertise can be seen as part of a broader challenge to elite power evident in Islamist arguments that Muslims have the right and obligation to determine when rulers are illegitimate and that those who prefer order to justice, security to freedom, and money to piety have forfeited any claim to authority.

This particular aspect of Islamism evokes the Protestant Reformation and, as Ellis Goldberg argues in his article "Smashing Idols and the State: The Protestant Ethic and Egyptian Sunni Radicalism," echoes Calvinists' attempts to transfer "religious authority away from officially sanctioned individuals who interpret texts to ordinary citizens." Such a comparison has sparked a great deal of speculation regarding a possible "Islamic Reformation," along with a range of arguments about whether and how Islamism might facilitate the democratization of Muslim societies, much as the Protestant Reformation is said to have heralded the emergence of European "liberal democracy." While such parallels are evocative, they are frequently overdrawn. A fuller understanding of Islamism requires first situating it in relation to a historical shift in the nature and locus of religious authority in Islam beginning in the 19th century. As scholars such as Muhammad Qasim Zaman have shown, mass higher education and a variety of new technologies enabling broad dissemination of information and knowledge have made available to amateurs what had previously been the purview of religious experts. At the same time, such processes have inaugurated a fragmentation of authority within the very ranks of the 'ulama' that continues to the present day. In this context, the ascendance and influence of autodidacts such as Qutb, Banna, 'Abd al-Salam Faraj, and Bin Laden simultaneously express and accelerate an ongoing renegotiation of authority over who may speak for Islam and on what basis.

This discussion requires an additional qualification, as the prevalence of autodidacts among prominent Sunni Islamists contrasts sharply with recent developments in Shiʻi Islamism, particularly as articulated by one of its best known figures, Ruhollah Khomeini. A jurist and learned *mujtahid* (legist), Khomeini is most widely known as a spiritual leader of the revolutionary movement that overthrew the Shah of Iran in 1979, as well as expositor of the "guardianship of the jurist" (in Arabic, *wilāyat al-faqīh*; in Persian, *velāyat-i faqīh*), the doctrine that would become the foundation of rule in the Islamic Republic of Iran. Like many Sunni Islamists, Khomeini understands the legitimacy of sovereignty in terms of Allah's exclusive right of legislation and defines justice as the rule of revealed law. Yet Khomeini also argues that, as law requires both institutions and executors, the best guarantor of legitimate sovereignty is rule by those jurists (*fuqahā'*; sing. *faqīh*) most knowledgeable in matters of shariʻa. As Islamic law encompasses both matters of worship and human relations, Khomeini reasons, so must the authority of those with the expertise required to implement Islamic law extend to political as well as religious domains.

Here Khomeini augments the already formidable authority of the Shiʻi *fuqahā'*, who had previously been designated custodians of Shiʻi religious belief and practice in the absence of the Hidden Imam (the legitimate leader of the Muslim community believed to have disappeared into occultation in the late ninth century). Such justifications for institutionalizing clerical authority and broadening its scope bear little resemblance to the arguments of Sunni Islamists such as Qutb, Banna, and Faraj, whose writings often exhibit a palpable frustration with religious scholars who they contend have a greater stake in stability than justice. At the same time, several prominent Sunni Islamists are also religious scholars, from Yusuf al-Qaradawi (b. 1926), the founder of the influential website Islam Online, to 'Umar 'Abd al-Rahman (b. 1938), the Egyptian cleric linked to the assassins of Sadat, now serving a life sentence in an American federal penitentiary for "seditious conspiracy" in connection with the 1993 World Trade Center bombing. Both Qaradawi and 'Abd al-Rahman are credentialed scholars in Islamic law from Azhar, Egypt's preeminent university and mosque. These and other trained Islamist scholars exemplify the political coming of age of what Malika Zeghal has called peripheral 'ulama': products of Azhar whose sympathies and affiliations with Islamists undermine conventional wisdom about a sharp divide between establishment Sunni 'ulama' and untrained, anticlerical Islamist upstarts.

Islamism and the Politics of Gender

Gender is frequently considered tangential to the knotty problems of defining Islamism and charting its central dynamics. Yet scholars from a variety of disciplines have shown that gender is consistently the terrain over which battles for political control and cultural identity are fought. In times of internal crises and external threats, women's bodies and behavior are frequently transformed into symbols of moral purity or vessels of cultural corruption. This is especially true of contemporary fundamentalists who, as Martin Riesebrodt argues in *Pious Passion*, tend to "idealize patriarchal structures of authority and morality," endorse gender dualism as God-given or natural, and vigorously condemn recent changes in gender relations as a symptom and symbol of secularist moral bankruptcy. Islamists are a case in point. Their concerns with the place and purity of Muslim women reveal the unwritten gender norms—in other words, standards of masculinity and femininity that organize human beings into political, social, and reproductive roles and reflect and reinforce prevalent assumptions about the "nature" of men and women— arguably at the heart of Islamist politics and political thought.

Despite important differences among Islamist thinkers, many explicitly or implicitly endorse gender norms in which female nature is inextricably tied to the domestic realm, and women are symbolically transformed into an index of moral and cultural virtue. This view is built on the premise that men and women are equal in belief but perform fundamentally different and complementary functions in society. While men are naturally made to rule in both the public and private domain, a woman's primary role is to be a wife and mother as well as to ensure the integrity of the family, the first school of moral education. As such functions are rooted in an inescapable human nature expressive of divine will, a woman's inability or unwillingness to perform her duties signals a disobedience to God and presages the corruption of the Muslim family from within. From this vantage, the Western insistence on full equality between the sexes only liberates women from moral constraint, enslaving them to mutually reinforcing sexual and capitalist exploitation. As women are responsible for producing the next generation of Muslim men destined to restore Islam to its former glory, it is not only the virtue of women or the integrity of the family that hangs in the balance but also the future of Islamic civilization itself.

Several Islamist thinkers make these arguments explicitly and in detail, but in much of Islamist thought and rhetoric, the nature and significance of women are established indirectly and symbolically and through three recurrent images in particular. The first of the three images is of women as silent symbols of cultural, moral, and sexual vulnerability—voiceless figures in need of masculine protection or defiled bodies that mutely demand vengeance. So, for example, 'Abdallah 'Azzam, one of Bin Laden's mentors, graphically details the agonizing humiliation of young men unable to act when the Afghan woman is "crying out for help, her children are being slaughtered, her women are being raped, the innocent are killed and their corpses scattered." In the second image, women function as a chorus that speaks in permitted cadences to ratify masculine endeavors. Such is the case, for example, in Bin Laden's 1996 "Declaration of War against the American Occupying the Land of the Two Holy Places," where the women exhort men to jihad in the following way:

> Prepare yourself like a struggler, the matter is bigger than words! Are you going to leave us . . . for the wolves of Kufr [unbelief] eating our wings?! . . . Where are the freemen defending free women by arms?! Death is better than life in humiliation! Some scandals and shames will never be otherwise eradicated.

In the third image, women are creatures not of this world but of another: they are virginal rewards for the courageous martyr in the afterlife. This is evident in the final instructions for the 9/11 hijackers, for example, in which Muslim "brothers" are urged to purify their carnal impulses, sharpen their knives for the slaughter (*dhabh*), and heed the call of the *hūr 'ayn* (the black-eyed ones) awaiting them in paradise.

Such rhetoric primarily registers women as an extension, mirror, or measure of masculinity and, in tandem with explicit Islamist arguments about the proper nature and purpose of men and women, embeds gender within a divinely ordained social hierarchy. So understood, deviance from this gendered script tends to signal disruption of a much broader religiopolitical order it both presumes and seeks to bring into existence. When precipitated by foreign aggression, such disruption exacerbates a predisposition to translate conflict into an assault on Muslim masculinity and to conceptualize women as potential conduits for Western corruption in need of guiding, guarding, and covering. Such a gendered script has posed a significant challenge to Muslim women who have sought a place and voice within the Islamist movement. Despite significant differences among them, such women have had to navigate carefully between Islamist characterizations of women's visibility and agency as symptomatic of *jāhiliyya* on the one hand and essentializing arguments that equate Islam with veiling, female genital mutilation, and honor killings on the other.

Zaynab al-Ghazali (1917–2005) and Nadia Yassine (b. 1958), two of the few women who have risen to positions of leadership in the Islamist movement, have negotiated such constraints and pressures quite differently. Ghazali founded Jama'at al-Sayyidat al-Muslimat (the Muslim Women's Association, or the MWA), an organization devoted to educating women in the Islamic tradition and training them in the practice of *da'wa* (call to greater piety), in the 1930s. She even stepped in to help reconstitute the Muslim Brotherhood in the 1950s, after the Egyptian state formally dissolved the organization and executed or incarcerated virtually all of its ideological leadership in response to a member's alleged attempt to assassinate President Gamal Abdel Nasser. Ghazali was in many ways a pioneer whose own life demonstrated a fierce resistance to conventional norms of domesticity, even as much of her early work articulated an Islamist gender ideology that defines women as wives, mothers, and "builders of men." Yassine, by contrast, has come to prominence as the daughter of the founder of Morocco's Justice and Spirituality Association (JSA) and its unofficial spokeswoman. Unlike Ghazali, Yassine has positioned herself as a dedicated wife and mother who embraces an "Islamic feminism" that urges women to engage the sacred texts directly through *ijtihād* (independent reasoning, judgment, or interpretation). If women and men do, in fact, have distinct perspectives on the world, Yassine suggests, women have a special obligation to recuperate what they see as the gender parity of the Qur'an buried beneath those "macho interpretations" of Islam on which men have built their privilege and power.

Importantly, Yassine and Ghazali are only among the most visible examples of a larger trend: the increasing participation of women from diverse social backgrounds in *da'wa* (practices and arguments meant to exhort, invite, and guide Muslims to what is regarded as proper conduct and moral devotion). Women's participation in *da'wa* is not a brand new phenomenon, as is evident in Ghazali's work with the MWA. Yet scholars have shown that the number of *dā'iyyāt* (those engaged in *da'wa*) is significantly increasing in places such as Egypt, Pakistan, Saudi Arabia, and the United States. This reflects, in part, current doctrinal emphases on *da'wa* as incumbent on both men and women and less dependent on technical knowledge than moral virtue and practical familiarity with Islamic tradition. This increase is also tied to a number of political and socioeconomic transformations in Muslim-majority societies. Crucial among them is the expansion of mass education that has simultaneously increased women's literacy and social mobility and made Islamic texts more accessible. Also crucial are the proliferation of technologies—from the tape cassette to the Internet—that facilitate the circulation of religious knowledge even among those who cannot read or travel, the precedent set by the vigorous participation of Iranian women in postrevolution debates about Islam, and the model of legal activism evident in the Islamist movement's own challenge to the status of the 'ulama' as gatekeepers of religious knowledge.

If Ghazali and Yassine exemplify the feminization of *da'wa* among elites, the mosque movement in Egypt illustrates the growing participation of women from diverse social backgrounds in religious classes devoted to studying and debating what Islam requires for a woman to be virtuous in the contemporary world. As Saba Mahmood shows in *The Politics of Piety*, participants in the mosque movement conceptualize piety in terms of a deep and holistic commitment to self-transformation. Consequently, they are concerned less with matters of sovereignty and politics conventionally understood and more with the "moral cultivation" of those daily practices seen as crucial to becoming closer to God. Some Islamists have criticized this focus on practices of worship as apolitical and overly privatized, yet such criticism misses the force of Islamists' own insistence on religion (*dīn*) as a way of life in which the domains of public and private are inextricably linked. As Mahmood argues, these women's intense efforts at "retraining ethical sensibilities" have a "sociopolitical force" that extends well beyond matters of governance, facilitating no less than the emergence of a "new social and moral order." Evidence of its transformative power may be found not only in the sheer numbers and variety of women—wealthy and poor, literate and illiterate—participating in the mosque movement but also in the rhetorical and political efforts by the state and some Islamists to curtail, control, or discredit it.

Taken together, these examples show how Muslim women from different perspectives and social classes are increasingly insisting on engaging the sacred texts directly for and with one another without the mediating authority of men, who have traditionally held the monopoly on such activities. Despite the proliferation of voices intent on claiming for themselves the authority to demarcate what is authentically Islamic and un-Islamic once and for all, contestation over Islam's scope and meaning proceeds apace, facilitated at least in part by women formerly excluded from the conversation. This is true despite the fact that Islamist women's agency and claims to authority are frequently still predicated on a willingness to follow fairly patriarchal rules about where, how, and with whom they may practice their vocation.

Islamism, Political Action, and Violence

If gender is frequently an implicit preoccupation among Islamists, jihad is arguably Islamists' most consistently explicit concern. Jihad is derived from the Arabic verb that means "to struggle" or "to strive," yet it is a particular kind of struggle of concern to many of the most prominent Islamists: the often violent struggle against apostates and infidels both at home and abroad to which every individual Muslim must contribute. Many (though not all) Islamists represent this understanding of struggle as jihad tout court, yet it is a historically specific interpretation derived from a selective use of texts and precedents, foremost among them the claim by Ibn Taymiyya that Muslim rulers who had violated Islamic law could be subject to forcible removal. It is, moreover, an interpretation that breaks with much of antecedent doctrine and practice. The claim that fighting unbelievers is the preeminent enactment of individual Muslim piety, for example, is a departure from the distinction Muslim exegetes had developed between a "collective obligation" (*farḍ kifāya*, a duty a group of people within the community may perform on behalf of the rest) operative in jihad against foreign enemies and an individual duty (*farḍ ʿayn*) that must be fulfilled by every Muslim in the event that the *umma* is under attack. This interpretation also explicitly rejects Muslim modernists who emphasized the largely defensive character of jihad and sought to show that relations between Muslims and non-Muslims were normally peaceful rather than antagonistic.

Within Islamist terms, jihad is a means and an end rolled into one: it is a form of action necessary to eradicate obstacles to restoring a just community on Earth that simultaneously brings human action into accord with God's plans and purposes. While the Qur'an states (2:256) that "there is no compulsion in religion," for many Islamists, it is only in a state in which Islamic law reigns supreme that human beings are free from enslavement to one another's rule and all are equal by virtue of their common submission to God. From this perspective, the realization of justice, liberty, equality, and choice itself necessitates the forcible removal of the constraints imposed by *jāhiliyya*, along with those who aid and abet it. This entails action on two distinct yet interrelated fronts: domestic and global. Within the *umma*, jihad is in the service of challenging the legitimacy of Muslim rulers who claim for themselves the sovereignty that belongs only to Allah. By rereading Qur'an 5:44 (conventionally rendered as "He who does not judge by what God has revealed is an unbeliever") as "Those who do not *govern* by what God has revealed are unbelievers," Islamists contend that rulers who have abandoned the prescriptions of Islamic law have forfeited any claims to obedience and are lawful targets of jihad. In this way, revolt becomes an act of restoration rather than destruction. Much as the 17th-century English philosopher John Locke sought to legitimize revolution by characterizing a government that violates the purposes for which it was created as unlawful, Islamists depict the ruler who violates shari'a as the outlaw rather than those who justifiably rise up to depose him.

At the same time, jihad is regarded as a necessary response to the pervasive power—both actual and perceived—of those outside the *umma* who have demonstrated hostility to Muslim lives, lands, pieties, and sensibilities. This view of jihad reframes it as a matter of self-defense, in language that subsumes individuals into archetypes of "infidels" and "believers" and vitiates more conventional distinctions between, for example, soldier and civilian or collective and individual responsibility. Indeed, for many Islamists, the scope and depth of this physical as well as symbolic assault ultimately renders fine distinctions between offensive and defensive jihad irrelevant. As Qutb famously argued in *Ma'alim fi al-Tariq* (*Signposts along the Road*), jihad must be regarded as a "permanent condition, not an occasional concern," one that in current circumstances requires deeds rather than words, struggle rather than contemplation, and revolution at home as well as resistance abroad. Muhammad 'Abd al-Salam Faraj, author of the pamphlet justifying the assassination of President Sadat, argues along similar lines that the nature of the attack makes political authorization by a legitimate caliph (deputy, referring to a legitimate successor to the Prophet's leadership) unnecessary. As Faraj writes, leadership "over the Muslims is (always) in their own hands if only they make this manifest. . . . If there is something lacking in the leadership, well, there is nothing that cannot be acquired."

These arguments about jihad may be said to constitute a common grammar and framework of analysis, yet, as in so many other matters, Islamists disagree with one another not only about strategy but about substance. Challenges to the equation of jihad with violence against infidels have come not only from non-Islamist exegetes but also from within the ranks of Islamists themselves. A case in point is Yassine of Morocco's JSA, who insists that jihad is the dedicated struggle against arrogance (*istikbār*), particularly in its common form as the lust for power and domination. As jihad against *istikbār* is both a final goal and a prescription for action, Yassine contends, it is antithetical to violent practices that aim at domination. For Yassine, the primary instruments of jihad are not bombs but words, particularly those deployed in the art of persuasion. When Islamists seek to legitimize violent revolution by recourse to Islamic texts, they contravene the true meaning of jihad to serve their own arrogant ends. By the same token, Yassine argues, Bin Laden's decision to "fight evil with evil and barbarity with barbarity" not only violates specific Islamic prohibitions against harming civilians, women, and children but also betrays the ethical imperative to embody the message of a merciful God who cautions believers that "you have no power over them" (Q. 88:22).

Even Islamists who endorse the more radical view of jihad adapt this framework and grammar to suit the distinct public spheres in which they operate and to which they carefully calibrate their political commitments. In his justification for the assassination of Sadat, for example, Faraj depicts the struggle to reclaim the moral foundations of the Egyptian state as a fight against *jāhiliyya* from within and further argues that the jihad against a corrupt nationalist regime at home must take precedence over fighting enemies elsewhere. The charter of Hamas welds Islamist rhetoric to that of nationalist resistance in an effort to both fight Israeli occupation and compete for adherents with the Palestinian Liberation Organization, yet simultaneously insists that all Muslims recognize the primacy of the jihad for Jerusalem. In contrast to both Faraj and Hamas, Bin Laden embraced a global jihad that essentially collapses distinctions between national and international, offensive and defensive fighting, and enemies at home and those from afar.

Here as elsewhere, these Islamists claim to speak for an unchanging authentic Islam that exists outside of time and space. Far from transcending history and local circumstances, however, this understanding of jihad mirrors the very state-sanctioned violence against which Islamists have struggled for almost a century. Indeed, along with thousands of Muslims caught in the machinery of 20th-century state violence, prominent Islamists from Qutb to Ghazali to Zawahiri are well known to have been radicalized by extended and often brutal terms of incarceration. It is thus unsurprising that Islamists forged by interrogation torture in prison camps would conclude that the preeminent enactment of Muslim piety is violent struggle. In this context, as scholar of Middle Eastern politics Timothy Mitchell argues, Islamist views of the world can be characterized as both a mode of resistance to state mechanisms of coercion and an expression of them. This is powerfully illustrated in Ghazali's memoirs *Ayyam min Hayati* (Days of my life), where she describes how the "darkness of prisons, the blades of torture and the vicious beatings only increase the endurance and resolve of the faithful."

Conclusion

The example of jihad shows why any definition—let alone understanding or explanation—of Islamism requires attending not only to the multiple and various ways Islamist thinkers reinterpret Islam but also to the specific conditions and cultures in which they are embedded and the partisans and audiences they seek to address. These conditions and contexts determine the extent to which an Islamist framework resonates with Muslims who live in a wide range of cultural contexts and geographic locations. Such resonances are, in turn, facilitated by a concatenation of forces that mark this particular moment in history. These include the ways in which contemporary global inequalities compound the legacy of European colonialism to reproduce a sense of Muslim powerlessness relative to the West; ongoing Euro-American political and financial support of corrupt autocrats, many of whom preside over nation-states stitched together by Western fiat; the persistence of authoritarian regimes eager to control domestic unrest by catalyzing "Muslim rage" toward external targets; the sense of emasculation produced by decades of political repression and economic frustration; and the flow of images of bloodied Muslim bodies delivered by a burgeoning array of video, satellite, and electronic media. Islamism is thus constituted by a complex dialectic between the selective appropriation of texts and precedents by Islamist thinkers and leaders, and the ways such ideas are enacted and reworked by Islamist activists forged in the crucible of Egyptian prisons, Pakistani villages, Gazan refugee camps, Saudi schools, French housing projects, British mosques, and the battlefields of Afghanistan, Bosnia, Chechnya, and Iraq.

Further Reading

Talal Asad, "The Idea of an Anthropology of Islam," Center for Contemporary Arab Studies Occasional Paper Series, March 1986; Aziz al-Azmeh, *Islams and Modernities*, 1993; James Barr, *Fundamentalism*, 1978; Osama bin Laden, "Declaration of War against the Americans Occupying the Land of the Two Holy Places," 1996; Norman J. Cohen, *The Fundamentalist Phenomenon*, 1991; Roxanne L. Euben, *Enemy in the Mirror: Islamic Fundamentalism and the Limits of Modern Rationalism*, 1999; Roxanne L. Euben and Muhammad Qasim Zaman, *Princeton Readings in Islamist Thought: Texts and Contexts from al-Banna to Bin Laden*, 2009; Muhammad Husayn Fadlallah, "Islamic Unity and Political Change: Interview with Shaykh Muhammad Hussayn Fadlallah," *Journal of Palestine Studies* (1995); Zaynab al-Ghazali, *Ayyam min Hayati* [*Days of My Life*], 1978; Yvonne Haddad, "The Qur'anic Justification for an Islamic Revolution: The View of Sayyid Qutb," *The Middle East Journal* 37, no. 1 (Winter 1983): 14–29; Johannes J. G. Jansen, *The Neglected Duty: The Creed of Sadat's Assassins and Islamic Resurgence in the Middle East*, 1986; Bruce Lawrence, *Defenders of God*, 1989; Saba Mahmood, *Politics of Piety: The Islamic Revival and the Feminist Subject*, 2005; George M. Marsden, *Fundamentalism and American Culture: The Shaping of Twentieth-Century Evangelicalism, 1870–1925*, 1980; Sayyid Qutb, *Ma'alim fi al-Tariq* [*Signposts along the Road*], 1964; Martin Riesebrodt, *Pious Passion: The Emergence of Modern Fundamentalism in the United States and Iran*, translated by Don Reneau, 1990; Max Weber, *The Sociology of Religion*, 1964; Nadia Yassine, "Inside Bin Laden's Head," 2005; Muhammad Qasim Zaman, *The 'Ulama of Contemporary Islam: Custodians of Change*, 2002; Malika Zeghal, "Religion and Politics in Egypt: The Ulema of al-Azhar, Radical Islam, and the State (1952–94)," *International Journal of Middle East Studies* (1999).

Government 〜〜〜〜〜〜〜〜〜〜〜〜〜〜〜〜〜〜〜〜〜〜〜

Emad El-Din Shahin

The term commonly used to refer to "government" in Arabic is *ḥukūma*; the term in Turkish is *ḥükümet*; and the term in Persian is *ḥukūmat*. They all refer to the holders of authority, the members of the cabinet, and more generally to the authoritative structures of the state. These specific meanings were acquired only in the 19th century. Traditionally, Muslim jurists used a variety of terms, sometimes interchangeably, to refer to the acts of government in Islam, including *amr*, *imāra*, *wilāya*, *khilāfa*, *imāma*, *dawla*, *mulk*, *ḥukm*, *tadbīr*, *siyāsa*, and *sulṭān*. The historian Ibn Khaldun (1332–1406) considered *al-khilāfa*, *al-imāma*, *al-ri'āsa*, and *al-sulṭān* to mean the same thing: the succession to the political authority of the Prophet. Following the same tradition, a prominent 20th-century Muslim scholar, Muhammad Rashid Rida (1865–1935), used *al-khilāfa*, *al-imāma al-'uẓmā*, and *imārat al-mu'minīn* as synonymous terms that refer to the leadership of the Islamic government in religious and worldly matters. The Egyptian constitutional jurist 'Abd al-Razzaq al-Sanhuri (1895–1971) used *al-khilāfa* and "Islamic government" interchangeably.

The traditional usage of the term *ḥukūma* refers to the act of arbitration between disputing parties and of deterring others from transgression. The word *ḥukūma* derives from the root *ḥ-k-m*, which in classical Arabic generally means "judgment, knowledge, and wisdom." *Ḥukm* is an ancient Arabic word and is mentioned in the Qur'an, as a root or its derivatives, 192 times with a wide range of meanings, including wisdom, judgment, perfection, deterrence, knowledge, and arbitration. Traditionally associated with the acts of adjudication and arbitration, the word gradually acquired broader meanings and entered into a variety of fields such as jurisprudence, logic, philosophy, linguistics, literature, and politics. In politics, *ḥukūma* denotes a binding authority that dispenses justice, deters people from wrongdoing, and directs them to fulfilling their welfare (*maṣlaḥa*).

In Islamic history, the word *ḥukm* has had a critical association with authority and justice. The Qur'an 4:59 commands believers to "obey Allah and obey the Messenger and those in authority (*ulū al-amr*) from among you; then if you quarrel about anything, refer it to Allah and the Messenger." The term *ulū al-amr* was interpreted in various ways and covered different groups that include political authority.

'Abdallah b. 'Abbas (619–87), a prominent interpreter of the Qur'an, explained "those in authority" as referring to the learned scholars. It also denotes "those who unbind and bind" in society. The term was then commonly used to refer to the "rulers." Ghazali (ca. 1058–1111) used the term for those with military authority (*aṣḥāb al-shawka*). The Egyptian reformer Muhammad 'Abduh (1849–1905) expanded the meaning of the term to include the rulers, the scholars, the army commanders, and all the heads and leaders to whom the people refer for their needs and public interests.

The question of who rules, or the qualities of the head of the Islamic government, has been critical in Islamic history. The first political conflict between the members of the early Muslim community took place immediately after the death of the Prophet (632) over the issue of *ḥukm*, or rule. The disagreement was not over the necessity of the establishment and continuation of political authority after the death of the Prophet but instead over who should succeed the Prophet as ruler of the Muslim community. Early Muslims also believed in the necessity of establishing one government under a single leader. This was indeed the source of the second conflict that took place between the fourth caliph, 'Ali b. Abi Talib, and Mu'awiya b. Abi Sufyan, the governor of Damascus, over who had the right to select the caliph and the source of the political legitimacy of the head of state.

Constitutional Theory of Government

Classical Muslim writings on government were drawn from the fundamental sources of Islam: the Qur'an and the sunna of the Prophet and the practices and consensus of the members of the early Muslim community, particularly of the Companions of the Prophet and the Rightly Guided Caliphate. The early views on government and rule were often dispersed along the various sections of the classical jurisprudential sources. The classical manuals of Islamic jurisprudence included discussions of government and administration as separate sections of *imāra* or *wilāya* or under sections dealing with zakat (alms giving), jihad, *kharāj* (revenues), and obedience. In the Muslim worldview, politics was viewed primarily in terms of welfare (*salāḥ*), justice, avoiding corruption, and leading people to fulfill their religious obligations. Several prominent jurists discussed issues of government and administration, such as Ibn al-Muqaffa' (ca. 720–56), Abu Yusuf (ca. 731–98), Ibn Abi al-Rabi' (d. 864), Jahiz (d. 868), Baqillani (d. 1013), and Baghdadi (d. 1037). However, it was not before the 11th century that a comprehensive and systematic juridical theory of government and administration developed. This was marked by the writing of Mawardi's (974–1058) influential book *al-Ahkam al-Sultaniyya* (The ordinances of government), which laid down many of the tenets of the classical political theory of government and became an influential reference for later generations of political theorists.

The classical constitutional theory of government revolved around six essential principles: (1) the establishment of authority is a religious and rational necessity;

(2) the leader of the community is selected by *ahl al-ḥall wa-l-ʿaqd* (those who unbind and bind, i.e., the influential elites in the community) or by testamentary designation; (3) the leader combines political and religious functions and has jurisdiction over the legislature (in cases where there is no ruling from the Qurʾan or the traditions of the Prophet [sunna] or preexisting consensus) and the judiciary; (4) the leader is a successor to the Prophet and is obliged to implement the rules of Islam; (5) the leader has authority over the entire Muslim territories; and (6) as long as the ruler performs his functions, he is entitled to the obedience and support of the *umma*.

The Principles of Government

Muslim jurists, classical and modern, agree that the Qurʾan does not stipulate a specific form or system of government. The Prophet died without designating a successor or delineating certain structures of government. Shiʿis differ on this issue and believe that ʿAli was designated as a successor. Juwayni (1028–1105) asserts that there is no point trying to find a text in the Qurʾan that addresses the details of the imamate. The Prophet's act has been interpreted to mean that as a primarily worldly issue he wanted the Muslims to devise the form of government they found suitable for the needs of the time and circumstances. The jurists concur, however, that the Qurʾan sets forth several guiding principles for government. These principles are open to a variety of interpretations. Modern Muslim thinkers expand the scope of these principles to include up to 12 social and political values that guide the government of Islam, of which the most common in classical and modern writings on government are justice, equality, and *shūrā* (consultation).

Justice

The value of justice is a central principle in Islam and an essential source for legitimizing the government. The Qurʾan contains about 300 verses that directly relate to justice and a similar number dealing with injustice, attesting to the centrality of this concept. The injunctions to adhere to justice take a variety of forms ranging from establishing justice—in the best of ways—to pursuing this value with those one disagrees with or even hates. The Qurʾan sets a universal rule: "God enjoins justice, doing good, and giving to kinsfolk, whilst He forbids indecent conduct, disreputable deeds, and insolence. He admonishes you so that you may be reminded" (Q. 16:90). According to Fakhr al-Din al-Razi (1149–1209), a prominent commentator on the Qurʾan, the entire Qurʾan is an elucidation of this principle. With those that may hold different, even hostile positions, the Qurʾan urges Muslims, "O you who believe, be steadfast for God, bearing witness with equity. Let not the hatred of any people induce you to act unjustly. Act justly—that is nearer to fear of God—and fear God" (Q. 5:8). The impartial delivery of justice is a fundamental value for government in Islam.

The traditions of the Prophet list the "just" imam among those whom God protects in His shade on the Day of Judgment. It is part of the Islamic tradition that justice is the basis of rule and government and that God supports the just state even if it is not Muslim. The jurists have considered justice as one of the qualities of the imam and a requisite for his selection. According to Ghazali, the true sultan was he who acted with justice and refrained from tyranny and corruption. This condition is also required for the appointment of judges, the people (*ahl al-ikhtiyār*) who have the right to select the ruler, and government officials. Justice as a value is central in defining the relationship among the members of the community as well as between them and other communities.

Equality

The concept of equality rests on the belief in One Creator and in the equal nature of all human beings: men and women, Muslims and non-Muslims. Human beings have rights and responsibilities regardless of their color, religion, or social status. Of course, Islam considers the inevitability of distinctions between people based on knowledge, reason, faith, and functions. However, the Qur'an asserts the principle of the equal nature of humanity, "O people, fear your Lord, who created you from a single soul and who created from it its fellow and who spread many men and women from the two of them; and fear God, through whom you seek rights from one another and from the ties of relationship. God is a watcher over you" (Q. 4:1). No one could lay claim to superiority over others, for all people are equal in origin and in creation or nature. In his farewell address, the Prophet emphasized the equality of all people and the criteria for distinction: "O people, your Lord is One, and your father is one: all of you are from Adam, and Adam was from the ground. The noblest of you in Allah's sight is the most god-fearing: Arab has no merit over non-Arab other than god-fearingness." The concept of equality was perhaps one of the reasons for the appeal of Islam among the poor and slaves, as it stressed the human equality of everyone, regardless of wealth or status.

The confirmation of the principle of equality has clear and direct implications for government. The equal membership of the community necessitates equality of rights and duties and the supremacy of the shari'a over everyone. As equals, Muslims have the same political rights in assuming public positions, running for an office, and voting. Muslim political theorists often refer to the incidents of Muslim rulers, particularly some of the Rightly Guided Caliphate, who were subject to the rule of law and obligated to carry out judgments made against them.

Shūrā

Muslim political theorists agree on the principle of *shūrā* (consultation) as an essential component of government in Islam. Modern thinkers consider the *shūrā* the most important constitutional principle of the Islamic system of government.

The Qur'an refers to this principle of *shūrā* twice. In verses 3:159 and 42:38, *shūrā* is associated with two important pillars of Islam, ritual praying and almsgiving, or salat and zakat, attesting to the fundamental significance of the concept. The sunna of the Prophet stresses the value of *shūrā*. It is reported that the Prophet frequently consulted with his Companions on various important issues that pertained to the affairs of the community. The Maliki scholar Abu 'Abdallah al-Qurtubi (1214–73) asserts, "When [a ruler] does not consult with the learned scholars, then it becomes necessary to depose him. There is no disagreement among the scholars on this [issue]." 'Abduh argues for the necessity of the *shūrā* on the basis of a third verse that states, "Let there be [one] community from you, summoning [people] to good and enjoining what is reputable and forbidding what is disreputable. Those will be the ones who prosper" (Q. 3:104). He relates this verse to the need for a group of people with the authority to encourage the rulers to do good and forbid them from wrongdoing. 'Abduh equates good with justice and wrongdoing with tyranny.

While acknowledging the importance of *shūrā* as a fundamental concept of government, scholars debated its nature and implementation. They differed on whether the *shūrā* was of an obligatory or advisory nature, whether or not it was binding, its scope, and which people (*ahl al-shūrā*) the ruler ought to consult. Classical scholars did not devise a structure or an institution for regulating the practice of the *shūrā*; such developments arose only many centuries later. The conventional views and practice established that while the rulers needed to consult with advisors and experts, the *shūrā* was neither compulsory nor binding. Highlighting the importance of *shūrā*, some jurists reduced the whole issue of government to an imam and his council of advisors (*imām wa-ahl mashūrātihi*).

The Islamic views of government are anchored in the premise that God has revealed the necessary principles, laws, and rules and has obligated Muslims to follow them in their relations with Him, among themselves, and with others. These principles, laws, and rules are contained explicitly or implicitly in the shari'a, which should be the guiding frame of reference and the source of legitimacy for an Islamic government. It is exactly this point that captures the essence of an Islamic government and distinguishes it from other types of government. The Islamic government draws its principles, laws, and practices from the shari'a. Classical jurists realized fully the implications of this orientation and placed the shari'a and God as the sovereign supermen, not the government, the state, or the people. Many attribute the development of this concept to the contemporary Muslim thinkers Mawdudi and Sayyid Qutb, but, in fact, classical jurists underscored this principle as well. Ghazali stated, "*Ḥukm* (rule, judgment, or sovereignty) belongs only to Allah; there is no sovereignty for the Messenger, or for a master over his slave, or a creature over another. All of that falls under God's jurisdiction and his stipulations; there is no ruler except him." Sayf al-Din al-Amidi (d. 1233) made a similar argument: "Know that there is no ruler except Allah and that there is no law except what he has revealed." Based on this concept, the classical scholars understood, first, that the shari'a preceded the government and the state. Second, God and the shari'a have legislative sovereignty in the Islamic government. Third, the shariʿa, or the legislature, is independent of the authority of the government. Fourth, the government and the ruler are not above the law, but their main function is to uphold the shariʿa and implement the law.

The classical theory of government has had a formative and lasting impact on the formulations of political theory in Islam. The early writings on government concentrated on several fundamental issues: the necessity of establishing a government, the qualities and source of the authority of the right imam (i.e., the qualifications of the head of the state), those who have the right to select the imam (*ahl al-ikhtiyār*), the qualifications of the people who unbind and bind (*ahl al-ḥall wa-l-ʿaqd*), the transfer of rule or succession, obedience and rebellion, the unity of the authority, and usurpation of power. The jurists tried to devise the legal frameworks that would preserve the general order and unity of the Muslims. In many cases, they had to extend the juridical principles to accommodate the changes in the forms and practices of government. In these early formulations, the caliphate was central to the discussion of the ordinances of government among Sunni theorists, and the imamate was central to the Shiʿi jurists. A major concern was to provide juridical arguments for accepting the existing institutions and the continuation of the religious and social life of the community as preferable to anarchy or civil disorder.

The Necessity of Government

Muslim political theorists considered government or the caliphate or imamate a necessary institution for fulfilling certain religious and temporal functions. They differed, however, on the justification for this principle and whether it was provided by divine law (*sharʿ*), reason (*ʿaql*), or both. Sunni theorists base the necessity of an authoritative entity on the concept of *ijmāʿ*, the consensus of the Prophet's Companions, who realized the need for political authority to continue managing the affairs of the Muslims after the death of the Prophet. The consensus of the early community of learned scholars is one of the fundamental sources of legislation, and, accordingly, the establishment of government becomes obligatory. Ayatollah Murtada al-ʿAskari (d. 2007) explains that the *amr* has always been understood as the issue of the imamate and government for the Muslims, Shiʿi and Sunni alike. The Qurʾan refers to the necessity of obeying those with authority. It also mentions that the Prophet stressed the need for the establishment of a ruling authority: "People are bound to have a just or unjust authority (*imāra*). They also need a ruler (imam)." According to another hadith, "The imam is a shield behind which people fight and defend themselves." The law therefore requires the establishment of an authority.

The Muʿtazilis and the philosophers justify the necessity of government based primarily on reason. Government is necessary for the welfare of the community, which consists of individuals who need to interact in an orderly fashion to ensure their welfare and prosperity. Government therefore is a natural form of social association, because individuals are incapable of living alone and tend to transgress against each other. An authority is necessary to keep order and promote the well-being of the members of the community.

Shi'is consider the imamate, the leadership of the Muslim community, a fundamental pillar of religion that should not be left to the discretion of the *umma* but instead must be designated by God and the Prophet. According to the Shi'i jurist Nasir al-Din al-Tusi (1201–74), the imam is *lutf* (divine bounty) and therefore should be designated by God. In Shi'i political theory, the Prophet has designated an imam, 'Ali b. Abi Talib, who in turn has designated a successor. Therefore, government for Shi'is is necessary because of the *naṣṣ* (or designation) and is a *farḍ 'ayn* (an obligation on every Muslim).

The Kharijis, particularly the Najadat sect, and some Mu'tazilis do not consider government to be necessary. For them, the main purpose of government is to establish justice and implement the rules of the shari'a. If the people can achieve these objectives on their own, then an established authority or government becomes unnecessary. A few contemporary thinkers like 'Ali 'Abd al-Raziq (1887–1966) and other secular Muslim intellectuals hold similar views and do not consider the government a fundamental part of Islam.

The Prophet's Model

Muslim political theorists believe that Islam, unlike Christianity, was born to develop a state and a government. They concur that the Prophet established a form of political authority that reflected the basic components of a government. The state of Medina included a territory, a community, and a form of authority and sovereignty entrusted with managing the affairs of that community. The Prophet maintained dual functions and exercised both religious and temporal authority. He performed many of the functions of a government. He acted as a ruler, judge, and military commander and appointed *'ummāl* (officials) to represent him to the far regions under his control. This model represented a clear intertwining of religious and political authorities.

The Rightly Guided Caliphate (632–61)

Following the footsteps of the Prophet, the government of the Rightly Guided Caliphate continued, in the eyes of many Muslims, to merge the ideals with the practices. This government, however, was viewed as civic and not divine. The caliphs had religious functions, but they did not rule by divine authority or assume the religious nature of the Prophet. The members of the community were the main source for the selection of the caliph, the leadership of the community was based on a contract and consensus, the supremacy of the shari'a was closely observed, and the members of the community had the right to depose the rulers if they violated the essential principles of Islam. This "ideal" or idealized form of government lasted for about 30 years and was followed by a dynastic or imperial model that shaped the forms and functions of government in Islam for centuries to come.

The Dynastic or Imperial Model

Government in the imperial or dynastic model during the reigns of the Umayyad caliphate (661–750) and Abbasid caliphate (750–1258) rested on different principles and practices. This model reflected a clear separation between the Islamic ideals of government and the actual practices. It witnessed significant political developments such as the rise of the political sects or parties, increasing political rivalries and disputes, the formulations of systematic and comprehensive writings on political jurisprudence, and the establishment of elaborate administrative and legal institutions. The classical political writings tended to perceive the government as a functional post. The most important of its functions were to protect and defend religion, to establish an organized authority, and to maintain order to enable people to fulfill their religious and social life. As long as the government was able to achieve these objectives, it was considered legitimate, or at least acceptable. To consolidate power and prevent the disintegration of political authority, the dynastic model instituted the practice of the designation of a successor who presumably possessed the qualities of leadership. As usurpers and less-deserving rulers took over power, however, these qualities were overlooked and the theory allowed for the rule of the less competent (*imāmat al-mafḍūl*) as long as they possessed the requirements of leadership (i.e., controlling and maintaining order). The prominent jurist Shafiʿi (767–820) was the first to sanction the leadership of the less competent. This became known historically as the "imamate of necessity."

The imamate of necessity became an accepted form, though viewed as irregular, and eventually replaced the rightful government. It was sanctioned by the jurists who were concerned for the continuation of the religious and social life of the community. In the 11th to 12th centuries Ghazali admits to this development and necessity: "There are those who hold the imamate is dead, lacking as it does the required qualifications. But no substitute can be found for it. What then? Are we to give up obeying the law? Shall we dismiss the qadis, declare all authority to be valueless, cease marrying and pronounce the acts of those in high places to be invalid at all points, leaving the population to live in sinfulness? Or shall we continue as we are, recognizing that the imamate really exists and that all acts of the administration are valid, given the circumstances of the case and the necessities of the actual moment? The concessions made by us are not spontaneous, but necessity makes lawful what is forbidden." The imperial model disintegrated in the tenth century and was replaced with empire states, the last of which was the Ottoman caliphate that was abolished in 1924.

Institutions and Structures of Government

The traditional theories of government centered on the institution of the caliphate and on the caliph. The issue of the caliphate of the Prophet is critical in Islamic history. It was a main cause for the emergence of political parties. Shi'is and Kharijis had different views on who should rule and on the authorities of the leader of the Muslim community. They often questioned the legitimacy of the existing authority. Sunni jurists formulated their theories on government largely in response to these views and in an attempt to accommodate the growing disparity between the Islamic ideals of government and the actual practices. They were concerned about maintaining the unity of government and the existing political institutions. Their discussions of the sources of legitimacy and political authority focused on the qualities of the ruler, the qualities of those who select him, and the main functions of government.

The Caliphate and the Caliph

Muslim jurists have provided various definitions for the caliphate, all focused on the nature and functions of this institution or on the position and the caliph himself, his qualities, and jurisdictions. Mawardi refers to the caliphate as the succession of the Prophet in the protection of religion and the management of earthly affairs. Ibn Khaldun considers the caliphate to be associated not with kingship but with religion and prophethood, as the Islamic government is a vicegerent to the Prophet in protecting religion and managing worldly affairs on its basis (*ḥirāsat al-dīn wa-siyāsat al-dunyā bihi*). Ibn Khaldun's definition qualified Mawardi's by stressing the role of religion in government. Both, however, rejected the notion that the caliph was the successor of God on Earth, a title that was used during the later days of the Abbasid caliphate. Stressing the importance of this post, Ghazali contends that the "shari'a is the basis of rule and authority (*mulk*) is its guardian. Whatever has no basis is bound to collapse and whatever has no guard is bound to disappear."

Based on the example of the Prophet and the Rightly Guided Caliphate, political theorists drew an idealistic image of the caliph and required certain qualifications that gradually became difficult to uphold. Mawardi specified seven qualifications: justice or moral probity, knowledge and the ability to exercise independent legal reasoning (*ijtihād*), the soundness of the senses, physical soundness, prudence, bravery, and descent from the Prophet's tribe of Quraysh. As less-competent or even unqualified rulers assumed power, however, the conditions of knowledge and *ijtihād*, prudence, or even moral probity were overlooked under the argument that the ruler could use the *ijtihād* and the knowledge of expert advisors. Similarly, as non-Qurashi and even non-Arab usurpers assumed actual control of the caliphate, the condition of lineage was reinterpreted primarily as an issue of solidarity and the capacity to exercise influence and power. The Kharijis rejected the condition of descent and reasserted the right of every Muslim to assume the caliphate.

The issue of the election or selection of the caliph and those who exercised this privilege was problematic. The caliph could not be duly invested and his authority could not be legitimate until he secured an oath of allegiance (*bayʿa*) from the *umma* through its representatives, *ahl al-ḥall wa-l-ʿaqd* (those who unbind and bind), or the elites who exercised influence over their constituencies and who also had to possess certain qualities, such as moral probity, knowledge, and prudence. With the changes in actual practices, the number of the people who could make the selection was reduced to less than five, thus depriving the *umma* from a true voice in the selection process. At some point, the actual seizure of power became a sufficient condition for the existence and acceptance of authority. Ibn Taymiya tried to redress this and considered the selection of *ahl al-ḥall wa-l-ʿaqd* an act of nomination that did not replace the general *bayʿa* of the members of the community, the decisive process for the election of the caliph.

Another process for the investiture of the caliph was by testamentary designation, or *istikhlāf*. The jurists used the precedent of the first caliph, Abu Bakr, and his designation of ʿUmar as his successor to sanction the later practice of hereditary rule as incumbent imams designated their heirs as successors. Shiʿis acknowledged designation and not selection as the proper process for the selection of the imam. They bestowed on the imam innate and extraordinary qualities.

Jurists did not set limits for the term of the caliph. He could stay in power as long as he was capable of carrying out his functions and did not commit a violation that required his removal from power. Practically, however, the term of the caliph ended with his death, abdication, or an usurpation of his power. The classical political writings do not elaborate on the means by which the caliph could be removed peacefully from power, and in fact removals often involved armed takeovers (*istīlāʾ* or *taghallub*), which were then sanctioned as de facto situations that ensured the continuation of authority and order. The seizure of power gave de facto authority to the government.

When the caliphs were strong, they exercised expansive powers. The early writings on the caliphate did not refer to any separation of powers and gave the head of the government expansive authorities. The caliph by definition was the successor of the Prophet in defending religion and managing the earthly affairs of Muslims. As the head of the Islamic state, the caliph was expected to perform religious and political functions. He had to defend religion, launch jihad, uphold the main pillars of Islam, collect and distribute the revenues, manage public affairs, defend the state, maintain public order, dispense justice, and appoint the governors and officials. The caliph was not expected to perform all of these functions personally. He could appoint whomever he wished to help him carry out these tasks. The caliph had the right to appoint (and dismiss) governors (*walīs*), officials (*ʿummāl*), ministers, and judges. As long as the caliph performed his functions and did not commit clear infractions, he was entitled to the obedience and assistance of the members of the community. While enjoying broad executive powers, the head of the government was in theory subordinate to the shariʿa and was not free to contravene its rules.

The Legislative Functions of Government

Legislation in Islam is divided into two types: divine and human. The divine legislation is revealed in the Qur'an as general principles or explicit rulings and is stipulated in the sunna of the Prophet. The human legislation is driven from the understanding of the fundamental sources of Islam (the Qur'an and sunna) and through the independent reasoning (*ijtihād*) of the scholars and jurists to come up with rulings to address new issues. During the time of the Prophet and the Rightly Guided Caliphate, the Prophet, his Companions, and learned scholars performed the legislative functions. As a messenger and ruler, the Prophet combined the executive and legislative functions. The Rightly Guided Caliphate addressed worldly issues based on the Qur'an, the sunna, and their own judgment. As mentioned earlier, it is reported that the Prophet and the Rightly Guided Caliphate consulted regularly with learned Companions on developments for which the Qur'an had not provided a specific stipulation.

With the flourishing of the sciences of jurisprudence over the first three centuries of Islam, the functions of legislation were performed by the jurists (learned scholars) who were not elected or appointed by rulers but recognized in society for their knowledge of the fundamental sources of Islam, their integrity, and their capacity to deduce new rulings to address societal changes. The caliphs, governors, and political elites exercised legislative authorities for administrative and temporal matters. The gap between the two authorities, scholars and rulers, increasingly widened. Another significant development in the legislative process was the limited exercise of *ijtihād* by the tenth century and the stagnation of legislation in general. Scholars tended to follow the footsteps of preceding jurists, and the gap between legislation and reality grew. Most contemporary Muslim countries adopted modern, Western-inspired structures of government and established legislative institutions (elected or appointed parliaments, assemblies, or consultative councils) to carry out the legislative functions. With the adoption of foreign-inspired laws, many of these parliaments did not fully follow a system of codified shari'a laws and even contradicted the shari'a in their legislation, thus creating a state of tension and a problem of legitimacy.

The Judicial Functions

Islam has required the establishment of justice, equity, and fair adjudication among people. The early Islamic system of government did not distinguish between the structures of authority. The rulers combined executive and judicial functions. The Prophet assumed the judicial functions and also appointed judges to the far regions under his jurisdiction. The early caliphs followed this practice. With the expansion of the Islamic state and the responsibilities of the rulers, the position of judge was created. The second caliph, 'Umar, appointed judges to the different provinces to represent him in his judicial authority. Later, governors delegated by the caliph had the authority to appoint judges to look into legal and civic issues. The implementation of rulings and penalties (*ḥudūd* and *qiṣāṣ*), however, remained the responsibility of the executive authority (the caliphs and governors). During the Abbasid caliphate, the judicial system became more elaborate. The caliph Harun al-Rashid (r. 786–809) established the position of the head judge (*qāḍī al-quḍāt*), who was given the authority to appoint other judges. The first to assume this position was the famous jurist Abu Yusuf, the student of Abu Hanifa (699–767). The appointed judges assumed their judicial responsibilities in or outside the mosques or in specially designated places, like *dār al-qaḍāʾ* (court). Though the jurists produced elaborate literature on the judiciary, the judges, their qualification, and best practices, the rulings and the judicial process at large were left up to the judge and often went unrecorded. In fact, the Islamic law was known as "the judges' law." The judges based their sentences on the shariʿa, when applicable, and on customary laws. This created inconsistencies and contradictory rulings in many cases. The failure to delineate the judicial and the political establishment (rulers) created problems with regard to the jurisdictions of each and the implementation of sentences, which were left up to the authorities to carry out. The courts' structure was simple and did not allow for an appeal process.

Two institutions were associated with judicial functions: the *ḥisba* and the Court of Grievances. The system of *ḥisba* is directly drawn from the principle of enjoining good and forbidding wrongdoing. As a concept, the main purpose of the *ḥisba* was to safeguard the implementation of Islamic principles and protect society against their violations. The *ḥisba* official's, or *muḥtasib*'s, main functions combined those of a qadi and a policeman. The *muḥtasib* was expected to maintain public order and prevent public acts of immorality. In many cases, judges assumed this function, which focused on preserving public virtues and upright social standards; overseeing the marketplaces; inspecting the scales and commodities; making sure roads were open; forcing people to make house repairs; and protecting Muslims from fraud, extortion, and exploitation.

The Umayyad caliph ʿAbd al-Malik b. Marwan (r. 685–705) established the Court of the Redress of Grievances as a separate institution. It resembled an administrative court and fell directly under the jurisdiction of the caliph, who appointed deputies or judges to address grievances against state officials (e.g., governors and tax collectors) and to arbitrate administrative disputes. In some cases, the caliph assumed this task himself. The jurisdictions of the Court of Grievances addressed the use of public funds, endowments, and complaints from public or state employees. This system continues to exist in several Muslim states.

The Administrative System

With the expansion of the Islamic state and functions of government, rulers needed to expand their administrative machinery. They appointed governors and officials to help them in the administration of the provinces. The administrative unit in the

Islamic state was the *wilāya* or *iqlīm*, which was governed by a *walī* or amir. 'Umar organized the territories under his control into 8 main provinces. These were expanded into 14 under the Umayyad caliphate and 24 under the Abbasid caliphate. The governor of the province performed administrative, judicial, military, and religious functions on behalf of the caliph. The Umayyad and Abbasid caliphates followed a centralized system of government, and as the caliphate began to weaken, some provinces became practically autonomous or pledged nominal allegiance to the caliph. The revenues that were collected from the provinces were spent first to meet the needs of the province, and then any surplus was sent over to the central authority.

The system of government adopted some Sasanid and Byzantine administrative structures. The *dīwan* system was among the first to be adopted. The *dīwāns* were administrative departments with specialized tasks for facilitating government business and transactions. Their functions covered the collection of revenues and taxes and the distribution of financial benefits. They evolved from a main *dīwān* for the revenues during the reign of 'Umar to many other *dīwāns* for the military, correspondences, records and archives, postal service, grievances, and the police during the Umayyad and Abbasid dynasties. To manage the vast Islamic state, the central *dīwāns* had branches in the various provinces of the empire.

The *wizāra*, or ministry, was the second most important structure after the caliphate. The term "vizier" (*wazīr*) was mentioned in the Qur'an to mean supporter or assistant. The Arabs considered Abu Bakr as Prophet Muhammad's *wazīr*. As an institution, however, the position of the minister became important during the Abbasid caliphate. Gradually, some *wazīr*s assumed extensive powers as they took charge of the administrative structures, the *dīwāns*, and even the army. In some cases, the position became hereditary and was monopolized by certain families. The early political writings focused on the *wizāra*, its different types, the qualities and functions of the *wazīr*, and efficient administration. To keep up with the actual developments of the position, Mawardi and others classified the ministry into execution and delegation. The functions of the former were mainly to carry out the directives of the caliph, while the minister of delegation exercised almost similar executive and administrative authorities as the caliph, except for designating a successor, resigning without the consent of the caliph, or deposing the caliph. The power and authority of the *wazīr* vis-à-vis the caliph fluctuated depending on the qualifications and skills of either. Some *wazīr*s became more influential than the caliphs and exercised full control over the government.

Additional institutions of significance for the management of the state affairs included the *ḥājib* (court chamberlain) and the *kātib* (scribe, secretary, or counselor). All of these institutions, including that of the caliphate, were historical and administrative institutions for government that had no stipulations in the fundamental texts. They were adopted out of the need for expediency in order to govern and administer the rapidly growing Muslim state. The caliphate, however, acquired a symbolic significance. It was the product of the consensus of the early Muslim community and was a uniquely Islamic institution. The caliphate represented for centuries the symbolic unity of the vast Muslim *umma* and combined both religious and political functions, which made the position more in tune with the Islamic frameworks and set it apart from the modern positions and titles of heads of state.

Modern Formulations of Government

The early jurists addressed the issues that concerned their time and circumstances. They concentrated on the functions of the government and on the fulfillment of specific functions that were necessary for considering a government legitimate, even if it committed injustice. These formulations preserved the continuation of the institutions of Islamic government for centuries. In retrospect, several elements were clearly absent in the classical formulations of government: the mechanism for exercising the principles of *shūrā* (consensus) or *ḥisba* (enjoining good and forbidding evil), the mechanisms necessary to rectify the government when it abuses its authority or deviates from the fundamental principles of Islam, and the practical role of the members of the *umma* in the political process. All of these issues became significant in the modern formulations of government.

Rida raised these concerns. He attributed the gradual disintegration of the system of government in Islam to the practice of hereditary rule, the failure of Muslims to devise a system of accountability to obligate the government to work for the welfare of the community and in accordance with the principles of Islam, and the ability of despots to undermine the control of *ahl al-ḥall wa-l-ʿaqd*. He also lamented the deterioration of the qualifications of the caliphs—namely, knowledge, moral probity, and *shūrā*—that led to the weakness of both the state and the Muslim *umma*.

The formulations of the modern theory of government were influenced to a large extent by classical theory, modern Western political theory, and developments in Muslim societies. The collapse of the Ottoman caliphate in 1924 caused vigorous debate among Muslim thinkers. Secularist intellectuals, like the Egyptian ʿAli ʿAbd al-Raziq and the Kemalists in Turkey, denied that government and political authority were an integral part of Islam. Abd al-Raziq maintained that the essence of the Prophet's message was religious and spiritual and that Islam, understood properly, never intended to establish a state and a political authority. Therefore, the restoration of the caliphate or the establishment of an Islamic government was neither necessary nor a religious obligation. Abd al-Raziq's views stirred up heated debates. Scores of books on the caliphate and government in Islam were produced during the 1920s and 1930s to refute his ideas.

A few political writings on government followed the classical theory and continued to focus on the head of the state, his qualifications, and his functions. They discussed the requirement of the Qurashi descent as a condition for the imamate or gave the head of the state the same idealized status and extraordinary powers. Certain intellectuals and parties proposed modern Islamic constitutions that gave the head of the Islamic state and the executive extraordinary powers at the expense of the *umma* and the modern principles of an accountable and representative government.

Several Muslim reformers, on the other hand, tried to reconstruct a modern theoretical basis for government in Islam. The modern reformulations often concentrated on the sovereignty of the people and the assertion that the people were the source of the government's authority. They also focused on restricting the power of the government either by the constitutional checks of the shari'a or by the people. They revisited the classical Islamic principles of government and early political theory through the prism of the modern Western structures of government (the executive, legislative, and judiciary) and deduced "Islamic stands" on the separation of powers and the system of checks and balances. Many modern thinkers stressed the civic nature of the government and authority (in response to Western criticisms and to a fresh reading of the principles) and advocated term limits for the ruler. In their view, the Islamic government rested on three main constitutional principles: *shūrā*, accountability of the rulers, and the general will of the people (expressed in the *bay'a*) as the source of authority. They reinterpreted the Qur'anic verse "Obey Allah, obey the Messenger, and those in authority from among you" as *ahl al-ḥall wa-l-'aqd*, who derive their authority from the *umma* and act as its representatives. They referred to the hadith "my community does not concur on error" and to the concept of consensus to reassert the authority—and, for some, the sovereignty—of the people. The reformist intellectuals expanded the principles of government to include, in addition to justice, equality, and *shūrā*, such principles as freedom, the accountability of the ruler, and the monitoring right of the *umma*. In most cases, they remained vague on the specifics and instruments of a modern Islamic government.

Rida attempted to synthesize the Islamic and modern principles of government. He described the Islamic government as the government of the caliphate and at the same time a civic government. In this government, the authority lies in the hands of the *umma*, the management of the state affairs is conducted by consultation, and the ruler assumes power through election or the *bay'a* of the representatives of the *umma*. Acknowledging the difficulty of restoring the traditional type of government, Rida accepted "the caliphate of necessity" as a temporary phase that, after serious preparations, would eventually lead to the establishment of a legitimate caliphate. In this temporary caliphate, the caliph would not assume actual responsibilities but would act as a symbolic figure and represent some sort of a religious legitimacy for an assembly of local Muslim governments.

Writing during the collapse of the caliphate and almost at the same time as Abd al-Raziq, the Egyptian legalist 'Abd al-Razzaq al-Sanhuri (1895–1971) considered the restoration of a proper Islamic government necessary to the unity of Muslims and the preservation of the law. He proposed a systematic and practical framework for a modern government in Islam. Sanhuri drew on the standard sources of Islam (Qur'an, sunna, and *ijmā'* of the members of the early community) to formulate a constitutional theory of government. He considered *ijmā'* as the basis of a parliamentary and representative system in Islam. Sanhuri listed several fundamental principles for the Islamic government that included popular sovereignty, the necessity of the *shūrā*, and the accountability of the rulers. For him, the democratic republican system was the closest to the Islamic type of government. He considered the abuse of power as an act of *fisq* (transgression) that led to the removal of the ruler. He also viewed foreign domination and influence as signs that the leader must end his *wilāya* (authority) and remove himself from power. The true Islamic government for Sanhuri performed three main functions: it combined religious and temporal authorities, defended the unity of the Muslim people, and adhered to the shari'a. Sanhuri advocated the establishment of a league of Muslim governments to replace the abolished caliphate until the Muslims were able to establish a rightful and proper one.

The Algerian Muslim reformer 'Abd al-Hamid b. Badis (1889–1940) welcomed the collapse of the Ottoman caliphate, which for him had deviated from the true Islamic principles of government. He used the accession speech of Abu Bakr and reformulated a modernist perspective of government. Written in 1938, these principles emphasized the consensual nature of government, equality before the law, the shared responsibility of state and society, the accountability of the government, conditional obedience and loyalty, and public participation in policy making. While considering these principles as intrinsic to Islam, Ibn Badis recognized the West for enabling contemporary Muslims to reformulate these principles and read them along modern perspectives.

In his formulations of the government in Islam, the influential Pakistani Muslim thinker Mawdudi emphasized the concept of *ḥākimiyya* as the main criterion for the legitimacy of an Islamic government. For him, society and state should be subordinate to the authority of Islamic law as revealed in the Qur'an and the sunna of the Prophet. If a government discarded the revealed laws, it became illegitimate, and its authority ceased to be binding. He defined the proper Islamic government as a "theo-democracy" or a "democratic caliphate," which was based on the sovereignty of God and the vicegerency of men (i.e., man as God's caliph). This government conducts the affairs of its citizens on the basis of consultation. Many criticize Mawdudi for his adoption of contradictory terms inspired by a particular Western political experience—namely, theocracy and democracy. But his formulation demonstrates the reformers' struggle to synthesize modern and Islamic principles.

Ayatollah Khomeini (1902–89) is credited with infusing the doctrine of *wilāyat al-faqīh*, or the guardianship of the jurist, into modern Islamic government in Iran. In a series of lectures delivered in Najaf in 1969, under the title of "The Guardianship of the Jurists: The Islamic Government," Khomeini presented the main tenets of his thoughts on government. According to him, Islam necessitated the establishment of a government to uphold the principles and laws of the shari'a and implement its injunctions. In this government, the jurists should play a major role as the most knowledgeable about Islamic law and as representatives of the imam. Since the *faqīh* is the source of emulation and represents the imam in religious matters, he can assume his "worldly authority" and preside over an Islamic government. Following the success of the revolution in Iran, the 1979 Constitution of the Islamic Republic carved a prominent role for the *faqīh* and entrusted Khomeini with overseeing the general policies of the republic. The new constitution adopted the modern structures of government and the system of checks and balances, but it also ensured the control of religious authorities over political processes.

The contemporary Iranian Islamic scholar Abdolkarim Soroush (b. 1945) has written against this tendency to "ideologize" religion. Such views have put him in disfavor with the Iranian government. Soroush is critical of the monopoly of the clergy over the interpretation of religious texts and the institutions of government. He stands against an a priori right of rule and the imposition of the government's will on the people. While the government may draw on religious values, it should be based on rational methods and the recognition of pluralism in society and the freedom of the individual.

The prominent Sudanese Islamic thinker and politician Hasan al-Turabi (b. 1932) bases his views on government on both the doctrine of *tawḥīd* (monotheism) and the consent of the people. This makes the government accountable to the higher authority of the shari'a in the first place. However, the government for Turabi is not an absolute or sovereign entity because it is subjected to the constitutional checks of the shari'a and to popular consent. It is a form of a representative democracy. Though the Islamic government is a government of the shari'a, it is in a substantial sense a popular government since the shari'a represents the dominant value system of the people. Turabi advocates limited government. He considers the *umma* the primary institution in the state and claims that not every aspect of Islam is entrusted to the government to enforce.

In his book *Public Freedoms in the Islamic State*, Rachid al-Gannouchi (b. 1941) elaborates on the specific structures and the institutions of the Islamic government. He acknowledges that several political concepts in Islam, such as *shūrā* and political parties, have not been turned successfully into stable institutions for administering differences in society. The West, by contrast, established various mechanisms for popular representation and controlled government. This realization affects Gannouchi's perception of the Islamic government as he attempts to devise a systematic and institutionalized design. Gannouchi underscores the centrality of the human being as the basis of government and highlights the concept of freedom. He considers political authority necessary to achieve justice and uphold religion. The nature of this authority is civic, however, not divine; its source of authority is not God but the people. The *shūrā*, which represents for Gannouchi the real empowerment of the members of society, can take place at various levels: a direct form (referendum and public elections), through parliamentary representation, and through councils of scholars and experts specialized in their fields.

With regard to the modern institutions, form, or specifics of government, modern Muslim intellectuals tend to adopt an instrumentalist approach that allows for the emulation of modern Western political institutions while preserving the fundamental Islamic principles of government. They justify this position on the basis of necessity and historical precedent. In their view, the efficient running of government requires the adoption of modern institutions that the West had already developed, such as constitutions, parliaments, separate structures for government, political parties, and a free press. This requirement makes the adoption of these institutions an obligation (*mā lā yatimm al-wājib illā bihi fa-huwa wājib*). They also argue that historically the early Muslims did not shy away from adopting Sasanid and Byzantine institutions of government to manage the affairs of the Muslim state. Therefore, the adoption of modern political institutions is beneficial to Muslims as long as they do not infringe on the general principles of the shariʿa. Hasan al-Banna, the founder of the Egyptian Muslim Brotherhood, accepted the parliamentary/constitutional form of government as the closest to an Islamic system, which stands on the accountability of the ruler, the unity of the *umma*, and the respect of its will.

Government as a concept, a set of principles, and a structure is an evolving notion within modern Islamic political thought. Contemporary Muslim intellectuals struggle to devise a coherent and systematic modern theory of Islamic government, a modern and at the same time indigenous framework of government that enjoys wide acceptance.

Further Reading

Charles Butterworth, "State and Authority in Arabic Political Thought," in *The Foundations of the Arab State*, edited by Ghassan Salame, 1987; Patricia Crone, *God's Rule: Government and Islam*, 2004; Rashid al-Ghannoushi, *Al-Huriyat al-Amma fi al-Dawala al-Islamiya*, 1993; Ruhollah Khomeini, *Islam and Revolution*, translated by Hamid Algar, 1981; Ann K. S. Lambton, *State and Government in Medieval Islam: An Introduction to the Study of Islamic Political Theory: The Jurists*, 1981; Bernard Lewis, *The Political Language of Islam*, 1988; Idem, *Political Words and Ideas in Islam*, 2008; Ali b. Muhammad al-Mawardi, *The Ordinances of Government*, translated by Wafaa H. Wahba, 2006; Muhammad Rashid Rida, *Al-Khilafa aw al-Imama al-ʿUzma*, 1922; Abd al-Razzaq al-Sanhuri, *Fiqh al-Khilafa wa-Tatawwuruha li-Tasbah ʿUsbat Umam Sharqiyya*, 1993; Hasan al-Turabi, *Al-Siyasa wa-l-Hukm: Al-Nuzum al-Sultaniyya Bayna al-Usul wa-Sunan al-Waqiʿ*, 2003.

Jihad ∞∞∞∞∞∞∞∞∞∞∞∞∞∞∞∞∞∞∞∞∞∞∞∞∞∞∞∞∞∞∞∞∞∞∞∞∞∞∞

John Kelsay

Literally meaning "struggle," jihad may be associated with almost any activity by which Muslims attempt to bring personal and social life into a pattern of conformity with the guidance of God. Nevertheless, early in the development of Islam, jihad came to be associated particularly with fighting or making war "in the path of God." In thinking about jihad, then, we may learn a great deal through a focus on war.

Muslims have written about war in a variety of genres. A.K.S. Lambton once remarked that philosophical treatises, the Mirrors for Princes compiled by court officials such as Nizam al-Mulk (d. 1092) who were interested in communicating the lessons of statecraft, and the compendia of juridical opinions collected in the schools devoted to shariʿa reasoning constitute three distinctive and important styles of Muslim political writing. One could speak similarly about war. For political thought, legitimation is the great issue: what form of order best coheres with the good, with practical wisdom, or with the guidance of God? And because experience indicates that establishing and maintaining political order often involves the use of military force, discussions of war ordinarily follow. A comparison of world civilizations shows that questions like "When is war justified?" "Who decides?" and "How is war to be conducted?" are typically tied to notions about the purpose of politics and the distribution of power: both are related to ideas about the nature and destiny of human beings, so religion comes into the mix as well.

In tying religion, politics, and war together, Muslims are hardly unique. They continue to speak and write in the distinctive ways previously mentioned. Indeed, Lambton's list of three types of writing is probably too short. For the fullest possible exposition of Muslim thought about war, one would need to consult the treatises (*adab*) of men of letters like Jahiz (d. 868 or 869) or the histories compiled by Tabari (d. 923) and others. Works of fiction would have their place in such a survey, as would poetic texts.

Nevertheless, one can speak of the relative importance of certain forms. The compendia of opinions or responses to questions by experts in the practice of shariʿa reasoning constitute a source of inestimable importance for understanding the Islamic experience of war. This is true because the shariʿa (i.e., the "path" or way of living most conducive to human happiness in this world and the next) suggests a focus on the questions of when, who, and how outlined earlier. In addition, the practice of shari'a reasoning, in the sense of a transgenerational argument about the guidance of God, goes to the heart of what it means to submit or to bring oneself and one's world into a pattern of behavior consistent with the purposes of the Creator. The attempt to relate the "sources of comprehension" (i.e., the Qur'an, the sunna of the Prophet, and the consensual precedents set by recognized experts) to contemporary situations (by means of reasoning, especially analogy) is perhaps the most characteristic attempt to think about war in an Islamic "voice." As such, changes in *aḥkām al-jihād* (the judgments pertaining to armed struggle) across the generations reflect the changing fortunes and political conditions of Muslims, thus opening the door to wider areas of Muslim experience.

Foundational Motifs

In speaking about shari'a discourse about war, it is useful to be aware of the following issues: (1) the story of Muhammad and his Companions, (2) theological ideas, and (3) accounts of the development of Islam across the centuries.

The Story of Muhammad

While the historical accuracy of traditional biographies of Muhammad may be in question, the outline of the story Muslims tell about the struggles of the Prophet and his Companions are not. Once the Prophet began his public ministry, the primary response in Mecca was resistance. The small community that gathered around Muhammad experienced discrimination and persecution. When this rose to the level of physical abuse, some of the Prophet's Companions urged retaliation. According to the story told by Muslims through the centuries, Muhammad refused, saying that he had been given an order only to preach.

This was not the final word, of course. Sometime during the negotiations by which Muhammad and his community moved to Medina, God sent the verses recorded in Qur'an 22:39–40: "Those who have been attacked are permitted to take up arms because they have been wronged. God has the power to help them; those who have been driven unjustly from their homes only for saying 'Our Lord is God.' If God did not repel some people by means of others, many monasteries, churches, synagogues, and mosques, where God's name is much invoked, would have been destroyed." The clear import of this text is that the Muslims now had different orders. In Medina, Muhammad added the roles of military commander and statesman to his preaching in the effort to achieve security for the believers.

As the story continues, we understand that the "permission" of Qur'an 22:39–40 evolves into the "destined" or "ordained" of Qur'an 2:216 ("Warfare is a thing written for you, though you do not like it") and the direct command of Qur'an

2:190–94 ("Fight those who are fighting you, but do not become aggressors"). In Qur'an 4:75, God challenges the believing community: "And why should you not fight in God's cause and for those oppressed . . . ?" In Qur'an 8:39, the order is to fight until God's cause succeeds, and in chapter 9, fighting against those who violate treaties or otherwise prove dishonorable is authorized "wherever you find them." The order of the verses is given in the story so that the intensity and expansiveness of the order to fight mirror developments in the military and political struggle with unbelievers. When in the end the Muslims prevail, Muhammad proclaims that "Arabia is solidly for Islam." The narrative of struggle thus ends on a note of hope.

It also ends by reinforcing the message that runs throughout: from the Muslim point of view, the question is not whether the Muslims should go to war or not. Rather, the issue from beginning to end is obedience. When the Companions in Mecca urge retaliation as a means of justice against mistreatment, the response is negative, not because of any direct rebuttal or refutation of their appeal, but because of God's order. Similarly, when fighting is justified in connection with the migration to Medina, the decisive factor is the command of God. The emphasis on obedience suggests the ongoing importance of ascertaining God's directives. The development of the shari'a discourse on judgments pertaining to armed struggle provides a noteworthy attempt to address this issue.

The Natural Religion

This emphasis on obedience has its corollary in the notion that Muhammad's entire career constitutes a divine summons—a "calling" of humanity to the condition signified by *islam*, or "submission" to God. Whether by the "beautiful words" of preaching or the strong persuasion of military force, the point is to bring human behavior, both personal and social, into a pattern consistent with the guidance of God.

In this, the story of Muhammad and his Companions suggests a certain view of the nature and destiny of human beings. Qur'an 7:172–73 describes the primordial encounter between God and humanity: "When your Lord took out the offspring from the loins of the Children of Adam and made them bear witness about themselves, He said: 'Am I not your Lord?' And they replied, 'Yes, we bear witness.'" The text goes on to say that the establishment of this covenant means that, on the Day of the Resurrection, no human being will have an excuse. All are bound by the fact that human beings are creatures of God whose very purpose is to serve the divine will. In accepting this—that is, in submitting themselves to their Maker—human beings find happiness, purpose, and dignity. Those who reject the divine calling do harm to themselves. Their fights with one another mirror conflicts within themselves. They suffer in this life, and if they do not make things right, they will also suffer eternal punishment in the next.

The point here is that nothing in Muhammad's approach to unbelievers is an imposition on or violation of their rights. He is God's messenger, calling human beings to act in accordance with their true nature and thus their best interests. Like other messengers before him (most importantly, Moses and Jesus), Muhammad summons people to submit to, or obey, God. Even the strong persuasion of war should be seen in this light, with one important proviso. War may create a sphere of security for the practice of true religion. It may be used to enhance such security by bringing non-Muslims under the protection (*dhimma*) or "superintendence" of Muslims. But it should not be used to bring about faith in the sense of heartfelt acceptance of God's service. It should not because it cannot—in Islam, as in other faith traditions, unwilling faith is a contradiction in terms. The Prophet and his Companions are a blessing to humanity because they call everyone to live as God intended, according to the "natural" religion. And they give particular groups, with their individual members, as much of the blessing as possible. For those who believe, full participation in the community of Muslims leads to rewards in this world and the next. For those who cannot believe but are willing to accept Muslim governance, the protection of Muslims keeps them secure from the disobedience of others and limits their own errors.

Historical Development

The Prophet died in 632. According to tradition, he sent letters to the Byzantine, Sasanid, and Abyssinian rulers prior to his death and invited them to accept Islam. In this account, acceptance could mean profession of faith or the payment of tribute indicative of the kind of protection or superintendence already mentioned. Failing this, the Prophet's letter promised to put these rulers and their armies to the test of war.

Muslim accounts take this report to indicate Muhammad's plan to enlarge his ministry beyond the confines of the Arabian Peninsula. Whether or not such letters were sent, in the generations following the Prophet's death, Muslim armies conducted campaigns to establish Islam in most of the Middle East and North Africa. Eventually, Islam became the driving force behind a world civilization, with adherents in every part of the globe and with special influence in North Africa, Asia, and central and southern Europe.

Muslim tradition attributes many of that civilization's most characteristic patterns of political and military organization to the earliest period (632–61) and especially to the leadership of 'Umar b. al-Khattab (r. 634–44). Again, it matters little whether tradition matches historical fact on this point. Later generations would cite early practice as precedent for a form of governance dedicated to the notion that human beings should administer their affairs according to the guidance of God. In order to fulfill this ideal, Islam should be established as the religion of state. The ruler should be a Muslim and should consult with recognized specialists in the Qur'an and other approved sources in the formation of policy. There should be a clear distinction between those who profess Islam as a faith and those non-Muslims living under the protection of Islam. While both should enjoy basic rights, the former should be viewed as citizens of the first rank, and the latter should pay additional taxes, observe limits on the public expression of religion, and in general behave or be regulated in ways suggestive of the priority of Islam.

We have already noted the theological motifs suggestive of the view that the imposition of such patterns of governance ought to be considered a blessing. Limits on Jewish or Christian religious expression, for example, were construed as a way of "reminding" or "recalling" members of these communities to the true or natural religion. According to this line of thinking, Moses had not founded a religion called "Judaism" any more than Jesus founded "Christianity." Both had proclaimed Islam. Where contradictions between the practice of Jews or Christians and that of Muslims became manifest, the judgment of Muslim tradition would be that the former had corrupted the preaching of the prophets. Muslim protection thus provided a kind of oversight or superintendence by which corruption could be contained.

It is in connection with these theological views that we may understand the insistence of Muslim tradition that the expansion brought about by Muslim armies was not precisely a matter of "conquest." Muslim thinking about war proceeded on the assumption that this expansion was a matter of "opening" or "liberating" territory in order to create opportunities for human beings to hear the call to practice Islam. A state led by a Jewish or Christian (or some other non-Muslim) establishment could be viewed as tyrannical by definition or, at the very least, not the best for human welfare. Given this assumption, experts in shari'a reasoning would develop their teaching on war in connection with a concern for the relations between the "territory of war" and the "territory of Islam."

Expansion of Islamic governance and of the Islamic profession of faith were not the same thing, although the establishment of a Muslim state did create incentives for conversion. Expansion into more established centers of trade and culture led to disputes and redistributions of power. Thus it was not long before Muslims located in Egypt complained of unjust treatment to the caliph 'Uthman b. 'Affan, who had succeeded 'Umar. 'Uthman's assassination in 656 led to the great intra-Muslim conflict known as the first *fitna*, or "test" of the community. When 'Ali b. Abi Talib, son-in-law of Muhammad and one of the earliest to profess Islam, pursued reconciliation with those accused of conspiracy against 'Uthman, the latter's relative Mu'awiya used his position as governor of Syria to mount a challenge to 'Ali's leadership. The resulting impasse led to further divisions—accounts speak not only of the partisans of 'Ali and Mu'awiya but also of a third party, the Kharijis, whose name indicates that they seceded or separated themselves from either side. 'Ali's death in 661 at the hands of members of this latter group did not resolve the issues of leadership. The dominance of Mu'awiya and his family—and thus the hegemony of Damascus in the territories now under Muslim rule—would not be set until the partisans of 'Ali, now under the leadership of his son Husayn, were defeated at Karbala in Iraq in 680 and opposition in the holy cities of Mecca and Medina quelled by forces under the command of 'Abd al-Malik in 692.

But matters did not remain settled for long. By the 740s, a disparate yet growing opposition to the Umayyads united under the banner of the Abbasids, whose victory moved the imperial capital once again, this time to Baghdad. The extent of religious difference in Islam can be shown by any number of developments in the period of Abbasid rule, but none made a greater impact on Muslim memory than the *miḥna*, or the test of scholars with respect to the nature of the Qur'an. Ma'mun (r. 813–33) and his successor determined that all recognized experts in religious matters should publicly adhere to the judgment that the Qur'an is God's "created" speech. The political import of the test was considerable. Resistance to Abbasid authority on this matter and the subsequent change of policy so that the contrary view became the official norm exemplify the intense competition between adherents of distinctive notions of Muslim practice. Abbasid authorities coveted the legitimacy associated with Islam. But this would be a long time coming; the Abbasids never really obtained control over significant sectors of the population, particularly portions of Egypt and Syro-Palestine. The resulting divisions, in which a consensus associated with "the people of the sunna and of the community" held sway in the Abbasid regions, while Shi'ism, particularly in its Fatimid/Isma'ili forms did so elsewhere, would be reflected in Muslim accounts of the progress of the faith for centuries to come.

Thus one might speak of a Sunni version of the expansion of Islam in which the story recounted thus far constitutes the gradual progress of a community elected by God to bring the world into a condition of submission to God's will. The *fitna* involving Mu'awiya and 'Ali, the Abbasid revolt, the *miḥna*, and other instances of conflict constitute a series of tests by which God refined the community. The story of Islamic expansion is a story of God's providential care, in which the believers may for a time become unsettled, but the saying of the Prophet eventually proves true: "My community shall never agree on an error."

By contrast, one may speak of a minority point of view in which claims of progress are offset by Muslim disobedience. Mu'awiya's challenge to 'Ali was wrong, and the subsequent defeat of Husayn at Karbala was an act of betrayal. In the generations following, Abbasid authorities ignored the claims of those designated by 'Ali's successors to lead the community of Muslims. In doing so, they preferred might to right, and their marginalizing or even conspiratorial policies constituted a kind of theft by which the Muslim community was deprived of the wisdom of persons possessing extraordinary piety and knowledge of the esoteric, as well as the exoteric, dimensions of religious practice. While the expansion of Islam throughout the world indicates that God has not rejected the believers, they will not enjoy the success for which they are destined until the family of 'Ali takes its rightful place at the head of the *umma*.

The Sunni-Shi'i divide has had enormous implications for the practice of Islam, not least in connection with the conduct of war. These distinctive modes of Muslim practice achieved political instantiation during the middle periods of Islamic development. The Ottoman and, in a somewhat different way, the Mughal empires reflected the Sunni consensus, while the Safavids constituted a Shi'i state. The latter in particular allowed for a considerable elaboration of the Twelver or Imami form of Shiʻism, with its distinctive eschatological emphasis. According to the doctrine of this school, the 12th in the series of imams or designated successors to the Prophet went into hiding in 874. He did so by the will of God and in response to the disobedience of the majority of the Muslims; this served to protect the imam from the fate of his predecessors, almost all of whom became victims at the hands of hypocrites. Imam Mahdi (i.e., the rightly guided leader) remains somewhere "in the Earth" and will do so until God decides that the time is right for his appearance. In his absence, a number of appointed "deputies" serve as guardians of the Shiʻis. By the time of the Safavids (1501–1722), this role largely belonged to the experts in shariʻa reasoning, whose view of the state was similar to that of their Sunni counterparts: an Islamic establishment in the service of adherence to the shariʻa, a Muslim ruler with settled modes for consultation with the religious class, and distinctions between Muslim and non-Muslim citizens reflective of the primacy of Islam. The authority of the Hidden Imam served to relativize the authority of the ruler, however, with important consequences for the justification and conduct of war.

In the modern period (beginning ca. 1750), the decline and ultimate demise of the great empires altered the political standing of Islam. That these changes occurred largely as a result of the advance of European powers, followed in the second half of the 20th century by the United States, only served to reinforce the judgment: the political and military precedents associated with the early expansion of Islam no longer held. Muslim thinking about war reflected the changed situation. Some authors wrote as apologists, arguing that Muslim approaches to war were consistent with the norms of civilization, as defined by the norms of Europe and the United States. Others wrote polemical tracts arguing that Muslim approaches constituted the measure of truly civilized warfare and that Europe and the United States should learn from Islam and thus add a spiritual and moral dimension to their obvious prowess in science and technology. Other interpreters of Islam used their position as diplomats to bring precedents from the history of Islam to bear on international law. In particular, the protocols added to the Geneva Conventions in the 1970s showed the influence of Muslim interlocutors, especially the provisions respecting the status of resistance movements. In this, the diplomatic contributions of Muslims mirrored the strongest trend in 20th-century Muslim thinking about war. Proponents of armed resistance attempted to stretch premodern precedents to fit circumstances in which believers found it possible to ask whether any established state actually constituted a Muslim, and therefore legitimate, form of political order.

Warfare and the Norms of Islam

The earliest compendia of scholarly opinions related to the rules of war seem to be those associated with the Iraqi jurists who styled themselves as working in the tradition of Abu Hanifa (d. 767). A collection of opinions related to jihad and *jizya* (i.e., to questions about military affairs and taxation in the regions that came under Muslim rule during the postprophetic expansion) is associated with the work of Abu Yusuf (d. 798). Even more significant is the collection associated with Muhammad b. al-Hasan al-Shaybani (d. 804), which later generations knew by the title *Kitab al-Siyar*, or the "book of movements." As the contents indicate, the movements in question are those between the territory in which Islam is established (*dār al-islām*) and the territory where it is not (*dār al-ḥarb*). As the Arabic suggests, the latter is, under certain conditions, the object of war intended to expand the dominion of Islam.

Given this interest, the text is preoccupied with the rules of engagement for Muslim forces: how they should approach the foe, what targets and tactics are appropriate, what is to be done with enemy persons, and how war prizes are to be distributed or managed. The opinions collected in the text are presented as responses to particular questions: Must the Muslim forces issue an invitation to the opposition so that its people have an opportunity to submit voluntarily and thus avoid war? What if the Muslim forces find themselves in a situation in which they must employ tactics that will result in the death of children? Are enemy captives to be killed, or must they be transported to the territory of Islam? May the Muslim fighters keep prizes (horses, money, etc.) they capture, or must they place these at the disposal of their commander?

In these and other cases, the text reports the opinions of Abu Hanifa, Abu Yusuf, or Shaybani—and sometimes of all three. Answers are crafted in consultation with verses of the Qur'an, reports of Muhammad's words and deeds, and the practice of the early Muslims, but these scholars also appeal to the notion of "that which is salutary," meaning (at least in part) "that which works, in order for the Muslim community to carry out its mission." Here, their interest is in the ability of the Muslim forces to attain victory. Thus, when faced with questions regarding tactics that will result in the death of children, the responses grant considerable latitude in the interests of the Muslims' ability to carry out their mission. Looking at the text as a whole, we may reconstruct the argument as follows:

1. The Prophet forbade the killing of children (along with a number of other categories of persons whose noninvolvement in fighting classifies them as noncombatants).
2. There are cases in which Muslim armies must employ tactics that would result in the death of children or else stop fighting. These include siege warfare, in which the use of hurling machines does not allow for precise targeting, and cases in which an enemy tries to deter the Muslims by tying children to the city walls, so that archers firing into the city are likely to hit at least some of the children.
3. In cases like those previously mentioned, the Muslim armies should do their best to avoid harming children and other noncombatants. But they cannot be prohibited from doing what is necessary to win. As Shaybani puts it, "If the Muslims stopped attacking the inhabitants of the territory of war for any of

the reasons that you have stated, they would be unable to go to war at all, for there is no city in the territory of war in which there is no one at all of these you have mentioned."

The overriding imperative is the expansion of the dominion of Islam. To drive the point home, the text mentions questions that focus on the possibility that the residents of a besieged city or the children tied to the city walls may be Muslims and then asks whether Muslim fighters deploying tactics that may lead to the death of these innocents should be required to pay blood money or to otherwise make up for the damage. The answer is an unequivocal no.

If such answers suggest the importance of the Muslim mission, others point to a concern that armies conduct themselves in an orderly fashion. Thus the responses make clear that war is authorized by a public authority and follows on an invitation to voluntarily submit. Enemy captives who might pose a threat to Islam—for example, adult males whose physical capacity suggests their ability to fight—should be killed, unless their capture occurs in territory that is already under Muslim control. Women, children, the old, the lame, and other noncombatants must be transported to the territory of Islam, even if this is expensive or dangerous for the Muslim forces. Part of the rationale for this restriction is the concern that fighters abstain from taking "private" booty. All prizes, including potential wives and slaves, must be placed under the administration of the authorities, who will (upon return to Muslim territory) distribute them according to rules governing the shares of various fighters.

Such concerns for regulation suggest the placement of the text in the early Abbasid drive to develop a standing professional fighting force. Tabari's history relates stories indicative of the way Abu Yusuf, Shaybani, and others crafted some of their opinions in response to questions from the caliph, and biographies compiled by later generations of Hanafi scholars report that these early scholars served in official capacities. Coupled with the fact that Shaybani's text appends a number of judgments related to the conduct of fighting within Muslim territory (e.g., against rebels or against *ahl al-dhimma*, "the people of protection," meaning Jews, Christians, and others living under Muslim rule, when these communities violate their agreement with the Muslims), the evidence suggests a set of opinions that draw on and reflect the condition of an imperial state. The rules of engagement bear comparison with those of Imperial Rome and other states governing an extended territory. The caliph's authorization makes war a public act, and the rules of engagement crafted by the scholarly community serve as norms for commanders in the field.

The condition of the empire changed, however, and the formulation of norms for the conduct of war shows similar alterations. Mawardi (d. 1058) is famous for his discussion of the ways the caliph can designate "lesser" rulers as his deputies. The powers assumed by those deputized include the authority to initiate war. In this respect, as in the more general question of public authority, Mawardi's opinion is crafted to serve the cause of continuity, even as it responds to a situation in which the notion of power centralized in Baghdad is at best a useful fiction. Particularly with respect to norms governing war, the idea that the caliph designates a deputy to serve as sultan preserves the idea that war is a public act fought in accord with standing notions of the mission of the Muslim community and for the benefit of humanity.

Mawardi's contributions do not end with his judgment about authority, however. In response to questions familiar from Shaybani's *Kitab al-Siyar*, Mawardi provides judgments that are quite distinct. For example, regarding the questions dealing with tactics that may bring about the death of children and others, Mawardi argues that if the Muslim forces cannot attain victory without killing large numbers of innocents, then they should cease fighting and offer the enemy a chance to surrender. If this does not work, then the Muslim forces should withdraw and wait for a more favorable opportunity. There is no appeal to the overriding importance of victory here. Mawardi maintains the authority of those reports in which the Prophet condemns the killing of noncombatants and thus the notion that Muslim forces should occupy the moral high ground. Given that Mawardi is usually presented as a follower of Shafi'i (d. 820) rather than of Abu Hanifa, one might suppose this is a difference between schools. However, Shafi'i is usually more aggressive than Shaybani on questions related to the issuing of an invitation to voluntarily submit and avoid war. For example, Shafi'i holds that the knowledge of Islam is universal and thus that the Muslim forces need not repeat the summons issued by the Prophet. On questions about the disposition of prisoners taken in the territory of war, Shafi'i says that all may be killed at the discretion of the commander. Mawardi's distinctive opinion may thus simply reflect a sensibility that the means employed by fighters must allow Muslim fighters to maintain the moral superiority of the Muslim community.

In any case, it is clear that judgments pertaining to military force are subject to interpretation. In this, the development of norms related to war is consistent with other areas in which scholars issued opinions developed in conjunction with shari'a reasoning. Finding a "fit" between textual precedents and the particular conditions of one's age is more an art than a science. Muslim reasoning about war, while indicating the outlines of a set of criteria or touchstones for believers in different times and places, nevertheless provides evidence of various opinions.

A move forward to the time of Ibn Taymiyya (1263–1328) points to serious debate on a number of questions addressed by Shaybani and Mawardi. Ibn Taymiyya stands at the end of the period in which the imperial model represented by the Abbasids was fading. Not only did the notion of central authority suffer from the rising power of lesser (Muslim) rulers, as suggested by Mawardi's development of the notion of "designated" authority, but by the 14th century the Crusades and the Mongol invasions posed new military and political challenges. With respect to the Crusades, the Book of Jihad, attributed to Sulami of Damascus (d. 1106), adapted the device of fighting as an "individual duty" to encourage Muslim rulers outside the province of Syro-Palestine to aid those bearing the brunt of the Christian advance. The leadership provided by the Kurdish military leader Saladin (d. 1193) seems in some ways to be a response to this, while in other ways he fits the model outlined by Mawardi. While Sulami's appeal to individual duty does not seem to be entirely original, it does mark a development by which later figures would discuss the norms of war in relation to conditions of emergency: if the opinions outlined by Shaybani and Mawardi related to conditions in which Muslims held power, what is their purchase in times when Muslim power is threatened or even overcome by foreign invaders?

Ibn Taymiyya issued his opinions in response to questions raised by the Mongol sacking of Baghdad (1258) and subsequent incursions into Syro-Palestine. Working primarily from Damascus, Ibn Taymiyya discussed issues posed when non-Muslim invaders came to dominate the territory of Islam but then converted. He argued that the Mongols continued to rule by a "mixed regime" of Muslim and Mongol law and should thus be regarded as illegitimate. In such a case, the notion of fighting as an individual duty authorized any Muslim authority able to mount resistance to do so. Ibn Taymiyya's primary appeal was to the Mamluk sultan in Cairo, although his own troubles with that ruler (Ibn Taymiyya served time in a Cairo prison at the order of the sultan) suggest that relationship was not entirely satisfactory. In any case, the collections of Ibn Taymiyya's opinions show a serious engagement with the set of precedents provided by the Qur'an, the sunna of the Prophet, and the rulings of outstanding scholars like Shaybani and Mawardi. Styling himself as a follower of Ahmad b. Hanbal (780–855), Ibn Taymiyya clearly does not feel bound to simply imitate earlier scholars. He does relate his opinions to theirs, however, and thus discusses a number of standard cases. Who may authorize fighting? Who should serve in the Muslim army? What targets are legitimate? What tactics may the Muslim armies employ? In these and other cases, Ibn Taymiyya's judgments reflect the quest for a fit between precedent and present circumstance characteristic of the practice of shari'a reasoning. Thus authority for war rests with an established leader so that fighting is a public act. However, the emergency presented by the advance of the Mongols means that "establishment" may not follow the most obvious lines. The Mamluk sultan's historic interest in Syro-Palestine suggests he should organize the resistance, but if he fails to do so, nothing in Ibn Taymiyya's texts suggests that another, more distant leader should not rise to the occasion. As to who should serve in the Muslim army, Ibn Taymiyya cites the standard norms about believers who are physically able and can provide their own weapons, horses, and other equipment. He notes that in ordinary circumstances, those who do not wish to fight may fulfill their duty by providing money or equipment for those who do. But the emergency condition is different. In this case, everyone able should fight—and this could include women and children, at the leader's discretion. Necessity makes the forbidden things permitted in the sense that every believer can and should support the leader's efforts at resisting invasion.

Necessity does not affect the question of means, however. Ibn Taymiyya follows established precedents regarding the restrictions on targets, with one exception: he says that women who support the enemy by means of propaganda may be viewed as combatants. That is, they need not actually take up arms, although the opinion does not specify the nature of "propaganda." Overall, however, Ibn Taymiyya suggests that the standard rules of engagement apply even in an emergency.

New Conditions and Alternative Views

Ibn Taymiyya's rulings draw on and point to striking changes in the political structure of the areas dominated by Islam. In the centuries that followed, these would include, first, the growth and expansion of the three great dynasties of the middle period of Muslim history and, second, the modern expansion of European power, with its legacy of colonialism.

With respect to the first, the Ottoman and Mughal empires represent the continuation of the standard majoritarian or Sunni discussions of the norms of war. Scholarly discourse sought to build on the opinions formulated by Shaybani, Mawardi, Ibn Taymiyya, and others like them.

The Safavid dynasty and its successor (the Qajar dynasty) represent something a bit different, however. As noted earlier, the Safavids ruled in conjunction with an establishment of Twelver Shi'ism. They sponsored a discussion of judgments pertaining to war that bears the imprint of the sect's characteristic doctrines. Particularly with respect to the authorization of war, the Shi'i view that God appoints one ruler for every generation, coupled with the Twelver notion that all of those so appointed were, from the death of the Prophet forward, prohibited from carrying out his mandate by the unbelief of the Muslim majority, meant that authority for jihad belonged only with the Imam of the Age. According to the compendium associated with Muhaqqiq al-Hilli (d. 1277), for example, mature men who are physically able and are not slaves are obligated to fight in the cause of expanding the hegemony of Islam. This obligation only holds, however, when the imam or his deputy is present. Since God responded to the unbelief of the majority by taking the Twelfth Imam into hiding, the conditions for jihad seem not to hold. Assuming that the reference to the imam's "deputy" indicates one of those who, according to Twelver tradition, served as intermediaries during the period of "lesser" occultation (roughly from 874–914), even this authorization may be in question.

The fighting authorized in the absence of the imam or his deputy is defensive in nature. That is, if an enemy attacks, the ruler is authorized to organize a resistance; indeed, in certain cases, any individual may defend himself or herself or even other victims from aggression. In the ordinary case, though, Hilli's text indicates that the ruler organizes forces in order to deter or preemptively attack a potential enemy.

With respect to other matters, Hilli follows standard precedents in that the Muslim fighters are required to avoid direct attacks on noncombatants. In the case of siege warfare or an enemy's use of children as shields, his opinion is closer to that of Mawardi than that of Shaybani. In a judgment that runs contrary to one of Ibn Taymiyya's views, Hilli says that even women or children who provide support to the enemy should be regarded as noncombatants, except in cases of emergency.

The consensus represented by Hilli becomes important in considering the effects of European expansion on Muslim judgments about war. In the early 19th century, Russia's advance to great power included increasing influence in the affairs of Iran. Shi'i scholars issued opinions advising the Qajar ruler of his authority as defender of the Shi'i faith and distinguished between an imposed war (*al-difa'*, a war of defense) and the jihad for which authority belongs only to the imam or his deputy. The distinction would appear again following the Iranian Revolution and the establishment of the Islamic Republic of Iran. The argument of Ayatollah Khomeini (1902–89) that the Shi'i scholars as a whole, or one of them having the requisite learning and piety, fill the office of deputy is enshrined in the Iranian Constitution. The notion that the scholar or scholars filling this role may authorize active resistance to an established ruler provides important background to the 1979 revolution. With respect to war, Khomeini called on the notion of defense, as well as of resistance to rebels, when he spoke about the war with Iraq (1981–88). Ongoing debates in Iran regarding the state's role in world affairs, its sponsorship of groups like Hizbullah and Hamas, and its nuclear program all show the import of traditional judgments like those collected in Hilli's compendium.

On the Sunni side, the erosion of Ottoman and Mughal power set off debates that similarly reflect the attempt to articulate a fit between historic precedents and changing circumstances. When a well-known Sunni scholar ('Abd al-'Aziz, grandson of the famous Shah Waliullah of Delhi) declared that the advance of British power rendered India a part of the territory of war rather than of Islam, he may or may not have meant to authorize popular resistance. Some groups in India thought it so, however, and organized the series of uprisings that led to the Sepoy Mutiny in 1857. Britain's brutal suppression of this rebellion suggested to many Muslims that a different strategy would be necessary, and Sayyid Ahmad Khan (d. 1897) advanced his well-known argument that jihad (at least in the sense of armed struggle) is obligatory when the Muslims are strong and not when they are weak. Post-Sepoy India would yield some of the most interesting examples of apologetic and polemical writing regarding jihad, with Syed Ameer Ali's (d. 1928) best-selling *Spirit of Islam* presenting the military campaigns of Muhammad as consistent with the highest standard of "humanity," while Mawdudi's (1903–79) treatise on jihad argued that fighting to establish a political order in which Islam is established is a duty for Muslims and a boon to an otherwise disorganized and heedless world community. For Mawdudi, the jihad is not only a necessary aspect of Muslim practice; it is also a feature of justice, because polities that are not organized around the norms of Islam tend to fight wars as they conduct domestic affairs—that is, by way of oppression, indiscriminate killing, and genocide.

Analogues to the apologetics of Ameer Ali and the polemics of Mawdudi appeared in other regions of the historic territory of Islam. In Egypt, for example, Mahmud Shaltut's (d. 1963) treatise on the "fighting verses" of the Qur'an combined a novel reading of the text with an account of the early Muslim expansion that rendered it a campaign of humanitarian intervention. For Shaltut, the account of the "occasions" connected with the revelation of the verses on fighting outlined in traditional biographies of Muhammad does not provide an adequate guide. Instead of reading the verses in relation to an escalating set of tensions between Muslims and their Qurashi rivals, one should read the text as a whole and thereby understand that the Qur'an meant only to authorize wars of defense. Similarly, Shaltut's understanding of the facts of the early expansion, by which for example the Christians living in Palestine petitioned 'Umar b. al-Khattab to defend them against their Jewish neighbors, presents a paradigm of one nation coming to the aid of another. In a modern context, Shaltut's point was that Muslim norms are fully consistent with those of the emergent tradition of international law.

More akin to Mawdudi is the essay on jihad by Hasan al-Banna (1906–49), the founder of the Muslim Brotherhood movement. Here, jihad is a duty laid upon Muslims for the benefit of humankind: the goal of jihad is the establishment of a state governed by Islamic values. As such values are consistent with the true nature of humanity, the jihad is a beneficent act. Left to their own devices, human beings will prove tyrannical and foolish, as the Qur'an indicates. Governed by Islam, human beings can live with dignity in the context of a political order that makes peace and justice possible.

Apologetic and polemical writing on jihad continued to develop throughout the 20th century and into the 21st. In the work of Sayyid Qutb (1906–66), this type of writing took a new turn, as the Egyptian writer and activist fused the style and arguments of the authors mentioned with arguments pertaining to resistance. In *Milestones, Social Justice in Islam*, and especially in his commentary on the Qur'an, Qutb argued that Muslims criticized global trends associated with the dominance of Europe and the United States and asserted that Islam alone provides a way of ordering life that accords with true human nature. In this sense, Muslims are always in a condition of resistance, because the way of submission is always opposed to *jāhiliyya*, that "heedlessness" to which, the Qur'an teaches, humanity is prone.

For Qutb, the notion of resistance becomes a characteristic trait of the Muslim life. Jihad, in the broad sense of struggle to bring oneself and the world into conformity with the path of God, is the principal theme of Muslim ethics. According to Qutb this struggle should focus on building communities of character, small groups of Muslims whose association would encourage personal discipline. These would be the seed from which a Muslim social movement might grow, with the aim of transforming the world. The use of military force would likely be a part of this aim, just as it was in the time of Muhammad. For the most part, however, Qutb focused on the need for these communities of character; as he put it in several places, if tyranny is overthrown and there is no group ready to assume leadership so that a truly Islamic social order might be put in place, the result will only be a new form of tyranny. Muslim devotees must thus undergo a time of purification and preparation, not unlike the Prophet and his Companions during the Meccan period.

Qutb is thus an important transitional figure for modern discussions of war, and many surveys point to his work as a foundation for later discussions of resistance, from the apologia of the assassins of Anwar Sadat (*The Neglected Duty*, 1981) to the *Hamas Charter* of Hamas (1988) and the World Islamic Front's *Declaration Concerning Armed Struggle against Jews and Crusaders* (1998). Such documents contain echoes of Qutb's ideas, but their authors also typically cite earlier precedents such as the Qur'an, the sunna of the Prophet, Islamic history, and standard contributors to the discussion of the judgments pertaining to jihad. In the end, texts like those mentioned attempt to develop a rationale for a certain kind of fighting, in conjunction with the establishment of political goals. As such, they make a series of claims and are the subject of much debate among Muslims engaged in shari'a reasoning.

Thus *The Neglected Duty* speaks of the duty to struggle for the purpose of establishing an Islamic state, meaning one in which public law is derived according to the sources and procedures characteristic of shari'a reasoning. Such "government by divine law" is distinguished from other forms, in which "human law" is the measure of political and personal behavior. In the current circumstance, the author writes, such a government does not exist in Egypt. He believes this judgment holds elsewhere in the territory of Islam, but his particular concern is with Egypt. In such a circumstance, Muslims are called to exert themselves to bring about change, and their efforts can include armed force. This is especially so if the ruler fails to heed numerous calls for change. Appealing to the time and judgments of Ibn Taymiyya, the idea is that Egypt, like the territory governed by the Mongols, is governed by a "mixed" legal regime. A truly devoted leader would institute a program of reform and move the state toward fidelity to Islam. But, according to the author, the Egyptian leader has not; he is thus an apostate and deserves punishment by death.

Herein lies the problem of resistance, and the author understands it clearly: who can carry out the punishment when the criminals are in power? Ultimately, says the text, the authority to punish belongs to God, who gives it to the Muslim community as a whole. The recognition of a ruler is a kind of "vesting" of this communal duty and right in a particular person or group. If these become corrupt, however, responsibility devolves to the community as a whole, or to those who understand the situation. Jihad thus becomes an "individual duty" incumbent on every Muslim able to fulfill it. As the author writes, in this case, jihad is like prayer and fasting: everyone must perform as he or she is able or else be complicit in injustice.

In this way, the text calls on Ibn Taymiyya and other historic figures. As described earlier, however, Ibn Taymiyya's appeal to individual duty was actually aimed at neighboring Muslim rulers. The author of *The Neglected Duty* thinks more of a mass appeal and of a kind of popular uprising. Not surprisingly, his argument has been controversial, so authorities like Shaykh al-Azhar suggest that the theory of resistance developed in the text is an invitation to anarchic violence. This fear stems not only from the possibility that the argument of *The Neglected Duty* comes close to suggesting that every Muslim serves as his or her own commander. It is also fostered by the author's claim that any Muslim who fails to support the uprising is prima facie complicit in injustice and may be killed with impunity. The text does admit that some supporters of a corrupt government may be innocent, or at least affected by factors that mitigate guilt (e.g., coercion or ignorance). In the event some of these supporters die in a military action, however, the author suggests that the "sorting" between innocent and guilty will be done by God. The calling of the faithful is to struggle for justice, and the killing of Sadat, in particular, is understood as an execution or an administering of just punishment.

The *Charter* of Hamas makes a similar appeal to emergency and argues that in a circumstance where an enemy has occupied territory belonging to the Muslims, jihad becomes an individual duty, akin to prayer and fasting. The focus in this case is Palestine, and the text asserts that Muslim claims to the land are not simply a matter of history or of property wrongly taken from individuals. Rather, it argues that Palestine (and with it, Jerusalem) was given to the Muslims as a trust. Defending this territory, or struggling to restore it to the territory of Islam, is thus a religious duty. Similarly, the enemy is defined in religious rather than ethnic or national terms: "the Jews" are an individual and collective target of resistance, and the struggle is part of a long-term, even eschatological, contest between faith and disobedience.

The *Charter* does not discuss the details of fighting, so one does not find arguments about combatants and noncombatants or about various tactics or weapons. Hamas has of course used techniques that suggest a lack of concern with traditional shari'a judgments regarding the distinction between combatants and noncombatants (e.g., the firing of rockets into Israeli villages), and "martyrdom operations" (also known as "suicide bombings") raise many questions for Muslims. Shaykh al-Azhar, for example, allows that martyrdom operations may be an appropriate tactic, but only if the direct target is military. By contrast, the popular scholar Yusuf al-Qaradawi seems to suggest that there are no civilians in Israel, since all men and women between the ages of 18 and 60 are at least eligible for military service.

The clearest example of a Muslim argument that justifies resistance and also connects it with something close to a strategy of total (i.e., indiscriminate) fighting is the World Islamic Front's *Declaration*. Published in a London-based Arabic-language newspaper in February 1998, the *Declaration* quickly attracted attention as an attempt by the leaders of a number of resistance movements to advance an argument in the form of traditional shari'a reasoning. After the September 11, 2001, attacks on New York and Washington, D.C., the text became known as "Bin Laden's fatwa or normative opinion." Muslim critics of the document complained that neither Osama bin Laden nor any of the other signatories actually had standing to issue legal opinions. Bin Laden's subsequent replies make clear that he believed such criticism reinforced one of the basic claims of the *Declaration*, which is that the contemporary Muslim community, while numerous, is dominated by leaders whose faith is superficial. As with *The Neglected Duty* and the *Charter* of Hamas, the *Declaration* interprets current circumstances in the language of emergency. By way of analogy, rulings offered by historic scholars indicate that such circumstances render fighting a duty incumbent upon "any Muslim able . . . in any country where it is possible." In this interpretation, one need not wait for authorization from an established ruler; the corruption and/or impotence of those holding power in the territory of Islam renders this point moot.

The *Declaration* also declares total war on a specified enemy. Fighting as an individual duty targets Americans and their allies, civilians and soldiers alike. This point has proven highly controversial among Muslims, and Bin Laden and other resistance leaders have attempted to respond. The duty to avoid direct harm to non-combatants is a well-established precedent, according to Bin Laden, but it is not absolute. To indicate the possibility of exceptions, he cited rulings that allow the Muslim forces to continue fighting an enemy that hangs children on the walls of a besieged city. The fighters know their tactics are likely to kill at least some of the children, but the children's blood is on the enemy's hands. Then, too, Bin Laden and others insisted that killing American and allied civilians is reciprocal justice or repayment in kind for the death of Muslim innocents. Finally, in a document published in November 2002, Bin Laden advanced the claim that the citizens of democratic states cannot claim innocence, since they have the ability to change governments and thus to alter objectionable policies. When Bin Laden released a video aimed at the American people just before the November 2004 presidential election, he reiterated this point, indicating that peace was at hand if the U.S. electorate would just choose the right candidate.

The issue of distinguishing civilian and military targets continues to trouble Muslims, however. Since 2005, this question has divided advocates of resistance: the indiscriminate killing of Muslim civilians by fighters associated with the late Abu Mus'ab al-Zarqawi, commander of al-Qaeda in Iraq, brought warnings from several advocates of resistance, including Bin Laden's associate Ayman al-Zawahiri. In 2009, Mulla 'Umar, leader of the most important Taliban group involved in fighting in Afghanistan, issued orders that fighters associated with him should avoid the direct killing of noncombatants. It seems that the weight of precedent and the weight of Muslim public opinion complement one another in this matter; at least with respect to fighting in areas inhabited by a majority Muslim population, one might expect fighters to alter the strategy articulated in the *Declaration*.

The debate over resistance is perhaps the strongest trend in contemporary Muslim argument about the rules of war. Resistance is also the topic of what is generally considered the most significant contribution of diplomats representing Muslim states in international forums.

The record of those agreements constituting the modern law of war shows that Muslim states, and particularly representatives of the Ottoman court, took part as early as the 1856 Paris Declaration Respecting Maritime Law. The various Hague Conventions also indicate Muslim participation, as does the Geneva Accord. More recently, Muslim diplomats played a part in the development of the 1993 Chemical Weapons Convention.

With respect to resistance, the most important contribution of Muslim states may be seen in the 1977 Geneva Protocol I. Together with a second protocol, this agreement responds to changes in the character of armed conflict since World War II. In particular, Geneva Protocol I expands the application of the law of war so that it includes conflicts in which "peoples are fighting against colonial domination and alien occupation and against racist regimes in the exercise of their right of self-determination." The text also eases the requirement imposed by earlier agreements that combatants "distinguish themselves from the civilian population." For example, the fourth Hague Convention specified that combatants should fulfill this requirement by wearing a "fixed distinctive emblem recognizable at a distance"; the Geneva Accord reiterates this directive. Geneva Protocol I recognizes that there are times when a combatant cannot do this, "owing to the nature of the hostilities." Combatants are still required to carry their arms openly. The relaxation of the requirement of emblems, together with the expansion of the scope of application of the laws of war, seems clearly designed to take account of the activities of guerrillas and other irregular or nonstate forces. From the perspective of Muslim states, support for these changes correlates with sympathy for Palestinian resistance to Israel. Such sympathy does not transfer to other conflicts involving Muslim resistance groups, however. Diplomats representing historically Muslim states during a term on the United Nations Security Council have consistently supported the sanctions and other counterterrorism measures adopted since 1999 by the council in its effort to deal with al-Qaeda and the Taliban.

Conclusion

The centrality of resistance in contemporary Muslim argument about war reflects the larger debate about political authority in which Muslims have engaged since the passing of the imperial states of the middle period (from ca. 1258 until the modern era). In particular, the abolition of the Ottoman caliphate or sultanate set off a great debate over the proper form of government in an Islamic state.

This lack of consensus certainly has an impact on the attempt to regulate war. Historically, Muslims in positions of leadership appealed to shari'a norms in order to harness war to appropriate ends and to ensure that the harms associated with war (death, destruction of property, etc.) might be proportionate to the goods at which it aimed. Without an agreement over the location of authority, regulation of ends and means alike comes into question. "Who decides?" is always a relevant question, not least with respect to war.

At the same time, one must note the persistence of a number of historic features of Muslim thought about war. Even in a situation characterized by disagreement, some of it deadly, respect for precedent seems very strong. When resistance groups are criticized for violations—for example, in controversies over martyrdom operations and al-Qaeda's doctrine of total war—the responses point to the enduring appeal of the notions enshrined in tradition: that the means of war should be proportionate to its ends and that fighters claiming to engage in a just war should not themselves engage in injustice.

In all this, Muslim thinking about war bears a strong resemblance to that developed by Christians, Jews, and other groups. This does not minimize the objectionable nature of certain judgments, such as al-Qaeda's doctrine of total war. But the question of war is present for every historic and contemporary group, and the attempt to regulate it, to see war as a tool that is sometimes appropriate for attaining or defending justice, is difficult. In the end, the question of war for Muslims is this: in what ways, or under what conditions, is war an appropriate means of jihad, in that it is consistent with the guidance of God? And a second question quickly follows: how do human beings comprehend this guidance?

Further Reading

Khaled Abou El Fadl, *Rebellion and Violence in Islamic Law*, 2001; James Turner Johnson and John Kelsay, eds., *Cross, Crescent, and Sword*, 1990; John Kelsay, *Arguing the Just War in Islam*, 2007; John Kelsay and James Turner Johnson, eds., *Just War and Jihad*, 1991; Rudolph Peters, *Jihad in Classical and Modern Islam*, 1996.

Knowledge ∞∞∞∞∞∞∞∞∞∞∞∞∞∞∞∞∞∞∞∞∞∞∞∞∞∞∞∞∞∞∞∞∞∞∞∞

Paul L. Heck

Knowledge informs us about the reality of existence, providing guidance for decision making. In Islam, such knowledge, based in scripture (Qur'an and sunna),
exists to generate a moral order pleasing to God. Loss of such knowledge is a sign
of the end times, ignorance being the cause of moral disarray. Knowledge is thus
not simply a source of prestige for scholars but truth from God to guide society to
prosperity in both this world and the next. Embodied in a corpus of laws known as
shari'a, this knowledge is overseen by religious scholars with jurisprudential expertise to apply God's will with wisdom to life's situations.

Arguably more than other systems of belief, Islam makes knowledge the measure of its claim to be God's final message to humanity. It is not about God's intervention in history to save humanity or reaffirmation of perennial human values. It
is incomparable knowledge of Judgment Day, along with norms for worship and
behavior to garner God's favor. However, the worth of such knowledge for human
well-being has never gone uncontested. Its truth depends on its efficacy alongside other forms of knowledge, including secular knowledge obtained not from
divine revelation but by human effort (such as philosophy and science). Alternative forms of knowledge can work in tandem with shari'a but can also challenge
it. A towering figure of classical Islam and counselor to caliphs, Abu al-Hasan
al-Mawardi (d. 1058) spoke of those who prefer the rational sciences (*al-'ulūm
al-'aqliyya*) over religion for the organization of society, a viewpoint he rejected
as wayward. Similar observations are heard today. Past and present, the value of
revealed knowledge has been defended, whether through a willingness to fight and
die in its cause, skill in persuading others to accept it, use of power to establish it
as a political order, or personal struggle to display noble character as evidence of
its "empirical" impact.

The struggle for revealed knowledge traditionally took place at the scholarly
level. For example, a prophetic saying (hadith) is considered true if it can be reliably
traced back to Muhammad through a sound chain of transmitters. In contrast, the
truth of other kinds of knowledge, such as geometry or politics, depends not on
prophetic origin but rationality. Does the mind accept it? Thus, revealed knowledge
has importance for the community of Muslims (*umma*), not for the prestige of the

scholars who oversee it but for its status as divinely given truth, making it vital to transmit it across generations as the source of moral guidance.

This role is considerably diminished when other forms of knowledge are more efficacious in guiding society. Knowledge with prophetic origin has always had its competitors, but the advent of European domination during the colonial period posed a profound and pervasive challenge to the truths of Islam, marginalizing the prestige of religious scholars by introducing critical analysis—apart from sound transmission—as the ultimate arbiter of truth claims. To be credible, knowledge from God had to hold up to human verification. The irrelevancy of such knowledge in the face of European power meant not only the loss of a way of life but also new standards for determining truth. This did not completely end the worth of knowledge from God. (Its ascendancy in some circles today is partly due to the failure of secular knowledge to live up to its own quasi-utopian promise.) But it now has to compete on new terrain where knowledge is valued for utility rather than prophetic origin.

This has had the effect of expanding the scope of religious knowledge, which, traditionally, is limited to select domains, notably ritual and moral affairs corresponding to information transmitted from the Prophet. Now, redefined by modern assumptions, it is to apply to the entire political order. While traditional conceptions of religious knowledge persist, alternative versions, unbound by a chain of transmission, now exist alongside it. Knowledge from God now competes in all spheres of life, including political and economic no less than ritual and moral. This association of religious knowledge with secular criteria for determining truth has led reformists to claim unprecedented scope for religious knowledge, presenting it as a total system, tying Islam to public utility as much as to otherworldly vision. As a result, modern innovations, from banking to constitutional law, are now seen as part of the domain of revealed knowledge.

Defining the Scope of Religious Knowledge

This dialectic between revealed and secular is not new but has been intensified by modern suspicions of revealed knowledge, leading to its redefinition according to secular comprehensibility rather than as divine communiqué. One example is Abdolkarim Soroush (b. 1945), who challenges the claim of religious scholars to rule in Iran, arguing that since religious knowledge is ever-changing, those trained in its traditional forms have no special privilege to guide society. But this makes it difficult to distinguish religious from secular knowledge. The flip side of the coin is Sayyid Qutb (d. 1966), revolutionary voice of the Muslim Brotherhood, who, like Soroush, views religious and secular knowledge through a single lens but, unlike him, makes the Qur'an the litmus test of all knowledge, whereas Soroush would subject all knowledge to historical (i.e., secular) processes. Thus, for Qutb, the Qur'an becomes the exclusive agent of political as well as ritual life. Traditional approaches continue amid the modernist divide. Mohammed Shabestari (b. 1936) rejects the secularization of revealed knowledge, to preserve its sacred character, but acknowledges its limits. It exists for human relation with God, not the political order.

The Qur'an says that all knowledge (*'ilm*) comes from God (e.g., Q. 2:32), but this does not make knowledge a simple phenomenon. God bestows knowledge both as scripture and wisdom (e.g., Q. 4:113). The Qur'anic term for "wisdom" (*ḥikma*) would be identified with philosophy, and a well-known hadith speaks of wisdom as the lost possession of the believer, who can claim it wherever he finds it. Such concepts enabled the integration of secular and religious knowledge in Islam.

Scripture is silent on the constitution of rule, and shari'a manuals do not include chapters on the state (*al-dawla*). Islam's teaching extends to behavior in the world (*al-dunyā*) no less than to acts of worship (*al-dīn*), but rule was traditionally not seen as essential to religion (although for Shi'is, leadership [*imāma*] is essential). God has not revealed the form of rule, leaving it to believers to decide what makes political sense, as witnessed in the development of political institutions in early Islam. Still, politics forms a juncture between religious and secular knowledge. The Qur'an calls for righteous prosperity, along with justice, as opposed to corruption, but does not specify how to achieve it. Muhammad acted as lawgiver and governor in Medina, but this model was hardly workable in Islam's later imperial context.

Farid al-Ansari (1960–2009) of Morocco argues that while Islam never defined the state, it does need a political system to enforce its teachings, that is, God's decrees as set out in shari'a for certain crimes (e.g., adultery, alcohol consumption, slander, theft, and brigandage), family affairs (marriage, divorce, and inheritance), and commercial and financial matters (e.g., prohibition of usury and deceptive business). A state, even if not essentially religious, is still needed to back Islam's way of life. Others argue that a state is derivable from revealed knowledge. For example, Mawdudi (d. 1979), a pioneer of Islamism, conflated God's ruling (*aḥkām*, a feature of shari'a) with the executive branch of government (*ḥukūma*, a political system) in a formula known as divine rule (*ḥākimiyya*), which left its impact on Qutb and Ayatollah Khomeini (d. 1989), as well as Hasan al-Turabi (b. 1932) of the Sudan, who built upon Mawdudi's concept of theodemocracy to link shari'a procedures such as interpretation (*ijtihād*) and consensus (*ijmā'*) with democratic ideas of voting and popular will, making it seem as if the modern nation-state was derivable from revelation.

Traditionally, however, Islam does not classify rule as religious knowledge. It was hoped that rulers be pious, but they also had to be astute in using mechanisms unspecified in revelation (e.g., tax collection, security forces, public works, military organization, and diplomatic correspondence) to preserve the worldly interests of the *umma*. Rulers—sultans and shahs—were not religious authorities but were expected to support religious institutions and heed the counsel of religious scholars, leaving them to adjudicate affairs that fell under the aegis of shari'a rather than that of the state. Indeed, a pious society was seen as a source of prosperity, and rule and religion, while not the same, were twinned, working in complementary fashion for the well-being of the *umma*.

The recognition of the limits of religious knowledge means that secular knowledge is part of Islam's political heritage, not secularism as a total way of life but rather religious appreciation of human wisdom in securing justice and prosperous rule. A tenth-century work by Qudama b. Ja'far (d. 948), administrative official under Abbasid rule, shows how a range of knowledge informed methods of governance in classical Islam. Indeed, governance (*siyāsa*) constitutes its own branch of knowledge, weaving together Persian notions of statecraft, Greco-Hellenistic theories of political community, universal ethical norms expected of rulers, and a system of bureaucratic institutions consciously built on a Sasanian and Byzantine past, as well as the experiences of Muslims as rulers of vast domains stretching from Andalusia to Central Asia. This is not at all to suggest neglect of shari'a, which does determine some matters of governance, such as penalties for certain crimes and principles for assessing the land tax (based on the manner of conquest, i.e., by force or by peaceful capitulation). This "religiosecular" character of rule in Islam features in the varied writings of Mawardi, in which he draws upon religious and secular sources of knowledge to construct a single framework of rule with three sets of "laws" at work in society: divine law (shari'a norms regulating moral life), public law (administrative norms regulating governing institutions), and natural law (processes by which rule naturally exists in the first place).

Appreciation of the complex nature of rule in Islam continues in diverse ways today. Morocco's Party of Justice and Development (PJD), for example, considers the common good as a divine mandate but does not tie its achievement to particular religious knowledge, only to just politics, along with careful policy planning based on the country's actual conditions. The party's 2007 electoral program contains no religious sloganeering, only technical proposals for national development. The PJD emerged from the Islamist Monotheism and Reform Movement (Harakat al-Tawhid wa-l-Islah) in Morocco, where the king is commander of the faithful and enjoys final authority over the religious arena, which he manages through a ministry of religious affairs and religious knowledge councils (*majālis al-'ilm*). The PJD exists in ambiguous relation to the court but acknowledges the authority of the king, while Monotheism and Reform works to fill a gap in society that resulted from the transformation of traditional religious authorities into state functionaries, leaving the nation's religiomoral character exposed to secularizing forces. The goal is to establish religion (*iqāmat al-dīn*) in society, not doctrine but righteous prosperity. As stated by Muhammad al-Hamdawi (d. 1957), the movement's aim is service to society, including religious education to ensure morality in society, but it measures its activities in terms of their worth to society, not as a predetermined set of rulings. Islam in this sense is as much about the nation's future as its past, the ethical reform of society serving as the key marker of its overall health as a civilization.

Another nuance of Islam's view of secular power is found in Yusuf al-Qaradawi (d. 1926), known as the global mufti for his widespread influence. He is hostile to secular rule in the abode of Islam but does not condemn rule that does not fully implement shari'a. He refers to kings and presidents not as agents of idolatry (*tawāghīt*) but as sultans, a traditional category to define rulers who are politically competent but who do not "wage war" against Muslims by preventing them from performing religious duties.

A final example involves the legal heritage of many Arab nations that once belonged to the Ottoman Empire, such as Egypt, Jordan, and Syria. The laws of these nations have developed in response to colonial and postcolonial realities but also retain shari'a material from the Ottoman legacy. 'Abd al-Razzaq al-Sanhuri (d. 1971), architect of the 1949 Egyptian Civil Code (as well as other Arab constitutions), worked to harmonize Egyptian laws with both Islam and international standards of justice. Many countries in the Middle East have constitutions that recognize secular processes (e.g., parliamentarianism) and shari'a as sources of lawmaking, further highlighting the religiosecular character of rule.

The Religious Value of Secular Reality

Is secular reality, not "controlled" by revelation, also part of God's plan? One can speak of two trends: (1) religious knowledge is the singular source of communal identity, setting Muslims apart from (and perhaps in opposition to) the wider society; and (2) religious knowledge inspires positive engagement with the world at large. The first can be seen in movements in South Asia such as Deobandism (including the Taliban) and Tablighism, the second in the movement known as Hizmet under the leadership of Fethullah Gülen of Turkey.

Islam in South Asia is known for devotion to saints as intercessory figures, mediators of divine favor, and spiritual guides—and also for powerful reformist movements that emerged in the 19th and 20th centuries in response to British colonial rule, which categorized its Indian subjects according to religion, making it the primary marker of communal identity. This was only intensified with independence when Muslims in India found themselves as a minority amid a predominantly Hindu nation. Some activists, notably Mawdudi, saw in secular reality, whether in the form of British rule or Hindu culture, a threat to the integrity of Islam. In 1941 he founded a group, Jama'at-i Islami (the Islamic Group), to protect and promote Muslim identity, humiliated, in his view, due to its loss of power in the form of Mughal rule. With the establishment of Pakistan, the group turned its attention to politics, advancing a view of Pakistan not simply as a land for Muslims but a nation under divine sovereignty. Its success at the polls has been limited, but it has done much to create the belief that rule exists for the establishment of Islam. Jama'at-i Islami is diversely present across South Asia. In Pakistan, it oscillates between political participation and protest of the nation's failure to implement shari'a fully.

Other groups in South Asia conceive religious knowledge in terms of communal identity but apart from politics. Deobandism, with a network of madrasas (religious schools) across South Asia, recognizes traditional forms of religious authority but seeks to form a communal identity circumscribed by religious knowledge. It is locked in a polemical discourse with another reformist movement, Barelwism, which also operates a network of madrasas but diverges from Deobandism in its devotion to saints, both living and dead. For Deobandism, divine favor is not mediated by saints but is earned by adherence to a body of religious knowledge untarnished by secular thought, namely, the corpus of prophetic sayings. Deobandism does acknowledge saintly figures as moral exemplars but views them, as it does the prophets, as merely human (*bashar*) and not as carriers of divine light.

By emphasizing a closed corpus of religious knowledge as the singular source of communal identity, Deobandism illustrates how Islam can assume a hostile stance toward the wider society. The Taliban, after all, represents one of its offshoots. Out of a desire to protect believers from secular influence, Deobandism molds Islam as a shari'a enclave. This can also be seen in the devotional movement loosely associated with Deobandism, Tablighi Jama'at (TJ), which is dedicated to religious revival at a popular level. It is "modern" in encouraging all believers to take responsibility for Islam but "antimodern" in its disdain for secular reality. Its central activity is the collective reading of common texts that recount the lives of the first Muslims, which limits its religious vision to a historical past deemed to be the exclusive source of virtuous behavior: how the first Muslims ate, laughed, bathed, and so on. This focus on Islam-specific activity fosters a sense of existential separation from the modern world. Islam is to be restored not by political but by ritual means (i.e., by accruing religious merit through imitating a sacred past, not by establishing a religious state in today's reality).

TJ's negative view of this world recalls jihadism, but TJ aspires to a favorable standing in the next world. However, it is a relatively easy step to jihadist activity for individuals who seek political expression of TJ-inspired otherworldliness. But the official TJ view of jihad is missionary activity, not fighting. While the secular reality of the world makes it displeasing to God, the goal is not to attack it but to separate from it through a group experience that allows one to live in the time of the Prophet and his companions, when religious knowledge prevailed over worldliness. Having turned its back on Islam's political heritage, TJ shares al-Qaeda's antiworldly stance but rejects the idea of religious action for worldly objectives, such as establishing a state. It aims to revive Islam by enlivening the religious identity of Muslims, not by sending them to death in battle against infidels. TJ's disinterest in the world can indirectly foster secularism. This world has no religious value, making it pointless to want to Islamize it. However, even if it does not organize politically, TJ is supportive of shari'a-based politics, as is true of Deobandism, which does not see politics as essential to Islam, defining itself simply as "people of the sunna" (*ahl al-sunna*), but it does have views on the political struggles of the age. It supported India's drive for independence and also the caliphate in Istanbul. It is partial to causes in defense of Muslims against the West or Hinduism but also speaks of the political rights of all peoples. Islam here is essentially a shari'a-oriented life free of "popular" customs, seen as innovations, but can play into shari'a-exclusive rule, as with the Taliban. Still, by refusing to make politics essential to Islam, Deobandism,

Tablighism, and Barelwism diverge from the Islamism of Jama'at-i Islami. Millions of Muslims associated with these movements thus have very diverse views on politics and secular reality overall. Support for Islamist politics exists but is not clearly linked to the vision of these groups.

In contrast, the movement led by Fethullah Gülen, a spiritual figure committed to the secular state but also to the teachings of Islam, seeks to engage the world and serve humanity irrespective of religious identity. Its members, generally conservative, helped foster the renewal of civil society in Turkey by creating networks of relations based on the ethics of Islam rather than the secular ideology of the state. They adhere to the particulars of Islam so as to embody universal virtues (honesty, humility, generosity, and kindness). This allows them to engage the world while witnessing to the ethics of Islam. The movement, global in its activities, has interests in education, business, and mass media, as well as interfaith initiatives. Gülen has not always been successful in his attempts to accommodate the Kemalist state, the secularist ideology of which has dominated the Turkish Republic since its founding by Atatürk (1881–1938), and his pro-Western outlook and network of schools have put him at odds with the interests of the ruling Islam-oriented Justice and Development Party (AK Party).

The fact that the Turkish state has control of official religious institutions is not inconsistent with the Ottoman past. The difference, of course, is that the modern state defines itself in secular categories, leading it to refashion Islam in its own image. For example, the religious curriculum of state schools is geared to the glorification of the Turkish nation rather than the beliefs and practices of Islam as ends in themselves. However, since the founding of the republic in 1923, figures associated with Sufism (particularly the Naqshbandis) have kept alive non-state visions of Islam even while diverging in their attitudes toward the secular state. Sufism is a religiosity that does not depend on state recognition or even social visibility—in contrast to shari'a, which defines the externals of people's lives (e.g., what they wear and how they act). Thus, the Naqshbandis in Turkey, despite the political diversity of their affiliates, have worked to foster Islam as an alternative to Kemalism, not political challenge but rather a spiritual life beyond the control of the Kemalist state. This has offered pious Turks a way to live the spiritual life of Islam within a public order defined by Kemalism.

Eventually, this would have political consequences. A key leader of the Naqshbandis was Mehmet Zahit Kotku (d. 1980), who encouraged his followers to engage the political arena first by allying with non-Kemalist secular parties and then by creating religious-oriented parties. Three prime ministers were disciples of his: Turgut Özal (d. 1993), Necmettin Erbakan (leader of the Islamist movement in Turkey known as Milli Görüş), and Recep Tayyip Erdoğan (leader of the AK Party, now ruling). The speeches of Kotku's successor, Esad Coşan (d. 2001), castigated the secularist ideology of Kemalism by proxy through verbal attacks on the West. He called for greater freedom for Islam but not for all (e.g., religious minorities, atheists, gays) and was a great advocate especially of free markets, seeing economic vitality as a way to protect the nation from foreign control. Not only pious believers but also nonobservant Muslims appreciated this counternarrative, even if religiously framed, as a more effective guarantor of freedom than Kemalism. The Kemalist state did permit a democratic process, which brought the AK Party to power, but it vigorously sought to program the nation to see secular modernization as the purpose of life, although now, with the success of the AK Party, it is no longer clear what the relation of the state to Kemalism will be even if the ideology of Kemalism continues to shape national identity.

From this background the Gülen movement emerged not as a spiritual brotherhood but as a socioreligious force to pave the way for the transformation of Turkish politics, a transformation symbolized in a religiously oriented party ruling a Muslim nation on behalf of a secularist state. This is not to suggest a formal relation between the movement and the party (and relations have been strained between the two), but Gülen set the conditions for the AK Party to navigate between the hammer of Kemalism and the anvil of Islamism as represented by Erbakan. The stage was set in 1997 when the state removed Erbakan as prime minister. This event made Islam in Turkey not only a force for economic liberalization but also for political liberalization—human rights, democracy, and civil liberties—which were previously castigated as products of the West. In short, Kemalist repression of Islam helped link Islam with political freedom (although this is now in question as a result of some of Erdoğan's policies, notably his repression of the press). Long before 1997, the nation as a whole aspired to greater freedom from the state, but the aspiration was realized only when key religious voices saw it as a necessary precondition for the well-being of Islam. However, the emergence of Islam as a proponent of civil society in Turkey is not wholly explicable as a response to state action. Political liberalization, to make religious sense, needs religious language, including the liberalization of religious attitudes toward secular reality: a religious message of tolerance and love for all without undermining the uniqueness of Islam. Gülen symbolizes this vision, articulating national harmony through a religious lens—not as a state policy but as a shaper of the character of society. The AK Party drew on Gülen's ideas to forge its approach to politics: a dynamic religiosity engaged with a global secular reality that is seen as part of God's created order.

Here, the aim of Islam is primarily ethical, not political: to restore the character of a nation disfigured by the materialist ideology of the state. However, renewal of national character is not reducible to philosophical abstracts but depends on a message that speaks to the cultural particularities and ethical loyalties of the people, including Islam, while also resonating with the national and global whole. Gülen is not so much in dialogue with Kemalism as he is with Turkish society at large and the entire world, defining a framework for the nation in which a dynamic concept of religious knowledge is freely at play. Gülen was a disciple of Sa'id Nursi (d. 1960), erstwhile affiliate of the Naqshbandis, who broke with institutional Sufism but drew on its intellectual heritage to defend faith in the face of secularizing trends in modern Turkey. His voluminous commentary on the Qur'an, *Risale-yi Nur* (Epistle of light), widely studied in Turkey and available on the Internet in multiple languages, weaves together questions of modern science with a spiritual vision of the cosmos, leaving the impression that secularity is itself part of the sacred narrative of Islam. Gülen in turn added civic activism to Nursi's legacy, inspiring his followers to bring piety to life in the form of service to the nation and the world. Indeed, the movement refers to itself as "service" (*hizmet*). Its promotion of piety operates not by preaching (*teblig*) for the sake of a religious identity but by representing (*temsil*) the ethics of Islam in the service of the common good. Islam has its particular norms, to which Gülen's followers are committed, seeing them as a belief system that encourages harmonious engagement with secular reality.

The Political Demands of Religious Knowledge

Religious knowledge makes demands on society in diverse ways. In general, the role of religious scholars, as heirs of the prophets, has been to give advice (*naṣīḥa*). Some see scholars as sharers in rule, but advice is often given from a distance, as in Morocco, where the leader of the Butshishiyya, Sidi Hamza, backer of the monarchy, calls the nation to support it as the protector of national harmony, while 'Abd al-Salam Yasin (d. 2012), founder of the banned Jama'at al-'Adl wa-l-Ihsan (Group of Justice and Charity), denounced it as a source of political injustice. A message from God can raise expectations of a perfect society, making deviation from God's decrees cause for fighting. The movement in early Islam known as Kharijism took shape in response to the Battle of Siffin in the year 657 between two of the Prophet's Companions, 'Ali b. Abi Talib and Mu'awiyya. The resulting arbitration was seen by proto-Kharijis as a compromise of the Book of God. Scandalized that the community's affairs would be governed by human negotiation, they famously declared that there could be "no rule but God's."

A combination of religious and material motives inspired the earliest affiliates of Kharijism to fight any Muslims willing to recognize human authority (*wilāya*). This did much to stimulate Muslim thinking about the ambiguous relation of religious knowledge to power and, indeed, about the religious status of "politics" in general. The basic conviction of Kharijism—that secular considerations are not to prevail over God's decrees—still exists. One example is jihadism with its strong resistance to rule that is religiously ambiguous even if politically effective. Al-Qaeda adjudicates political realities wholly through a scripturally informed narrative where the forces of God do battle against his enemies. Qutb, especially, shaped this narrative, overturning centuries of Muslim appreciation of secularity. His dismissal of nonrevealed explanations of human existence was partly a reaction to secularizing processes that would put authority over the moral character of the nation in the hands of state authorities. Still, the resulting jihadist narrative ignores long-standing reservations about utopian thinking. For al-Qaeda, the failure to incarnate religious knowledge as rule casts suspicion on its veracity, making it necessary to "stage" the truth of revelation by enacting the divinely revealed victory of belief over unbelief in the battlefield.

In this outlook, there can be no compromise between divine sovereignty and powers that place worldly considerations before divine speech. (Doing so is seen as a kind of polytheism.) The concern is that Islam's truth will be suspect if it is not guiding society. Here, then, divine speech is made the sole criterion of action in the world. The rhetoric of al-Qaeda speaks of tyranny as a deviation, humiliating for the *umma*, from knowledge given by divine speech. The jihadist reading of politics through the lens of a revealed narrative makes it necessary to "rescue" Islam from the political ambiguities that religiously imperfect rule casts on the certainty of religious knowledge. Jihadism is not merely a religious form of violent protest against injustice but more a battle (equating piety with fighting) for the supremacy of religious knowledge over secular reality.

Muslims, past and present, have been wary of calls for religiously perfect rule, seeing perfection (*kamāl*) as spiritual, not political. Leaders claiming to be the Mahdi, the figure who will deliver the world from injustice at the end of time, occasionally appear with the intention of fulfilling the prophetic project on Earth, but Mahdism has limited endurance. Wariness of utopian calls comes from the fact that governance (*siyāsa*) has no revealed status. Leading scholars, such as Mawardi, wrote on governance without making it a branch of shari'a. Others, such as Ibn Qayyim al-Jawziyya (d. 1350), would do just that, but this was the minority view. To be sure, rule came with expectations, chiefly the preservation of the *umma*'s worldly interests (protection of life and property, preservation of justice and security, and promotion of prosperity). Such expectations were articulated in literature known as "counsel-for-rulers," which drew upon secular (and even pre-Islamic) wisdom no less than shari'a norms. As a result, Muslims have long judged the exercise of power against the standards of worldly interests. These may include the dissemination of religious knowledge as a public good, but rule is not evaluated in terms of religious knowledge exclusively.

This outlook is partly traceable to the so-called people of postponement (*al-murji'a*), who refused to judge the religious status of 'Ali or Mu'awiya on the basis of their governance. The Shi'is, too, while making leadership integral to religion, would also adopt a position of political accommodation once the last imam went into concealment in the ninth century. However, the imam's absence did not leave the Shi'is bereft of religious knowledge but only meant that its scope was limited to areas such as rituals and morals, where God's rulings do not change, in contrast to politics and economics. This is one reason that the rise of constitutionalism in the abode of Islam, beginning in the 19th century, caused a good deal of confusion. Was it religiously legitimate? Traditional indifference to the nature of rule, so long as it preserved order, meant that Sunni and Shi'i authorities alike would take varied positions on democracy, provided it did not threaten the integrity of religious knowledge as a moral guide for society. But this is exactly what modernity put at risk by challenging the verifiability of religious knowledge.

It thus became necessary to rethink the relation of religious knowledge to the political order. In the past, rulers—sultans and shahs—posed no threat to the supremacy of religious knowledge, even if sometimes manipulating it for their own interests. Also, Islam has generally respected the autonomy of secular knowledge in its own spheres, such as astronomy, geography, and medicine. There was little sense of a clash between the pursuit of secular knowledge and the otherworldly purposes of religion. But the modernist assertion that only secular knowledge has a claim on truth posed a profound challenge for the place of Islam in public life. Some reacted with the claim that religious knowledge is applicable in all spheres of life, including politics and economics. Is there a way of pursuing the science of politics and economics that is unique to a religious community? Scholars have long sought to extend religious knowledge into the political domain by applying general principles culled from shari'a to areas with no clear shari'a precedent, allowing scholars to extend their authority into the public sphere. Qaradawi leaves it to the judgment of the leader (ra'y al-imām) to determine the public interest in shari'a-unspecified areas but requires him to do so in light of "the intentions of religion" (maqāṣid al-dīn) that only scholars can verify. Abu Yusuf (d. 798), one of the early shari'a masters, also recognized the authority of the leader's judgment but did not qualify it as Qaradawi, leaving it to the ruler to do what he sees best for Muslims as long as he does not contradict God's rulings.

Past scholars, such as Ghazali (d. 1111) and his teacher, Juwayni (d. 1085), did define public interest (maṣlaḥa) in terms of shari'a considerations, but in contrast to Qaradawi, the motive was not to link politics to religion but rather a concern for the corruption of shari'a knowledge and the corresponding need to construct a "rational" system where the essence of shari'a, defined as "the universal interests" (al-maṣāliḥ al-kulliyya), could be known in spite of the decline in religious learning. The point, then, is that such premodern attempts to define public interests in terms of maqāṣid al-dīn were motivated by scholarly anxieties and not the desire to construct a political system out of religious knowledge as in the modern context.

The Politics of Religious Diversity

To be sure, scholars of the past thought systematically about the relation of religious knowledge to political order as much as Islamist thinkers today, but they did so for different reasons than those motivating Islamism today. Tensions between the truth claims of religious knowledge and political realities can be compounded by competing definitions of Islam, a confessional pluralism that sometimes lends itself to conflict. Sectarian strife is nothing new in Islam, but there have also long been attempts to view confessional pluralism within philosophical categories. Farabi (d. 950) was one of the first to do so. His political works should not be seen simply as Greek thought in Arabic but rather as a cogent response to sectarian divisiveness: a conception of truth able to embrace multiple confessions. As a result, political order is geared not to the particulars of one religious community (*milla*) but to universal conceptions of justice. Thus, community-specific knowledge (shari'a), while a source of *milla* coherency, is relative next to allegedly higher forms of knowledge that only the philosophical elite can attain, making it futile to fight and spill blood on behalf of religiocommunal knowledge, which is not truth per se but only an approximation of it.

Another philosopher of this period, Abu al-Hasan al-'Amiri (d. 992), argued for the priority of religiocommunal knowledge (*milla*) over philosophical knowledge (*ḥikma*), since the former provided guidance for life's details, the latter for only abstract truths. Still, in his view, revealed knowledge exists for a rational goal—the political good—which implies that *milla* knowledge can be applied only in view of the greater interests of the polity. The idea that God's will exists for a rationally identifiable purpose—the common good of Muslim society—rather than as a test of obedience would climax in the thought of Abu Ishaq al-Shatibi (d. 1388), a jurist of the Maliki branch of Islam, who would draw on Islam's various intellectual streams to advance a rational understanding of shari'a in service of the common good of Muslim society.

Contrast this with the Muslim Brotherhood, a transnational group that in Egypt is known to set the religiocommunal specifics of Islam above national harmony. 'Amiri places them at the service of political ends, whereas the Muslim Brotherhood makes them ends in themselves. The Brotherhood sees political empowerment (*tamkīn*) as the logical consequence of the religious mission (*da'wa*). Certainly, the events of the Arab Spring raise many questions, but the Brotherhood's approach to power has generally been gradualist, not revolutionary; unlike 'Amiri, it would identify the constitution of the polity with shari'a rather than a secular good in which Muslims can enact their specific religiocommunal obligations.

A final example in this regard is Ghazali, who saw all knowledge, religious and secular, through the lens of a higher knowledge of the other world (*'ilm ākhira*). He defended the truth of religious knowledge in a confessionally divided community but was less sanguine about a political solution for the religious morass than his teacher, Juwayni, who proposed in his political treatise, *Ghiyath al-Umam* (Salvation of the nations), that Nizam al-Mulk (d. 1092), celebrated Seljuq vizier, enforce religious conformity by the sword if necessary in order to eliminate belief contradictions among Muslims that only subvert all claims to religious truth.

Despite misgivings about a political defense of religious truth, Ghazali was no esotericist. He was committed to the particular wordings of religious knowledge and shared his teacher's concern that religious knowledge be visibly represented. His use of the idea of spiritual brotherhood (*ukhuwwa*, a concept from the Qur'an, e.g., Q. 3:103, and title of a chapter in Ghazali's magnum opus, *The Revivification of the Religious Sciences*) was not a turn from the world's realities so much as a witness that religious knowledge remained efficacious in the *umma* even without a strongman to back it and despite the corruption of the community's scholars.

Religious Knowledge and the Modern State

The battle for the enduring relevance of religious knowledge marks every age, but in the modern context, it is as much a political endeavor as a scholarly one, blurring the lines between religious knowledge and political authority. One example is Muhammad Baqir al-Sadr (executed by Saddam Hussein in 1980). Sadr countered secularization with the claim that religion could define all aspects of life, speaking of "the empty region" (*manṭiqat al-farāgh*; that is, the legislative void that can be filled despite the imam's absence) first in *Our Economics* (1961) but also in *Islam Leads Life*, a treatise written shortly after the Iranian Revolution of 1979 that would leave its mark on the constitution of the Islamic Republic. In his view, religious knowledge consists not only of specific rulings (*aḥkām*; e.g., no interest, no deceptive business) but also of concepts (*mafāhīm*) that inform all areas of Muslim life. In other words, Islam embodies a narrative: God created the world and entrusted it to humans to care for it and make it prosper justly and righteously. The Qur'an encourages humans to enjoy the fruit of God's creation but discourages the hoarding of wealth. For Sadr, this narrative embodies principles applicable to economic matters: consumption, production, capital, labor, and so on. Indeed, the religious heritage—both revealed texts and scholarly treatises—contains a wealth of principles applicable to modern life. The void could be filled and Shiʿis could once again live Islam to its fullest, as if the imam were present, without needing to succumb to Western conceptions of life simply for want of a total knowledge system of their own.

It is left to those in command (*ulū al-amr*, a highly exploited Qur'anic phrase) to issue rulings for the governance of society. These rulings are not fixed and permanent, as if revealed by God, since new situations arise, but the failure to issue them puts society at the mercy of elite interests. For Sadr, the gross shortcomings of capitalism and communism only demonstrated the need for a divine system of governance to ensure justice and brotherly relations. Thus, Islam has a philosophy of its own, embedded in the religious heritage; its concepts—equity and liberation from exploitation, ignorance, and tyranny—could dynamically engage the nation to engender a religious polity.

Such a polity requires not merely rule by Islam but the involvement of the jurist (*faqīh*), who alone possesses the qualifications to guarantee the process. The exact role of the *faqīh* in the polity is a matter of debate. Khomeini claimed that he is to rule, but how is he to be checked when he is the imam's representative? Such questions were less of a concern to Sadr than the need to restore society on the basis of monotheism, where people would be free of oppression, harmonious, and productive. But he acknowledged that a divine society does not depend on legislation alone. The citizens needed to be educated in Islam's virtues in order to be willingly ruled by its principles. Sadr was favorably disposed to democracy but cautioned against its manipulation by partisan interests; democracy needs to be corrected by Islam, the parliament supervised by the *faqīh*.

Sadr sought to bring ethical standards to economics and politics. However, by greatly expanding the boundaries of religious knowledge, Sadr opened the door to religious supremacy. In his view, since Islam was a total system, Muslims could only be Muslim if ruled by Islam. Religiously undetermined areas of life could become religiously determined through Islam's concepts along with its precedents. All of this has created a troubled legacy for Shi'ism, and various figures have tried to deflate Khomeini's idea of rule by the *faqīh*. However, while Khomeini's politics have been discredited, Sadr's notion of filling the legislative void has had lasting influence on such groups as Hizbullah. One can debate whether the supreme leader in Iran is fully qualified to fill the void, but it is more difficult to argue that life in all its aspects should not be guided by some measure of truth. Is everything relative? Are the powerful to dominate the world's resources? Intense discussions on the nature of truth in Iran have important political implications. Those who say that heaven should rule can look to Sadr for inspiration: if not addressed, the powerful will exploit the void, leaving society to the law of the jungle. Truth must be brought to bear on the void, and where else to find truth than in God's revelation, which only the *faqīh* fully comprehends. This renders politics quasi-apocalyptic, as seen with President Mahmoud Ahmadinejad (2005–13), who was not a shari'a scholar but claimed to implement Islam's truths, obviating the voice of the people. Long the preserve of scholarly circles, religious authority is now refashioned according to worldly criteria: political astuteness and a willingness to use force to bring about rule by God. Religion is unbound, making economics and politics, and ultimately power, integral to divine favor no less than ritual and morals.

Religious Knowledge as Guidance for Society

Despite the ascendancy of Islamism, many Muslims, even within Islamist circles, speak not of divine sovereignty but rather "the civil state" (*al-dawla al-madaniyya*), where religious and secular knowledge are equally at play in determining what is best for the nation. This shift emerged from the conclusion—after a painful learning process—that the idea of a religious state is actually contrary to the teachings of Islam, since that idea has been used to justify authoritarianism in the name of Islam.

If religious knowledge is a question not only of prestige and power but also of truth, what is this truth in a secular age? The response will vary, but the truth of religious knowledge cannot simply be a matter of historical contingency. The knowledge that Islam offers is a tightly regulated economy of rights (*ḥuqūq*) owed to others, both God and fellow humans. God has the right to be worshipped and has revealed sanctions against theft, adultery (and false accusation of adultery), alcohol consumption, and brigandage. Believers who commit such crimes will have to pay the penalty in this world or the next, but God can "cover over" (*satr*) people's sins in His mercy (*raḥma*). Muhammad is thought to have embodied this "godly" character as a model ruler, ensuring justice and righteousness but also forgoing retribution for the sake of peace in society. Members of society also have duties to one another, and God forbids transgression of the life, property, and dignity of others without just cause (e.g., a murderer judged to deserve death or an unrepentant blasphemer who wages against religion). Spouses have duties to each other and to their children. Society as a whole has a duty to care for the weak and poor, and relations between individuals are to be guided by justice; in other words, everyone gets his or her due, especially whether in commercial or marital relations. Islam places great emphasis on keeping promises and fulfilling contracts. When obligations are not met, justice can be sought or mercy extended. Rulers are to be obeyed as long as they do not transgress the rights of God and of His slaves (i.e., humans). This could imply just rule or rule that does not offend Islam or, at a minimum, rule that does not prevent believers from performing religious duties.

How exactly is such religious knowledge relevant? The concept of a system of rights and duties sanctioned by God has enormous value in societies under authoritarian rule. In such a context, the concept of *ḥaqq*, a complex term meaning "right" in the sense of something owed to others (in the plural, it can refer to human rights), is very powerful as the measure of all relations. Indeed, especially when transgressions occur, the concept has most resonance as a way to preserve moral standards. One might have to pay a bribe but can still declare it to be without *ḥaqq*. Some associate the concept with democracy, but it is not a precise match. It is not about an equal say in policy making (although not opposed to the idea) but about preserving a just balance in society. People make decisions in accordance with their interests (as well as their hope for familial and societal acceptance) but are limited by the framework of *ḥaqq*—what is owed to them and what they owe others. They may forgo what is owed them, but this must be by choice and not forced, as an act of magnanimity, forbearance (*tasāmuḥ*), or simply out of a desire to please God.

Thus, despite the existence of realpolitik, society is still guided by morals ultimately rooted in religious knowledge. The point is not to enthrone the voice of God as national sovereign, although that remains a goal of some Islamists, but rather to maintain a society pleasing to God through the preservation of values (justice and mercy) as communicated by religious scholars. Thus, religious knowledge, encoding ethical values, remains vital for the coherency of society, especially but not only when the state shows little commitment to these standards.

In this sense, those with expertise in religious knowledge continue to offer advice to their local societies in the modern age, impacting society by conveying such counsel but also by embodying it in their own persons as models of piety, in line with a long-standing tradition as epitomized in the figure of Shaykh Arslan, the 12th-century holy man and patron saint of Damascus, who is still remembered today as "the protector of piety in Syria" (*ḥāmī al-birr bi-l-shām*).

Religious knowledge in this traditional formula is thus morally operative irrespective of the nature of political power. Scholars may or may not cooperate with the regime. They may or may not harbor hostility to secular politics, but they do not look to the state as guarantor of the moral integrity of the *umma*. The "rights of

God" can be respected within communities of piety apart from state enforcement. They may want the state to enforce shari'a rulings (e.g., on alcohol and adultery) but are confident that Islam's purposes can be met without the state. Mediators of traditional religious knowledge also play a role at "secular" ceremonies, such as weddings and funerals, where their presence is seen as a blessing and a reminder of the higher purpose of life. This, along with teaching and preaching (and also counseling troubled marriages), is seen as part of the work of reforming society (*iṣlāḥ al-mujtamiʿ*). It is thus not the state officials but traditional custodians of religious knowledge who maintain the religiomoral character of society. To be sure, Islamist and non-Islamist sentiment can and does overlap within a single religious milieu. As purveyors of piety, the shaykhs are often united with Islamists against secularism but are able to coexist with an authoritarian and ideologically secular state in a way Islamists cannot, as seen in the modern history of Egypt and Syria, among other places. As promoters of a religiosity that does not depend on political power for success, the shaykhs also temper the "urgency" of the Islamist call and even offer the state passive support in exchange for freedom to promulgate religious knowledge on their own terms (in contrast to the state-defined version of Islam as taught in national schools). They see their role as teaching, preaching, and guiding, not confrontation with the power of the state.

This posture is not simply political caution. It comes from the widely recognized belief that piety is worthless if coerced and that such top-down attempts to enforce piety inevitably lead to strife (*fitna*), producing more harm than good for Muslim society. Their commitment to Islam as a guide to society is not simplistic but is qualified by the means used to pursue the goal: teaching and preaching to refine both individual souls and society as a whole in Islam's virtues. A state also guided by Islam, in their view, will help achieve the purpose of politics (i.e., the common good), but rule by Islam cannot be pursued at the cost of the common good, making it necessary to protect Islam from too close an association with worldly power. Of course, traditional religious scholars themselves represent a range of attitudes toward modernity: some more critical, others reconsidering Islam in light of it.

Cities in the so-called world of Islam are replete with references to religious knowledge. There is, of course, a wide assortment of pious literature: scholarly tomes in well-known bookstores or popular pamphlets on sale on the street, as well as a host of religious television programs available on satellite and viewed at home and in cafés. But there are also signs and banners of all kinds to remind one of knowledge given by God. In Damascus, where the state is clearly not the moral leader, the values of religion become all the more important for maintaining standards of ethics to facilitate the daily business of society. For example, a sandwich shop in the Halbuni section of Damascus displays a hadith in full view of its clients that speaks of God's protection and provision, making the point that one should be satisfied and respond gratefully by fulfilling duties to God. Across from the main entrance to the University of Damascus, recitation of the Qur'an resounds from a newspaper kiosk, offering perspective, and perhaps a moral reminder, at a highly congested intersection. Down the road, beyond the Baramika traffic circle, a motor-oil store displays a banner referring to the Prophet as a mercy for the universe. A 15-minute walk from there, in a mosque named for 'Ammar b. Yasir, a Companion of the Prophet, in a middle-class neighborhood called Bikhtiyar, children sit in groups before middle-aged mentors, memorizing the Qur'an and imbibing Islam's values. Just a bit farther, at a mosque at the Kafarsusa Circle, children are dropped off throughout the day for religious instruction.

All of this is not simply religious knowledge in the service of prestige but rather of a society's moral coherency. To speak again of Damascus (at least prior to the Arab Spring) is to speak of a city known as a regional center for sex tourism, among other things. Employment opportunities were limited. Prices were on the rise, partly due to urbanization. The state sought to extract revenues from all economic activity, its institutions hives of corruption that state leaders pretended to combat. The economic woes heightened concern for self-preservation, encouraging erosion of clan ties and neighborly solidarity (although social relations remained strong in principle). Caution, if not mistrust, was increasingly the norm, a creeping individualism, not in the sense of people doing as they please in public but in reduced expectations of support from others. Many religious leaders privately blamed the rampant vice on the state's introduction of secular ways, which they saw as a pollutant to the city's reputation as "honorable Damascus," long known for attracting both scholars and merchants. They concluded that the economic misery was due to the loss of morality that followed the abandonment of "the dear principles of Islam."

In the midst of this, pious people cultivate parallel societies, alongside and in interaction with state institutions, through the communication of religious knowledge in concrete ways as described above. To be sure, questions of power and prestige are at play, but more fundamental is the question of moral integrity in the face of modernity's challenges. Alongside interests, there is also aspiration for righteousness in society, and religious knowledge is the key to achieving it. The truth of religious knowledge today may be less oriented to its sound transmission and more to its demonstrable worth for society, but even by this "modern" criterion, the facts suggest that religious knowledge remains a contender for the mantle of truth.

Further Reading

Farid al-Ansari, *al-Bayan al-Daʿwi wa-Zahirat al-Tadakhkhum al-Siyasi*, 2003; Dale F. Eickelman, *Knowledge and Power in Morocco: The Education of a Twentieth-Century Notable*, 1985; Wael Hallaq, "Caliphs, Jurists, and the Saljuqs in the Political Thought of Juwayni," *Muslim World* 74, no. 1 (1984); Muhammad Al-Hamdawi, *al-Risaliyya fi al-ʿAmal al-Islami*, 2008; Paul L. Heck, "Doubts about the Religious Community (*Milla*) in al-Farabi and the Brethren of Purity," in *In the Age of al-Farabi: Arabic Philosophy in the 4th/10th Century*, edited by P. Adamson, 2008; Idem, "Eschatological Scripturalism and the End of Community: The Case of Early Kharijism," *Archiv für Religionswissenschaft* 7 (2005); Kai Kress, *Philosophizing in Mombasa: Knowledge, Islam, and Intellectual Practice on the Swahili Coast*, 2007; Brinkley Messick, *The Calligraphic State: Textual Domination and History in a Muslim Society*, 1993; Barbara Daly Metcalf, *Islamic Revival in British India: Deoband, 1860–1900*, 1982; Felicitas Opwis, "*Maslaha* in Contemporary Legal Theory," *Islamic Law and Society* 12, no. 2 (2005); Paulo Pinto, "Sufism and the Political Economy of Morality in Syria," in *Sufism and Politics: The Power of Spirituality*, edited by Paul L. Heck, 2006; Franz Rosenthal, *Knowledge Triumphant: The Concept of Knowledge in Medieval Islam*, 1970; Yoginder Singh Sikand, *The Origins and Development of Tablighi Jama'at (1920–2000): A Cross-Country Comparative Study*, 2002; Thierry Zarcone, *La Turquie moderne et l'islam*, 2004.

Minidorities ∞∞∞∞∞∞∞∞∞∞∞∞∞∞∞∞∞∞∞∞∞∞∞∞∞∞∞∞∞∞∞

Yohanan Friedmann

This chapter treats both Muslim minorities under non-Muslim rule and non-Muslim minorities under Muslim rule. Due to the limitations of space, it includes only the most significant minorities.

Muslim Minorities under Non-Muslim Rule

The question of the majority-minority relationship has been relevant to Muslims since the emergence of Islam. Muslims began their history in Mecca as a minority persecuted by the polytheistic establishment of the city (610–30). This situation, however, did not last long. Following the conquests of the seventh century, the Muslims became an elite ruling over non-Muslim majorities in the vast expanses of the emerging empire. The process of conversion to Islam was much slower than the conquests themselves; scholars disagree on when Muslims became a majority in the Middle East and North Africa. It is clear that this transformation did not take place before the 11th century, but some argue that it did not occur until the beginning of the Mamluk period in the 13th century. In the Indian subcontinent, the Muslims never exceeded a quarter of the population, although various Muslim dynasties ruled substantial parts of India from the 13th to the 19th century. Historians of Indonesia—where Islam spread by slow penetration of traders and divines rather than by conquest—have not been able to chart demographic developments with great confidence, but Islamization apparently started there (probably in the 15th century) with the ruling elite so that Muslim rulers initially controlled a mainly non-Muslim population. It is not possible to say when exactly Muslims became a majority in Indonesia, which at the time of writing is the state with the largest Muslim population. Similar difficulties face the historians of sub-Saharan Africa. The coastal region of East Africa became a Muslim majority area between 1200 and 1500, while comparable development in West Africa differed from region to region. The Chinese Muslim minority developed during the Tang dynasty (618–907); its growth accelerated during the period of the Mongol invasions, and in 2006 it numbered 20 million, according to government estimates.

In the formative centuries of Islamic history, when Islam was constantly expanding, Muslims who lived as minorities under non-Muslim rule were rare. Early tradition (hadith) considered living under such conditions undesirable, and a tradition makes the Prophet denounce Muslims who live among polytheists. Later jurists do not distinguish between situations in which the Muslims formed a majority or a minority of the population: what matters is the religious affiliation of the ruler.

When the Muslims were forced for the first time to abandon significant areas previously under their control, the legal thinking on the permissibility of living under non-Muslim rule began to change. While some schools of law continued to reject the legality of living under non-Muslim rule, others weighed such issues as the ability to practice Islam freely in a non-Muslim area and the possibility that Muslims living there would bring about the conversion of the non-Muslims to Islam. In Spain, the process started with the fall of Toledo into Christian hands in 1085. Further Christian advances in the 12th and 13th centuries left substantial numbers of Muslims, known as Mudejars (those who were allowed to stay), under Christian rule, but the Muslim population eventually would vanish from Spain completely. In Syria and Palestine, on the other hand, the Crusaders' takeover at the end of the 11th century was followed by a Muslim restoration at the end of the 13th century. Nevertheless, for almost two centuries, the Muslims of Syria and Palestine lived under Frankish-Christian rule. In some areas they were a subjugated majority, while in others they were reduced to minority status. In the 12th century, the non-Muslim Central Asian empire of the Qara Khitay treated the Muslim population with tolerance and won the general appreciation of its subjects. The 13th century, on the other hand, saw the destructive Mongol invasion of Persia and Central Asia, although this episode of non-Muslim rule over a Muslim population came to an end with the conversion of the Mongol Ghazan Khan to Islam in 1295.

During the era of the three great Muslim empires—the Ottoman, the Safavid, and the Mughal—barely any Muslim minorities lived under non-Muslim rule. This situation began to change in 1774 when the Ottomans were forced to surrender Crimea and its Muslim population to Russia in the Treaty of Küçük Kaynarca. A substantial Muslim minority came into being when the Ottomans ceded Bosnia and Herzegovina to the Habsburg Empire in 1878. The Muslims of India were a minority, but since the government of most areas of the Indian subcontinent was in their hands, they experienced few problems until 1858, when the gradual takeover of India by the British was formalized. India was incorporated into the British Empire, and the Muslims of India were transformed from a ruling elite to a subjected minority. After the partition of the Indian subcontinent and the establishment of Pakistan in 1947, a substantial Muslim minority came into being in the newly established independent and professedly secular Republic of India. The difficulties initially experienced by this minority because of its connections with the rival and professedly Islamic state of Pakistan were brilliantly analyzed by W. C. Smith in his *Islam in Modern History* (chapter 6). The question of living Islamically in a non-Muslim environment has long been the subject of public debate among Indian Muslims in terms of Islamic law: is India the abode of Islam (*dār al-islām*) or the abode of war (*dār al-ḥarb*)? How should this question be answered in a region that had been under Muslim rule in the past and in a situation in which the sovereign is non-Muslim but where Muslims enjoy unrestricted freedom of worship? A comparable analysis could be attempted concerning the Muslim minority in Israel.

The 20th century—and especially the years after World War II—saw the development of significant Muslim minorities in Europe and the Americas. In the medieval period, very few Muslims were ruled by others or lived in a non-Muslim environment, but in contemporary times millions of Muslims find themselves under non-Muslim rule. This has become a significant issue of debate among Muslims themselves and in the scholarly literature. The Muslim minorities that emerged in the West are diverse. They differ in their countries of origin, their mode of integration into the local society, and their vision of life in their adoptive countries. In England, most Muslim immigrants originated from Pakistan and Bangladesh, in France from North Africa, and in Germany from Turkey. The Russian Muslim minority has been estimated at 15 to 20 million. The Muslim minority in the United States, now estimated at about 4 million, is also of diverse origins. The first substantial number of Muslims entered the United States as slaves brought from Africa between the 17th and 19th centuries. In late 19th century, Muslims started immigrating to the United States from the Arab provinces of the Ottoman Empire. Beginning in the 1970s, the number of North American Muslim institutions and organizations increased dramatically. The Islamic Society of North America (ISNA), an umbrella association of a few hundred mosques and Islamic centers; the Muslim Public Affairs Council (MPAC); and the Council on American-Islamic Relations (CAIR) brought the problems of the American Muslims to the attention of the government and into public awareness. The debate concerning the Muslim minority in the United States grew in intensity and gained importance in the wake of the terrorist attacks on New York City and Washington, DC, perpetrated by radical Muslims on September 11, 2001.

Among the most important issues in the relationship between these minorities and their adopted countries are their involvement in politics, their economic integration, their mosques, their educational institutions, and their relations with the other religions. As of 2003, there were Muslim members of Parliament in England, the Netherlands, Denmark, and Sweden. All were elected in the framework of existing political parties; attempts to organize specifically Muslim parties in Belgium, England, France, and Germany were not successful. Muslim participation in local governing bodies was substantially greater than on the national level. Organizations that claimed to represent the generality of Muslims in various countries were established; prominent among them were the Muslim Council of Britain, Union des Organizations Islamiques de France, and Zentralrat der Muslime in Deutschland. Radical Muslim organizations with small memberships but considerable visibility also developed: among them, the Jama'at-i Islami (The Islamic Group) was active among Muslims of Indian and Pakistani extraction and the Hizb al-Tahrir

(The Party of Liberation) promoted a radical Muslim agenda in several European countries.

In the early 21st century most Muslim children in Europe and America studied in state schools; additional instruction in Islam frequently was given in mosques or prayer rooms after school or on weekends. In recent years, Western Europe experienced a remarkable increase in the construction of mosques, estimated at 212 in 2003, and prayer rooms, of which several thousand were in operation. Countries with the largest number of mosques were England (80), Germany (66), and France (8). Hundreds of mosques from the Ottoman period survived in Bulgaria, Western Thrace, and Romania.

Since the 1990s, the emergence of significant Muslim minorities in non-Muslim countries provided the impetus for the development of a new branch in Islamic thinking called "legal theory for Muslim minorities" (*fiqh al-aqalliyyāt*). *Fiqh al-aqalliyyāt* addresses the problems encountered by Muslims who want to live according to Islamic precepts in a non-Muslim environment. The most prominent figures in the development of this branch of Muslim thought are Yusuf al-Qaradawi and Taha Jabir al-Alwani. Alwani was born in Iraq, studied at Azhar, taught in Saudi Arabia, and then became the president of the School of Islamic Social Sciences in Ashburn, Virginia. Qaradawi, a prominent public figure in contemporary Muslim thought, was born in Egypt, also studied at Azhar, and moved to the emirate of Qatar in 1961. Among the matters discussed in the framework of this legal theory are the nature of the Western countries when analyzed according to the classical division of the world into *dār al-islām* (abode of Islam), *dār al-ḥarb* (abode of war), and *dār al-ʿahd* (abode of covenant); the question of jihad; economic questions such as the permissibility of trading in stocks and bonds (i.e., if doing so violates the Muslim law that prohibits paying or receiving interest); the problems of child adoption (which is prohibited in classical Muslim law); and, in general, the permissibility of deriving new rulings from the sacred sources of the shariʿa (*ijtihād*). Qaradawi maintains that since Muslims are a community with a global mission, they must have a presence in the West since the West is a leading force in the world and they must influence its policies. He devotes considerable attention to the question of marriages between Muslim men and non-Muslim women. Classical Muslim law allowed Muslim men to wed Jewish or Christian women, though many jurisprudents expressed reservations concerning this practice. The Qurʾan permits marriage to scriptuary women, and while, in principle, Qaradawi accepts this rule, he considerably restricts its applicability. The Christian woman must be a real believer (being born of Christian parents is not sufficient proof of this—she herself must not be an atheist, an apostate, a communist, or a member of the Bahaʾi faith), and it is forbidden to marry a Jewish woman as long as there is war between the Muslims and Israel. Another interesting ruling by Qaradawi concerns what happens when a non-Muslim woman married to a non-Muslim man embraces Islam while her husband retains his original religion. After surveying the views of classical jurists—most of whom believed the woman must leave her husband—Qaradawi rules that in the

West such a woman should stay with her husband. The purpose of this rule is to encourage married women to embrace Islam, to spare them the hardships facing women without husbands, and to give the husband an incentive to follow his wife into Islam.

The growing importance of Muslim minorities in Europe and America in the second half of the 20th century gave rise to a growing interest in public debate, academic study of interfaith relations, and interfaith dialogue. Numerous conferences, along with journals dedicated to this field (*Islamo-Christiana*; *Islam and Christian-Muslim Relations*; *Studies in Muslim-Jewish Relations*; *Journal of the Institute of Muslim Minority Affairs*; *Encounters: A Journal of Intercultural Perspectives*), have served as significant venues for adherents of diverse faiths to share their sensibilities and points of view.

Non-Muslims under Muslim Rule

This section focuses on non-Muslims living under Muslim rule, whether the non-Muslims constitute a majority or a minority in a given area. Medieval Muslim law initially distinguished among Jews and Christians ("People of the Book" or scriptuaries [*ahl al-kitāb*]), Zoroastrians, and polytheists. According to the Qur'an, the Muslims are obliged to fight the scriptuaries "until they pay the poll tax (*jizya*) out of hand while being humbled" (9:29). This has been taken to mean that the purpose of the war against the scriptuaries is not their conversion to Islam but rather their submission to Islamic rule. The scriptuaries who submitted to Islamic rule were described as "protected communities" (*ahl al-dhimma, dhimmīs*). Their rights and obligations were defined in a series of documents referred to as the Treaty of 'Umar (*al-shurūt al-'umariyya*), which probably dates from the eighth century, despite being attributed to 'Umar b. al-Khattab, the second caliph (r. 634–44). These "conditions" promised the *dhimmīs* the right to retain their religion and perform their rituals, though various restrictions were placed on religious observance in public. The granting of this right was conditioned on the payment of the poll tax (*jizya*) and on the acceptance of a lowly status reflected in numerous rules relating to the construction and maintenance of places of worship and behavior in the public sphere.

The *dhimma* concept, which initially included only Jews and Christians, was broadened as a result of the huge expansion of the areas under Muslim control. The first religious group to be added to the *dhimma* category was the Zoroastrians, adherents of a dualistic religion that had been dominant in Iran before the Muslim conquest. Though the Zoroastrians are not mentioned in Qur'an 9:29, and though most schools of law do not consider them scriptuaries, they were included in the *dhimmī* category on the basis of a Prophetic tradition. As for polytheists, two of the four schools of law (the Hanafi and the Maliki) were willing to bestow *dhimmī* status on non-Arab polytheists. Only Arab polytheists were excluded from this category and therefore forced to choose between conversion to Islam and the sword; however, according to the perception of most jurists, all Arabs embraced Islam during the Prophet's lifetime. The exclusion of Arab polytheists from the *dhimmī* status therefore had little practical significance after the Prophet's death in 632. Hence, according to the Hanafi and Maliki schools of law, all non-Muslims living under Muslim rule—except for the apparently nonexistent Arab polytheists—are eligible for the *dhimmī* status; whereas, according to the Shafi'is and the Hanbalis, only Jews, Christians, and Zoroastrians are eligible.

The question of the relationship between Islam and the non-Muslims under its rule developed in the earliest period of Muslim history as a result of the major conquests in the first century. The non-Muslim communities of the Middle East, which was the first area conquered by Muslims, included Christians, Jews, Zoroastrians, and Manicheans (the latter were persecuted and never attained the status of *ahl al-dhimma*). In some regions of the Indian subcontinent, adherents of Indian religions lived under Muslim rule from the eighth century; this phenomenon grew dramatically in the 12th century and lasted until the 19th. Since the Hanafi school of law was predominant in India, the Hindus of the subcontinent were treated in most periods as *dhimmī*s; the few attempts to change their status and consider them unprotected polytheists came to naught. The Ottoman Empire had substantial Christian and Jewish minorities and developed the *millet* (from Arabic *milla* or "community") system for their governance. This system brought the non-Muslim communities (mainly the Greeks, the Armenians, and the Jews) into the framework of Ottoman law while giving them a substantial measure of religious and cultural freedom. The Iranian Safavid Empire had Armenian, Zoroastrian, and Jewish minorities whose situation was, in general terms, worse than that of the minorities of the Ottoman Empire. In the 19th century, the Babi and Baha'i religions came into being in Iran; as religions founded after the revelation of the Qur'an, their adherents never received the *dhimmī* status and have been persecuted by successive Iranian governments. In Egypt, muftis have repeatedly declared the tiny Baha'i minority as apostates who are not entitled to the free exercise of their religion.

During the medieval period, several groups that began as Muslim sects developed beliefs so remote from Islam as to constitute distinct religions and therefore are considered minorities. The Druze community originated in the 11th century, developing out of the Isma'ili movement and named for Muhammad b. Isma'il al-Darazi, one of the early supporters of the Fatimid caliph Hakim (r. 996–1021) in his quest for recognition of his supernatural status. After Darazi's death in 1019, the leadership of these supporters passed to Hamza b. 'Ali, who is considered the founder of the Druze faith. The Druze call their faith "the Unitarian Way" (*madhhab al-tawhīd*) and call themselves the "Unitarians" (*muwahhidūn*). God is one, incomprehensible and undefinable by humans. The intricate cosmogony of the Druze faith cannot be discussed here. The faith has major ethical components, including truthfulness and solidarity within the community. The community is divided into the "learned," initiated into the secrets of the religion (*'uqqāl*) and the "ignorant" (*juhhāl*), who are not initiated but are nevertheless members of the faith. Of the principal commandments of Islam, only the Feast of Sacrifice ('Id al-Adha) is observed. Polygamy as well as divorce against the wife's will are forbidden. The Druze live in Syria, Lebanon, Israel, and Jordan. Their number is estimated at slightly above one million.

The Nusayris (or 'Alawis), whose main concentrations are in Syria and Turkey, are a syncretistic group that originated in ninth-century Syria among radical Shi'is. They are named after Muhammad b. Nusayr, who proclaimed the divine nature of the Shi'i imams and supported the transmigration of souls and antinomianism. They believe in the divine nature of 'Ali b. Abi Talib, as well as in the trinity of 'Ali, Muhammad, and Salman al-Farisi. They celebrate some Muslim and some Christian festivals, but the way in which these festivals are performed and the meaning given to them by the Nusayris are not the same as in Christianity and in Islam. It is noteworthy that despite their minority status, the Nusayris have held power in Syria since the early 1970s.

Mention should also be made of the Yazidis, a Kurdish-speaking group. They believe in one God who created the world and entrusted it to seven archangels, whose leader is the Peacock Angel (*Ṭāwūs-i malak*). This angel has been identified by outside observers with the devil; this identification has not yet been satisfactorily explained, but it resulted in the description of the Yazidis as "devil worshipers" and has increased the scholarly interest in their history and system of belief. The Yazidis were not considered as *dhimmī*s and their religion was not protected in any way until the period of the Tanzimat (Reforms) in the Ottoman Empire. Their origins can be traced to the activities of 'Adi b. Musafir, a Sufi shaykh who was born in Biqa' (now in Lebanon) in 1073 or 1078 and moved to Kurdistan at the beginning of the 11th century, where he established the 'Adawi order and acquired a considerable following. According to Maqrizi's (1364–1442) account, the order was transformed after 'Adi's death: his followers engaged in excessive veneration of their founder, claimed that he sits together with God, refused to accept any livelihood that is not from him, disregarded sexual taboos, and abolished the ritual prayers, saying that 'Adi prayed on their behalf. Consequently, 'Adi's tomb was destroyed in 1414–15; his bones were exhumed and burned. Since the 17th century, the Yazidis have experienced several waves of persecution and were even forced to convert to Islam. At the present time, most Yazidis (estimated by Kreyenbroek at about 120,000) live in Northern Iraq; in Syria they number about 15,000. In the 1980s, most Yazidis who lived in Turkey found refuge from religious persecution in Germany, where they number between 20,000 and 40,000. Modern Yazidis deny any relationship with Islam, but their religious vocabulary is still influenced by Sufism.

An important minority in the Indian subcontinent are the Sikhs. Their religion was founded in the Punjab province by Nanak (1469–1539). His creed centered on a preference for devotion as opposed to ritual and on a fierce criticism of the Hindu caste system. His followers in the leadership of the community were known as gurus, or teachers. They affirmed the existence of one God and rejected both Hindu and Muslim rituals. The Sikhs started as a peaceful religious group bent on bridging the gap between Hinduism and Islam but transformed themselves, since the 17th century, into a militant movement. This development was caused mainly by the change in the policies of the Mughal Empire from toleration during the reign of Akbar (r. 1556–1605) to persecution, which started during the reign of Jahangir (r. 1605–27), who executed Arjun, the third Sikh guru, in 1606. In the modern period, the number of Sikhs is estimated at 23 million, of whom more than 19 million live in India (according to the census of 2001).

In the medieval period, the *dhimma* system was the legal framework for the treatment of non-Muslims by the various Muslim governments. It seems to have been changed for a limited period only by the Mughal emperor Akbar, who abolished the *jizya* in 1581; the tax was restored in the framework of orthodox measures carried out by Emperor Aurangzeb (r. 1659–1707) in 1679. Though the exact nature of the *jizya* in India is open to debate, the symbolic significance of both its abolition and its restoration is not in any doubt. A much more significant change that heralded the end of the *dhimma* system took place during the Tanzimat period in the Ottoman Empire. The Hatt-ı Sherif of Gülhane (1839) proclaimed the equality of all Ottoman subjects, regardless of religion. In 1855 the *jizya* was abolished and the principle of equality of all subjects reaffirmed.

The question of non-Muslim minorities in Muslim majority countries entered a new phase in the 20th century with the emergence of numerous new states in the Middle East, Asia, and Africa. There are Hindu and Sikh minorities in Pakistan and a Hindu minority in Bangladesh. The Jewish minorities in Egypt, Syria, Iraq, and North Africa practically disappeared when most of the Jews emigrated to the newly established state of Israel and elsewhere. Significant Christian minorities exist in Egypt (the Copts), Syria, Iraq, and Jordan.

The Shi'is

The minority with the most ancient roots in Islam is the Shi'is. In general, Shi'is have not been denounced as non-Muslims by mainstream Islam, and they are therefore different from the other minorities discussed in this entry. The term "Shi'i" is derived from the expression "Shi'at 'Ali," the party of 'Ali. Shi'is support the principle that the leadership of the Muslim community after Muhammad's death must be retained by the Prophet's descendants (*ahl al-bayt*) and that religious authority must be derived from the same source. Several attempts to implement these principles and place the Shi'is in positions of leadership were foiled during the Umayyad period. There is no way to estimate the size of the Shi'i community during this period, but its minority status does not seem to be in doubt. Similarly, in the premodern period it is not possible to estimate the size of the Shi'i population in any given region.

Despite being a minority, Shi'is succeeded in establishing major political units in the medieval period. The Buyid dynasty, which ruled from Baghdad between

945 and 1055, was significant for the development of the Twelver Shi'a. During Buyid rule, important developments took place in the development of Shi'i thought and ritual. Shi'i luminaries such as Ibn Babuya (d. 991), Mufid (d. 1022), Murtada (d. 1044), and Muhammad al-Tusi (d. 1067) flourished during the Buyid period. The lamentations of the Day of Ashura on Muharram 10 (the first month of the Islamic calendar), commemorating the killing of Muhammad's grandson Husayn and his supporters in Karbala on October 10, 680, as well as the festival of Ghadir Khumm, commemorating the alleged appointment of 'Ali b. Abi Talib as the Prophet's successor, were granted recognition during this period.

The main political achievement of the Isma'ili branch of Shi'is in the medieval period is the Fatimid state. Established by 'Ubaydallah al-Mahdi in the early tenth century, it progressively extended its power throughout North Africa; during the reign of Mu'izz it conquered Fustat in 969 and established the city of Cairo in 970. Thus began two centuries of Shi'i domination in Egypt, ending with the Ayyubid takeover in 1171 and the restoration of Sunnism. It is noteworthy that the Fatimid period does not seem to have brought about a substantial increase in the number of Shi'is in Egypt.

The political achievement of Shi'is that had the most durable results is the establishment of the Safavid state in Iran in the 16th century. In contrast to the Fatimid case, the establishment in Iran of the Twelver Shi'a as the official religion of the Safavid state by Shah Isma'il in 1501 launched the process by which Iran became, in the modern period, the most important concentration of Shi'i population.

Reliable statistics on the size of the Shi'i community are hard to come by, but it is estimated to constitute 10–15 percent of Muslims. Despite their minority status in the Muslim world in general, the Shi'is constitute a majority in Iran, Iraq, and Bahrain. In Iraq until 2003, the Shi'is were dominated by the Sunni minority. Since the establishment of the Iraqi monarchy in 1921, the government strove to marginalize the Shi'i majority. This was done by using citizenship criteria, such as holding Ottoman citizenship before the collapse of the Ottoman Empire, to restrict the civil rights of the Shi'is. In the late 1960s, the Ba'th government used the nationality law, first introduced in 1924 and amended several times in the 1970s, in order to deny Iraqi nationality to a large number of Shi'is. During the Iran-Iraq War of 1980–88, according to Yitzhak Nakash's *Reaching for Power*, about 300,000 Iraqi Shi'is were forced to leave the country.

The Shi'is are the largest community in Lebanon. Substantial Shi'i minorities exist in Pakistan, India, Saudi Arabia, Yemen, the Gulf states, Afghanistan, Syria, and Turkey.

The Shi'is are not proponents of a single political attitude. In contradistinction to the idea propagated by Ayatollah Khomeini and his successors in Iran, according to whom scholars of religious law should rule (*wilāyat al-faqīh*), Ayatollah 'Ali Sistani, the most prominent religious leader of Iraqi Shi'is, has been reluctant to be drawn directly into worldly affairs.

Other Minorities under Muslim Rule

Minorities that adhere to religions known to the classical Muslim tradition (Judaism, Christianity, Zoroastrianism, polytheism) have their place in the scheme developed by Muslim jurisprudents. However, other types of minorities also developed during Muslim history. The Ahmadi movement emerged in the last decade of the 19th century in British India. The Ahmadis maintain that they are Muslims in the fullest sense of the word but are not recognized as such by many mainstream Muslim organizations and were declared a non-Muslim minority by the Pakistani parliament in 1974. This happened because their prophetology can be interpreted as contradicting the doctrine claiming Muhammad as the last prophet (*khatm al-nubuwwa*). Since then, and especially since the introduction of the Islamization policy of the Pakistani president Zia-ul-Haq in the 1980s, the Ahmadis suffered serious persecution in Pakistan, and the headquarters of their movement was relocated to London in 1984.

On the other hand, there are groups whose status as Muslims is not disputed but who are considered minorities because of their ethnic affiliation. A prominent example is the Kurds. The Kurds are a people who speak various Iranian languages and whose territory is divided between Turkey and Iraq; significant Kurdish minorities live also in Syria and Iran. Most Kurds are Sunni Muslims of the Shafi'i *madhhab*. In modern times, the Kurdish minority of Turkey rebelled several times in order to achieve the independence that was envisaged in the Treaty of Sèvres (1920) but abandoned in the Treaty of Lausanne (1923). The Turkish government suppressed these rebellions and went as far as denying the very existence of a Kurdish people, officially calling the Kurds "mountainous Turks." As recently as 1967, a presidential decree prohibited the import into Turkey of any written or recorded material in Kurdish. In northern Iraq, the secessionist tendency was also in evidence in the wake of World War I, and several Kurdish revolts were suppressed both during the monarchy and after its fall in 1958. The most brutal suppression of the Iraqi Kurdish minority was committed during the so-called Anfal ("spoils," after the name of sura 8 in the Qur'an) campaign in 1987–88 when the Iraqi army massacred tens of thousands of civilians. In Iran, the most important event for the Iranian Kurds in the 20th century was the establishment of the ephemeral Kurdish republic of Mahabad (January to November 1946).

Concluding Observations

The issue of minorities in the Islamic world is complex. The minorities are not restricted to Jews and Christians, who are frequently given exclusive attention when the issue is addressed. Some minorities belong to religious communities that existed before the emergence of Islam (Jews, Christians, Zoroastrians, Hindus, Buddhists); among these can be included the Manicheans, who were not tolerated and are now extinct. Others were related to Islam when they came into being but developed into distinct religions (Yazidis, Nusayris, Druzes, Babis, and Baha'is). Another group considers itself Muslim but has been placed beyond the pale of Islam by the Muslim mainstream (Ahmadis). It is important to note that whatever tolerance was practiced in most historical periods in relation to the Jews, the Christians, the Zoroastrians, and even the non-Arab polytheists was not accorded to adherents of religions that came into being after the emergence of Islam. The prime examples of such minorities are the Baha'is in Iran and the Ahmadis in Pakistan. There are also minorities that are not religious but ethnic, such as the Kurds in Turkey, Syria, and Iraq and the Arabs in the Iranian province of Khuzistan.

The Muslims were a ruling minority for at least four centuries in the Middle East and for more than six centuries in various parts of India. The Arabian Peninsula, the birthplace of Islam, is an area with special rules: it was declared a region in which there would be no two religions, though there is evidence that Christians lived in Najran for some period after the Prophet's death. There was also a substantial Jewish community in Yemen, an area that was considered distinct from the rest of the peninsula according to most early jurists. The Yemeni Jews fared reasonably well until the 17th century, which brought a series of intermittent persecutions and oppressive policies. After 1948, most Yemeni Jews emigrated to the newly established state of Israel. In modern times, a considerable number of foreigners work in Saudi Arabia, but citizenship is conferred on Muslims alone: according to the "Saudi Arabian Citizenship System" (para 14.1), applications for citizenship must include "a certificate signed by the imam of the mosque at the applicant's area." This seems to preclude any non-Muslim from submitting an application.

In practical terms, the fortunes of the non-Muslims living under medieval Muslim rulers varied. Modern historians generally agree that non-Muslims under medieval Muslim rule fared better than non-Christians or heretical Christians under medieval Christendom. The prominent historian Bernard Lewis aptly observed that "there is nothing in Islamic history to compare with the massacres and expulsions, the inquisitions and persecutions that Christians habitually inflicted on non-Christians and still more on each other. In the lands of Islam, persecution was the exception; in Christendom, sadly, it was the norm." This must not be taken to mean that freedom of religion was unrestricted in the Islamic world or that the non-Muslims minorities also enjoyed equality. Nor was the relationship between the Muslims and their non-Muslim subjects as idyllic as it is sometimes described. Various disabilities were imposed on the non-Muslims and they were at times persecuted. The Abbasid caliph Mutawakkil (r. 847–61), for example, ordered his officials to destroy newly built churches, to confiscate parts of non-Muslim homes, to prevent the public performance of some Christian and Jewish rituals, and to impose distinctive clothing on the non-Muslims. It is not clear to what extent these instructions were carried out. The Fatimid caliph Hakim (996–1021) ordered the demolition of churches, the dismissal of non-Muslim officials, and the prohibition of various non-Muslim religious rituals, though he reversed this policy toward the end of his reign. The Almohad dynasty of North Africa and Spain (12th century) denied any tolerance to the Christian and Jewish communities and even engaged in forced conversions. This was also the policy of some Safavid rulers in 17th century Iran. Nevertheless, it seems that the treatment of non-Muslims under various Muslim governments in the Middle Ages was, overall, better than that of non-Christians or "deviant" Christians under medieval Christian rule. Modern Muslims frequently take pride in this comparison and draw from it conclusions concerning the tolerance inherent in the Islamic civilization.

In the modern period, the above-mentioned comparison is no longer tenable. Since the Enlightenment, there has been a marked increase in religious tolerance in the West. With the glaring exceptions of Nazi Germany and some communist regimes, countries whose population is predominantly Christian generally have shown more tolerance than countries whose population is predominantly Muslim. Massacres of Assyrians and Armenians in the late Ottoman Empire and the massacre of the Assyrians in Iraq in 1933 are significant examples of the harsh treatment of minorities in the modern Muslim world. Likewise, the growing strength of radical Islam in recent decades and the persecution of minorities such as the Baha'is in Iran and the Ahmadis in Pakistan and elsewhere go a long way to undermine the argument for the inherent toleration of religious minorities in Islam.

Further Reading

Meir Bar Asher and Aryeh Kofsky, *The Nuṣayrī–'Alawī Religion: An Inquiry into Its Theology and Liturgy*, 2002; Allan D. Austin, *African Muslims in Antebellum America*, 1997; Robert Brenton Betts, *The Druze*, 1988; Rainer Brunner and Werner Ende, *The Twelver Shia in Modern Times*, 2001; Michael Dillon, *China's Muslim Hui Community: Migration, Settlement and Sects*, 1999; Shammai Fishman, *Fiqh al-aqalliyyāt: A Legal Theory for Muslim Minorities*, 2006; Yohanan Friedmann, *Prophecy Continuous: Aspects of Ahmadī Religious Thought and Its Medieval Background*, 2003; Idem, *Tolerance and Coercion in Islam: Interfaith Relations in the Muslim Tradition*, 2003; John S. Guest, *Survival among the Kurds: A History of the Yezidis*, 1993; Heinz Halm, *Shi'a Islam*, 1997; Idem, *Shi'ism*, 2004; M. Ali Kettani, *Muslim Minorities in the World Today*, 1986; Philip G. Kreyenbroek, *Yezidism—Its Background, Observances and Textual Tradition*, 1995; Philip G. Kreyenbroek and Stefan Sperl, eds., *The Kurds: A Contemporary Overview*, 1992; Donald Leslie, *Islam in Traditional China: A Short History to 1800*, 1986; Milka Levy-Rubin, "Shurut 'Umar and Its Alternatives: The Legal Debate on the Status of the Dhimmis," *Jerusalem Studies in Arabic and Islam* 30, 2005; Bernard Lewis, *The Jews of Islam*, 1984; Otto F. A. Meinardus, *Christians in Egypt*, 2006; Matti Moosa, *Extremist Shiites: The Ghulat Sects*, 1987; Yitzhak Nakash, *Reaching for Power: The Shi'a in the Modern Arab World*, 2006; Vali Nasr, *The Shi'a Revival: How Conflicts within Islam Will Shape the Future*, 2007; Jørgen Nielsen, *Muslims in Western Europe*, 2004; Wilfred Cantwell Smith, *Islam in Modern History*, 1957; Yosef Tobi, *The Jews of Yemen: Studies in Their History and Culture*, 1999; Raquel Ukeles, *The Evolving Muslim Community in America: The Impact of 9/11*, 2003.

Modernity ∞∞∞∞∞∞∞∞∞∞∞∞∞∞∞∞∞∞∞∞∞∞∞∞∞∞∞∞∞∞∞

Armando Salvatore

The idea of modernity combines a variety of vectors and paths of transformation: economic factors linked to the rise of capitalism, sociopolitical dynamics related to the formation of increasingly centralized and bureaucratized states, and cultural orientations putting a premium on individual autonomy and collective agency, on self-reflexivity, self-steering, and a capacity for creative innovation, and new, pervasive forms of solidarity. This complex yet well-profiled idea reflects in a first instance the historical experiences and achievements of European societies, or better, of some parts of northwestern Europe. It is also important to consider that the transformations that ushered in the advent of modernity concerned religion, both institutionally and conceptually. It was in modern transformations that religion became a clearly circumscribed—optimally, a privatized—sphere, one increasingly differentiated from the realm of politics.

The social science literature that, from the founders of sociology at large (Marx, Durkheim, and Weber) onward, has delineated the key traits of modernity (including its relations to religion) and has postulated that the historical breakthrough to modernity is a Western prerogative, focused on Western Europe and on some of its former settlement colonies overseas (mainly North America and Australia)—primarily because of some allegedly "Occidental" cultural and institutional conditions that did not exist or did not come to maturation in other civilizations. Such civilizations, including Islam, were by contrast considered lacking in one or more crucial features of modernity, in particular the fundamental capacity to spawn creative innovations and to liberate new transformative energies from the "shackles of tradition." According to this vision, non-Western civilizations could at best achieve limited degrees or dependent forms of modernity through their introduction from outside, via a modernization process induced from the West.

More recent theoretical work has revised both the assumption of the uniqueness of the West and the corresponding conception of modernity as singular. In order to reframe the issue of modernity from the perspective of Islamic political thought, a sound conceptualization of the relation between tradition and modernity cannot approach the former as a mere relic of premodern cultures that is destined to be either neutralized or erased in the course of modernization. Specifically, the relation between modernity and Islam cannot be reduced to an analysis of deficits to be measured by Islam's alleged insufficient capacity to supersede its rooting in tradition or in a set of combined traditions, by Islam's dependencies on Western hegemonic patterns of modernity, or by alleged Islamic idiosyncrasies reflected by distorted outcomes of a dependent modernization.

Questions such as "What went wrong?" with Islamic civilization vis-à-vis the modern world hegemonized by the West are the result of static and unilateral views of both tradition and modernity. The famous British Orientalist Bernard Lewis was not the first author to ask this type of question with regard to Islam, nor was 9/11 the first event that prompted such interrogations. The question has been repeatedly formulated from the perspective of a long-term Western hegemony extended over the entire modern world and therefore facing recurrent traumas (from the Indian revolt of 1857 through the oil embargo of 1973, to the terrorist attacks of 2001 and after) resulting in a continual challenge of this same hegemony, often occurring on a symbolical level more than on a material one. The formulation of the question therefore already presupposes that the Western path to modernity is unique, though exposed to challenges.

The heyday of modernization theory, which articulated ideas of modernity as monopolized by the West but exportable, under certain conditions, to the rest of the world, go back to the 1950s and 1960s. The approach suffered a lethal blow in the wake of various events unfolding on the global level during the 1970s and in particular the Iranian Revolution of 1978–79, which raised the banner of Islam against the Shah's authoritarian rule and Westernizing programs. Seeds for an alternative conception, according to which modernity is not a uniquely Western prerogative and cultural and religious traditions are not just detritus left behind by the waves of modernization, were sown in the decolonization struggles, which sparked reinterpretations and critiques of modern ideas and institutions. Their combined result was to challenge the West's monopoly over the definition of modernity.

With even greater intensity since after the demise of modernization theory, key voices within Western social sciences and in particular within social theory have concurred in observing that modernity was never singular, neither was it homogeneous, not even within Europe. A major contribution to make this simple insight productive in theoretical and comparative terms has been the development of a civilizational approach to modernity itself, according to which the civilizational heritage of a given country or macroregion has an impact on the type and outlook of the modernity to come. Yet even within this revisionist approach it is also admitted that modernity—as a global condition affecting cultural life and institutional forms as much as capitalist cycles and hegemonic contentions—equally impinges on a plurality of civilizational tracks differentiating the hegemonic West from the institutions and cultures developing in other macroregions like China, India, and the Islamic world. In spite of such significant theoretical revisions, the older patterns of Western appraisal of Islam vis-à-vis modernity that were cumulatively built over time have retained a considerable influence on a variety of levels, from scholarship to the media—not least, as mentioned earlier, due to the periodical reiteration of traumatic events.

The branches of scholarship that happened to deal with the issue of Islam's otherness from a Western viewpoint saw the light during the 19th century in coincidence with the European colonial encroachment upon the Muslim world. They underwent important changes during the 20th century, mainly as a consequence of the two world wars and of the ensuing processes of decolonization. Yet they were also influenced by earlier views of Islam propagated by leading European thinkers who were not academic specialists within Islamic studies but who contributed to shaping the Enlightenment and post-Enlightenment self-understanding of the West—thinkers such as Hume, Voltaire, Hegel, and even Nietzsche. Both the discourse on Islam's insurmountable otherness on issues of modernity and the attempts to critique and revise it are therefore neither a merely scholarly enterprise nor the inexorable reflex of malign media campaigns. The debate has profound philosophical roots and widespread intellectual implications. Any attempt to develop a critical viewpoint should be aware of such deep ramifications in order to avoid falling into a facile counterhegemonic posture.

A host of historians and social theorists—from Ernest Renan through Max Weber to Rémi Brague—have provided the key link between intellectual manifestations of a Western modern self-understanding and scholarly programs for investigating specific cultural factors that were held responsible for the blockage or delay of the political and economic development within Muslim-majority societies. Within such a body of Western scholarship, it was argued that the doctrine of divine command proclaimed by Islam led Muslims and particularly the 'ulama' to deny a full legitimacy to government and therefore hindered a full-fledged, modern state formation. In a similar vein, the presuppositions to capitalist growth that enlivened the early modern sociopolitical formations of Western Europe have been considered too frail within Muslim lands. The cause for this deficit was often identified in cultural mechanisms of self-limitation of the entrepreneurial and innovative spirit. This self-limitation was in turn explained with the deeply religious commitments of both cultural elites and popular classes.

Such views have been elaborated upon within the specialized scholarship of Islamic studies. An influential antecedent to the discourse propagated by Bernard Lewis in the academic world of the post–World War II era is the work of another leading Orientalist of the 20th century, Gustave E. von Grunebaum. His approach capitalized on selected Weberian insights revolving around a keen understanding of Western cultural uniqueness and its universal normativity. Even more than Weber himself, von Grunebaum engaged in the study of Islam as a representative of the Western cultural elite deeply imbued with its civilizational values. While he was convinced that the Weberian approach held the key to understanding the West's rationalist spirit, he considered Islam to be at the mercy of the Western-led process of modernization. Not least, von Grunebaum followed Weber closely in explaining Islam's purportedly unsuccessful encounter with modernity by seeing in it a dilution of the inner impetus of Christian faith.

This idea aggravated Weber's derogatory view of the Islamic orientation toward immediate rewards in contrast to Christianity's focus on the "inner" realm of pure values. According to this interpretation, the inherent deficit of Islamic faith was magnified in the modern era by the fact that Islam did not undergo the process of self-renewal that the West had been going through since after the Protestant Reformation. This stress on reformation often became an obsessive theme in Western approaches to the issue of Islam and modernity. The Protestant Reformation was seen as anchored in a reform of the self that was facilitated by an increasing reflexivity and rationality. Von Grunebaum denied to Muslim cultural elites and political leaders such a capacity for intellectual renewal, which could enable them to successfully cope with the challenges and requirements of modernity.

Modernization theorists introduced some important distinctions into the picture. According to Manfred Halpern, the Muslim as a social actor is not completely paralyzed by the legacy represented by Islamic traditions. It was evident to him that many Muslim actors were not idle but on the move in postcolonial society. While the process and its predictable outcome amounted for him to a gradual collapse of Muslim culture, some key Islamic ideals may not only survive modernization but can even feed into it, if separated from the traditional system to which they originally belonged. Within this more dynamic picture, Islam appears ambivalently positioned toward modernity: while modernization theorists (wrongly) predicted the demise of Islamist forces, they did allow that selected elements of Islamic traditions could enliven the forces of change.

For all these Western scholars the ambivalence toward the West and Western modernity manifested by subsequent generations of Muslim leaders and thinkers, including the so-called modernists or reformists, was deeply problematic. What most Western observers neglected to see was a cumulative trend among Muslim reformers consisting in rejecting the view of either "Islam" or "modernity" conceived as comprehensive entities, as Western scholars were used to seeing them. The idea that Islam is internally plural and that modernity is a process not entrenched in a singular culture seemed alien to most Western observers, while it gradually became a main avenue of reasoning for key Muslim thinkers. A rare and early recognition of this insight came with the observation of Lothrop Stoddard (1883–1950), a non-Orientalist, who in spite of being a WASP supremacist wrote in the early 1920s that Muslim thinkers were not simply obsessed with the West but rather intent on developing "a new synthesis."

A more comprehensive appreciation of original Islamic approaches to modern thought as well as to modernity as a social process could only take form after the slow agony of modernization theory. A major change was prompted by the innovative work of younger Islamologists and historians. They saw that patterns of intellectual modernity, in their multiple ties to specific developments within capitalist production and markets, were seeing the light within the Muslim world prior to any overt confrontation with the encroaching Western modernity. They placed such developments in the context of comprehensive social processes and intellectual trends that linked Western Europe with the Muslim and in particular with the Ottoman world.

The two scholars who most coherently worked on the idea of largely endogenous seeds of an Islamic modernity were Peter Gran and Reinhard Schulze. In order to tackle the weakest point of the Orientalist argument about the decline of the Muslim world in the modern era prior to the advance of the West on Muslim lands, they challenged head-on the "Napoleon's theorem"—namely, the assertion that the issue of modernity, with its spirit of enterprise and innovation, was first brought to the core of the Muslim world by Napoleon's occupation of Egypt and other parts of the Near East at the end of the 18th century. The main point of convergence between the work of Gran and Schulze is the intent to show the existence in 18th-century Ottoman society, including Egypt, of thriving bourgeois-like intellectual cultures, many of them significantly connected to some Sufi brotherhoods. According to the two scholars, such cultures reflected commercial and capitalist interests and revealed a new, genuinely modern emphasis on social autonomy and individual responsibility. Accordingly, the Islamic 18th century, far from being the stagnant counterpart to a flourishing European Enlightenment, might have manifested innovative dynamics both at the level of culture and politics.

In the debates that followed their scholarly challenge, Gran and Schulze also stressed that the analysis of texts is meaningful only if situated in the context of wider sociopolitical processes of transformation. Therefore, neglecting the sociopolitical context might lead students of Islamic civilization to lose touch with more general academic debates about the internal reform of tradition and the singularity versus the plurality of modernity. In other words, belittling the diversity of sociopolitical context encourages essentializing both Islamic traditions and Western modernity. The emergence of this new type of scholarship prefigured the possibility of interpreting the relation of Islam and modernity no longer as an oxymoron but as a theme in its own right, opening the way to thinking about the capacity of actors to creatively recombine endogenous resources with exogenous stimuli and challenges.

Secular Subjectivity and Social Solidarity

Against the deeper background of Western theorizing about the allegedly deficient capacity of Islamic civilization to fit into a modern world—not to mention its ability to initiate autonomous modern transformations—the new challenge strengthened the argument, supported by a general reflection on Islamic history (including a new attention to earlier works like *The Venture of Islam* of Marshall Hodgson), that a differentiation of state power and religious authority was integral to the development of Islamic civilization. Hodgson in particular anticipated interpretations that became familiar to a larger academic public only from the late 1970s onward, ranging from the critique of Orientalist worldviews to a plural and civilizational approach to modernity. Hodgson stated that at the dawn of the modern era, Islamic civilization reached the zenith not only of its political power but also of its cultural creativity. Key Muslim actors and institutions, he argued, worked to selectively blend the resources of power and culture that constitute a civilization within the three different but equally flourishing early modern Muslim empires: the Ottoman, the Safavid, and the Mughal or Timurid.

In the early 21st century, comparative civilizational analysts are revising the older bias of Western social theorists by valorizing selected Orientalist contributions like the work of Hodgson. As stated by Johann P. Arnason—a social theorist and leading practitioner of comparative civilizational analysis, who has thoroughly studied and commented on the work of Hodgson—the idea that any differentiation of religion and politics was alien to Islamic civilization has given way to the more nuanced view that this civilization displays specific trajectories of differentiation that cannot be measured on a homogeneous scale via a comparison with purported normal standards, usually taken from simplified Western models. Edward Said was right in suspecting that Orientalists were not alone with their essentialist bias concerning Islam. The mother of all essentialisms lies indeed in the way Western social scientists and social theorists have conceptualized religion and its role within modern societies. The work of revision within Western social theory concerning the issue of modernity is therefore no less crucial than the challenge launched by new historians and Islamologists.

In order to throw more light on the vexed question of the differentiation, or lack thereof, of religion and politics within Muslim societies, we need to extend our purview to the wider context that overloaded the study of religion in the West with heavy presuppositions closely tied to the Western self-understanding and its hegemonic discourse. In a variety of academic disciplines that attempted to locate the sources of human sociability, religion was identified as a key sphere of human endeavor, whose emergence basically coincided with the formation of organized community life. From comparative linguistics and comparative mythology through text criticism and history to anthropology and sociology, an army of Western scholars has worked since the 19th century to investigate the role of religion in the constitution of human society and the social bond. The issue of religion figured centrally in the genesis of sociology.

It was Karl Marx who defined religion as a crucial instrument of domination in human history and as a token of human alienation. Émile Durkheim and the school associated with his name reinterpreted religion as the pristine force of social cohesion through which the subject first alienates but then appropriates the power located in the collective world of social relations. According to this school, religion became the overarching category for investigating the nature of the collective forces providing cohesion to society via ever more abstract—and in this sense purportedly rational—models of solidarity. The idea itself of a modern society based on a rational division of labor became with Durkheim the key to postulate an evolutionist trajectory through which the integrative potential of traditional religion is transformed into a civic religion that is strictly functional to the maintenance of the social bond—a trajectory that sees its completion in Western, modern, and complex societies. In this perspective, secularization as a chief characteristic of modernization does not occur by suppressing religion but by transforming its cohesive potential in parallel with the deepening of the social division of labor. In the process, religion takes on increasingly abstract, and nonetheless civil, forms.

The purported role of a "civil religion" within modernity gained further prominence in the latter part of the 20th century, in particular in the United States, where civil religion was interpreted as a cultural capital of society capable of reconciling tradition and modernity. This approach was also represented, though in original ways, in the work of the anthropologist Clifford Geertz, for whom the role of religion as a source of stability is found both in the most modern of Western societies—especially in those with a strong Protestant background, characterized by an increasing individualist ethos—and in the new postcolonial nations, including many Muslim-majority societies, where the cultural function of religion as a provider of collective identity comes to the fore. This interpretation overlapped with the idea, well represented within modernization theory, that elements of Islamic traditions were on their way to being reabsorbed as fragments of a new collective identity, in forms suitable to new development imperatives. Unlike the idea, dominant during the rise of European colonialism, that the Islamic doctrine of divine authority prevented a real legitimization of political power and justified the colonial supremacy of the West over Muslim lands, Geertz argued that in the postindependence polities of the Muslim world, cultural elites and political leaders might be able to culturally construct and politically legitimize new and sophisticated forms of social power and political organization—different from those of the West, but nonetheless modern or at least sufficiently compatible with the modern world.

The chief latent issue underlying the cohesion of modern, Muslim-majority societies, however, does not concern so much the role of "religion," on which Geertz focused his attention as the configuration of the domain of "politics." The specter of Western essentialism pushed out by the main door comes back through the window when it is assumed that a secular subjectivity aligned with the model nation-states of the modern West is surrogated within Muslim societies by hybrid formations favoring a basically authoritarian fabrication of a developmental ethos, whereby a conveniently reduced type of Islam remains a key component of collective identity. The relentless critique performed by Talal Asad, targeting a wide arch of Western scholarship stretching from Durkheim to Geertz, puts in evidence the vicious circle between the affirmation of secular subjectivity as the banner of Western culture and values and the reiteration of essentialist knowledge of the West's other, as incarnate in Islam. Western norms of modern governance remain both in the metropoles and in the former colonies connected to ideas of individual autonomy rooted in a secular subjectivity. Hereby the "secular" should not be equated with a rejection of "religion" but rather presupposes an essentialized, reformed religion as the necessary condition for the formation of self-governing agents.

Asad has stressed that practitioners of Islamic Studies often wrongly assumed that Islamic traditions had no notion of subjective inwardness, in spite of sufficient evidence of the importance of subjective intention and cultivation of the self, both in Islamic worship and in mysticism. Certainly, modern Western subjectivity is different in its emphasis on individual autonomy and dependence on state law, regulation, and administration, as well as on consumer choices mediated by the market. Asad warns, nonetheless, that based on a reiteration of such patterns across various stages of world politics (e.g., from the colonial to the postcolonial age), a full normalization of politics in Muslim-majority societies will always be deferred to some form of direct or indirect, benign or violent intervention by Western powers.

The historical reality is far more complex. Muslim intellectuals from the Maghrib to the Ottoman Empire viewed modern Europe not as culturally unique but as a frontier of new ideas and programs for the rational steering of society. The trauma of colonialism fractured this potentially positive perception of Europe, yet the continuous development of solidarity within modern European societies continued to impress subsequent generations of several Muslim reformers, for whom modern power could be attained within and through a variety of cultural settings. According to these Muslim reformers, there was nothing wrong with Islam per se, provided that its pristine forms of social cohesion and power were restored and reenergized. Yet most reformers remained caught in a polarizing dilemma, also evidenced by Asad's critique: Is the "organic solidarity" envisioned by Durkheim a legitimate goal for Muslim leaders intent on pushing for the reform of their societies? Does it necessarily require turning religion into mere civic morals? Or can it help instead retrieve the full power of Islamic normativity and even promote a transnational dimension of solidarity extended to the entire Islamic *umma* (community of believers)? Is the price to be paid the acceptance of the secular subjectivity of the citizen as reflected in the historic trajectory of Western nation-states: a type of subjectivity requiring a privatization of shari'a? While the latter option seems unattractive to the majority of Muslim intellectuals, all other responses risk becoming trapped in facile formulas of reconciliation of "tradition and modernity" that hide the node represented by the normative requirements of the secular subjectivity rooted in the Western historic models and experiences.

Premodern Forms of Collective Action and the Role of Sufism

Revising the postulates of the Western monopoly of modernity entails a questioning of its universally normative power. Western Europe accomplished a compromise between the state's control of the religious field and the sovereignty of the soul, between publicness and inwardness. This normative arrangement, however, does not match the historic dynamics through which the Islamic *dīn* (religion) was incorporated within sociopolitical structures. The *dīn* and the *dawla* (state) designated different, though at times overlapping, fields of social activity. Bernard Lewis's typical assertion that the state and the church are identical in Islam is fundamentally flawed, since neither "church" nor "state" are concepts that can be neatly translated into the institutional grammar of Islamic traditions. The conceptual pair *dīn* and *dawla* designates two poles of activity that permanently contribute to each other's definition while retaining their principled, though conditional, autonomy: they are not absolutely autonomous; rather, they are autonomous within the boundaries defined by Islam. Even at face value, the slogan *islām dīn wa-dawla* (Islam is religion and state), which became particularly popular as a modern Islamic response to a state whose autonomy was compromised by colonial dependency, does not proclaim the identity of religion and state but the possibility of their concomitant and, optimally, mutual legitimation "in Islam." The problem in the formula is not an alleged identity of religion and state but rather a strong essentialization of Islam and of its univocal normative force—a presumption that was maintained with particular energy by Western Orientalists in the first place and by some Islamic actors concomitantly or subsequently.

Therefore, one cannot impute a deficit to Islamic civilization for having largely shunned the fully autonomous powers of Western models. Yet in the reiteration of historical processes under Western norms of autonomous agency—inscribed in constitutional formulas, sanctioned by human rights provisions, and prescribed in the form of good governance—this specific type of autonomy becomes an absolute value, in proximity of which any other tradition of self-governance is rarely recognized as fully legitimate from a Western viewpoint (be it "absolutist" or "relativist"). Modern associations invoking a specifically Islamic ethos and adopting organizational forms and funding patterns that refer directly or indirectly to Islamic tenets have had to prove their loyalty to the state in Egypt, while in France they have sometimes claimed a secular identity in order not to incur the suspicion of the authorities and of the public alike.

Invocations of an Islamic legitimacy of forms of organization cannot be reduced to a mere counteressentialist reflex prompted by the need to respond to the affirmation of the universality of Western standards. Once more we need the help of unbiased Orientalist scholarship to understand the relation of tradition and modernity in Islamic history. Hodgson stressed in particular the seminal role of Sufi movements, especially in the later phase of the Middle Periods, during the three centuries that preceded the modern era and the nearly simultaneous rise of what he termed the three dynamic and powerful "gunpowder empires" of the Muslim world: the Ottoman, the Safavid, and the Mughal or Timurid. According to Hodgson, Islamic civilization gained from the 13th to the 15th century the profile of a transstate ecumene, thanks to a steady expansion across the Afro-Eurasian landmass.

Orientalists before (but also after) Hodgson have mainly characterized this "medieval" period as an epoch of decadence and lack of creativity. It cannot be denied that in this phase, which followed the Mongol invasion of the mid-13th century, political domination was weak and fragmented. Yet at the same time, the cultural elaboration on the relationship between *siyāsa* (a term of Mongol origin that means sheer government) and shariʻa (designating the comprehensive idea of Islamic normativity more than simply "law") reached a high point. During this period, Muslim society was a society of networks more than states, so that social governance and its legitimacy were effectively divorced from state power. In the Middle Periods, and especially in its latest phase, Sufi *ṭuruq* (brotherhoods) played a key role in Islam's expansion into the Eurasian depths—particularly into the Indian subcontinent and Southeast Asia—and across sub-Saharan Africa. Their flexible and semiformal model of organization and connectedness, of balancing competition, cooperation, and hierarchy, was well suited to the political characteristics of the epoch. As synthetically put by Hodgson at the end of this period, at the threshold of the modern era, thanks to the expansive capacity of this crystallizing model of soft governance, the dynamics of Islamic civilization exhibited a markedly hegemonic potential.

The most interesting question to ask from a contemporary perspective, which witnesses the erosion of the West-centered state system and the advent, in the wake of globalization, of new forms of governance and solidarity, concerns the aborted yet still latent potential of religious cosmopolitanism that Islamic civilization inherited from the Middle Periods and ambivalently invested into the structures of power of the modern Muslim empires. Viewed from the perspective of the seminal developments of the Middle Periods, these empires, in spite of displaying impressive political power, military organization, and promotion of high culture, and basing their power on specific patterns of differentiation of state and religion, could only partially inherit the creative impetus of the Middle Periods, when a cosmopolitan high culture thrived alongside a dense social autonomy balancing horizontal cooperation and solidarity with hierarchy and command—a pattern that facilitated the penetration of the Islamic message into the lifeworld of lower population strata across new territories.

Western scholars and Muslim reformers alike predicted that the Sufi networks would vanish as several colonial and postcolonial societies of the Muslim world adopted a greater separation between the religious sphere and a civic domain or "civil society." Yet in the colonial era some Sufi orders expanded their constituencies, and some actually participated in or even led movements of resistance against colonial occupation, most notably in North and West Africa and in Southeast Asia. Several scholars have noticed major shifts in some Sufi orders toward more formal and hierarchical modes of organization since the 18th century—a development that demonstrated their ability to push for social and even political change. While this thesis is well reflected in the previously examined work by Gran and Schulze, earlier scholars like Fazlur Rahman and John O. Voll already spoke of a distinctive "neo-Sufi" associational form characterized by a sociopolitical activism nurtured by a commitment to Islam's potential for mobilizing various social groups in order to implement Islamic ideals of justice.

Some such Sufi groups cultivated the study of hadith in ways that are comparable to some puritan movements—like the Wahhabis—of a decidedly anti-Sufi inclination. The decentralized nature of studies of hadith and the latitude allowed within this branch of study to reinterpret norms of social interaction, including those affecting trade and business, appeared in some cases to further the interests of a rising commercial class. Some urban reformers of the 19th century seemed to be influenced by selective Sufi ideas even in the absence of solid organizational ties to any *ṭarīqa* or Sufi master. Those reformers who attacked Sufism stigmatized types of practices (like saint worshipping, shrine and grave visits, and above all the "abominable" display of superstition and promiscuity at Sufi saints festivals) that most "neo-Sufi" leaders also shunned.

Sufi orders were overall in good health during the 19th and early 20th century and able to absorb the challenge of colonialism in order to partially renew their social goals and organizational forms; yet by the middle of the 20th century, during the formation of postindependence states, observers registered a state of stagnation if not an outward crisis of Sufism. Nonetheless, this moment of difficulty was overcome in the 1970s via the larger phenomenon commonly dubbed Islamic resurgence, which took a firmer root in a nonovertly political, "civic" field and therefore also favored a revival of Sufi types of affiliation. Nonetheless, especially in late-colonial and postindependence settings, Sufi orders in many countries underwent a process of bureaucratization through their subjection to a more centralized control under ultimate state supervision and patronage. In the new context, however, Sufi leaders often sought connection and influence with various, sometimes high echelons of the state bureaucracy. In this sense, while the formula of incorporation of *awqāf* (plural of *waqf*: "pious foundation") into the state administration was streamlined and could be roughly compared to secularization processes in European settings (whereby the first meaning of secularization was the confiscation of church properties by the state), the way Sufi orders renegotiated their space and autonomy in a postcolonial, nation-state setting was open to arrangements that did not necessarily erase the earlier autonomous dynamism of Sufism and in some cases even reinvigorated it. In republican Turkey, the Naqshbandis (almost reflecting a prototype of neo-Sufi ethos) reenergized themselves in the second half of the 20th century in spite of the thorough secularization measures of earlier republican governments. Most notable in Turkey is the capacity of Sufism to mutate into a new type of movement that is no longer formally a Sufi order but incorporates a rationalization of the Sufi ethos and its flexible organizational and disciplinary forms. This is the case of the Nur movement founded by Sa'id Nursi and its presently most successful spin-off initiated by Fethullah Gülen: increasingly pervasive in the media world and in the educational sector, aiming at the formation of new elites and audiences alike, imbued of a modern Islamic ethos, and active transnationally, not only in Turkey but also in several other countries of West and East.

Modern Politics and the Reform Program

In contrast to the pursuit of the social idea of human connectedness inspired to the "common good"—an idea that cuts across the divide between tradition and modernity—the prime theme of modernity lies in the issue of differentiation between societal spheres, a process governed by the new forms of power and regulation deployed by modern states. This process affected the original forms of organization and collective action historically promoted by Sufi orders in their pursuit of interconnectedness over distant spaces. The process of differentiation did not destroy or absorb the patterns of connectedness promoted by Sufism—but by affirming the centralization and monopolization of the state's power on the territory on which it exercised sovereignty, it inculcated in the state subjects the disciplines of the rational agent, increasingly identified with the social agent acting on the basis of narrowly defined personal interests (*homo economicus*). As an unexpected consequence of the process, these subjects started to reclaim more control of governance and tried to compensate the emerging dominance of economic rationales within social relations by mobilizing the ties of affection and solidarity entailed by ideals of civility—intended as a form of social intercourse, politeness, and interconnectedness that cuts across closed communities and confessional divides. The observation of the unfolding of such highly ambivalent processes in Muslim-majority societies first in the colonial era and then in the postindependence settings also drew the attention of observers to the programs of a host of self-proclaimed Muslim reformers. Many of them still saw in the Sufi ethic a resource, and not a hindrance, for encouraging a new ethos of participation.

Within Muslim societies, the path to modern transformations cannot be therefore reduced to an adaptationist twist of an older model of "Oriental despotism," which never existed except in the imagination of Western thinkers. Unless we want to identify the access to political modernity of Muslim-majority societies as a process entirely induced by colonial domination or indirect Western pressures (as in the case of the Ottoman Empire, whose kernel regions were never controlled by colonial powers), we should look at the transformations of the cohesive and mobilizing potential of discourses on the "common good" cutting across the conventional divide between traditional and modern social worlds. Islamic notions of the common good (*maṣlaḥa*) were appropriated by some early reformers in the 18th century (some of them linked to neo-Sufi groups) and were later reinvigorated both intellectually and politically by subsequent generations of thinkers and activists in the context of colonial and postcolonial politics, or, in the Ottoman Empire, in the framework of administrative reforms, known as Tanzimat, and which started in the 1830s.

It is noteworthy that the culture of those reformers who were also members of the high echelons of the state bureaucracy was particularly close to the *adab* tradition—distinct from the core Islamic traditions based on Qur'an and sunna—inherited from Persianate court culture. *Adab* denotes the catalogs of the ethical and practical norms of good life that were cultivated by a class of literati in the framework of life at court: a tradition that was central to Islamic civilization, even if detached from the core religious traditions. Far from being abandoned at the passage to the modern era, the cultivation of the *adab* tradition provided the background culture to the scribal class during the period, from the 18th century onward, when it increasingly acquired the ambitions of a modern bureaucracy. We might conceive of the transformations of *adab* as the cultural engine of a civilizing process in the sense highlighted by Norbert Elias: initiated in court milieus but with the potential to reach down the social ladder and encompass wider populations, and therefore as a substantial aid to "state-building." The upgrading of *adab* into the matrix for a self-sustaining civilizing process starting in the era of the Tanzimat (during which printed administrative bulletins first saw the light) was followed by the rise of a full-fledged public sphere based on a largely free press and the emergence of new genres of public speech. This process suggests that conceptual syntheses of the essence of modernity in terms of either autonomy or self-mastery neglect the more complex social layering effected by a "civilizing process" also via the communicative sophistications allowed within a modern public sphere. Both phenomena are particularly well visible in a sociopolitical world, as in Ottoman and other Muslim, post-Ottoman and postcolonial societies, which are neither the modern incarnation of Oriental despotism nor the exact antithesis of liberal civil society.

By the time, in the late 19th century, when the reform discourse started to be formulated in the context of emerging public spheres by urban personalities who were in most cases both thinkers and activists and sometimes state servants, the Western diagnosis of the inherent deficits of Islamic cultural traditions was already gaining currency. Starting with Afghani (1838–97), reformers were faced with the task both to ground a shared cultural perspective and institute its communicative infrastructure in order to challenge their Western colonialist counterparts on their own terrain while relying on select elements of their own intellectual traditions and institutional legacies. With later reformers such as Muhammad ʿAbduh (1849–1905), the operational conditions were complicated by the fact that colonial (and later postcolonial) rule at the same time empowered the reform discourse and channeled it into a modern, positive view of the law as a key tool of reform controlled by the state.

The resulting visions could no longer be reconciled with the traditional approach to *maṣlaḥa*, in spite of the rising popularity of this concept among many Muslim reformers who were interested in its potential to provide the hub for a Muslim theory of social agency and autonomous judgment. The way the Islamic traditions ingrained into the newly emerging sphere that became the battleground of the civilizing process marks an interesting difference with regard to developments in northwestern Europe, where the moral subject was, initially, effectively integrated in the governance machine of the modern state before it claimed autonomy in the public sphere. In the Ottoman Empire and especially in Egypt, the public sphere, though still dependent from conditions dictated by the colonial regimes, developed from the beginning an autonomous potential distinct from the state by virtue of its reposing on a newly recombined discourse of shari'a and *adab*—a discourse that, though focused on the building of a new moral subject, was not entirely functional to the sovereign domain of state law and was still to a large extent related to ideals of connectedness and self-governance. This is best illustrated by 'Abdallah al-Nadim (1845–96), a committed Muslim reformer but also one major disseminator of *adab*, who defined virtue not just in terms of the canonical injunction *al-amr bi-l-ma'ruf wa-l-nahi 'an al-munkar* (commanding right and forbidding wrong) that is at the heart of the normative system of shari'a, but as tied to economic development and "industriousness." *Adab* thus acquired a meaning close to "civility," understood as an ensemble of moral dispositions entailing good manners and mastery of the self as well as a sense of social circumstances. While initially reflecting a classic notion envisioning models of cultivation of the self, in the course of the reform process the concept of *adab* evolved into defining a quite homogeneous field of public morality that the state could not fully control by legislating measures.

Global Civil Society and Transnational Islam

The reform project has left a strong imprint on popular movements inspired by Islamic tenets until our era. Yet the rise of such movements since after the late 1920s can also be considered the symptom of a backlash in the attempt to autonomously articulate an Islamic modernity in the context of an ongoing colonial dependence and postcolonial weakness. Instead of increasing the power of the Islamic sphere through inculcating cultured behavior in the masses, as earlier reformers had tried to do, with the formation of Islamist sociopolitical movements like the Muslim Brothers, the reform program ended up justifying a more one-sided focus on the power of engineering a morality-based public culture. One major test of the development of the branch of Muslim reform that has morphed into modern Islamism has been whether it can renounce a prioritization of power as an instrument to enforce public morals and thus fit into modern visions of "civil society." Civil society is in the first instance the outcome of specific developments within northwestern Europe. The long erosion of ideological unity since medieval Christianity and the social fragmentation that resulted from the commercial and industrial revolutions led several modern authors, in particular those from the 18th-century Scottish Enlightenment, to view the social bond as resting on a combination of interest and affection and ultimately on mutual trust among individuals. This formulation replaced a more traditional notion of community as a partnership of faith in God among individuals. The emerging vision stressed new factors of cohesion in society, made "civil" by the simultaneously spontaneous and necessary bond of trust that linked individuals without any divine mediation. The "moral sense" theorized by the Scottish moralists was a form of pristine trust facilitating contractual exchange among private individuals and providing the necessary stability to social relationships spurned by the commercial and industrial revolutions.

Trust among individuals within civil society became the key tool to redefine a social bond increasingly exposed to the impersonality of factory work and of contract-based labor relationships within capitalist economies, as well as to the faceless bureaucracies that were replacing the arbitrary rule of absolutist autocrats. Civil society was considered distinct from the modern state, while it entered a rather symbiotic relationship with it. Optimally, civil society expresses legitimate interests and produces ties of solidarity, while the state guarantees the rules that protect those interests and provides a legal framework for warranting social order. Far from being an antistate, civil society contributes to both solidarity and governance from the bottom up. With the present processes of globalization, however, solidarity at the national level has been eroded, while governance gains ever more transnational contours. In this sense, globalization as a whole denotes the long-term process of adaptation of practices, discourses, and institutions of a given society or civilization to standards dictated by the rationality of world capitalism and of the international political system of nation-states. The latter increasingly includes—especially since the 1990s—narrowly defined liberal norms, aligned with the governance standards of international organizations like the International Monetary Fund (IMF) and the World Bank. A response to the combined economic and political dynamics of globalization can be found at the level of sociopolitical movements that act on a global scale to challenge the hegemonic paradigms of globalization and propagate alternative global visions, typically subsumed under the slogan "Another world is possible" of the World Social Forum. To describe these developments, the term "global civil society" has been coined—an idea that happens to stress solidarity much more than ties of interest.

As a result, globalization does not weaken either solidarity or governance per se but deterritorializes and redeploys them across conventional borders. Solidarity in particular becomes less tied to locales and potentially more expansive, while governance can be either concentrated in transnational centers or delegated to local power centers less bound by conventional notions of citizenship. The obverse of this process is a looming sense of rootlessness that is caused by the weakening of the incorporation of individuals and groups into nation-state jurisdictions. Sociopolitical integration comes to increasingly depend on market rules and consumption preferences.

The contemporary unfolding of a globally Islamic, post-Westphalian sphere of connectedness, solidarity, and communication builds on the earlier illustrated historical experiences of global interconnectedness within Islamic civilization, while it also responds to Western norms raising the banner of civil society and global governance and to the deep ambivalence of the current processes of globalization, which create new dependences and constraints but also new occasions and spaces for collective action. Although the eyes of Western observers are mainly focused on so-called global jihadism and transnational networks of migration, Islamic globalism includes far more components and facets, which should be carefully taken into consideration. Underlying all forms of Islamic globalism is an abstract notion of a global *umma*, which superimposes social relations and political contests that are still mainly framed within nation-state frameworks and their narrow patterns of governance and solidarity.

In the extensive literature on Islam in Europe and in the West, several Muslim spokespersons and public intellectuals report a rising feeling of participation in a universal *umma*—a perception that is sharpened by critical events, from the Rushdie affair of 1989 to 9/11 and the ensuing "war on terror," which have nourished renewed patterns of Muslim global solidarity in the face of a threatening Western posture. This phenomenon is particularly intense in the Muslim diasporas of the West, and an increasing number of Muslim intellectuals who were born or reared in the West have led struggles for Muslim participation within global networks of solidarity. Such battles are often intended to transcend narrowly defined Muslim interests and to join broader efforts for global justice. While increasing attention has been paid to radical groups, particularly remarkable in this context is the flourishing of Sufism. Throughout Islamic history, one strength of Sufi networks was their capacity to support travelers across wide distances. Postcolonial labor migration has been, since the second half of the 20th century, similarly intertwined with the thriving of Sufi *turuq* in the West. These orders are often linked with the regions of origins of the migrants, such as South Asia and West Africa, but sometimes initiate new networks that cut across traditional regional localizations and attract Western members, including practitioners and sympathizers who are not Muslims in the conventional sense.

To conclude, the significance of Islamic globalism at the present stage of entanglement of multiple modernities might support the decoupling of modernization from Westernization and a reconstruction of modernity along specific civilizational paths conforming to their foundational images, symbols, and discursive patterns. Mass cultural production can further this process but can also increase the chances of building new ties and coalitions across communal or national domains. The growing Islamic focus on transnational interconnectedness transcends a Eurocentric modernist approach to modernity confined within the rationales of nation-states or of new aggregations thereof, like the European Union.

Further Reading

Said A. Arjomand, "Coffeehouses, Guilds and Oriental Despotism: Government and Civil Society in Late 17th to Early 18th Century Istanbul and Isfahan, and As Seen from Paris and London," *European Journal of Sociology* 45, no. 1 (2004); Johann P. Arnason, "Marshall Hodgson's Civilizational Analysis of Islam: Theoretical and Comparative Perspectives," in *Islam in Process: Historical and Civilizational Perspectives*, vol. 7, *Yearbook of the Sociology of Islam*, edited by Johann P. Arnason, Armando Salvatore, and Georg Stauth, 2006; Talal Asad, *Formations of the Secular: Christianity, Islam, Modernity*, 2003; Karen Barkey, *Empire of Difference: The Ottomans in Comparative Perspective*, 2008; Dale F. Eickelman and James Piscatori, *Muslim Politics*, 1996; Shmuel N. Eisenstadt, "Fundamentalist Movements in the Framework of Multiple Modernities," in *Between Europe and Islam: Shaping Modernity in a Transcultural Space*, edited by Almut Höfert and Armando Salvatore, 2000; Clifford Geertz, *Islam Observed: Religious Development in Morocco and Indonesia*, 1971; Haim Gerber, "The Public Sphere and Civil Society in the Ottoman Empire," in *The Public Sphere in Muslim Societies*, edited by Miriam Hoexter, Shmuel N. Eisenstadt, and Nehemia Levtzion, 2002; Ralph D. Grillo, "Islam and Transnationalism," *Journal of Ethnic and Migration Studies* 30, no. 5 (2004); Robert W. Hefner, ed., *Remaking Muslim Politics: Pluralism, Contestation, Democratization*, 2005; Marshall G. S. Hodgson, *Rethinking World History: Essays on Europe, Islam and World History*, 1993; Bernard Lewis, *What Went Wrong? Western Impact and Middle Eastern Response*, 2002; Saba Mahmood, "Secularism, Hermeneutics, and Empire: The Politics of Islamic Reformation," *Public Culture* 18 (2006); Şerif Mardin, *Religion, Society and Modernity in Turkey*, 2006; Muhammad Khalid Masud, Armando Salvatore, and Martin van Bruinessen, eds., *Islam and Modernity: Key Issues and Debates*, 2009; Brinkley Messick, *The Calligraphic State: Textual Domination and History in a Muslim Society*, 1993; Timothy Mitchell, *Colonizing Egypt*, 1988; Armando Salvatore, *Islam and the Political Discourse of Modernity*, 1997; Adam B. Seligman, *The Idea of Civil Society*, 1992; Georg Stauth, ed., *Islam, a Motor or Challenge of Modernity*, vol. 1, *Yearbook of the Sociology of Islam*, 1998; Martin van Bruinessen and Julia D. Howell, eds., *Sufism and the "Modern" in Islam*, 2007; John O. Voll, *Islam: Continuity and Change in the Modern World*, 1994; Björn Wittrock, "Social Theory and Global History: The Periods of Cultural Crystallization," *Thesis Eleven* 65 (2001); Muhammad Qasim Zaman, "The Scope and Limits of Islamic Cosmopolitanism and the Discursive Language of the 'Ulama," in *Muslim Networks from Hajj to Hip Hop*, edited by Miriam Cooke and Bruce B. Lawrence, 2005; Sami Zubaida, *Law and Power in the Islamic World*, 2003.

Muhammad ⋙⋙⋙⋙⋙⋙⋙⋙⋙⋙⋙⋙⋙⋙⋙

Gerhard Bowering

Muhammad's Career and Achievements

In Muslim belief, the religion of Islam is based on divine revelation and represents a divinely willed and established institution. In the perspective of history, the origins of Islam can be traced back to the prophetic career of Muhammad, its historical founder in the first third of the seventh century. Born around 570 in Mecca, a town in a rocky valley of the Hijaz—the northwestern quarter of the Arabian Peninsula—Muhammad began his prophetic proclamations circa 610. He appeared not as a mystic or visionary but as a prophet with the mission to convert the Quraysh, his fellow Arab tribesmen who had settled there.

The town of Mecca flourished on trade and commerce. It was built around a well, which provided a reliable yearlong water supply and held in its center the Ka'ba, the sanctuary of the Black Stone and seat of the tribal deity Hubal. Most importantly, it was a pilgrimage site where fairs and festivals were held every year. Muhammad's message to his fellow townsmen was based on the religious synthesis that had formed and fermented in him since his youth and that he understood to be the divine revelation that God had sent to him to proclaim. This message eventually became known as Islam, or "submission to God," and grew into a universal and missionary religion whose current followers represent about a fifth of the world's population. Muhammad experienced his revelations as inner promptings that inspired ad hoc utterances that he recited piecemeal to his listeners over about 20 years. These recitals were collected after his death in the Arabic Qur'an (literally, "recitation"), the holy book of Islam. They were couched in rhymed prose (*saj'*), a mode of expression that facilitated memorization and distinguished them from Muhammad's personal instructions.

Muhammad broke forth with his message, proclaiming faith in the one God (Allah), whose messenger he perceived himself to be. In God, the Prophet Muhammad recognized the divine creator of the universe and humanity as well as the final judge of all human beings on the Day of Judgment, which would bring this world to its end in an apocalyptic cataclysm. On that final day, all human beings would be raised in the general resurrection to account for their lives on Earth and enter into everlasting life in the world to come. The life offered in the hereafter would be either God's reward of eternal bliss in paradise for those who had surrendered to His will in this world, obeying His commandments and putting them into practice, or His punishment of never-ending suffering in hellfire for those who had acted against His will by violating the divine commands and interdictions.

For some ten-odd years, Muhammad tried to convert his fellow tribesmen at Mecca to his newly found faith of Islam. Rejected by the majority of the Quraysh, however, he took flight from Mecca with a small group of followers, becoming a tribal dissident who breached the bonds of common descent with his clan, and, in 622, immigrated to Medina, situated about 200 miles to the north. Medina was a cluster of fortresses and compounds scattered over a large area. It was known as Yathrib at the time, but it later came to be called "the city of the Prophet" (*madīnat al-nabī*) after Muhammad had settled there. Medina was an agricultural settlement inhabited by two major Arab tribes and three smaller Jewish tribes that had assimilated to the Arab way of life and its customs, adopting the Arabic language but not the beliefs of the pre-Islamic Arab tribal religion. Medina offered the emigrants (*muhājirūn*) the livelihood of its fields, palm groves, and orchards and extended to them the welcome of the helpers (*anṣār*), a group of Medinan Arabs who accepted Islam and became brothers in faith with the emigrants. Muhammad's emigration, known as the hijra and occurring in September 622, became the moment in history in which the small Muslim community of Medina was launched on its meteoric rise; by the time of Muhammad's death, it had established its hold over the entire Arabian Peninsula. In the centuries after his death, both the religion and the empire of Islam spread over the Middle East, advancing westward along the North African shores of the Mediterranean into Spain and Sicily and pushing eastward across the Iranian plateau into Central Asia and the Indian subcontinent. The first day of the lunar year in which the hijra took place came to mark the beginning of the Muslim era, and the Muslim calendar reckons its own lunar calendar from this year.

Muhammad's time at Medina was characterized by a struggle for preeminence vis-à-vis the Meccan leadership of the Quraysh; his success in Medina represented a threat both to their authority and to their caravan trade that passed Medina on its route to Syria and Palestine. It also drew him into serious confrontations with the Jewish tribes of Medina, whose memory of their religious legacy was at variance with Muhammad's proclamation of events surrounding major biblical figures, such as Abraham and Moses. In addition, Muhammad faced the challenge of providing leadership for his Meccan emigrants and Medinan helpers while arbitrating issues between the two Arab tribes (the Aws and Khazraj and their clients) who had emerged exhausted after a long history of fraternal feuds and their ensuing blood revenge and adjudication of blood money. Especially in the first few years at Medina, Muhammad had to deal with the "waverers" (*munāfiqūn*): those Medinan Arabs on whose loyalty and zeal he could not rely and whom it took time to convert. Furthermore, he had to find a means of channeling the tribal raiding tradition of the Arab clansmen away from fraternal warfare and into the constructive building of a community.

At the end of his life in 632 in Medina, Muhammad was able to claim three major achievements: the foundation of the Muslim community (*umma*), the proclamation of the Arabic scripture (Qur'an), and the dynamism of the "struggle on the path of God" (jihad). For the first time in history, he had united all the Arabs living in the Arabian Peninsula into one *umma* based no longer on the tribal principle of blood kinship and descent from a common ancestor but rather on the religious basis of a common faith expressed in the Muslim profession of faith (*shahāda*) that "there is no god but Allah and Muhammad is his messenger." This achievement resembled a social revolution because it transformed Arab society from an unwieldy conglomeration of rivaling kinship groups into an ordered whole of individuals united by a common bond of faith. Rather than resting in the hands of freely elected tribal elders (shaykhs), community leadership rested thenceforth in the divinely chosen messenger (*rasūl*), to whom all owed obedience next to God. For the first time in history, Muhammad had given the Arabs a scripture in their own language that would remain the basis of their faith throughout the ages. It signified a religious revolution that uprooted the polytheistic beliefs and cultic practices of the pre-Islamic Arabs and substituted for them a strong monotheistic faith. The proclamations of this faith in the one God, understood as divine revelation, were written down and collected about two decades after the Prophet's death in the first Arabic book ever produced: the holy writ of the Qur'an. From now on, each Arab was charged to surrender to God alone and to justify his actions before God rather than seeking protection as a clan member and living in submission to the customs of his forefathers and tribal ancestors. For the first time in history, the tribal energy of the Arab clansmen, spent in the past on nomadic raids or tribal blood feuds, became directed toward the common goal of building a coordinated polity. This polity was to be driven by jihad, which marshaled all means, whether peaceful or militant, available to the members of the community. Jihad became the engine that, through conquest, empowered the Arabs to establish a global empire and, through proselytization, propelled Islam in its missionary thrust toward its goal of a universal religion.

Muhammad's Life from ca. 570 to 610

Western scholarship has studied the life of the Prophet assiduously and meticulously, beginning in earnest in the 19th century with F. Wüstenfeld and J. Wellhausen. The harvest of scholarship since then on the biography of the Prophet has been synthesized in two standard works: the one-volume masterpiece of F. Buhl, *Das Leben Muhammeds* (1934), and the two-volume set of W. M. Watt, *Muhammad at Mecca* (1953) and *Muhammad at Medina* (1956). Many studies, monographs, and articles have been added since World War II, but none has produced a radically new analysis that would change the basic assessment of Muhammad's achievements or alter the historical development of his career. Western scholarship is ultimately based on the principal work of the traditional Islamic biography of the

Prophet, known as his "way of life" (*sīra*). This work of Ibn Ishaq (704–767), the famous *Sirat Rasul Allah* (Life of God's Messenger), is extant in the recension by Ibn Hisham (d. 833). Compiled more than a century after Muhammad's death, it portrayed the Prophet as a revered figure and the glorified founder of the religion. Other early Islamic works that include important information on the Prophet's life are those on his "campaigns" (*maghāzī*), such as the one by Waqidi (d. 823), as well as the history of Tabari (d. 923), which includes the valuable reports of 'Urwa b. al-Zubayr (d. 712). The Qur'an itself offers limited historical data for the construction of Muhammad's biography. On the whole, the traditional biographical literature on Muhammad neglects the early phase of his life, focusing instead on his career as a prophet, which began with his call to proclaim the Qur'an in about 610. For the early period (ca. 570–610), only a small number of historical facts were recorded, such as those concerning his humble origins, his early career as a merchant, and his marriage to a widow in Mecca.

Muhammad was born into the family of the Banu Hashim, one of the clans of the Quraysh tribe. That his birth occurred in the "Year of the Elephant" (Q. 105:1–5), when Mecca was unsuccessfully threatened by a group of Abyssinian invaders, is not based on a reliable tradition. Because his name, Muhammad (worthy of praise), can be understood as an Arabic epithet, some scholars doubt whether this actually was his given name; yet it is the name by which he is mentioned four times in the Qur'an (3:144; 33:40; 47:2; 48:29) without, however, being addressed by it directly. In general, Islamic literature addresses him by his Qur'anic titles—"the Prophet" (*al-nabī*) and "God's Messenger" (*rasūl Allāh*)—and frequently calls him "the Chosen One" (*al-muṣṭafā*) and honors him with the eulogies such as "peace be upon him" and "may God bless him and grant him salvation" after his name, while Muslim mystics tend to revere him as "the beloved of God" (*ḥabīb Allāh*). Muhammad grew up in poverty as an orphan, his father, 'Abdallah, having died before his birth. Raised by his mother, Amina, and looked after by his grandfather, 'Abd al-Muttalib, he may have spent a year with a wet nurse among the nomads. His mother died when he was six years old, and his grandfather died two years later. After passing into the custodianship of his uncle Abu Talib, the young boy showed an interest in the life of a trader and merchant, possibly making a trade journey to Syria while still a young man. Noticed for his business skills by Khadija, a well-to-do merchant's widow who was twice married before and possibly divorced, Muhammad became an agent in her employ. According to tradition, Khadija was 40 years old when she proposed marriage to him, and Muhammad was about 25 years of age. They had four daughters, who later were given in marriage to some of Muhammad's Companions, and several sons, all of whom died in infancy.

The legendary stories that Muhammad's breast was cleansed by angels shortly after his birth and that, in his youth, Muhammad placed the Black Stone in the wall of the Ka'ba during its reconstruction, thereby solving a squabble of the tribal elders of Mecca for the privilege of doing so, are later creations of tradition to signify immunity from sin and leadership qualities already manifested by Muhammad as a youth. Equally doubtful are encounters in his youth with a Christian monk, named either Bahira or Nastur, who is presented as prophesying Muhammad's later career. In his early life, Muhammad proved his mettle as a merchant, and he used a good portion of commercial vocabulary in his Qur'anic proclamations. He proved to be a responsible father, an energetic member of his clan, and a sound and capable person; this is in contrast to many discrediting assessments of his personality in European accounts from medieval times until today. Unfortunately, the traditional biographical literature tells us little about the provenance of the religious ideas Muhammad acquired during his early life. These ideas came from two principal sources: on the one hand from the religious environment into which he was born, the tribal Arab cult of pre-Islamic Arabia with its fatalistic notions and pagan practices that were observed in his hometown, and on the other hand from a medley of mainly Christian sectarian beliefs, certain Jewish practices, and some Manichean notions that he encountered during his youth in Mecca.

In Islamic historiography, the epoch of Arabia prior to the promulgation of Islam is generally called the age of "ignorance" (*jāhiliyya*), against which Islam is contrasted as the age of enlightenment and knowledge. The *jāhiliyya* was a time when the Arabs were known for their virtues of courage and bravery, their generosity and hospitality, their excesses in eating and drinking, their drinking songs and love poetry, their worship of idols and stone cults, and their beliefs in a variety of local and tribal deities, both male and female. Muhammad grew up in this environment of the *jāhiliyya*, as indicated by some scattered references in the Qur'an: he was found erring (93:3), did not know scripture and belief (42:52), offered animal sacrifices to deities (cf. 108:2), once brought a sheep as a sacrifice to the female deity al-'Uzza, and believed in spirits (*jinn*) and demons (*shayāṭīn*). His uncle Abu Lahab, cursed in the Qur'an (111:1), was a violent defender of paganism, and his uncle and tribal protector Abu Talib never embraced Islam. Furthermore, Muhammad's early Qur'anic proclamations were expressed in cryptic rhymed prose that resembled the oracles of the pre-Islamic soothsayers (*kāhin*). To assert their truth, he would introduce them with oaths, swearing by natural phenomena, such as the heavens and the Earth, the sky and the constellations, the sun and the moon, the stars and the planets, the dawn and the forenoon, or the fig tree and the olive tree.

Muhammad speaks of the Jews and Christians with whom he came into contact cumulatively as "possessors of the scripture" (*ahl al-kitāb*) without specific reference to their religious differences. It is possible that the occasional reference to Sabians in the Qur'an (*Ṣābi'ūn*, 2:62; 5:69; 22:17) implies contact with Manicheans as well. The biblical lore of Jews and Christians made an overpowering impact on Muhammad; he firmly believed that his revelations agreed with the content of their original scriptures, and on occasion he asked them for clarification of his newly found ideas (Q. 10:94). In our present state of research, it is impossible to pinpoint the sources from the Jewish-Christian background that Muhammad may have had for his religious ideas. It is certain, however, that he received his knowledge by oral information and that he had not read the scriptures of Jews and Christians. In his time, the Bible had not yet been translated into Arabic, and Muhammad was unable to read either Hebrew or Greek. In fact, only one verse of the Bible (Psalms 37:29) is quoted verbatim in the Qur'an (21:105). As a merchant he may have had a rudimentary knowledge of Arabic writing and record keeping, though it is a general Muslim perception that he was illiterate (*ummī*—a term that in the Qur'an means not "illiterate" but rather denotes Muhammad as "the heathen prophet," *al-nabī al-ummī*; 7:157–58).

Most of the biblical lore included in the Qur'anic proclamations shows similarities with the Book of Genesis and signals midrashic or apocryphal origin. In the case of Christianity, it points to sectarian rather than normative and orthodox beliefs and possibly includes some traces of Manichean ideas. The significant number of Syriac and Ethiopic loan words in the Qur'an further document that Muhammad not only assimilated elements of biblical and extra-biblical lore but also absorbed some foreign ritual vocabulary. Furthermore, the Qur'an retains traces that reveal Muhammad's rather distinct knowledge of circumstances linked with Mount Sinai, its monastery, and the tradition of the burning bush (28:29–30, 44–46; 52:1–6; 95:2). It also shows some familiarity on his part with Christian prayer practices and some awareness of the lives of Christian hermits. There is not sufficient evidence, however, to link Muhammad with particular Christian monks as his teachers. In general, all information about Christian themes and topics came to him by word of mouth, probably through contact with Christian traders or slaves in Mecca itself. Some scholars refer to accounts in Muslim tradition that signal Waraqa b. Nawfal, a cousin of his wife Khadija, as a possible channel of Christian ideas for Muhammad. Most of these accounts, however, treat him as one of the *ḥanīf*s, or seekers of a pure worship of God, who were dissatisfied with idol worship and inspired by an innate monotheistic belief. It should not be overlooked, however, that pre-Islamic Arabia was exposed on its borders to Christian beliefs. There were Christians living in Najran in Yemen in the south of the Arabian Peninsula, and Arab principalities had formed on the northern fringes of the Arabian desert: these included the Ghassanids, who adhered to a Monophysite creed, and the Lakhmids, who had adopted Nestorian beliefs.

Muhammad's Career in Mecca from ca. 610 to 622

In about 610 Muhammad began to proclaim his message at a decisive moment of his life when he suddenly broke through to the unshakeable conviction that he had to proclaim to the people of Mecca the inner promptings he received as the word of God. Muslim tradition places this event—"his call to prophecy"—in a cave on a mountain outside Mecca, when he was impelled to recite, "Recite in the name of your Lord who created . . ." (Q. 96:1–5). Tradition describes him as experiencing states of spiritual excitement and ecstatic seizures; at times he asked to be wrapped (Q. 73:1; 74:1) in a mantle, and his cryptic speech resembled the words of a magician (*sāḥir*) possessed by demonic forces (*majnūn*). According to tradition, he hesitated for an "interval" (*fatra*) of three years before he came forward publicly with his message, but then he continued fearlessly persevering in proclaiming it until his death. When explaining his revelations, Muhammad conceived of them as originating from an archetypal book (*umm al-kitāb*, Q. 43:3), a guarded tablet (*lawḥ mahfūz*, Q. 85:22), kept in the presence of the angels, its noble scribes (Q. 80,15–16). Rather than reading this heavenly book, Muhammad received from it individual revelations of a few verses at a time, orally communicated to him by a spirit of revelation later identified as the angel Gabriel (Q. 2:97).

The content of his proclamations was focused on praise for God the Creator and the warnings of God the Judge, the one and only God, Allah. Muhammad saw himself as both a "warner" (*nadhīr*) of an apocalyptic end of the world followed by an eschatological punishment for unbelievers and a "bringer of good tidings" (*bashīr*) about God as the bountiful creator of the heavens and the Earth as well as the fashioner of each and every human being. His most prominent role was that of a prophet who proclaimed an uncompromising monotheism centered on God who had neither partners nor associates. He singled out the prophets of old as prototypical recipients of revelation in history and referred to them by their biblical names in Arabic, such as Nuh (Noah), Ibrahim (Abraham), and Musa (Moses), as well as certain heroes of pre-Islamic Arab lore. He made no reference, however, to any of the great prophets of the Bible, such as Isaiah, Jeremiah, or Ezekiel, yet he mentioned central figures of the gospels, such as Yahya (John the Baptist) and 'Isa b. Maryam (Jesus, son of Mary), the Messiah (*masīḥ*); he saw himself standing in line with these prophets of old as their final representative, the "seal of the prophets."

At first, Muhammad's proclamations were given little attention by most Meccans. They made an impact, however, on a small group who became his followers, honored in history as the first Muslim converts. Among them were his wife Khadija; his cousin 'Ali, a youth at the time; the well-to-do merchant Abu Bakr, who adhered to him with unswerving loyalty; as well as a handful of young men who would later play a significant role in the succession struggles to Muhammad's leadership of the community. One early convert to Islam, perhaps the first, was Zayd b. Haritha, a slave bought in Syria and given by Khadija to Muhammad, who freed and adopted him. Ten years younger than Muhammad, he hailed from the region of Dumat al-Jandal, an oasis halfway between Mecca and Damascus, where the idol Wadd was worshipped and a considerable Christian colony had found shelter. Until his death in 629 as standard bearer of the Muslim forces on an unsuccessful expedition at Mu'ta against Arabs on Byzantine soil in Transjordan, Zayd b. Haritha remained very close to the Prophet; his extreme solicitude for Muhammad may be seen in the fact that he divorced his wife Zaynab a few years after the hijra so that the Prophet might marry her.

The Meccans stiffened in their opposition to Muhammad's revelations when they realized that his message attacked their tribal religion and its polytheistic pantheon, threatening their authority and trade by challenging their tribal oligarchy and endangering their fairs. When their opposition turned into persecution, Muhammad sent a group of weaker followers away to seek the protection of the Christian ruler of Abyssinia in a migration (hijra), which occurred about 615 (most of these emigrants drifted back later to rejoin their Muslim brethren). In Mecca itself, Muhammad tried to gain the goodwill of the Meccans by accepting as special intercessors with God their three favorite female deities, whom they worshipped as "daughters of Allah." These three goddesses were al-Lat, a solar deity, who had her sanctuary in a valley near Tai'f, a neighboring town of Mecca; al-'Uzza, an astral deity, to whom animal sacrifices were made at her sanctuary in an acacia grove located in a valley on the road from Mecca to Tai'f; and Manat, the goddess of fate and death, whose sanctuary was a Black Stone on the road from Mecca to Medina. Realizing that the recognition of "daughters of Allah" harmed his radically monotheistic message, Muhammad withdrew this compromise and abrogated it by altering the relevant verses included in the Qur'an (53:19–23). The most trying hostile scheme of Muhammad's Meccan adversaries, however, occurred about 616, when the tribesmen of the Quraysh engaged in a full tribal boycott of the Banu Hashim, Muhammad's clan. Although most of the Banu Hashim, including his custodian Abu Talib, had not accepted Islam, the clan stood by Muhammad in loyalty to their tribal code of honor and protected him during this difficult period. Only his uncle Abu Lahab, together with his wife, remained resolute in his hostility toward Muhammad (Q. 111:1). This boycott failed, however, because it proved to be more of a disruption to the communal life in Mecca than a successful step to silence Muhammad.

Most scholars place Muhammad's vision of a miraculous night journey (isrā') in the later period of his life at Mecca. According to the legend, Muhammad was carried by a flying steed in the company of the angel Gabriel from the sacred area of the Ka'ba to the "farthest place of worship" (Q. 17:1), interpreted as either the temple precinct in Jerusalem or the place of prayer of the angels in heaven. Furthermore, Muslim tradition links the nocturnal journey with Muhammad's ascension to heaven (mi'rāj). This heavenly ascent, seen as initiation to his prophetic career, would need to be placed at the beginning of his Qur'anic proclamations. Though connected with a vision recorded in the Qur'an (53:1–18; 81:19–25) in which Muhammad is approached by a heavenly figure rather than being carried off, this would seem to refer to a separate experience. The interpretation of the Prophet's ascension to heaven as an ascent through the seven heavens into the very presence of God, with Muhammad passing beyond the spheres of other prophets (among them Adam, Jesus, Abraham, and Moses), is a further elaboration of Muslim tradition. According to the legend, Muhammad began his heavenly ascent from the rock in Jerusalem, which became associated with the Dome of the Rock, the symbol of Islam's triumph over Judaism and Christianity, erected in about 694 by the Umayyad caliph 'Abd al-Malik on the temple precinct of Jerusalem and opposite the hill crowned by the Church of the Holy Sepulcher.

Certain significant events occurred during the last third of Muhammad's prophetic activity in Mecca. In about 618, 'Umar b. al-Khattab, a young man of a certain social status, converted to Muhammad's cause and became one of his strongest supporters as well as the founder of the Arab Empire about a decade after Muhammad's death. 'Umar's joining of the Muslims in Mecca, however, was followed in the next year by the deaths of Khadija and Abu Talib, resulting in a loss of both deep personal and strong tribal support. Exhausted and discouraged by the obstinate opposition of the Meccans to his reforms and unsuccessful in his initiative to find a welcoming audience for his proclamations in Tai'f, Muhammad came to despair of converting his fellow townsmen, convinced that God had destined them to unbelief. At this point in time, he realized that he had to cut the blood bonds with his tribe and find a new theater for his message to be accepted. At this juncture, something happened that was beyond his control.

The settlement of Medina had reached an impasse in its communal life due to tribal warfare and bloodshed between the Aws and Khazraj, the two major Arab tribes living in the town together with three smaller Jewish tribes that were drawn into the altercations. Because of this predicament, the inhabitants of Medina were looking for a political leader who could arbitrate their tribal conflicts. Muhammad, for his part, was looking for a new environment that would be receptive to his teachings. Medina answered this need. It had been prepared for a monotheistic message and the vision of a history of prophets through the presence of the three Jewish tribes—the Banu Qaynuqa', Banu al-Nadir, and Banu Qurayza—who had settled in the town before the arrival of the Aws and Khazraj. At the same time, it offered Muhammad a platform to combine his role as a prophetical reformer with that of a political leader. It so happened that some peasants from Medina, who had come as pilgrims to Mecca, saw Muhammad as the person who could provide the solution to their communal strife. Muhammad found willing listeners for his message among them, and in 621, he met about a dozen of them on the hill 'Aqaba outside Mecca. A year later, a formal pledge was made at the same place between him and a group of 73 men and 2 women from Medina that they would receive him and his followers as brethren into their community and offer them their tribal protection by the force of arms if necessary. On the basis of this "pledge of war" (*bay'at al-ḥarb*), Muhammad had successive groups of his followers leave Mecca for Medina and then finally left the town himself with Abu Bakr and 'Ali, hiding in a cave, according to tradition, as the Meccans were in pursuit. The Meccans failed in their attempt to prevent Muhammad's group of fugitive dissidents from forming a new polity allied with other tribal groups in the neighboring town of Medina.

Muhammad's Career in Medina from 622 to 632

The emigration from Mecca to Medina in 622, known as the hijra, was to become a key historical event, marking as it did the decisive moment Muhammad became an exemplary political leader. Muhammad integrated the people of Medina into one cohesive community by subsuming the Arab tribal elements into his community and by eventually eliminating the Jewish tribes altogether from the town. With re-gard to the Arabs, Muhammad could rely on two groups: the *muhājirūn*, who were firmly identified with his message and had given up their livelihood and left their homes, and the *anṣār*, the group of tribesmen (mainly belonging to the Khazraj but some also to the Aws), who welcomed him and his followers into their midst and accepted Islam wholeheartedly. Henceforth the Muslim community of believers, established by and loyal to Muhammad, would be founded on these two groups who acquired rights of kinship with one another rooted not in common blood but rather in common faith. Many people of Medina, however, remained noncommit-tal toward Muhammad and as such were identified as "hypocrites" (*munāfiqūn*), turncoats on whose loyalty Muhammad could not rely, and "waverers," who irritated him because of their reluctant support and persistent doubt about his message. They were led by 'Abdallah b. Ubayy, a rather irresolute leader of the Khazraj who did not manage to organize them into an opposition to Muhammad; he did, however, incite the three smaller Jewish tribes to resist Muhammad but left them in the lurch when it came to blows.

It is not known whether the three Jewish tribes living in Medina, each of them about 500 to 800 men, were descendants from Hebrew stock or Arabs who had adopted Judaism. They spoke Arabic, lived according to Arab customs, and were or-ganized as tribal units but held to basic religious principles and practices of Judaism. Muhammad called the Jews (*yahūd*) "children of Israel," knew that they followed the laws of Moses, and was aware that they had their own scripture (called Tawrat in the Qur'an) and the psalms of David (called Zabur). Among the Jewish tribes that settled in Medina, the Banu Qaynuqa' lived in two strongholds in the southwest of the town, becoming clients of the Khazraj; as they did not possess any lands, they made their livelihood by trading. Muhammad perceived them as a challenge to his message, obstructing his way with their religious claims and mockeries of his person. He would eventually expel them from Medina after the Battle of Badr in 624, de-manding that their arms and tools be left behind for the Muslims and taking a fifth of the spoils for himself. The Banu al-Nadir, believed to have come from Palestine at an unknown date, had connections with the Jews of the oasis of Khaybar and probably had an admixture of Arab blood in their veins. Though they bore Arabic names, they spoke their own peculiar dialect and lived in fortified compounds half a day's journey to the south of Medina. They were clients of the Aws and entered into alliance with Muhammad in the first year after the hijra. Muhammad, however, became suspicious of them and feared that they intended to kill him. Laying siege on them and cutting down their palm trees, he forced them to surrender and made them leave with their possessions to the oasis of Khaybar and Syria; he gave their lands to the emigrants and kept part of them for himself. The Banu Qurayza, related to the Banu al-Nadir, lived as agriculturalists of cereals and palms on lands out-side the city to the southeast of Medina. They were known to have adhered firmly to Jewish traditions and had intermarried with Arabs, becoming allied with the Aws. After the Battle of the Trench (*khandaq*) in 627, they were made to surrender unconditionally; the men were put to the sword and their women and children sold as slaves. It remains a mystery why the Jewish tribes did not rally together to prevent their expulsion from Medina.

In Medina, facing the task of creating a united community—bringing together emigrants and helpers, overcoming the reluctance of the "waverers," and dealing with the Jewish tribes—Muhammad displayed considerable political acumen. After establishing a link of brotherhood between the emigrants and helpers, he realized that he needed a practical mechanism to form a true unity of highly different and incongruous elements of the Medinan society. He pursued this end soon after the hijra by promulgating a document, recorded in his biography, known as the "Constitution of Medina" (*ṣaḥīfat al-Madīna*); it may be considered authentic. This legal document drafted on Muhammad's initiative had two sections: the first defining the duties of the believers (*mu'minūn*), including both emigrants and helpers from various clans of the Aws and Khazraj, and the second guaranteeing the rights of the *yahūd* and their clients. It was a significant document of brotherly solidarity that formed the foundation for the communal life of the *umma*, now no longer based on the traditional tribal system of blood kinship groups. Indeed, it broke up the tribal system of Medina by severing links of some of its tribesmen, based on common blood, and bonded the helpers with the emigrants who belonged to the Quraysh, a separate blood kinship group. From now on, this new political order of society would make a radical distinction between those loyal to Muhammad and those who did not follow him. As a consequence, it fortified Muhammad's position as the highest authority, next to God, of the newly established community and demonstrated the eminent practical sense of purpose with which he established himself as the political leader of the new polity in Medina.

When Muhammad arrived in Medina, he came with the firm conviction of his status as the bearer of a revelation in Arabic that confirmed the revelations "the possessors of the scriptures" had received in their own languages. In this spirit he tried to win over the local Jews by adopting their fast on the day of atonement (*'āshūrā'*), introducing the midday prayer (*al-ṣalāt al-wusṭā*, Q. 2:238) in emulation of Jewish custom, easing the rules of ablutions before prayer, and maintaining the direction (*qibla*) of the ritual prayer (salat) toward Jerusalem. He soon realized, however, that he misjudged their openness to his message when they ridiculed his version of biblical stories due to discrepancies with their own traditional lore. In a religious sense, it was not possible for the Jewish tribes of Medina to welcome an Arab as their promised Messiah or accept Muhammad's claim to be "the seal of the prophets" (*khātam al-nabiyyīn*, Q. 33:40)—a title Mani (216–77), the founder of Manicheanism, had applied to himself—and whose coming Jesus is said to have predicted in the Qur'an under the name of Ahmad (Q. 61:6). Faced with overwhelming rejection from the Jews, Muhammad abruptly reoriented his religion, transforming it into an Arab religion focused on the sanctuary of the Black Stone in Mecca and dismissing the existing Jewish and Christian scriptures as a corruption of their original revealed form. He ordered that the direction of ritual prayer be changed toward the Ka'ba, making Mecca the hub of the true religion (Q. 2:144). He stressed Friday as the day of congregational prayer (Q. 62:9) yet not as a day of rest like the Sabbath because, in his view, God did not rest after his work of creation. Substituting for the fast on *'āshūrā'*, he instituted, following Manichean custom, the lunar month of Ramadan (Q. 2:183–85) as a month of fasting from daybreak until sunset requiring abstention from food, drink, and sexual intercourse during daylight hours. He introduced what was to become an essential element of the Muslim pilgrimage (hajj) by celebrating the day of sacrifice on the tenth day of the month of pilgrimage (Dhu al-Hijja) in Medina, and most of all, he identified Islam as a restoration of the primordial religion of Abraham (*millat Ibrāhīm*). Abraham, neither a Jew nor a Christian, thus became the prototype of the true Muslim and *ḥanīf*, the monotheist who had rejected all pagan polytheism. He now maintained that Abraham, assisted by his son Isma'il, had erected the Ka'ba (Q. 2:127) and celebrated the rites there that Muhammad sought to restore to their original purity.

Distancing himself somewhat from his identity as a prophet called to warn people of an oncoming apocalyptic judgment and to confirm the revelations other groups of people had received in their own languages before him, Muhammad now embraced his new role as legislator and leader of the burgeoning Muslim community. It now became the duty of his followers to obey God and the Prophet. He pursued his newfound role not only in Medina but also in his relations with the Meccans, who constituted the major challenge he faced outside Medina. With Mecca as the focus of his religious thrust and with the responsibility of providing sustenance for his group of emigrants, Muhammad turned his attention to Mecca and focused the energies of the Arab tribesmen who were accustomed to raiding. His altercations with the Meccans, developing from skirmishes to full-fledged war, were driven by the idea of jihad, the all-out struggle on the path of God that demanded the total devotion of his Muslim followers such that they would go to war against the Quraysh of Mecca.

A new chapter began in the life of Muhammad and that of his community with a sequence of battles with the Meccans. A first instance of war was triggered by a raid made by some of Muhammad's followers on a caravan at the oasis of Nakhla. In it a Meccan was killed during the holy month of Rajab, in which raiding was forbidden by current pre-Islamic custom, and the spoils of his operations were taken to Medina. Emboldened by this success, Muhammad led a group of his Medinan followers in a new raid on a caravan of the Quraysh that was advancing from Syria to Mecca. In their attempt to ambush the caravan at Badr in 624, Muhammad's small contingent was forced to engage an army sent from Mecca to protect the caravan (Q. 3:123); surprisingly, however, they succeeded in routing the superior enemy, whose leader Abu Jahl was slain. Muhammad interpreted his glorious victory as divine confirmation of his religion and believed that angels fought at his side, enabling him to overpower the forces of the mighty commercial hub of Arabia. Islamic historiography upholds this day as a great watershed in the course of Muslim ascendancy as granted by divine assistance. To follow up on his victory, Muhammad not only expelled the Banu Qaynuqa' but, more importantly, sent letters to Bedouin tribes to contract alliances of mutual assistance with them, now recognized as a leader well beyond the confines of Medina. Trying to avenge their losses at Badr, the Meccans equipped an army of 3,000 men and sent them against Muhammad's forces in 625 under the leadership of Abu Sufyan, defeating them decisively at the hill of Uhud outside Medina (Q. 3:118, 121; 33:23). In this battle Muhammad was severely wounded and his uncle Hamza was killed. The Meccans, however, did not follow up on their victory and returned home thinking that they had put the upstart in Medina in his place; for his part, Muhammad expelled the Banu al-Nadir from the town and confiscated their possessions in order to replace the spoils his force had failed to secure in the battle.

Further harassed by Muhammad's raiders and realizing that their assessment of their victory at Uhud was premature, the Meccans assembled a force of Quraysh and tribesmen from the surrounding areas, specified as 10,000 men in the tradition, to advance against Medina in 627. Whether or not this was at the suggestion of a Persian by the name of Salman, Muhammad had a trench (*khandaq*) dug around the unprotected parts of Medina, which caused a long siege to drag on and gave Muhammad time to plot against the besieging force, who eventually lost heart and returned home without ever engaging in open battle. In the aftermath of the "Battle of the Trench," Muhammad felt free to deal harshly with the Banu Qurayza, executing their men and selling their women and children into slavery.

Still intent on bringing Mecca under his control, Muhammad called on a group of his followers in 628 to accompany him on a peaceful pilgrimage (*'umra*) to the Ka'ba in Mecca; in the process he tried to negotiate his way into the town. He encamped with his group at Hudaybiyya and sent 'Uthman b. 'Affan, who was related to the Meccan leadership, ahead to make arrangements for their peaceful passage. When 'Uthman did not return at first, Muhammad had his men swear an oath that they would fight for him to the last. This proved to be unnecessary when the Meccans offered the compromise proposal of a ten-year truce that would allow Muhammad to visit the town for a pilgrimage in the following year. Muhammad accepted this proposal, but his followers were disappointed by this apparent about-face, though history would later call it a stroke of brilliance on Muhammad's part to induce the Meccans to recognize a tribal dissident as an opponent of equal rank.

Muhammad made use of the lull in the struggle with the Meccans to capture the oasis of Khaybar in 628 and constrained its Jewish inhabitants to pay taxes every year. However, the tradition that holds that, in the same year, Muhammad began to send letters to the governor of Alexandria, the ruler of Abyssinia, the Byzantine emperor, and the Persian king, inviting them to adopt Islam, cannot be trusted. More certain is his dispatching of letters to chiefs of Bedouin tribes in different parts of Arabia, demanding that they join the fold of Islam, perform the ritual prayer, and pay the alms tax (zakat) incumbent on every Muslim. In the following year, 629, Muhammad performed the pilgrimage to the Ka'ba as agreed and welcomed Khalid b. al-Walid, later a great general of the Muslim conquests, into Islam. Khalid b. al-Walid proved his mettle soon thereafter in 630 when he subdued the inhabitants of Dumat al-Jandal and forced their leader to come to Medina to sign a treaty with Muhammad. Then in the Battle of 'Aqraba' in 632, Khalid b. al-Walid crushed the apostasy of the tribes after the Prophet's death and defeated Musaylima b. Thumama, the leader of the Banu Hanifa, who inhabited the oasis of Yamama in central Arabia. Musaylima rivaled Muhammad with his claim to be a prophet and to receive revelations from God the Merciful (al-Raḥmān). He aspired to be Muhammad's successor after his death, but when both of them met in Medina, the Prophet had him summarily dismissed, refusing to give him "even a splinter of a palm branch."

Using the pretext of a conflict that led to bloodshed between two tribal bands—one affiliated with him, the other with the Quraysh—Muhammad broke the ten-year truce of Hudaybiyya and set out to conquer Mecca at the head of an army of emigrants, helpers, and Bedouin tribesmen. They were met in the field by Abu Sufyan, the leader of the Quraysh, who accepted Muhammad's terms and received lavish gifts for himself and other chiefs of the Quraysh. The town of Mecca was opened to Muhammad's forces, and its inhabitants nominally adopted Islam en masse; the idols were destroyed and some poets who had ridiculed Muhammad were executed. In 630, then, Muhammad achieved his ultimate victory, the conquest of Mecca, and was able to defeat a remaining hostile alliance of Bedouin tribes from central Arabia at Hunayn, after which the town of Ta'if was opened to him as well. Muhammad sent letters to various tribes, demanding that they adopt Islam and pay tribute, and he received their embassies in Medina. However, there were some signs of inner division among the Muslims, caused by a rival "mosque of dissension" (masjid al-ḍirār, Q. 9:108–9) where Muhammad, in his early years at Medina, used to perform a ritual prayer on the Sabbath. In fact, this mosque was the first established in Medina, founded by the exiled Abu 'Amir, "the monk" (al-rāhib), of the clan 'Amr b. 'Awf, who lived in the compounds at Quba' in the southern part of the town. The unrest did not prevent Muhammad, however, from setting out in 630 on an expedition to Tabuk on the northern border of Arabia, where he received some petty Christian rulers and Jewish towns into Islam. New converts from tribes all over Arabia formally entered Islam—many out of fear, others more nominally than fervently—in hope of material and political advantages.

It is not fully clear to what extent Muhammad perceived his message to be a local or a universal one. At the beginning of his mission he directed his message primarily toward the people of Mecca (qawm), just as the prophets of old spoke to their own people, but he also addressed all of humanity (al-nās, al-'ālamūn) without confining his audience to a specific group. The expeditions to Mu'ta and Tabuk across the northern borders of the Arabian Peninsula in the latter years of his career may indicate a shift in his consciousness toward a more universal applicability of his message. In addition, Muhammad sent letters from Medina to numerous Arab tribes in the desert demanding their conversion and received tribal delegations in Medina from all over Arabia in the last years of his life. They pledged their allegiance to his cause, a phase described by the Qur'an as being characterized by "men entering God's religion in throngs" (Q. 110:2). The actual spread of Islam beyond the confines of Arabia, however, did not occur during Muhammad's lifetime but would come about with astonishing rapidity during the age of the Muslim conquests that began shortly after his death. In 631, Muhammad sent Abu Bakr to Mecca to read a declaration of "exemption" (*barā'a*) from the hajj that excluded all pagans from performing it. Then, in 632, at the climax of his career, Muhammad performed his "Farewell Pilgrimage"—referred to in the Qur'an with the words "Today I have perfected your religion" (Q. 5:3)—that reformed some of the pagan rites and became the standard of the pilgrimage until today. On his way back to Medina from the pilgrimage, Muhammad had stopped at the watering place of Ghadir Khumm and, taking 'Ali b. Abi Talib by his hand, apparently signaled him to be his successor as leader of the Muslim community with the cryptic words, "For whomever I am the patron (*mawlā*), 'Ali is also his patron." A few months later, Muhammad died in Medina after a short fever in the lap of his beloved wife 'A'isha on June 8, 632, a day that according to tradition saw an eclipse of the sun.

Throughout history all factions within Islam have maintained that prophecy, in the sense of the proclamation of a sacred scripture, had come to an end for all times with Muhammad's demise. In political terms, however, an intense struggle for succession began immediately during the preparations for his burial. Abu Bakr, 'A'isha's father and an early Meccan convert, managed to secure the leadership, backed by the majority of the clans of the Quraysh, who acclaimed him as Muhammad's successor (*khalīfa*, or caliph) at the Portico of the Banu Sa'ida. 'Ali, Muhammad's cousin, son-in-law, hero of many battles, and a man of great merits, was pushed aside despite his legitimate claim to being Muhammad's successor as champion of the family of the Prophet (*ahl al-bayt*) and leader of the Banu Hashim. A major bone of contention was that, during Muhammad's career at Medina, his family was assigned a certain religious privilege that entitled Muhammad and his kin to a fifth (*khums*) of the war booty as well as property (*fay'*) that came into possession of the community by means other than war. Upon his accession to leadership, Abu Bakr stripped the family of the Prophet of this entitlement and transferred it to the clans of the Quraysh, thereby solidifying their support for his caliphate (632–34). In this succession struggle lie the roots of the primary Islamic schism between the majority Sunnis and the minority Shi'is, the party of 'Ali (Shi'at 'Ali). In its origin, the ultimate issue driving the schism was political and material rather than religious and spiritual; in the history of the ideological development of orthodoxy and heterodoxy in Islam, however, it took on theological dimensions.

Muhammad as a Political Leader

That one man could achieve so much in such a short time is astounding. Muhammad can truly claim the status of one of humanity's greatest founders of religion who made a global impact over more than a millennium and whose cause continues to exert a worldwide attraction today. His message has stood the test of time for more than a thousand years, and his community has grown steadily over the centuries. Except in small corners of the Muslim world, Islam has never receded but rather has always expanded without losing any substantial region to any other religion. Throughout history, conversions from Islam to other religions have been rare and conversions to it plentiful.

Inasmuch as it can be gathered from the sources, Muhammad was a man of average height and sturdy build. He had a prominent forehead, a hooked nose, and black eyes. His hair was long and slightly curled and his beard was full and thick. His charming smile was endearing and his energetic stride difficult to keep pace with. He experienced periods of silence and withdrawal and was at times plunged into deep thought and meditation. He showed great self-control and spoke with clarity, frankness, and precision. He treated people with great friendliness, was fond of children, and was apt to break into tears during moments of grief and sadness. He lived in modest circumstances all his life and was known for his courage, impartiality, and resolve. Most of all, Muhammad was a deeply religious man whose strongest characteristic was, without doubt, his deep personal conviction that he was called by God. This consciousness of a call from God gave him an unshakeable faith in his divine mission. On the strength of this conviction, he persisted in proclaiming his message of an uncompromising monotheism over more than 20 years in the face of all adversities and hostilities, whether in times of disappointment or in moments of success. He was a charismatic personality with enormous leadership qualities, stupendous political gifts, and persuasive diplomatic skills. He commanded intellectual superiority at critical moments of his career and was capable of savvy and executive decision making, even if this required an abrupt reversal of approach. He was a very practical man who found ways to compromise and adapt when presented with unforeseen circumstances. He showed an uncanny ability to maneuver through the labyrinth of tribal bonds, rivalries, and compacts. His strong personality gave him real power to influence others and win them over to his cause. After his death, his followers began to regard him as the model of the ideal Muslim and the perfect Prophet, placing him on the highest pedestal and attributing to him the qualities of impeccability and infallibility as well as the powers of intercession for his community at the Last Judgment.

Contrary to the oft-repeated claim that Muhammad functioned as a religious reformer and prophet in Mecca and became a political leader and statesman only in Medina, his qualities of political leadership were already evident during his Meccan days. From the beginning of his preaching in Mecca, Muhammad showed great political skills in building a network of followers woven together from family relations, young men belonging to influential clans of Meccan society, men nominally related to clans but without close ties to them, and a few older men of considerable social standing. It was essential for him to establish these bonds because, as an orphan, he lacked the natural protective power of the nucleus of his family and faced hostility from his uncles Abu Lahab, a determined opponent, and 'Abbas, who joined his cause only reluctantly after the conquest of Mecca, while his uncle Abu Talib granted him loyal protection but never accepted Islam.

Muhammad's political acumen may also be seen in the way he strengthened his bonds with the core group of his followers through ties of marriage. Through his marriage with 'A'isha, Abu Bakr's daughter, and Hafsa, 'Umar's daughter, he established family bonds that tied him to the two caliphs who would succeed him at the head of his community. His marriages with widows of Companions who died in warfare or women who belonged to the group that early on had migrated to Abyssinia served to strengthen his bonds with his community early in the Medinan phase of his career. Other unions established links with a Jewish woman of the Banu al-Nadir in Medina and a Christian woman given to him by the ruler of Egypt. By giving his own daughters, Ruqayya and Umm Kulthum, to 'Uthman in marriage, he forged a bond with a representative of an opposing clan who became his third successor. 'Ali, the fourth caliph who became the leader of the Shi'a, received Fatima, a third daughter from Muhammad's union with Khadija, as his spouse and also married the daughter of Muhammad's oldest daughter, Zaynab.

Two other political moves of great consequence include his decision to send a group of weaker members of his following in Mecca to Abyssinia and his decision to go with his group of emigrants as dissidents and fugitives on the hijra to Medina. The negotiations he held with the emissaries of the Medinans and the pledges he made with them shortly before the hijra paved the way for his subsequent political leadership in Medina. The draft of his first legal document soon after his arrival in Medina shows his sharp political insight into the new circumstances he and his followers faced in the new urban environment. It constituted the foundation of the social unity of the community established by Muhammad, integrated the Meccan immigrants with the Medinan helpers, and provided clauses of security for Jewish believers. With regard to military planning and strategy, Muhammad's political gifts may be seen in the way in which he calmly conducted the Battle of Badr, decided on an innovative form of defense at the "War of the Trench," and pragmatically reversed his position to arrive at a solution at the truce of Hudaybiyya. In the years after the conquest of Mecca, he exhibited shrewd political instincts in drafting the many treatises he concluded and in exacting tribute from the inhabitants of a number of oases, such as those with the people of Dumat al-Jandal in 630 and the Christians of Najran in northern Yemen in 631. In these later years of his activity he also forged alliances of mutual assistance and established ties of political dependence with many Arab tribesmen by sending a large number of delegations all over Arabia that served to tie them to his personal political authority. In all these political actions, Muhammad was led by a sense of flexible and adaptable pragmatism rather than by preset principles of political theory and may thus be considered a genius in the field of applied political practice.

Further Reading

Tor Andrae, *Mohammed, the Man and His Faith*, 1936; Regis Blachère, *Le problème de Mahomet*, 1952; Frans Buhl, *Das Leben Mohammeds*, 1934; Alfred Guillaume, *The Life of Muhammad*, 1955; Harald Motzki, *The Biography of Muhammad: The Issue of the Sources*, 2000; Rudi Paret, *Muhammad und der Koran*, 1957; Maxime Rodinson, *Muhammad*, 1980; Uri Rubin, *The Eye of the Beholder*, 1995; William Montgomery Watt, *Muhammad at Mecca*, 1953; Idem, *Muhammad at Medina*, 1956.

Pluralism and Tolerance ∞∞∞∞∞∞∞∞∞∞∞∞∞∞∞

Gudrun Krämer

Pluralism and tolerance are considered constitutive elements of good governance, especially liberal democracy as it developed in the late 19th and early 20th centuries. For this reason they are widely debated among modern Muslims, including Islamists of various persuasions. For the same reason, this chapter will focus largely on modern debates. Pluralism and tolerance are clearly related and both cover a broad semantic field. They concern relations within the Muslim community, as well as between Muslims and non-Muslims, and are closely tied to understandings of freedom, liberty, and citizenship. However, there is a difference of emphasis between the two: Pluralism is discussed mostly with regard to the Muslim community, or *umma*, especially concerning the plurality of political views and interests and their institutionalization within civil society and a multiparty system. Discussions of tolerance, on the other hand, tend to focus on relations between Muslims and non-Muslims—more specifically Christians and Jews as the prime representatives of the People of the Book (*ahl al-kitāb*)—within a Muslim polity, or within an Islamic state.

On Method

The issue of (religious) authority has been of great relevance to Muslims from an early date, and it has always been controversial. As a result of mass education and new forms of mass communication spreading from the late 19th century onward, individuals, groups, and institutions who previously would not have been considered qualified to speak on Islam have asserted their right to do so. As a result, an unprecedented variety of speakers have made statements of uncertain status on Islam in general and pluralism and tolerance in particular. The 'ulama' (religious scholars) have by no means disappeared from the stage. But next to them, and often in competition with them, other voices employ different modes of expression, some of them decidedly modern. These include Islamic activists and intellectuals who share what has become known as the "Islamic discourse" (*al-khiṭāb al-islāmī*).

Islamists (*islāmiyyūn, uṣūliyyūn*) are defined here as a discursive community sharing a number of claims and assumptions: that Islam provides a comprehensive set of norms and values ordering human life in all its manifestations; that this set of norms and values derives solely from the Qur'an and the Prophetic traditions (sunna) and that it is enshrined in the shariʿa; and that to follow other sources of normative guidance, such as modern political ideologies, amounts to *shirk*, or "associating" other powers with God. From this they conclude that for Islam to be fully realized within a given community or territory, the shariʿa must be "applied" exclusively and in its entirety, and that the application of the shariʿa makes Islam into a unique, self-contained, and all-embracing "order" or "system" (*niẓām*) competing with other ideological systems. Islamists pursue various strategies to realize their goals, nonviolent as well as violent, in contrast to the majority of Muslims, who reject violence except in cases of legitimate self-defense. Distinctions among Islamists, Muslim scholars advocating an "Islamic solution," and other Muslims speaking on Islam are less clear when it comes to the precise shape of the "Islamic order" in general and definitions of pluralism and tolerance in particular.

Many of the positions reviewed here are not strikingly original. However, they illustrate a specifically modern legal-cum-political reasoning that aims to be true to the Islamic heritage (*al-turāth*) and at the same time fully attuned to present realities. Global power relations clearly affect the style of writing and the thrust of the argument, giving it a defensive ring. Even authors expressing themselves strictly in Islamic terms, condemning the adoption of un-Islamic concepts, do so against the backdrop of a challenge posed by the West and modernity as defined by the West. This includes understandings of pluralism and tolerance as core elements of modernity and good governance. At the beginning of the 21st century, debate has become overshadowed by the threat of militant Islamism and the fear of terrorism, calling forth attempts to define "true Islam," which is not what its enemies claim it to be. Opposition to Islamist violence also informs reflections on the status of pluralism and tolerance among Muslims and between Muslims and non-Muslims.

Faced with Western demands on the one hand and Islamist militancy on the other, Muslim scholar-activists have attempted to define a "middle ground," *al-wasaṭiyya*, a concept that came to the fore in the 1990s and is widely identified with the Egyptian-born scholar-activist Yusuf al-Qaradawi (b. 1926). The basis for this idea is Qur'an 2:143: "Thus, We have appointed you as a median nation (*wa-kadhālika jaʿalnākum ummatan wasaṭan*), to be witnesses for mankind, and the Prophet to be a witness for you." Advocates of *al-wasaṭiyya* search for broader principles reflecting the essence of shariʿa and at the same time responding to changing realities, enabling Muslims to find the "right place" between the extremes of Western demands for modernization in its own image and faith-based rejection of any kind of adjustment. Advocates of *al-wasaṭiyya* can build on solid support for the *juste milieu* in classical Islamic scholarship and adapt key terms found in the *turāth* (the classical heritage), such as balance, moderation, and a pragmatic realism (*tawāzun, iʿtidāl, iḥsān*). Men as different as Qaradawi and the Sudanese scholar-activist Hasan al-Turabi (b. 1932) propagate a "new *fiqh*," or jurisprudence, that takes into account conditions in the real world (*al-wāqiʿiyya* and *al-maydāniyya*), focusing on the need to balance different interests and aspirations (*fiqh al-muwāzanāt*) and to establish a list of priorities (*fiqh al-awlawiyyāt*) that privileges the essence of Islam and the shari'a over what they see as trivialities. At the same time, like prominent authors of the Salafi reform movement of the late 19th and early 20th centuries, they emphasize the "ease of Islam" (*yusr al-islām*) that aims to make life easy for Muslims as well as non-Muslims and not to impose hardship on them (*yusr lā 'usr*)—a view neatly opposed to the rigor exercised by certain traditionalist scholars and radical Islamists.

In the debate on pluralism and tolerance, proponents of different positions, "radical" as well as "moderate," basically adopt the same reasoning: selective reference to the Qur'an and sunna, supplemented by even more selective use of Islamic history on the one hand and the Islamic scholarly tradition on the other and expressed in the language of Islamic jurisprudence. In contemporary Islamic discourse, the theological dimension is generally weak, whereas political considerations loom large. Shifts of register from theology to history or from theology to law are frequent and are often made with little regard for either text or context. They are especially marked in the debate on the legitimacy of a multiparty system and concepts of citizenship that reinterpret traditional notions of religious tolerance (or toleration) to extend equal civic and political rights to all residents of the "Islamic homeland," irrespective of religious affiliation. This requires considerable investment in reinterpreting the sources as well as the scholarly tradition.

Muslims confront the basic challenge to all believers in a personal God who has revealed himself in scripture: the fact that according to their own normative tradition, revelation is precisely located in time and place and yet universally valid for all times and places, unbounded by the confines of origin. For virtually all Muslim authors engaged in the debate on pluralism and tolerance, revelation (*waḥy*) is enshrined in the Qur'an and the Prophet's example, or *al-kitāb wa-l-sunna*. They pursue a textual approach to certain knowledge—but textual does not necessarily mean literal.

Most Muslim authors regard the sunna as part of revelation and look to the Prophet as well as members of the early Muslim community, the *salaf ṣāliḥ*, as role models for Muslims. In spite of much critical scholarship on the sunna, especially among Western authors, the life of the Prophet and the Prophetic traditions continue to be among the most popular sources of inspiration to Muslims. The sunna documents (or purports to document) the social norms and practices of Arab tribal society in seventh-century northwestern Arabia—practices that were informed by the Qur'anic message but that cannot easily be transferred across time and space to be implemented in highly diverse sociocultural settings. Tribal factions in seventh-century Arabia are not the same as modern political parties, the treatment of Jews in the oasis of Khaybar cannot be taken as a timeless model of tolerance, and the so-called Constitution of Medina is no blueprint for organizing the state of law in the modern period. Many Muslims are aware of these facts. Yet only a minority hold that the exemplary practice of the Prophet is not just embedded in a particular "space" but also tied to it and thus not timelessly valid and binding. The issue is relevant to all conceptualizations of the Islamic state or order, including understandings of pluralism and tolerance.

Even more sensitive is the status of the Qur'an as the primary source of normative guidance for Muslims of all times and places. With regard to Qur'anic exegesis (*tafsīr*), modern authors can build on the classical tradition, but openly or tacitly many also go beyond it. Classical exegetes did recognize that the Qur'anic text is occasionally ambiguous and too complex to be ever fully exhausted by human minds; the Qur'an itself says so in more than one place. Certain features of the Qur'anic narrative and the hermeneutical strategies of Qur'anic exegesis, such as the use of metaphor, figurative speech, self-referentiality, and allegorical interpretation, are relevant to present discussions. However, these discussions are largely limited to academic circles. In a broader context, which tends to be more openly political, other methods of Qur'anic exegesis stand out more prominently, one based on contextualization and the other on abstraction. Both seek to define a hierarchy of commands and rules, one by placing them on a chronological scale, the other by assessing their validity within the overall context of revelation.

Contextualization includes, first, the exegetical subdiscipline of the "circumstances of revelation" (*asbāb al-nuzūl*), which aims to establish the context, or "seat in life," of all textual references, and second, abrogation (*naskh, al-nāsikh wa-l-mansūkh*), which seeks to ascertain their chronological sequence, with later revelations superseding earlier ones. Contextualization is a recognized element of both Qur'anic exegesis, *tafsīr*, and legal reasoning, *fiqh*, and indeed is indispensable to these disciplines. In contrast to most classical scholars, however, modern authors like the Egyptian lawyer Muhammad Sa'id al-'Ashmawi (b. 1932), an outspoken critic of the "application" of the shari'a, use contextualization as a tool not only to correctly locate specific rulings but also to restrict their binding force to this context. In doing so, they attempt to expand the scope of rational inquiry without abandoning the textual framework of the Qur'an (and sunna). There are obvious problems with this approach. One concerns history or rather historiography: the Qur'an does not represent a linear narrative and therefore does not establish an undisputed chronological sequence of divine commands and rulings. At best, this may be done with the aid of other materials, including the sunna and the Life of the Prophet (*sīra*), both of which, however, were not written down at the same time as the Qur'an. Very few Muslim scholars have ventured to deconstruct the historiography concerning the age of the Prophet and the early community. Seen from the perspective of modern historical source criticism, contextualization rests on shaky ground. Seen from the perspective of tradition-bound scholars, it threatens to undermine the foundations of Muslim belief.

Abstraction offers ample opportunities to rethink the Qur'anic message, especially when combined with contextualization, and it is widely employed in present debates on pluralism and tolerance. Here, too, modern authors can build on the Islamic scholarly tradition. A majority hold that the shari'a is divine law in the sense that it was laid down by God (or his messenger, Muhammad, which is generally less clearly stated), with respect to its fundamentals and certain specific rulings. The challenge is to identify these fundamentals, or universal principles, in order to do justice to the "spirit" of Islam and the shari'a rather than merely following its letter. These fundamentals or universal principles have been largely identified with the "objectives" of the shari'a (*maqāṣid al-sharī'a*), or its "finality." They have also been linked to the concepts of the common good or public interest (in modern terminology, *maṣlaḥa 'āmma*) and of certain underlying goods or benefits (*maṣāliḥ*) to be protected by the shari'a: religion (i.e., Islam), life, offspring, property, and intellect; often honor has been included in the list as well. In ways that are not always clear, the distinction between fundamentals and nonfundamentals has also been related to the distinction between general and specific rules (*'āmm* and *khāṣṣ*). While the fundamentals or universal principles constitute the unchanging essence of Islam and the shari'a, their realization is contingent on time, place, and circumstance. As a result, the shari'a is considered fixed and unchangeable in its essence but flexible in its detailed rules and regulations.

The distinction between the fixed and the flexible (*al-thābit wa-l-mutaghayyir*), between the basics and secondary matters, and between universals and specifics is crucial to modern conceptions of an Islamic order and more particularly to discussions of tolerance, equality, and citizenship. According to some, universal principles carry greater weight than specific injunctions of the Qur'an and sunna, and in case of conflict, can even supersede or suspend explicit textual injunctions (*naṣṣ*) if this serves the common good. Reference to *siyāsa shar'iyya*, or governance in accordance with the shari'a, and to respected theoreticians of *maṣlaḥa,* from Ghazali (d. 1111) to Abu Ishaq al-Shatibi (d. 1388), cannot obscure the fact that modern interpretations are set in a context quite different from the one inhabited by Ghazali or Shatibi. The rationalist, if not openly utilitarian, logic employed by writers such as 'Ashmawi to root modern understandings of liberty, pluralism, and tolerance in the normative tradition renders them vulnerable to critique from Islamists and Islamic scholars alike, who defend what they see as unchanging "divine law" against human whims and interests, especially because those whims and interests seem to be inspired by foreign models.

The Unity of the Community

The crucial importance of unity (*waḥda*) to Islamic thought past and present is undisputed. There are numerous references to unity in the Qur'an, and they are liberally quoted by modern authors. At the core is Qur'an 3:103–5:

> O believers, fear God as He should be truly feared, and die not except as Muslims. And hold fast, all of you, to the rope of God and do not fall into dissension (*lā tafarraqū*). Remember God's bounties upon you, when you were enemies to one another, and how He brought harmony to your hearts so that, by His blessing, you became brothers . . . Let there be among you a group who call to virtue, who command the good and forbid vice. These shall indeed prosper. Do not be like those who scattered (*tafarraqū*) and fell

into dissension (*ikhtalafū*) after manifest signs had come to them. These shall meet with terrible torment.

Qur'an 23:52 states simply, "This, your nation, is a single nation and I am your Lord. So fear Me." Qur'an 30:31–32 warns people not to be "among those who associate other gods with Him, those who have sundered their religion and turned into sects, each sect happy with what they have." Some modern authors refer to the doctrine of *tawḥīd*, denoting the unity of God, in order to explain the overriding need for the unity of the community, or *al-jamāʿa*. Critics have spoken of "political *tawḥīd*." In legal theory (*uṣūl al-fiqh*) the emphasis on unity corresponds to the principle of *ijmāʿ*, the consensus of the Muslim community as expressed by its religious scholars or the first generations of Muslims. (For Twelver Shiʿis, or Imamis, consensus has to be endorsed by the imams.) Many modern authors leap from religious doctrine and legal principle to historical practice: virtually all believe that at the beginning there was unity—a community firmly united around the Prophet as its sole spiritual and political leader—and that only later did unity yield to differentiation, giving rise to theological, legal, and political schools (*madhāhib*), sects (*milal*), or parties (*aḥzāb*).

The unitary vision can entail the rejection of all divergence of opinion, critique, or opposition to the dominant doctrines and practices as a menace to and sin against not just the given sociopolitical system but the divinely ordained order at large. Many writers do indeed view differentiation as fragmentation, entailing a weakening of the community of Muslims, as exemplified by the first and second civil wars, or *fitna*s, of the first century after the hijra (the migration of the Prophet and his Companions from Mecca to Medina). If broad moral-cum-religious categories such as true and false (*ḥaqq* and *bāṭil*), right and wrong (*maʿrūf* and *munkar*), or permissible and forbidden (*ḥalāl* and *ḥarām*) are employed to evaluate political opinions and decisions; if there is only one truth and only one correct "position of Islam" on any given issue; and if this truth can be clearly identified by the community of Muslims or a given group of Muslims, then critique and diversity cannot be admitted as legitimate, nor can it be institutionalized. Legitimate plurality remains confined to what the powers-that-be define as consistent with the public order. Many would not rule out plurality and diversity altogether but still perceive them as destructive and divisive. There is a widely shared feeling that Muslims should overcome internal divisions and restore the pristine unity of the age of the Prophet. Attempts to bring about a rapprochement between Sunni and Shiʿi Muslims (*taqrīb*) and to create a unified *fiqh* beyond the established schools of law and theology testify to this quest for unity.

The Logic of the Nation-State

Idealization of the early *umma* as an undivided community has been reinforced by the colonial experience and the opposition to Zionism, Israel, and the West as the perceived enemies of Islam. It has been further enhanced by the imprint of the modern nation-state. Modern authors are heirs to a legacy of conceptionalizing the community, homeland, and nation that was created by Salafi authors and activists, from Afghani (1838–97) to Hasan al-Banna (1906–49), largely in opposition to colonial domination. Even in the present era of globalization and mass migration, or perhaps precisely because of these phenomena, many (and not only Muslims) continue to think of Islam and the Muslim community in territorial terms, evoking the boundary between the "territory of Islam" (*dār al-islām*), in which the shariʿa is enforced by the prince or state, and the "territory of war" (*dār al-ḥarb*), in which this is not the case, either because the rulers are not Muslim or because they, though nominally Muslim, fail to apply the shariʿa. Even those who, in recognition of present realities, acknowledge a third category, the "territory of truce" (*dār al-ṣulḥ*) or the "territory of treaty" (*dār al-ʿahd*), in which the state of war between Islamic and non-Islamic territories has been suspended, adhere to a territorial logic.

Building on the binary notions of *dār al-islām* versus *dār al-ḥarb*, Salafi authors have proposed a territorial concept of Islam as the homeland (*waṭan*) of all Muslims as well as of the non-Muslims living in their midst. Thus in 1934, Banna, the founder of the Egyptian Muslim Brotherhood, wrote in a newspaper editorial that "every piece of land where the banner of Islam has been hoisted is the fatherland of the Muslims" (Krämer, 2010, p. 105). From earlier authors, he borrowed the neologism *al-jinsiyya al-islāmiyya* ("Islamic nationality") to describe the bond uniting all residents of the Islamic homeland. By the same token, earlier Salafi reformers had declared patriotism to be "part of faith" (*ḥubb al-waṭan min al-īmān*). Because of the close link between the Arabs and Islam in the formative period, relations between Arabism and Islam retained a special character throughout the 20th century. As a result, the vocabulary employed—especially in the context of tolerance and citizenship, with its characteristic combination of terms taken from the Islamic tradition (*umma, jamāʿa*) on the one hand and modern political vocabulary (*waṭan, jinsiyya*) on the other—suggests a certain level of conceptual confusion.

From Plurality to Pluralism

In spite of the high value attached to unity (of both the Muslim *umma* and the modern nation-state), most contemporary Muslim thinkers acknowledge plurality and diversity as facts of life willed by God and sanctioned by the Qurʾan. The recognition of plurality and diversity, however, does not necessarily entail a recognition of pluralism, which makes diversity into a founding principle of social and political organization and allows for its institutionalization through voluntary associations ("civil society"), political parties, and bodies of parliamentary representation. The important distinction between plurality and pluralism is not always made, though the key terms—difference or divergence of opinion (*ikhtilāf*), plurality (*tanawwuʿ*), and pluralism (*taʿaddudiyya*)—permit such a differentiation. On the theoretical as well as the practical level, there exist a range of positions, even among Islamists, that can be roughly divided into two opposing camps: one deeply suspicious of, or indeed opposed to, plurality and pluralism as menacing to Muslim integrity, power, and unity, and the other supporting plurality and pluralism as contributing to Muslim strength and creativity, rendering Islam, as the well-known formula has it, valid for all times and places. Even among the latter, finer distinctions emerge as soon as the legitimacy of a plurality of *interests* rather than mere *opinions* is addressed.

Opposition to plurality and pluralism is characteristic of militant Islamic groups and their spokespersons, while support of plurality and pluralism is common among Muslim thinkers and activists advocating a moderate, pragmatic course. The most widely shared view would seem to be that plurality and diversity are legitimate as long as they involve nonantagonistic groups operating "within the framework of Islam." Put simply, Muslim society and the Islamic state are conceived of as plural but not pluralistic. Differing opinions and interests should be balanced and harmonized to reflect the ideals of the equilibrium and the *juste milieu*. This limits both plurality and pluralism, though the actual imposition of restrictions may be subject to pragmatic considerations, including political reason weighing the options in light of the public interest, or what is identified as such.

Advocates of pluralism point to the elements of diversity in the religious, legal, and historical heritage of the Muslim community as one of the very sources of its strength and resilience. They quote the Qur'an and sunna, and, like their opponents, they do not hesitate to translate ethicoreligious concepts into sociopolitical ones. The most popular reference is Qur'an 49:13: "O mankind, We created you male and female, and made you into nations and tribes that you may come to know one another. The noblest among you in God's sight are the most pious." Potentially more powerful, though less often cited, is Qur'an 5:48:

> For every community We decreed a law and a way of life. Had God willed, He could have made you a single community—but in order to test you in what He revealed to you. So vie with one another in virtue. To God is your homecoming, all of you, and He will then acquaint you with that over which you differed.

In addition, there is a famous Prophetic saying (hadith) according to which the "diversity of opinion among [the learned of] my community is a blessing (*ikhtilāf* [*'ulamā'*] *ummatī raḥma*)." Though the hadith is considered weak, which restricts its legal force, it is often quoted in the literature on Islamic political thought, and pluralism and tolerance more specifically. The tradition of scholarly controversy, together with its specific body of literature (*kutub al-ikhtilāf*), is still known in erudite circles and serves to legitimize a plurality of views, even if antagonistic—provided they do not transgress the bounds of religion and morality.

As in other contexts, the shift from theology to law to politics is readily made. Thus the existence of the different Sunni and Shi'i schools of law (*madhhab*, pl. *madhāhib*) and of local legal practices (*'urf*, *'āda*) is often assimilated to political parties. The same is not true of the theological schools, which, at least among modern authors, are widely seen as divisive. Thus Qaradawi insists on the need to transcend the boundaries of the established schools of theology and law in order to create an inclusive vision of Islam that is meaningful to all Muslims. In various contexts, he asserts that what he practices is *ijtihād*, or independent reasoning on the basis of the Qur'an and sunna, freed from the ties to any particular *madhhab* with its specific rules and assumptions. Qaradawi acknowledges the historical embeddedness of *fiqh* and the controversies of its practitioners. In contrast to many others, he welcomes the existing plurality of legal opinions found in the legal tradition, but he also considers them a matter of the past that is no longer a concern for present-day Muslims, who should harness their energies to make Islam relevant to their own lives and those of others.

In the domain of politics, even conservative authors who take care not to be seen as borrowing from outside the Islamic tradition advocate consultation, or *shūrā*, as a key principle of political organization, enjoined by the Qur'an and incumbent on Muslim rulers past and present. *Shūrā* is premised on a plurality of opinions, at least within the community and within what is generally referred to as the "framework of Islam." *Shūrā* is a flexible device that allows for a variety of interpretations, all relevant to the issues of pluralism and tolerance. Some see it as mere advice to the ruler, similar to "good counsel," or *naṣīḥa*; others view it as the foundation of multiparty parliamentary democracy. Definitions of *shūrā* can be purely pragmatic, but they can also be based on philosophical reflection, for even though there may be only one truth, there is no guarantee that humans will be able to attain it with certainty. The Tunisian Islamist thinker and activist Rachid al-Gannouchi (b. 1941) is a prominent champion of this line of thinking. It has also been put forth in the context of Islamist self-critique. The Qur'anic text permits more than one reading. Accordingly, no individual or group of Muslims can have a monopoly on truth, or exert a tutelage (*wiṣāya*) over their fellow Muslims. This argument, which for lack of a better term might be called egalitarian, is directed against all kinds of religious authorities, from the Sunni 'ulama' of Azhar University in Cairo to the Shi'i leaders of the Islamic Republic of Iran. It is also directed against Islamist movements, first and foremost the Egyptian Muslim Brotherhood, whose claim to leadership over the "Islamic awakening" (*ṣaḥwa*) has been squarely repudiated by Islamist leaders such as Gannouchi and Turabi. Both insisted that Islamist activists, like all Muslims, have to interact with local realities if they wish to make their vision of Islam relevant to their own societies. Interaction with local conditions necessarily results in a plurality of interpretations.

Debate is therefore legitimate and indeed necessary. Under the conditions of modern mass society, debate may have to be institutionalized in voluntary associations and political parties to become effective. However, there is little agreement even among Islamists concerning institutionalization. Views range from a grudging recognition of political associations and parties as the lesser evil (compared to clandestine activities of undesirable political forces) to full acceptance of political pluralism as healthy and legitimate. Some recognize voluntary associations or even trade unions but not political parties. Others express more liberal views. The names adopted by Islamist organizations reflect this diversity of opinions. Many call themselves *jamāʿa, jamʿiyya,* or *tajammuʿ,* all derivatives of a verbal root stressing unison, to highlight their faith in unity; the Muslim Brotherhood (Jamʿiyyat al-Ikhwan al-Muslimin) is a prime example. Some call themselves "front" (*jabha*), using a more openly modern label to transport a similar message; examples include the Algerian Front Islamique du Salut and the Sudanese National Islamic Front or the Islamic Action Front in Jordan. Yet others call themselves parties, such as the Islamic Liberation Party (Hizb al-Tahrir al-Islami), founded in the early 1950s by the Jordanian Taqi al-Din al-Nabhani; the Malaysian Parti Islam Se-Malaysia (PAS), also established in the early 1950s; or the Tunisian Nahda Party (Hizb al-Nahda), founded in 1989 by Gannouchi.

However, the choice of the term "party" does not in itself signal an acceptance of political pluralism, as shown by the Hizb al-Tahrir or the Lebanese Hizbullah; at least in its early years, the latter was firmly opposed to a multiparty system. According to the binary vision adopted by both organizations, there are only two "parties" (or rather groups or communities): the party of God (*ḥizb allāh*) and the party of the devil (*ḥizb al-shayṭān*), or, with a significant change of register, the party of the downtrodden (*al-mustaḍʿafūn*) and the party of the arrogant (*al-mustakbirūn*). The former refers to Qurʾan 5:56 ("Whoso takes God and His Messenger and the believers for allies, the party of God shall be victorious") and Qurʾan 58:19, 22 ("They are the party of Satan and the party of Satan are assuredly the losers. . . . They are the party of God, and the party of God shall surely win through"). The latter uses categories popularized by the leaders of the Islamic Revolution in Iran. Here as elsewhere the argument rests on a transfer of ethicomoral notions to the sociopolitical field. Thus the Qurʾanic condemnation of whims and desires (*hawā,* pl. *ahwāʾ*) is used to denounce political parties and associations premised on a particular interest (*maṣlaḥa*) at the expense of the common good or public weal, resulting in a collective weakening of the Muslim community or the nation. Gannouchi is one of the few distinguished Islamist authors to defend interests as a legitimate component of political action and organization.

At one end of the spectrum, the prominent Egyptian lawyer and Islamist intellectual Muhammad Salim al-ʿAwwa (b. 1942) openly declared himself in favor of pluralism. In an article on "political pluralism" published in 1993, he wrote that pluralism means the recognition of diversity and that this diversity is an "expression of the marvelous divine achievement." With regard to political organization he argued that if one "recognises the pluralistic nature of humans, and recognises their rights to disagree and differ, one must inevitably, and without much effort, recognise pluralism in the political sphere." To reject political pluralism and to adopt monism, or a unitary vision, he continued, usually leads to an unjust despotic rule or tyrannical government. The reference to the Qurʾanic verses sanctioning plurality cited earlier comes out clearly, as does the seemingly effortless change of register from theology to politics.

In spite of some verbal stridency, pragmatism features prominently in modern Islamic discourse. The Egyptian Muslim Brotherhood, for example, under changing conditions gradually moved from a principled rejection of multipartyism to an acceptance of a multiparty system—provided that it stays within the framework of Islam. In the face of British colonialism, the Muslim Brotherhood propagated national unity combined with the denunciation of party politics or factionalism (*ḥizbiyya*). Faith, Banna declared, is unity; fragmentation and disunity equal unbelief (*kufr*). Considering that in Egypt the interwar period has often been called the age of party politics, this was not a minor point. Yet the Muslim Brotherhood was not alone in criticizing "partyism" and partisanship. Saʿd Zaghlul, the leader of the Wafd Party founded in 1918, did the same, claiming for the Wafd the role of representative of the nation at large; by the 1930s, the critique had become commonplace. For Banna, politics (but not party politics) was an integral part of Islam. In 1938, he sent an open letter to the king and leading politicians, which was later published under the title *Nahwa al-Nur* (To the light), urging them to dissolve all parties and to create a united front. Still, there is no compelling link between this dualistic vision pitting right against wrong and the endorsement of a one-party system as it was espoused especially during the 1950s and 1960s by Islamists in particular communities and countries. Changed sociopolitical circumstances resulted in modified political thinking. By the mid-1990s, the Egyptian Muslim Brotherhood had largely revised its earlier positions on multipartyism, exchanging earlier rejection for cautious endorsement.

At the same time, most authors would rule out the possibility that political parties explicitly representing non-Muslims (such as Christian parties) be recognized in the framework of an Islamic order. Lebanon, with its system of institutionalized confessionalism, or sectarianism (*ṭāʾifiyya*), is a special case; set quotas for non-Muslims and other minorities in countries such as Iran or Jordan do not allow for political parties to form on a confessional basis. The same applies to political parties based on what are labeled un-Islamic principles, such as Marxism, communism, or fascism. But this does not exclude the possibility of cooperation under certain circumstances, notably under conditions of duress, in which the established legal principle of necessity, or *ḍarūra*, can be invoked. Here the crucial distinction between the fundamentals of religion (*aṣl*) and its derivatives (*furūʿ*) comes into play. It allows for recognizing the existing plurality and diversity of opinion and interest without abandoning the ideal of unity. In a similar context, the noted Islamic scholar H.A.R. Gibb has spoken of "tolerance for the sake of unity" (Gibb, 1962, p. 15).

From Toleration to Tolerance

Tolerance covers a broad spectrum of positions, from toleration of the Other to respect for his or her beliefs and practices to the full recognition of these beliefs and practices as equally viable and legitimate. The Arabic *tasāmuḥ* does not distinguish between toleration on the one hand and tolerance on the other. Toleration can be based on pragmatic considerations and made contingent on certain conditions; it is thus revocable. It can be granted by autocratic rulers and authoritarian states irrespective of their own beliefs and ideologies. Toleration can also reflect philosophical insight into the impossibility of ascertaining truth, similar to the argument made by Gannouchi and others in the context of pluralism. Both pragmatic toleration and philosophical reflection can come together but need not do so. In modern debates, it is often conditional toleration that authors, especially Islamist authors, have in mind when they invoke tolerance as the distinguishing feature of Islam and any polity based on it. Respect for the Other as a different expression of toleration and tolerance presupposes a certain degree of familiarity among the different parties, especially concerning their religious beliefs and practices. However, respect need not translate into specific legal and political arrangements granting equal religious, civic, and political rights to the latter.

By contrast, tolerance in the sense of full recognition of the Other is inconceivable without such legal and political arrangements translating religious recognition into rights of citizenship. In the modern period, tolerance thus defined has been associated with human rights, freedom, and liberty. Tolerance entails recognition of individual self-determination in diverse fields of life, including the free choice of lifestyle and religion, the right to practice this lifestyle or religion, and the right to either change or relinquish them altogether. Tolerance thus bears on individual and collective rights and liberties in both the private and the public spheres and is premised on a differentiation between religion, morals, law, and the constitution. The distinction many authors make between the public and the private domain, with the private sphere protected against outside intrusion and intervention, is remarkable in light of contemporary debates on whether the distinction between public and private in Western contexts is relevant to Muslim contexts. Discussions of sexual freedom and apostasy suggest that it is indeed highly relevant to the latter.

Tolerance among Muslims

Even for innovative authors such as 'Awwa, there are limits to tolerance and diversity. These limits, defined by God's law and revelation, inform (or ought to inform) Muslim understandings of freedom, liberty, and tolerance. Freedom in its various dimensions—freedom of conscience, religion, thought, and expression; freedom of association; academic and artistic freedom—is widely discussed among contemporary Muslims. Personal freedom, entailing free individual choice, bears on concepts of tolerance and pluralism. With regard to personal freedom, 'Awwa, who supports political pluralism and tolerance toward non-Muslims that treats them as citizens, not as protected subjects, shows himself as much more conservative. In a monograph on Islamic penal law he argued that

> the Islamic concept of personal freedom is entirely opposed to that of the post-war generation in the West. Personal freedom, according to the Islamic concept, is permissible only

in respect to matters not regulated by the injunctions and prohibitions laid down in the Qur'an and the Sunna, which are expressions of the Divine Will. (El Awa, 1982, p. 18)

This does not address the question of how the community or the state should deal with transgression and whether under certain circumstances it might be tolerated, but it does underscore the necessity to distinguish among different fields to which individual groups and authors may apply different standards of rigor or leniency or toleration and tolerance.

The distinction between public and private is equally relevant to another key issue affecting tolerance among Muslims: the change of religion, which continues to be labeled as apostasy (*ridda*), suggesting the illegitimate nature of the act. Many would argue that within the Muslim community, public debate must fall short of any radical critique of religion or its dominant interpretations, which is readily denounced as blasphemy, heresy, or apostasy, raising the issue of *takfir*, or the exclusion from the community of Muslims. Modern Muslim authors are concerned not so much with the theological dimension (the definition of apostasy and how it can be distinguished from sin, unbelief, heresy, or blasphemy) but with its impact on the body politic. Discussions of apostasy provide a striking illustration of territorial logic and the modern nation-state's impact on much of contemporary Islamic discourse. Thus in a tract devoted to the issue of apostasy, Qaradawi claimed that the Muslim who openly declares his apostasy transfers his allegiance from his own community and homeland to another and thereby threatens the foundation of collective identity.

According to him, the apostate does not simply abandon the community; he joins the enemy, an act not to be tolerated. Lacking compelling evidence from the Qur'an and sunna to support the identification of religious conversion and high treason, Qaradawi follows standard practice by invoking memories of the historical *ridda*, the secession of Arab tribes after Muhammad's death, which he describes as treason on both religious and political grounds. Like many others, Qaradawi looks at apostasy from the perspective of the community, not the individual making a personal choice, and he identifies Islam with individual and collective identity. This has obvious consequences for conceptions of religious tolerance and the status of non-Muslims in a Muslim polity or Islamic state.

The Status of Non-Muslims

The Qur'an describes other religions in its own terms, and these terms have been adapted by Muslim scholars of the formative and classical periods; modern Muslims still use basically the same vocabulary. Monotheism and a book of revelation are the crucial criteria by which the Qur'an distinguishes between several categories of believers (*mu'minūn* and *muslimūn*) and unbelievers (*kuffār*): the People of the Book, which include the Christians, the Jews, the Zoroastrians, and the mysterious

Sabians; the polytheists or pagans (*mushrikūn*); and the hypocrites (*munāfiqūn*), who pretend to be Muslims while actually conspiring against the Muslim community. Qur'anic rulings on the theological and legal status of non-Muslims as well as on how Muslims should interact with non-Muslims are not entirely consistent. Interpretation rests on the methods of contextualization and abstraction outlined earlier. Some Qur'anic verses describe the commonalities of all believers; others draw a clear line between Muslims, the People of the Book, and pagans. Thus Qur'an 109:6 states, "O unbelievers! I do not worship what you worship, nor do you worship what I worship; nor will I ever worship what you worship, nor will you ever worship what I worship. You have your religion, and I have mine." Qur'an 5:48 makes a similar statement. Both could be taken as the basis of respect and religious tolerance, although they are by no means unequivocal. As for the modes of interaction among the adherents of different faiths, Qur'an 2:256 famously decrees that "there is no compulsion in religion," whereas Qur'an 9:29 calls on Muslims to "fight those who do not believe in God or the Last Day, who do not hold illicit what God and His Messenger hold illicit, and who do not follow the religion of truth from among those given the Book, until they offer up the tribute, by hand, in humble mien." Several verses warn Muslims not to take non-Muslims as their friends and allies, while others instruct them to act justly toward them and to respect their treaties with them.

In view of such diversity, modern authors rely on classical theological and legal scholarship to put forth the position of Islam on the status and treatment of non-Muslims in Islamic or Muslim society. Modern authors still discuss *dhimma*, the protection granted to non-Muslims living permanently under Muslim rule; *jizya*, the poll tax to be paid by all able-bodied adult non-Muslim males in exchange for protection; the rules of interaction, including intermarriage, the possibility of sharing a table and of consuming foodstuffs produced or meat slaughtered by the non-Muslim Other, and the risks of ritual pollution; the freedom of religious practice, including the construction and restoration of sites of worship; and (partial) autonomy within the Islamic polity, best known from the late Ottoman Empire as the millet system. Most of these issues are dealt with in the so-called Treaty of 'Umar, attributed to the second caliph, 'Umar b. al-Khattab (r. 634–44), and possibly composed in the eighth century. Modern writings are often apologetic in nature; religious polemic informed by theological issues has become rare. According to prevalent perceptions, tolerance was practiced from the time of the Prophet and the pious ancestors (*al-salaf al-ṣāliḥ*) up to at least Ottoman times. While early Muslim history is frequently invoked, the actual experience of coexistence, if not conviviality—not only in Andalus or in Fatimid Egypt but in various other times and places, too—is rarely explored. The conceptual framework is shaped by the territorial state, and the non-Muslims concerned are by and large local Christians. Muslim minority groups within Muslim-majority societies, such as Alevis in Turkey, Shi'is in Saudi Arabia or Morocco, or Sunnis in Iran, are hardly ever covered under the heading of tolerance. The status of Hindus and Buddhists is rarely discussed outside of South Asia and Southeast Asia, and contributions of South Asian or Southeast Asian Muslim intellectuals tend to be ignored by their Middle Eastern homologues. Reception is slightly better among Muslim intellectuals and activists residing in the West. New religious communities such as the Mormons or Jehovah's Witnesses are largely excluded from discussion and denied recognition and legal protection.

Discussions of tolerance accorded to non-Muslims under Islam, therefore, tend to be limited to the People of the Book in general and to Christians and Jews in particular. Within this narrow field, however, the range of positions is wide: At one end of the spectrum are those scholar-activists who are prepared to tolerate Christians and Jews as *dhimmī*s, subjects of the Muslim state or ruler protected on the condition that they acknowledge the superiority of Islam and the Muslim community and, as a token of this recognition, pay the *jiyza* "with humble mien" (Q. 9:29). They exclude non-Muslims from political participation and representation as well as all positions involving power and authority over Muslims (*wilāya*), including the judiciary, the military, and high state offices, which are classified as religious because in one way or another, they are charged with applying the shari'a. The distinction between "religious" and "nonreligious" spheres and offices at work here is intriguing given the Islamist conviction that Islam does *not* separate religion from politics—the bedrock of antisecular argument. It appears that within the framework of Islamic rule, as exemplified by the application of the shari'a, distinct fields or domains operate according to a different logic, provided that this logic does not contradict the "fundamentals" of Islam and the shari'a. Still, this is a minority view, mostly to be found among militant Islamist groups and theoreticians. At the other end of the spectrum are those scholars, intellectuals, and political activists who recognize Christians and Jews as citizens of the (Muslim or Islamic) nation-state with equal rights and duties, grant them autonomy in personal-status matters, and bar them only from the office of president, to which only male Muslims can be appointed. This position is much more common than the former, though also more diversified. Statements on the status of Jews must be seen in light of political conflict with Zionism and Israel rather than the principle of religious tolerance only. The same applies to anti-Semitism, which in certain milieus has arisen mainly as an element of the critique of Zionism and Israel or Israeli state policies.

In certain contexts, non-Muslims residing in Islamic territory are described as *dhimmī*s of the Muslim community, enjoying protection (*dhimma*) against the payment of dues and taxes including the *jizya*; in other contexts, they are described as *muwāṭinūn*, variously to be translated as compatriots or citizens. According to classical *fiqh*, relations between Muslims and non-Muslims are based on a contract involving reciprocal rights and duties, which were unequal, reflecting the religious and political superiority of Muslims. Except for certain militant Islamist activists, modern authors commonly assert that non-Muslims enjoy essentially the same civic and political rights and duties as Muslims, referring to the formula "same rights, same duties" (*lahum mā lanā wa-'alayhim mā 'alaynā*), which is also known in classical *fiqh*, especially the Hanafi tradition. Accordingly, Islam guarantees non-Muslims protection of their lives, bodies, property, and honor as well as respect for their religious freedom, covering the fundamental goods or benefits (*maṣāliḥ*) protected under the shariʿa. In the framework of the modern nation-state, it also offers them social benefits such as old-age pensions. It is only in the religious field that they cannot be considered equal.

With regard to politics, some authors argue that the protection accorded non-Muslims under Islam is the same as what is today described as nationality or citizenship (*jinsiyya*). They interpret the *jizya* as an equivalent of zakat or a substitute for military service. Accordingly, non-Muslims could not be expected to fight for Islam and the Muslim community, a fight identified as jihad, in the premodern era; however, the nature of jihad was transformed in the process of anticolonial struggle and modern nation building. Non-Muslims who joined their Muslim fellow countrymen in the fight against colonialism and for the nation earned the rights of citizenship, making special payment of *jizya* obsolete. Not all authors claim that the *muwāṭinūn min ghayr al-muslimīn* (non-Muslim countrymen and women) enjoy full equality with their Muslim compatriots in all spheres of life. Instead, they elaborate on justice, equity, and religious freedom properly understood, which does not force non-Muslims to convert but allows them to retain their cultural authenticity just as it protects the cultural authenticity of Muslims. In return, non-Muslims have to respect the religious sensibilities of the Muslims. Proselytizing missions among Muslims cannot be tolerated, highlighting once again the shifting meanings of toleration and tolerance.

Further Reading

S. Ghalib Khan al-Abbasi and A. de Zayas Abbasi, *The Structure of Islamic Polity. Part I: The One-Party System in Islam*, 1952; Mohammed Salim al-Awa, "Political Pluralism from an Islamic Perspective," in *Power-Sharing Islam?*, edited by Azzam Tamimi, 1993; Mark Cohen, *Under Crescent and Cross*, 1994; Hamid Dabashi, *Theology of Discontent: The Ideological Foundation of the Islamic Revolution in Iran*, 1993; Mohamed S. El-Awa, *Punishment in Islamic Law: A Comparative Study*, 1982; Rainer Forst, *Toleranz im Konflikt: Geschichte, Gehalt und Gegenwart eines umstrittenen Begriffs*, 2003; Yohanan Friedmann, *Tolerance and Coercion in Islam: Interfaith Relations in the Muslim Tradition*, 2003; H.A.R. Gibb, *Studies on the Civilization of Islam*, edited by Stanford Shaw and William R. Polk, 1962; Bettina Gräf and Jakob Skovgaard-Petersen, eds., *The Global Mufti: The Phenomenon of Yusuf al-Qaradawi*, 2009; Gudrun Krämer, *Gottes Staat als Republik. Reflexionen zeitgenössischer Muslime zu Islam, Menschenrechten und Demokratie*, 1999; Idem, *Hasan al-Banna*, 2010; Birgit Krawietz, *Hierarchie der Rechtsquellen im tradierten sunnitischen Recht*, 2002; Johanna Pink, *Neue Religionsgemeinschaften in Ägypten. Minderheiten im Spannungsfeld von Glaubensfreiheit, öffentlicher Ordnung und Islam*, 2003; Josef van Ess, *Theologie und Gesellschaft im 2. und 3. Jahrhundert Hidschra*, vol. 1, 1991; Muhammad Qasim Zaman, *The Ulama in Contemporary Islam: Custodians of Change*, 2002.

Qur'an ∞∞∞∞∞∞∞∞∞∞∞∞∞∞∞∞∞∞∞∞∞∞∞∞∞∞∞∞∞∞∞∞∞∞∞∞

Gerhard Bowering

The Qur'an, the holy book of Islam, is the most recent of the major sacred scriptures to have appeared in human history. It includes the prophetic proclamations of Muhammad (570–632) in Arabic, collected after his death in definitive written form and meticulously transmitted through the centuries. More than a billion Muslims around the globe consider the Qur'an to be the eternal word of God, who "sent down" the scripture as his final divine revelation and commissioned Muhammad to be the last prophet to proclaim his divine will for all of humanity to follow.

Muslims believe that as the most perfect and ultimate form of divine revelation, the Qur'an represents the final stage in a process through which divine speech is translated as scripture. In essence there is only one timeless revelation reiterated by the prophets, God's messengers throughout the ages, without any contribution of their own. From Adam, through Abraham, Moses, David, and Jesus, to Muhammad, the messengers are considered human beings as well as divinely chosen mouthpieces of revelation. God is the speaker of the Qur'an and Muhammad its recipient; the Qur'an itself is considered the verbatim word of God, revealed in clear Arabic to Muhammad.

Clearly understood, faithfully proclaimed, and accurately recited by Muhammad in historical time, the Qur'an, according to the normative Muslim view, was memorized with exact precision and also collected in book form by Muhammad's followers after his death. Then it was recited and copied with painstaking care in continuous transmission from generation to generation. Today, as in the past, the Qur'an is copied and recited in Arabic; it is pronounced only in Arabic in Muslim ritual worship by Arabs and non-Arabs alike. It cannot be rendered adequately into any other tongue, and, in the Muslim view, all translations are crutches, at best helpful explanations of its original intention and at worst doubtful makeshifts, obscuring its true meaning. Inasmuch as Muslims believe that the Qur'an has been preserved unchanged over time in its pristine Arabic, they also believe that it is superior to all other scriptures solely because of the faulty form in which other scriptures have been transmitted and preserved by their respective communities.

The Qur'an exhibits a significant relationship to the biblical tradition and echoes themes found in the epigraphical writings of Judaism and Christianity. No single collection of normative, midrashic, or apocryphal biblical writings, however, has been identified as the major source on which the Qur'an might directly depend. There is no evidence that this tradition had been translated into Arabic by the time of Muhammad, either as a whole corpus or in the form of single books. It is the widely shared view among historians of religion that Muhammad's knowledge of the biblical tradition came principally, if not exclusively, from oral sources. This oral lore, enriched by extrabiblical additions and commentary, was communicated to Muhammad in his mother tongue. However, it ultimately originated in traditions recorded mainly in Syriac, Ethiopian, and Hebrew, as evidenced by the vocabulary of foreign origin to be found in the Arabic Qur'an. Mainly, this foreign vocabulary had already been assimilated into the Arabic religious discourse of Muhammad's native environment.

The Qur'an is the first book-length production of Arabic literature and as such stands at the crossroads of the pre-Islamic oral, highly narrative, and poetical traditions of the Arabic language and the written, increasingly scholarly prose tradition of the subsequently evolving civilization of Islam. The beginnings of this transition in the Arabic language from the oral to the written tradition can be tied to the time and person of Muhammad and are clearly reflected in the rhymed prose style of the Qur'an. This rhymed prose (saj'), the mode of speech of the oracles uttered by the pre-Islamic soothsayer (kāhin), is a characteristic of the Qur'an, the first Arabic document of any length to exhibit this form of speech in written form. The roots of the Qur'an as the first Arabic book may also be detected in its content. In its verses, the Qur'an captures many topics that had formed an important part of the worship and cult of the nonscriptural tribal religion practiced in pre-Islamic Arabia. There is no doubt that the religious practice of Mecca exerted the most influence on the vision of Arab tribal religion that Muhammad acquired in his early life.

The Qur'an exerts a powerful spell on its listeners. It has a presence in everyday Muslim life, with its verses visible on the walls of mosques or inscribed in the hearts of men and women. For centuries, it has been copied in precious manuscripts and printed in definitive editions published all over the Islamic world. The Qur'an accompanies the Muslim believer from birth to death, and a copy of the book is kept in a special place in Muslim households. Words of the Qur'an are whispered into the ears of newborn children, daily prayers are taken from its verses, and particular words of its praise of God are exclaimed at set points in the daily routine of Muslims. All Muslims learn to recite essential passages of the Qur'an by heart from an early age and turn to them throughout their adult life. Some scholars commit its entire text to memory, and blind men often make it their profession to recite the Qur'an by heart at funerals and other special occasions.

Historical Origin and Development of the Qur'an

The most common translation of the Arabic word *qur'ān* is "recital," connoting that Muhammad heard the words from God and recited them without specific reference to a written text. If understood as rooted in a Syriac loanword, *qur'ān* would mean "a reading," such as a reading aloud of scripture in a liturgical context. In the actual text of the Qur'an, the word *qur'ān* refers to separate revelations made piecemeal to Muhammad or, more generally, to the revelation (*tanzīl*) that was sent down by God (specifically in the month of Ramadan). When it is understood to mean a book, the word *kitāb* (scripture) is used synonymously with "the Arabic Qur'an" that was revealed or, generally, as the manifest scripture that includes the wondrous "signs" (*āya*) sent down to manifest and expound God's power. The Qur'an calls itself a *dhikr* (admonition) and *ḥikma* (wisdom) as well as a *furqān* (salvation, discrimination) and even *sūra* ("section," i.e., a piece of revelation). Originally referring to component parts of the revelation, the terms *sūra* and *āya* eventually were chosen to denote "chapter" and "verse" of the Qur'an, respectively.

According to Qur'anic evidence, Muhammad understood his revelations as coming from a heavenly archetype, called "the mother of the scripture" (*umm al-kitāb*), that is described in the Qur'an as a well-guarded tablet, to be touched only by the pure angels—lofty leaves in the hands of noble scribes, unrolled sheets of parchment inscribed by the reed pen, a holy writ comprising all happenings in the universe. This heavenly scripture contains not only what is revealed through the Qur'an but also what previously has been revealed through the law (Tawrat) of Moses and gospel (Injil) of Jesus. Jews and Christians—"the people of the Scripture"—altered their own holy books, effecting serious discrepancies between their scriptures and the authentic Qur'an. Muhammad did not read this heavenly book but rather received words of revelation from it that no one may alter. They were brought down by the "spirit of holiness" (identified with the angel Gabriel) and induced trancelike moments of meditation or ecstatic states in which the shaken Muhammad had to be wrapped in a mantle. The words that he received were predominantly auditions rather than visions, some traces of visions in a few suras notwithstanding. The promptings came piecemeal and were couched in verses of rhymed prose. Some of these verses were clear and obvious, others obscure and ambiguous, but all of them were clearly distinct from Muhammad's ordinary words.

It is widely assumed that Muhammad proclaimed the Qur'an in the dialect of the people of Mecca and that the language of the Qur'an and its style originated from one particular person, Muhammad, rather than from a group of disparate individuals. Because Muhammad would add new revelations to the earlier ones throughout his career, when he died, there was not yet a collection of revelations in final form. Muslim tradition records the names of Ubayy b. Ka'b (d. between 640 and 656) and Zayd b. Thabit (d. between 662 and 675) as two followers who served Muhammad as scribes in Medina. In addition, Muhammad's wives Hafsa and Umm Kulthum could write, while his wives Umm Salama and 'A'isha could read but not write. Tradition also mentions that 'Abdallah b. Abi Sarh, foster brother of the third caliph 'Uthman b. 'Affan, claimed to have served Muhammad as a scribe and induced him on occasion to change the wording.

The actual collection of the Qur'an in book form was principally the work of Zayd b. Thabit, who knew Syriac and arithmetic. He was an expert on the division of inheritances during the time of Muhammad. He collected ransoms and calculated taxes during the caliphate of Abu Bakr, prepared written orders for the distribution of supplies during the caliphate of 'Umar b. al-Khattab, and oversaw the treasury during 'Uthman's caliphate. He was given the task of collecting the material that existed on various primitive writing materials and in the memoirs of men and wrote it down on "sheets" of uniform size (ṣuḥuf). Though there is some conflict in the traditions on this point, this collection seems to have been a process that may have begun during the caliphate of Abu Bakr and was furthered by the caliph 'Umar, whose daughter Hafsa (d. 665), a widow of Muhammad, is portrayed as the guardian of the ṣuḥuf. This process of collection came to a head during the caliphate of 'Uthman, who entrusted a commission, headed by Zayd b. Thabit, with the standard collection of the Qur'an in its rudimentary book form, considered the original copy of the Qur'an. It is known as the 'Uthmanic codex (muṣḥaf) and was established about 15 to 20 years after the Prophet's death.

Next to this standard codex established in Medina, tradition also attributes particular collections of the Qur'an to Companions of Muhammad that showed a somewhat different order of suras. Ubayy b. Ka'b's collection had two additional suras and 'Abdallah b. Mas'ud's (d. 652) lacked the last two suras of the 'Uthmanic codex. For a short time, these private collections enjoyed a measure of authority in the Syrian towns of Damascus and Homs and in the Iraqi towns of Kufa and Basra. They disappeared, however, after the 'Uthmanic codex had imposed uniformity as the authoritative standard, a standard in which Zayd's commission seems to have made the final order of the suras, many of which existed in a set order since the time of the Prophet while others show marks of having been put together in the final redaction. The order of the suras, 114 in number, was based on the principle of roughly decreasing length, which had the longest chapters in the beginning of the book and the shortest at its end. The short first sura, al-Fatiha ("the Opening"), numbering seven verses, was placed at the head of this authoritative standard, on which all Qur'ans are based.

Each of the individual chapters of the Qur'an is introduced by the formula, "In the name of God, the Merciful, the Compassionate" (except for the ninth sura, which might originally have formed a unit with the preceding chapter). The formula is also found once in the body of the Qur'an, at the head of Solomon's letter to the queen of Sheba. Immediately following this formula at the head of 29 suras, there are mysterious letters that are disconnected and convey no obvious meaning. Some of them occur only once and others are put together in patterns of two to five letters. Scholars have suggested a great variety of explanations about the meaning of these letters, but none of them has been accepted as probable, although they belong to the earliest stage of the Qur'anic redaction and cannot be explained as additions by later hands. The Qur'an does not refer to its suras by numbers; rather, each chapter has a particular name (or in some cases is known under a few different names). These names are clearly later additions to the Qur'an and were derived from catchwords that figure in the first few verses of a sura or are derived from a characteristic or odd word in the body of a sura. The division of the chapters into numbered verses, mainly based on rhyme, is likewise a later phenomenon that was not yet in use in the early centuries of the transmission of the Qur'an. The numbered verses, just like the numbers of the suras, have become standard, however, in the Qur'an copies in print today, although Muslims prefer to quote the suras by their names rather than their numbers.

The Analysis of the Qur'an in Scholarship

The 'Uthmanic codex established by the commission headed by Zayd b. Thabit was written in a rudimentary form, a "*scriptio defectiva*" constituting merely a consonantal skeleton lacking diacritical marks that distinguish certain Arabic consonants from one another. Oral recitation was needed to ascertain the intended pronunciation of the text by the addition of short vowels for its vocalization. As the Qur'anic orthography developed incrementally over more than two centuries and as the linkage between the consonantal skeleton and the oral recitation became increasingly robust, the deficiencies of the Arabic script were gradually overcome. The variants of recitation, the vast majority being of a minor nature, were either reconciled or accommodated, and the written text became increasingly independent of its linkage to oral pronunciation. This process culminated with the *scriptio plena*, the fully vocalized and pointed text of the Qur'an. This text may be considered a *textus recepetus, ne varietur* with the proviso that no single clearly identifiable textual specimen of the Qur'an was ever established or accepted with absolute unanimity.

The final, fully vocalized and pointed text of the Qur'an, accepted as normative and canonical, may best be understood as a construct underlying the work of Abu Bakr b. Mujahid (d. 936), who restricted the recitation of the Qur'an to seven correct readings, termed *ahruf* (literally, "letters") on the basis of a popular tradition. Ibn Mujahid accepted the reading (*qirā'a*) of seven prominent Qur'an scholars of the eighth century and declared them all to be based on divine authority. In 934 the Abbasid establishment promulgated the doctrine that these seven versions were the only acceptable forms of the text and all others forbidden. Nevertheless, "three after the seven" and "four after the ten" ways of reading were added somewhat later to form, respectively, 10 or 14 variant readings. Finally, each of the ten ways of reading was eventually accepted in two slightly varying versions (*riwāya*), all of which, at least theoretically, belong within the spectrum of the *textus receptus, ne varietur*. For all practical purposes, only two versions are in general use today—that of Hafs (d. 805) from 'Asim (d. 744), that is, Hafs's version based on 'Asims's way of reading, which received official sanction when it was adopted by the Egyptian standard edition of the Qur'an printed in 1924, and that of Warsh (d. 822) from Nafi' (d. 785), that is, Warsh's version based on Nafi''s way of reading, which is followed in North Africa with the exception of Egypt.

From the mid-19th century, Western scholars began to engage in serious literary research on the Qur'an, linking the scholarly findings of traditional Muslim scholarship with the philological and text-critical methods that biblical scholarship was developing in Europe. An intensive scholarly attempt was made to arrive at a chronological order of Qur'anic chapters and passages that could be correlated with the development and varying circumstances of Muhammad's career. This Western chronological approach to the Qur'an achieved its climax in the highly acclaimed *Geschichte des Qorans* (History of the Qur'an) by Theodor Nöldeke (1860), which was later revised and expanded by F. Schwally (1909 and 1919) and again by G. Bergsträsser (1938). The chronological sequencing of the suras elaborated by Western Qur'anic scholarship largely adopted the distinction of traditional Muslim scholarship between Meccan and Medinan suras already worked out in the *Itqan fi 'Ulum al-Qur'an* (Securing Qur'anic exegesis) by Jalal al-Din al-Suyuti (d. 1505), the major Muslim reference work on the Qur'anic sciences. However, it further subdivided the Meccan phase of Muhammad's proclamation of the Qur'an into three distinct periods. R. Bell, in his *The Qur'ān* and, posthumously, *A Commentary on the Qur'an*, took a radically different approach. He abandoned the chronological division into Meccan and Medinan periods and designed a disjointed dating system for individual verses in the Qur'an taken as a whole.

The overriding goal of the chronological framework of the Qur'an as elaborated in Western scholarship was to divide the Qur'anic proclamation into four distinct periods—Mecca I, Mecca II, Mecca III, and Medina. It linked these periods with a vision of the gradual inner development of Muhammad's prophetic consciousness and political career that Western scholarship had determined through biographical research on the life of Muhammad in conjunction with its research on the Qur'an. In general, the fourfold division of periods of the Qur'anic proclamation proceeded on the basis of two major principles. It related Qur'anic passages source-critically to historical events known from extra-Qur'anic literature, and it systematically analyzed the philological and stylistic nature of the Arabic text of the Qur'an passage by passage. It also placed clear markers between the Meccan periods at the time of the emigration to Abyssinia (about 615) and Muhammad's disillusioned return from Ta'if (about 620), and it retained the emigration in 622 as the divide between Meccan and Medinan suras.

The group of 48 short suras classified as belonging to the first or early Meccan period were identified by a similarity of style that gives expression to Muhammad's initial enthusiasm in a language that is rich in images, impassioned in tone, uttered in short and rhythmic verses, marked by a strong poetic coloring, and containing about 30 oaths or adjurations that introduce individual suras or passages. They are driven by a heightened awareness of the apocalyptic end of this world and God's final judgment of humanity. They include Muhammad's vehement attacks against his Meccan opponents for adhering to the old Arab tribal religion and his vigorous rebuttals to their damaging accusations against his claim of divine inspiration when they dismissively characterized him as a soothsayer (*kāhin*), sorcerer (*sāḥir*), poet (*shāʿir*), and a man possessed (*majnūn*).

The suras of the second or middle Meccan period, 21 in number, have longer units of revelation, which are more prosaic and do not exhibit a clearly distinct common character. They mark the transition from the excitement of the first phase to a Muhammad of greater calm who aims to influence his audience by parenetic proofs selected from descriptions of natural phenomena, illustrations from human life, and vivid depictions of paradise and hellfire. The stories of earlier prophets and elements from the story of Moses in particular are cited as admonitions for his enemies and as encouragement for the small group of his followers. The place of the oath is taken by introductory titles such "This is the revelation of God!" and by the frequently recurring "Say!" (*qul*), the divine command for Muhammad to proclaim a certain Qur'anic passage. The name *al-Rahmān* (the Merciful), a name for God in use prior to Islam in southern and central Arabia, although rejected by the pre-Islamic Meccans, is frequently employed yet dies out in the third period.

The suras of the third or late Meccan period, also 21 in number, cannot be seen as standing in any kind of inner chronological order. They exhibit a broad prosaic style with rhyme patterns that become more and more stereotyped, frequently ending in *-ūn* and *-īn*. In addressing his followers as a group, Muhammad frequently employs the formula, "O you people" (*yā ayyuhā al-nās*). Muhammad's imagination seems to be subdued; the revelations take on the form of sermons or speeches and the prophetic stories repeat earlier ideas. Overall, this group of suras could be understood to reflect Muhammad's exasperation at the stubborn resistance to his message on the part of his fellow Meccan tribesmen.

The suras of the Medinan period, 24 in number, follow one another in a relatively certain chronological order and reflect Muhammad's growing political power and his shaping of the social framework of the Muslim community. As the acknowledged leader in spiritual and social affairs of the Medinan community that had been torn by internal strife prior to his arrival, Muhammad's Qur'anic proclamation becomes preoccupied with criminal legislation; civil matters such as laws of marriage, divorce, and inheritance; and with the summons to warfare against opponents. Various groups of people are addressed separately by different epithets. The believers, the Meccan emigrants (*muhājirūn*) and their Medinan helpers (*anṣār*), are addressed as "you who believe," while the Medinans who distrusted Muhammad and hesitated in converting to Islam are called "hypocrites" (*munāfiqūn*). The members of the Jewish tribes of the Qurayza, Nadir, and Qaynuqaʿ are collectively called Jews (*yahūd*), and the Christians are referred to by the group name of Nazarenes (*naṣārā*). More than 30 times—and only in Medinan verses—the peoples who have been given a scripture in previous eras are identified collectively by the set phrase "the People of the Book" (*ahl al-kitāb*). They are distinguished from the *ummiyyūn* (gentiles) who have not been given a book previously but from among whom God selected Muhammad, called *al-nabī al-ummī* (the "gentile" prophet) in a late Meccan passage, as his messenger. A significant group of Qur'anic passages from Medinan suras refers to Muhammad's break with the Jewish tribes and his subsequent interpretation of the figure of Abraham, supported by Ishmael, as the founder of the Meccan sanctuary. Abraham is henceforth depicted as the prototypical Muslim (*ḥanīf*) who represents the original pure religion designated "the religion of Abraham" (*millat Ibrāhīm*), now reinstated by Muhammad.

The most radical chronological rearrangement of the suras and verses of the Qur'an, undertaken by R. Bell, concluded its elaborate hypothesis with many provisos. Bell suggested that the composition of the Qur'an followed three main phases: a "sign" phase, a "Qur'an" phase, and a "book" phase. The earliest phase of sign passages (*āyāt*) represents the major portion of Muhammad's preaching at Mecca, of which only an incomplete and partially fragmentary amount survives. The Qur'an phase included the later stages of Muhammad's Meccan career and about the first two years of his activity at Medina, a phase during which Muhammad was faced with the task of producing a collection of liturgical recitals (*qur'ān*). The book phase belonged to his activity at Medina and began at the end of the second year after the emigration, from which time Muhammad set out to produce a written scripture (*kitāb*). In the present Qur'an each of these three phases, however, cannot be separated precisely, because sign passages came to be incorporated into the liturgical collection and earlier oral recitals were later revised to form part of the written book. Regarding the redaction of the Qur'an during Muhammad's lifetime, the starting point for the Qur'an as sacred scripture, in Bell's view, had to be related to the time of the Battle of Badr in 624. For Bell, this was the watershed event, while the emigration did not constitute a great divide for the periodization of the suras.

None of the systems of chronological sequencing of Qur'anic chapters and verses has been accepted universally by contemporary scholarship. Nöldeke's sequencing and its refinements have established a rule of thumb for the approximate order of the suras in their chronological sequence. Bell's hypothesis has established that the final redaction of the Qur'an was a complex process of successive revisions of earlier material, whether oral or already available in rudimentary written form. In many ways, Western Qur'anic scholarship reconfirmed the two pillars on which the traditional Muslim views of Qur'anic chronology were based. First, the Qur'an was revealed piecemeal, and, second, it was collected into book form on the basis of both written documents prepared by scribes on Muhammad's dictation and Qur'anic passages preserved in the collective memory of his circle of Companions. All methods of chronological analysis, whether traditional Muslim or modern Western, agree that the order of the suras in Muhammad's proclamation was different from the order found in the written text we have today, where, in general, the suras are arranged according to decreasing length.

Political Elements in the Qur'an

As can be seen from his prophetical career, Muhammad's political actions were directed by an instinct for pragmatism. The Prophet did not act on the basis of preset principles of political theory but rather demonstrated a flexible and adaptable political practice. Examples of Muhammad's political documents are the Constitution of Medina, the treaty of Hudaybiyya, and the documents of alliances with Arab tribes.

The Qur'an, however, is foremost a religious message rather than a document of political theory. The Qur'an is an expression of Islamic beliefs, doctrines, rituals, laws, and practices; it is not a textbook of political theory, nor does it provide a system for political thought. Rather, it offers certain themes that constitute scattered building blocks for the eventual historical development of political thought in Islam. These elements do not represent a complete foundation or an articulated framework for the emergence of a systematic political vision in Islam, although some of them became cornerstones in the eventual political theories developed by Muslim thinkers over the centuries. The number of such elements is small, and, compared to the weight they carry in contemporary Islamic political thought, they appear to be at best stepping stones for political theories.

The core of the Islamic creed, the twofold Muslim profession of faith (*shahāda*)—"There is no god but God, and Muhammad is God's messenger" (*lā ilāha illā Allāh wa-Muḥammad rasūl Allāh*)—is intensified by the Qur'anic command, "Obey God and obey the messenger" (Q. 4:59) that is also embedded in the most articulate passage of the Qur'an on obedience and authority (Q. 24:47–56). The Shi'is augment this profession of faith by adding "and 'Ali is God's guardian" (*walīy Allāh*) and interpret the Qur'anic phrase "and those in authority among you" (Q. 4:59) as validating the authority of their imams as rulers of the community after the Prophet. The categorical command of obedience implies two basic dimensions for Islamic political thought. It defines the vertical axis of authority that intrinsically links obedience to God with obedience to the Prophet, intertwines the power of divine rule with human governance, and requires unquestioning submission to God combined with absolute allegiance to the Prophet. Furthermore, it marks the horizontal axis of an inextricable interrelation of religion and politics in Islam, the immutable religion (*al-dīn al-qayyim*, Q. 12:40) that the Prophet perfected (Q. 5:3) and proclaimed as the religion of submission to God, Islam.

The crux of the creed is Muhammad's self-perception as a prophet that developed from his early preaching in Mecca, where he presented himself as the reformer of the pre-Islamic tribal religion. He believed himself a "messenger" (*rasūl*) called by God for an Arab monotheistic and revealed religion that confirmed the revelations other peoples had received in their languages. In proclaiming his message, he drew inspiration from the example of earlier messengers (*rusul*), prophets (*nabiyyūn*), and biblical patriarchs, as well as leaders known from old Arab lore. Established in Medina after the hijra (emigration), he applied the term "prophet" (*nabī*) consciously to himself. Henceforth he had himself addressed as "O Prophet!" (*yā ayyuhā al-nabī*, Q. 33:45), and he understood himself as *al-nabī al-ummī* (Q. 7:157–58), the final prophet, and "the seal of the prophets" (*khātam al-nabiyyīn*, Q. 33:40). The authority of the earlier biblical prophets, who founded a community, was rooted in the covenant (*mīthāq*, *'ahd*) God had made with them. Yet only one passage, based on the small phrase "and with you" (*wa-minka*, Q. 33:7), refers to a covenant relationship with God on the part of Muhammad. Post-Qur'anic traditions recognized the tenuousness of this basis and tried to bolster it through legends such as the angelic cleansing of Muhammad's chest and his miraculous ascension to heaven (*mi'rāj*), symbols of a divine covenant with Muhammad.

The biblical background of the covenant is evident in Qur'anic references to God's covenant with pivotal prophetical figures of the Qur'an. On the day of the primordial covenant (Q. 7:172), humanity professed monotheism as its pledge in response to God's self-disclosure as their Lord at the dawn of creation. Since the dawn of creation, according to the Qur'an, God has made a covenant with humanity that is reinstituted from prophet to prophet throughout religious history. Although they are recipients of a covenant for their people, in the Qur'an the prophets are not immune to sin. Adam, "the father of the human race," carries in his loins the symbol of God's covenant, his progeny, the human race, as "the children of Adam," until the Day of Resurrection (Q. 7:172). Yet Adam broke the covenant together with Eve by eating from the tree of paradise (Q. 20:115)—an act, however, for which he repented. The symbol of Noah's covenant is the ark in which he is rescued together with his people (Q. 33:7). Abraham, the prototype of the true Muslim (*ḥanīf*, Q. 3:65–70), abandons the worship of astral deities (Q. 6:76–79), breaks the idols (Q. 21:58–67), builds the Ka'ba, and institutes the pilgrimage as the symbol of his covenant but violates the covenant through three lies: feigning illness (Q. 37:89), denying culpability (Q. 21:63), and passing his wife off as his sister (according to tradition). Joseph, whose mark of the covenant is his inspired ability to interpret dreams, showed his readiness to commit sin with the wife of the Egyptian (Q. 12:24) but was divinely protected from acting on it. Moses, in his encounter with God on Mount Sinai, receives the tablets as the symbol of his covenant (4:142–45), and in his desire to see God, he falls to the ground as if struck by lightning as the mountain is crumbled to dust (4:142–45). But he breaks the covenant by slaying another human being without any right to blood revenge, while his followers, "the Children of Israel," break the covenant made at Sinai through their idolatry of the calf (Q. 2:63).

David, who represents the covenant in his receiving the psalms (Zabur), slaying of Goliath, and appointment as God's viceroy (*khalīfa*) to dispense justice, asks for God's forgiveness (Q. 38:24). Solomon, heir to David's throne, receives as a symbol of his covenant immense knowledge and wisdom, giving him power over humans and demons (*jinn*) and the capacity to understand the speech of birds and command the wind. Solomon had to repent for idolatry (Q. 38:34). Jesus, the son of Mary, the Messiah and the recipient of the Gospel (Injil), is spirit from God (*rūḥun minhu*) and his word (*kalimatuhu*, Q. 4:171) as well as God's servant (*'abd Allāh*). He has his symbol in the power to give life by raising the dead and breathing life into figures of clay (Q. 3:47; 5:110). The Qur'an rejects the crucifixion of Jesus but accepts the ascension in an earthly body: "They did not kill him nor crucify him, but it was made to seem so to them" (*shubbiha lahum*, Q. 4:157). His death on the cross as a sign of defeat is therefore denied in the Qur'an, but his being raised to life directly from the cross is granted (Q. 4:158). It is God Himself who says in the Qur'an, "O Jesus, I am going to take you and raise you to Me" (*mutawaffika wa-rāfi'uka*, Q. 3:55). This position resembles the Gnostic Christian belief that only a counterfeit (simulacrum) of Jesus was crucified.

In the Qur'an, Muhammad stands in the line of the prophets, who are human beings with all their foibles and flaws and their sins and acts of disobedience before God. In the Qur'an Muhammad expressly states, "I am only a mortal like you" (Q. 18:110), who receives forgiveness for all the sins of his life, "may God forgive you your past sin and your sin that is to come" (Q. 48:2). Tradition explains that Muhammad was "erring" (Q. 93:7) when he toyed with a compromise of his monotheism by accepting three Meccan female deities as divine intercessors next to God, sacrificed to a heathen goddess before his call, and married Zayd's wife. The Qur'an portrays Muhammad as a human being as well as the carrier of a revelation and leader of his community. In post-Qur'anic literature, he was put on a pedestal; ranked above all other prophets before him; and attributed the power of intercession on the Last Day, sitting next to God on the divine throne. In his ascension to heaven, he passes beyond the other prophets who each rule one of the seven spheres. His colloquy with God, associated with his ascension to heaven and linked with his encounter of God's presence at the Lote Tree of the boundary (Q. 53:13–18), becomes the symbol of his covenant through the divine institution of the five daily prayers. Through association with the famous light verse (Q. 24:35), Muhammad is perceived created as "light from light" and taking the place of Adam—the last prophet taking the place of the first—as he swears his oath of fealty to God on behalf of all of humanity. His message, reconfirming the religion of Abraham, surpasses it by reflecting most perfectly the light of the innate primal religion (*fiṭra*, Q. 30:30), enshrined in all human beings since the dawn of creation.

There is hardly any emphasis in the Qur'an on Muhammad as a political leader or lawgiver. The Qur'an, however, juxtaposes the background of the history of the prophets and their covenants with the oath of allegiance, a ceremony rooted in a pre-Islamic tribal institution. Obedience to God is linked with obedience to the Prophet, and obedience to the Prophet is made manifest through entrance into the community by an oath of allegiance. The formal gesture of the oath of allegiance (*bay'a*) was the ceremonial handclasp. Exchanged with the Prophet, it implied a pledge of fealty to God (Q. 48:10). The *bay'a* guaranteed the gift of God's protection and reward, mediated by the Prophet, in exchange for the loyalty of the person who joined Muhammad's community and surrendered to God. It possessed the character of a contractual agreement rooted in the ceremonial of pre-Islamic commercial transactions. In this sense, submission to God became symbolized by "grasping the firmest handle" (*al-'urwa al-wuthqā*, 2:256), an act that meant abandoning idolatry and doing good works. "Whoever surrenders his face to God and does good, has grasped the firmest handle" (Q. 31:22).

New converts to Islam enter into the community by swearing allegiance to the Prophet, who represents the covenant humanity made with God at the dawn of creation and the fashioning of Adam as father of the human race. Sworn by an individual entering the fold of Islam, this oath manifests two aims. It recognizes the authority of the person to whom it is given and expresses the adherence to the message of the person who represents and proclaims it. On the power of this oath, the Qur'an prescribes fighting to Muhammad's followers in Medina and demands that military commands be obeyed (Q. 22:39–40). When decisive action had to be taken during crucial moments of his cause, formal oaths of allegiance were made to Muhammad (Q. 48:10). Such vows of obedience became the norm when Muhammad's polity in Medina grew in numbers (Q. 9:11–12), although the Qur'an indicates that Muhammad did not always find it easy to enforce compliance (Q. 9:38–57; 9:81–106). A particular case is the oath of allegiance to the Prophet sworn by women, traditionally linked with the treaty of Hudaybiyya that includes as its conditions the core commands of the Decalogue (Q. 60:12). The treaty made between Muslims and pagans at the sacred mosque of Mecca, however, is a pact ('ahd) and hence does not imply an oath of allegiance (Q. 9:7).

Three particular terms in the Qur'an, *umma, khalifa,* and jihad, have become highly valued fulcrums of Islamic political thought in Islamic history, although they do not appear in a prominent position in the Qur'an itself. The term *umma* (community), appearing about 60 times in the Qur'an, is a loanword from Hebrew and Aramaic that refers to groups of people who are included in the divine plan of salvation. In the view of the Qur'an, humanity consists of a plurality of communities, each to whom God sends messengers to guide and test them (Q. 6:42), but the messengers are usually attacked and accused of lying. When each *umma* is brought to judgment on the Last Day, God will call upon their respective messengers to give witness against those who did not follow their message (Q. 4:41). The Qur'an explains the plurality of the communities from the divine will. Originally, God created one *umma* (Q. 10:19), but humanity became disunited because of their malice and rancor. In the Meccan suras, the Qur'an envisages the Arabs of Mecca as forming an *umma*; in the Medinan suras a new "community surrendering to God" (*umma muslima,* Q 2:213) is founded on a religious basis that bids to honor and forbids dishonor (Q. 3:104, 110). The famous statement of the Prophet, "My community (*umma*) will never agree upon an error," is a post-Qur'anic tradition. Only twice does the Qur'an mention the related term, "the party of God" (*ḥizb Allāh,* 5:56; 48:22), and the term *jamā'a,* later so prominent and used to denote the whole body of the believers as a unified "community," does not appear in the Qur'an at all. The Qur'anic term, *milla* (religious community), an Aramaic or Hebrew loanword, appears 15 times in the Qur'an and 8 times as "Abraham's religion," in which sense it is applied to Muhammad's community. As such, however, it means "religion" and does not imply the aspect of solidarity and unity that is so predominant in Islamic political thought.

Another Qur'anic term that has only tenuous Qur'anic moorings with regard to political authority is the notion of *khalifa,* which appears only twice in the singular in the Qur'an and seven times in the plural. With reference to Adam, the Qur'an says, "I am setting a viceroy in the Earth" (Q. 2:30), and with reference to David, the Qur'an says, "We have appointed you a viceroy in the Earth" (Q. 38:26). The

Qur'anic reference to Adam represents a divine address to the angels who are being told by God that Adam, and with him the human race, will be their "successor" (*khalīfa*) inhabiting the Earth. The passage about David as "successor" has a political and juridical meaning in that David is commissioned by God to judge justly between people. The notion itself does not imply the idea of the caliph, conceived as representative of God's messenger or even as shadow of God on Earth, although in later political theories the term took on a politically charged meaning and, in Sunni interpretation, became the key term for the caliph as head of the Muslim polity, called somewhat ineptly the "vicar of God's messenger" (*khalīfat rasūl Allāh*). For their idea of supreme leadership, the Shi'is have erected impressive theological theories around the term "imam" (leader), which appears in the Qur'an seven times in the singular and five times in the plural. It refers to Abraham as "a leader for the people" (Q. 2:124); to the Book of Moses as "a model" (Q. 11:17; 46:12); to the prophets raised from the progeny of Adam, who will give witness about the conduct of their communities on the Day of Judgment (Q. 17:71); to pious Muslims as leaders in faith; and to both righteous and unjust leaders. Both Sunnism and Shi'ism employed the term *imāma* (leadership, imamate) for their theological discourse on leadership and authority.

Similarly, in the Qur'an, jihad, a highly prominent slogan of Islamic political thought, means "struggle" or "striving," which, coupled with the notion of fighting "in the path of God" (*fī sabīl Allāh*, Q. 2:190; cf. 9:24; 60:1), gained its predominantly political meaning of "warfare" through post-Qur'anic interpretation. As used in the Qur'an (the verbal noun, *jihād*, occurs but four times in the Qur'an: 9:24; 22:78; 25:52; 60:1), only a small portion of the term's semantic range can be linked with warfare. On the contrary, the majority of the relevant passages point to an origin in the pre-Islamic tribal perception that one must demonstrate oneself deserving of the deity's reward through hardship, pilgrimage, poverty, and perseverance in trials and tribulations. Rather, the Qur'an expresses warfare mainly by employing a semantic field that expresses the order to fight and slay the infidels (*qitāl*), as exemplified in Qur'an 9:1–14. There is no doubt that the Prophet encouraged his followers to fight and proclaimed fighting as a divine command, and Qur'an 22:40 may be the first Medinan verse that deals with fighting the unbelievers. Many other verses exhort the believers to fight "with their possessions and their selves." Those who "are slain or die in the path of God" (Q. 3:157–58) are promised eternal reward—they will be "living with their Lord" and rejoicing "in the bounty that God has given them" (Q. 3:169–70), while those who are not willing to fight are threatened with hellfire (Q. 9:81). Exhortations to fight and participate in warfare can be found many times in the Qur'an (e.g., Q. 4:84; 8:65), but it was not the term "jihad" that was their standard Qur'anic expression.

There is no one coherent doctrine of warfare in the Qur'an, and exegetes found it difficult to reconcile ambiguous and contradictory verses given both the inconsistent Qur'anic terminology on warfare and Muhammad's increasingly hostile relations with the Meccans that developed into open warfare after his emigration to Medina. Muslim exegesis tried to resolve these ambiguities and contradictions through the use of certain methodological techniques, particularly theories of abrogation and specification that regarded Qur'an 9:5 and 9:29 as ultimately superseding earlier verses. The basis for these theories may be found in the Qur'an itself in a passage (Q. 4:76–77) that implies an inner-Qur'anic evolution with regard to warfare. When relevant Qur'anic verses are read chronologically, one may construct four stages in the evolution of Qur'anic exhortations to warfare. Before his emigration to Medina, Muhammad was instructed by God to pardon the unbelievers and to desist from engagement in warfare. After the hijra, however, his followers were given permission to retaliate for injustices they had suffered from the Meccans (Q. 22:39–40). As the altercations with the Meccans increased, they were exhorted to fight against unbelievers as long as they observed certain conditions. Then they were given the divine command to rescind all treatises with the unbelievers and fight them unconditionally (Q. 9:1–4). Finally, God's ultimate and unconditional command to engage in warfare was given expression in the "sword verse" (Q. 9:5) with regard to the unbelievers and the "poll tax verse" (Q. 9:29) with regard to "the People of the Book." A group of Qur'anic verses (Q. 2:216; 4:71; 9:38–41; 9:120–22) provide the basis for the legal definition of jihad as a collective duty (*fard kifāya*) and not an individual obligation (*fard 'ayn*) that became the normative principle elaborated by the scholars of Islamic law.

The Qur'an not only exhorts to warfare but also stipulates a series of specific conditions that served as the basis for later Islamic thought on the purpose of warfare and the definition of a just war. A good number of Qur'anic verses counsel patience and forbearance with respect to the unbelievers, warn Muslims to avoid fighting, recommend forgiveness and generosity, and advise arguing with opponents in a peaceful manner, while other verses warn unbelievers of God's vengeance (Q. 3:19). Warfare against idolaters who are to be converted to Islam is differentiated from fighting against the People of the Book—whether they are Jews, Sabians (i.e., Manicheans or Mandeans), or Christians (Q. 2:62; 5:69, 82)—who are identified as enjoying a measure of tolerance. The famous and oft-quoted verse, "There is no compulsion in religion" (*lā ikrāha fī al-dīn*, Q. 2:256), however, does not proclaim the principle of tolerance as the Qur'anic ideal—it simply states that compelling acceptance of religion must prove a futile exercise in the face of obstinacy. As purposes for warfare other than subjection and nominal conversion, the Qur'an mentions revenge for violation of treaties and retaliation for attacks of adversaries as well as self-defense and the defense of weak members of the community. Exemption from warfare is granted to the physically handicapped (Q. 4:17). Other verses deal with the treatment of prisoners and safe conduct. Qur'an 8:67 exhorts the Prophet not to take prisoners—a norm judged to be abrogated by Qur'an 47:4, which accepts ransom for prisoners or offers outright pardon. Other very specific stipulations would be added in Islamic tradition, such as the interdiction against killing enemy noncombatants (women, children, and the elderly); mutilating bodies; harming infrastructure such as buildings and fruit trees; and embezzling spoils.

The idea of "holy war," however, is not present in the Qur'an at all, although warfare may be considered sacred to a certain extent because it is commanded and rewarded by God under certain conditions.

The Legacy of the Qur'an

Throughout its entire text, the Qur'an intertwines two basic traditions, the pre-Islamic tribal and the Judeo-Christian, through loanwords drawn from Aramaic, Syriac, or Hebrew and assimilated by the Arabic of the Qur'an. This power of association has been noted earlier in the typological history of messengers and prophets that include central biblical figures next to leaders and heroes of pre-Islamic Arabian lore. Similarly, the celestial messengers among the angels show an association with the spirits and demons (*jinn*) of tribal Arabia, as can be seen in the figure of the devil that merges Shaytan with Iblis (i.e., *diabolos*), the fallen angel. The intertwining of these traditions can also be seen in some of the central rituals of the Qur'an, the "pillars of religion," as for instance the daily ritual prayer, the obligation of almsgiving, the month of fasting, and the yearly pilgrimage. Ritual prayer (salat) combines recitation of scripture and liturgical worship at precise times of the day with gestures of submission offered in the direction of the sanctuary of the Ka'ba. The twin institution of almsgiving (zakat) links the practice of benevolence and charitable righteousness toward the poor and needy with taxes levied on property, crops, and merchandise, and it is collected for the necessities of warfare and from the dues paid by tribes adopting Islam. The ritual obligation of fasting (*sawm*) assimilates aspects of monastic asceticism and abstinence with the Arab month of Ramadan, established in the tradition of sacred months during which bloodshed was prohibited in pre-Islamic tribal Arabia. The Muslim pilgrimage (hajj) merges tribal festival traditions at the Meccan sanctuary and on the hill of 'Arafat with the story of Abraham and his sacrifice.

At the death of Muhammad, Abu Bakr (d. 634), the first caliph and Muhammad's direct successor, is said to have coined the slogan "Whosoever has worshiped Muhammad—Muhammad is dead. Whosoever has worshiped God—God lives and will not die." His message was that although Muhammad had died, God's word would endure. No new prophet was required to come and renew his message.

What counted throughout history was the membership in the community based on the Qur'an and the memory of the Prophet's sayings and actions, as demonstrated by two early monuments of Islam. The construction of the Dome of the Rock in Jerusalem in 692 was established as a sign of triumph over the power of the Byzantine Empire, facing the ruins of the Christian landmark, the Church of the Sepulchre, on the opposite hill of the city. Inscribed on the Dome's walls were words taken from sura 112, the Qur'anic manifesto aiming at Christianity: "Say, He is God, One. God, the Impenetrable, who has not begotten, and has not been begotten, and equal to Him is not any one." The Umayyad Mosque of Damascus, standing in the place of the destroyed church of John the Baptist, would bear the inscription of the year 706, "Our Lord is God alone, our religion is Islam and our Prophet is Muhammad," where the person of the Prophet seems to overshadow his message, the Qur'an. Although the Prophet proclaimed the Qur'an, Islam became supremely a religion of the book. The word of the Qur'an has a much greater weight in Islam than the New Testament does in Christianity, for in Islam the dogma of *incarnatio*, the Word become flesh, is transformed into the belief of *inlibratino*, the Word become book. Jesus did not manifest the urge to compose a book; Mani (216–76), the founder of Manicheanism, had done so, and Muhammad would proclaim the final holy book. The Qur'an was not "good news" proclaimed by a group of narrators but instead God's own speech, warning and reminding humanity of God's presence in his word.

The Qur'an came into being at a time of a paradigm shift in human history when myth was overtaken by history, and when, in Arabia, a book of parchment overpowered graffiti on the rocks. Breaking into the bright light of history from the dark ages of the Arab past, the Arabic language of the Qur'an became the idiom of a newly arrived "third world," pushing a wedge between the Greco-Roman and Indo-Persian culture zones. When the Qur'an entered the scene of world history, Judaism and Christianity read their respective Bibles in translations, rather than in the original idioms of Moses or Jesus. The Arabic Qur'an, however, has remained steady and fixed until the present in the idiom of its messenger and the language of the listeners to whom it had been addressed. Although the Qur'an was not a wholly coherent book, with its evidence of abrogation, and had weaknesses of repetition, it became understood as eternal by virtue of being the divine speech. It came to be regarded as the normative scripture of Islam, possessing inimitability (*i'jāz*) and rhetorical superiority even if linguistic elegance was granted to Arabic poetry.

As scripture the Qur'an was identical with the word of God recorded since eternity and, in the view of some, known in its entirety by Muhammad even before he was called to come forth as a prophet. By reproducing the word of God in this world, prophecy separated it from God as his revelation. As text it recorded the trace (*rasm*) that divine speech left in this world through its letters and consonants, distinguished by diacritical marks and carrying vowel signs. As divine speech it was considered the actual inner speech of God, eternal in nature and revealed from on high as sounds that were God's own voice (*sawt*) and his own pronunciation (*lafẓ*). God's speech, which had been heard in different historical epochs by other prophets, now was spoken forth by Muhammad, either directly as God's mouthpiece in the ecstatic utterances of the early Meccan period or mediated by Gabriel, the angel of revelation who "brought it down upon your heart" (Q. 2:97), in the extended passages of the Medinan period of its proclamation. The stage was thus set for the "Trial" (*miḥna*, 833–48), the great theopolitical struggle about the nature of the Qur'an defined by the antagonists as centering on the issue of the "created" versus "uncreated" nature of the word of God, a divisive contention Muhammad himself had neither anticipated nor offered guidance on in either direction.

Further Reading

R. Bell, *The Qur'ān*, 2 vols., 1937–39; Idem, *A Commentary on the Qur'an*, 1991; J. Burton, *The Collection of the Qur'ān*, 1977; M. Cook, *The Koran: A Very Short Introduction*, 2000; J. Jeffery, *The Qur'an as Scripture*, 1952; J. D. McAuliffe, *The Cambridge Companion to the Qur'ān*, 2006; A. Neuwirth, *Der Koran als Text der Spätantike: Ein europäischer Zugang*, 2010; R. Paret, *Der Koran: Kommentar und Konkordanz*, 1977; F. Rahman, *Major Themes of the Qur'an*, 1980; N. Robinson, *Discovering the Qur'an*, 1996; J. Wansbrough, *Quranic Studies*, 1977; W. M. Watt, *Introduction to the Qur'an*, 1970; S. Wild, *The Qur'an as Text*, 1996.

Revival and Reform ◇◇◇◇◇◇◇◇◇◇◇◇◇◇◇◇◇◇◇◇◇◇◇◇◇◇◇◇◇◇◇◇◇◇◇◇◇

Ebrahim Moosa and SherAli Tareen

Revival and reform, *tajdīd* and *iṣlāḥ*, are terms widely disseminated across a range of genres in Muslim literature. They are found in commentaries of prophetic traditions, political discourses, debates about shariʿa, and the integrity of learning and scholarship. Often these key words are rhetorically invoked in exhortations of moral awakening in order to advance a Muslim social and political gospel. Over time, these terms have been used together to represent a concept that links newness and creativity (renewal/revival) to wholeness and integrity (*iṣlāḥ*, reform). Whether the "renewal and reform" is aimed at the collective or the individual or both, the discourse of revival and reform addresses stability and change, the mutable and immutable in Muslim thought. In this larger semantic framework, two things loom large: political theology and the integrity of the learned tradition. Renewal and revival (*tajdīd*) stem from the root *j-d-d*, to make new, to innovate, to refresh and resuscitate. One may think of reform as a discourse of improvement, recovery, and healing. Indeed, *iṣlāḥ* (repair) is derived from the Arabic root *ṣ-l-ḥ*, which means to mend, restore, and improve.

Plain readings of the proof texts suggest that renewal will not only resuscitate the body politic of both community and society but also heal and restore the brokenness of the moral order. This restorative aspect made this conceptual category attractive and appealing to all kinds of public actors who advanced a political, spiritual, and intellectual agenda for the betterment of both individuals and society.

The key report attributed to the Prophet Muhammad on the question of renewal states, "Indeed, at the beginning of every century God dispatches to this confessional community (*umma*) a person who will renew its *dīn*—salvation practices (religion)." Another report on the topic says, "God shows benevolence to the people who are part of His order of *dīn* at the beginning of every century by dispatching a man from my family who will clarify to them matters related to their salvation practices (*dīn*)."

Paradox, however, lies at the heart of the renewal-reform concept. A countervailing concept, called illicit innovation (*bidʿa*), appears to ascribe dire consequences to expressions of newness and creativity. Generally, the prophetic statement "all innovation leads to misguidance" is understood to suggest that innovation in matters of *dīn* were forbidden. Thus alterations to normative standards of behavior (sunna) as well as those concepts associated with these normative practices were viewed as an egregious disruption of the paradigm of salvation. Even supplementing or altering the practices of *dīn*, without reference to the broader purposes of the Islamic ethics (shari'a), was frowned upon. Over time new paradigmatic shifts occurred that tolerated alteration to the practices of *dīn*, provided that they cohered with the overall goals of the shari'a. The tension generated by the enthusiasm to promote renewal-reform, on the one hand, and the proscription of illicit innovation in matters of *dīn*, on the other, required some explanation. The two conceptual categories were not polarities but rather mutually constitutive. Renewal and reform were providential promises for the continued betterment of God's approved faith community. This forward-looking momentum was sustained by traditions attributed to the Prophet, which said, "The parable of my community is like that of rain. It is not known whether the best part is when it begins to rain or when it ends." Twelver Shi'i Islam has a strong messianic dimension in the expectation of the return of the political-spiritual leadership of the imam who went into occultation, but it has no tradition of centennial renewal. Sunni Islam, however, rooted its notion of perpetual low-key messianism in the idea of centennial renewal. Coupled with the sentiment of a melancholic exilic framework (namely, "true" Islam's estrangement in the world), this cluster of concepts constituted Sunni Islam's political theology.

Political theology, in the words of contemporary theorist Jan Assmann, is the "ever-changing relationships between political community and religious order, in short, between power [or authority: Herrschaft] and salvation [Heil]." Muslim thinkers such as Mawardi articulated a similar idea somewhat differently through the prism of leadership and governance: "Leadership (*imāma*) was designed in order to succeed the role of prophecy by protecting the order of salvation (*dīn*) and managing the affairs of the world." There was a conjunction of the religious order and the political order for these Muslim thinkers, too. But what made Muslim political theology so different from its counterpart in Christianity was that the political-theological in Islam was intimately related to the idea of prophecy. With the death of the Prophet Muhammad, the responsibility of his mission passed on to those who were designated as the guardians of the knowledge produced by prophecy, namely revelation. Since salvation was a core idea of Islam, the knowledge of practices was integral to the order of revelation. The semi-sacrosanct character of the discursive tradition, in turn, elevated the status and power of the scholars ('ulama'), the mediators of the learned tradition. The learned in Islam were seen as the true heirs of prophetic charisma. Statements attributed to the Prophet suggested that the learned "were analogous to the prophets among the Israelites." Given the equivalence between the learned and the prophets of yore, the power and authority of tradition were inseparable from Muslim political theology. And given this rather elevated status of the learned, the tradition that they managed and interpreted also acquired a certain semi-sacrosanct status.

Another way of putting this was that the Prophet in Islam had two bodies that paralleled his two primary earthly roles. The first was the Prophet's political body in his capacity as God's messenger, who established a political order that favored the transcendent good. The second was his moral body in his role as teacher of wisdom and the transcendent good (*yuʿallimuhum al-kitāb wa-l-ḥikma*), whose embodied life (sunna) became the reference point of imitation. After Muhammad's death, the political body was continuously articulated through the concept of stewardship (*khilāfa* in Sunnism or imamate in Shiʿism), and the body of knowledge provided by the Prophet lived on in the Islamic knowledge tradition.

Reform and the Meaning of Tradition

The concept of reform was put to different uses by a range of Muslim actors and social movements. One can thus pose several questions: What do Muslims mean by revival and reform across time? What are the goals of revival and reform? Did revival and reform resonate differently over time and serve different functions at distinct periods of Muslim history?

Any conception of Muslim reform was intimately connected to tradition. To reform a tradition was to recover it, in order to rehabilitate it to its original form. If one understood tradition as a continuing moral argument that authoritatively connected a community's memory of the past to its present and future, then reform was the process of restoring that tradition, of sustaining the promise of its continued repetition and also inventing it simultaneously. Reform in Islam, therefore, did not have a singular meaning or trajectory. Modernist presumptions about reform imagined it to be progressive and incremental. To the contrary, apart from some recent modernist discourses, reform in Islam was usually mobilized to "re-form" what was already in place, to restore the original form of a practice or an idea to shield it from the specter of change and newness. Any attempt to restore an original form, however, was always vulnerable to the possibility of creating something new instead of restoring the original. Therefore reform, even when it ostensibly sought to resist change, could not escape the inherent dynamism of creativity and change.

In order for a project of reform to authorize itself, it had to identify an object of reform, a fractured object that was available and in need of healing, mending, and improvement. In that sense, reform was integral to the story of Islam from its very beginnings. Reform was in many ways at the heart of Prophet Muhammad's career. Moreover, the divine revelation transmitted through the Prophet told a particular story of moral fracture, disintegration, and chaos about the place and time in which it was revealed. The seventh-century Arabic context, so the story went, was enveloped by the corruptions of unbelief, polytheism, and idolatry. People valorized ancestral authority over divine command, tribal customs over divinely sanctioned law. The revelation of the Qurʾan, as embodied in the figure of the Prophet, intervened to mend, resolve, and reform that disorder.

The philosopher/historian Quentin Skinner wrote that certain modes of inquiry rest on what he called "a question and answer space." Skinner maintained that a proposition was only properly understood if the question that elicited an answer was properly identified and articulated. The meaning of a proposition, in other words, was relative to the question it answered and could not, as a consequence, be discovered by lifting it out of the discursive process or milieu of which it was a constitutive part. In order to conceptualize the narrative plot of Muslim reformist discourses, one must examine the nature of the questions the reformists imagined alongside the answers they provided. More precisely, the moral argument for submitting to the absolute sovereignty of the divine represented an answer to a society crippled by polytheism and idolatry. This original story of contestation between those who affirmed and detracted from divine sovereignty served as the paradigmatic narrative plot that haunted almost all subsequent moments of Muslim reform, in both the premodern and modern periods.

Indeed, the authority of any project of reform depended on its ability to establish the relevance of its own question and answer space within the context of the Prophet's time. Reform then emerged as the trope of reenacting the narrative drama of prophetic time in a new context or present. Such instances of narrative "translation" populate the intellectual history of premodern Islam.

Ibn Khaldun: History and Change

In his magnum opus, the *Muqaddima* (Prolegomena), the historian and polymath Ibn Khaldun (1332–1406) demonstrated that apocalyptic narratives in the prophetic traditions were by and large not reliable. Often the predictions made about the end times in the prophetic traditions were of a political character. Reports predicted the political fate of pious and impious rulers and the rise and fall of dynasties with great specificity and detail. Ibn Khaldun treated many of these reports as spurious. He used his skills as a historiographer of the hadith literature to show that some of the material recorded in the books of prognostications (*malāḥim*) were either weak reports or tied to the sectarian conflicts endemic to early Islam.

Acutely aware that many of these discourses were constructed, Ibn Khaldun then examined some of the narratives that explained the messianic coming of the guide or Mahdi before the apocalypse. Often these narratives, he stated, were deeply coded with political agendas that gave power to those who wielded them: "The time, the person, place, everything is indicated in these many spurious and arbitrary proofs. Then the time passes without a trace of the predictions coming true. Then they fabricate another narrative replete with linguistic equivocations, along with imaginary and astrological claims!" The idea of the imminent advent of a person who would renew both the moral values of the faith community (*aḥkām al-milla*) and the principles of truth (*marāsim al-ḥaqq*) was prevalent among his Sufi contemporaries, Ibn Khaldun wrote. He claimed to have been in touch with relatives of some saintly figures who expected the arrival of such a renewer at the beginning of the eighth Islamic century, corresponding to the 14th century on the Gregorian calendar. Ibn Khaldun did not cite any authority, such as a prophetic report about the centennial renewer from the collection of Abu Dawud, a collection with which he was familiar. Rather, Ibn Khaldun implied that such activities of renewal were part of the practice of the Sufis. He reminded his readers that charismatic authority on its own was insufficient to gain power. One needed something more fundamental in order to institutionalize change: hegemonic power. He explicitly stated, "No religious or political propaganda can be successful, unless hegemonic power (*shawka 'aṣabiyya*) prevail in order to support such religious and political aspirations and to defend them against adversaries until God's will materializes in these matters." Central to Ibn Khaldun's theory for any religious or political transformation to successfully occur was the need to be in a position to wield what he called group solidarity (*'aṣabiyya*): in other words, the acquisition of hegemonic power was necessary in order to make things happen. Any religious call or political mission had to be backed up by a form of social solidarity that became the basis and vehicle for the transmission of ideas.

Religion, in Ibn Khaldun's view, played a central role in leavening the hegemonic political power he regarded as fundamental to social organization. Political authority, what he called royal authority, needed some kind of compelling appeal that was provided by religion, which held people together. In fact, one might say that Ibn Khaldun used the notion of religion in the sense of an ideology. Arabs in their state of nature were uncontrollable, he said, and their traits were tailor-made for anarchy and the ruin of civilization. Then something transformative happened that rendered them capable of governance. That elixir, in his view, was *dīn*, a set of practices and behaviors central to salvation, which transformed the community that adopted it. He described the way *dīn* shaped both the individual subject and the community attached to it. Inspired by a Qur'anic expression of *sibghat Allāh* (the color of God), Ibn Khaldun freely used the expression *sibgha dīniyya* (religious coloration) to describe the deep transforming experience a people derived from prophecy or from their engagement with religion. "Arabs are by nature remote from political leadership," he said. "They attain power only once their nature has undergone a complete transformation under the influence of some religious coloring that wipes out all such [negative qualities] and causes the Arabs to have a restraining influence on themselves."

Even though Ibn Khaldun did not give much weight to prophetic materials, he was aware of the potential and limits of social reform based on religion. He was aware of reform initiatives taken by figures in North Africa whose theopolitical platform was to propagate the truth and reestablish the prophetic traditions. Ideally, such changes required the moral correction of humanity (*iṣlāḥ al-khalq*), but often such efforts, he claimed, resulted in superficial changes. The rhetorical keystroke of the reform initiatives was to connect people to the sunna of the Prophet Muhammad and to instruct them to desist from living a life of sin, he said. The rate of successful change in some of the folk he had observed, he admitted, was limited. Some merely desisted from a life of highway robbery and brigandage without really changing their conduct when they adopted a religious ethic. While such cessation of sin was by all accounts noteworthy, Ibn Khaldun's larger point was that internalizing a religious ethic required additional education. Merely raising the standard of the sunna and rooting out the wrongs were not sufficient.

Premodern Imaginaries of Reform

The sunna played a key role in the earliest discourses on renewal and the healing of the faith community. A report in the book of Abu Dawud stated, "Indeed, God deputes to this faith community (*umma*) at the beginning of every century one who will renew its salvific practices (*din*)." This pithy statement captured the redemptive utopia of Islam and also structured its sense of history. Not only did providence play an important role in the self-understanding of the faith community, human agency was explicitly affirmed in the renewal process. Furthermore, temporality and human agency were inseparable, while Islam as a faith was equipped with a reformist gospel. In other words, Islam as a discursive project was a human-God partnership or covenant. In order to keep the faith community vibrant and to render it temporally relevant, it would require a regular process of renewal—but the nature of this process and the spheres in which it would take place were points of contention among Muslims.

Given that the idea of revival and reform animated the Muslim moral and political imagination from a very early period, it also produced an illustrious genealogy of actors and players who had occupied the role of "renewer(s) of the age." The career of the jurist and eponymous founder of the Shafiʿi school of Sunni law, Muhammad b. Idris al-Shafiʿi (d. 820), was one such example. Shafiʿi's project of reform was animated by his desire to fashion the model of the Prophet into a coherent, universal, and consistent object of knowledge. Shafiʿi's offer of a system and a method to retrieve the epistemological body of the Prophet—namely, the sunna—catapulted him into prominence as a centennial renewer (*mujaddid*). His principal intervention was to introduce a hermeneutical understanding to the prophetic reports (hadith) and to end the reign of crass literalism perpetrated by the partisans of hadith. Moreover, he sought to counter the unbridled rational opinion advanced by the advocates of rationality—namely, the Hanafi scholars of Iraq. Shafiʿi's dissatisfaction was directed at what he perceived to be the potential ethical chaos that might result from a plurality of models or bodies of the Prophet. The central dilemma that Shafiʿi sought to address was this: how must a community affirm and embody the memory of the Prophet's model in a world that was becoming more and more distant from that prophetic past? Fashioning an answer to this question was central to multiple projects of reform, revival, and ethics in Islam. Moreover, with the movement of time, this question became increasingly pressing, and it engaged several Muslim scholars in the generation following the foundational architects of Islamic law and moral reasoning such as Shafi'i. Among the Shafi'is, Ibn al-Surayj (d. 918), Juwayni (d. 1085), and Ghazali (d. 1111) all became known as centennial renewers for their labors in recasting the body of knowledge in the Muslim tradition.

An excellent illustration of this trend can be found in the reformist project of Ibrahim al-Shatibi (d. 1388), the 14th-century Andalusian jurist aligned with the Maliki School of law. If Shafi'i's signature achievement was to systematize the knowledge of prophetic norms, then for Shatibi it was the elucidation of the underlying objectives that sustained the philosophical and doctrinal dimensions of Islamic law. Shatibi's most meticulous treatment of this project was found in his well-known magnum opus *al-Muwafaqat* (Concordances), although almost all his works were inspired by this central theme in some way.

Shatibi's conception of reform was driven by his attempt to align the practical implementation of law to its moral foundations. He argued that divine law could not be divorced from a larger program of ethics. For Shatibi, divine revelation was not a composite of haphazard discourses that lacked any cause or intentionality. On the contrary, revelation and the order that it generated were grounded in certain indispensable deeper objectives (*maqāṣid*), such as the safeguarding of life, property, salvational potentiality, intellect, and lineage. When law became separated from these objectives, Shatibi argued, it ceased to serve the welfare of the people for whom it was intended. In that situation, law no longer performed its primary purpose, to serve human interests in both this life and the next. Shatibi elaborated on this principle in his work that is now known as the discourse on the "objective-driven understanding of law and jurisprudence" (*al-fiqh al-maqāṣidī*). At the heart of Shatibi's legal reform, as exemplified in the category "objectives of the law," was his desire to establish a correlation between the values attached to particular practices and the higher ethical objectives that those values were supposed to foster and fulfill. Shatibi perhaps most emphatically articulated the foundational premise that informed his understanding of reform in Islam when he wrote, "[Divinely revealed] laws have all been established to preserve human beings' interests both in this life and the life to come." He further elaborated this principle when he said, "Normative rulings are intended to realize the welfare [of a community] and to repel harm and corruption. These, then [i.e., the realization of welfare and the repelling of harm], are the desired effects of normativity." To be engaged in reform signified, for Shatibi, the labor of preserving the synchronicity between the normative limits of the law and the ethical objectives that those limits were intended to secure. In other words, Shatibi sought to protect the marriage between law and ethics in Islam from separation or divorce.

But what kind of narrative about the past's relationship to the present (and the future) enabled the urgency of such agendas of moral reform? Shatibi provided some clues in his highly poignant introduction to his most extensive work on the concept of heretical innovation (*bid'a*), *al-I'tisam* (The adhering). Here Shatibi told a particular story about the tension produced by the polarities of normativity versus heresy in Islam through a narrative about becoming estranged from the world.

Shatibi's prophetic report has a melancholic mood. "Islam began as a stranger and will return as a stranger like it began, so blessed were the strangers." Shatibi narrated his own struggles against the heretical innovations prevalent in his time, such as offering a benediction (du'a) after formal prayers, and his resultant marginalization from the mainstream of his society. His suffering was unmistakably similar to the Prophet Muhammad's estrangement from society in the early years of his mission as God's messenger. In confronting heresy and adhering to the sanctioned path, according to Shatibi, one also became estranged from the sinful society.

In his political and theological writings in the 14th century, Ibn Taymiyya (1263–1328) used the hadith about the coming of a centennial renewer as a sign of the promised awakening and renewal of the dīn in two slightly different contexts. In a letter to the Crusader leader of Cyprus, he explained the virtues of Islam and commented on a number of practices and recent experiences of the Muslims. The Mamluk sultans, he explained, routed the Mongols, who had declared their loyalty to Islam but then reneged in their conduct and obstinate pagan beliefs. In terms of the providential promise, Ibn Taymiyya stated, God sent the "armies of God" in the shape of the Mamluks in order to protect the community of Muslims from sure destruction. In this instance he invoked the hadith about awakening and renewal after the Muslim political entity was saved from destruction at the hands of enemies. In another citation of the same hadith, Ibn Taymiyya talked about messianic times, when Islam would become estranged from the world for some time until it was announced again to the world. Under such conditions, according to the authority of another hadith report, the true people of faith would stand up for the truth, fearless of the consequences and suffering they might endure at the hands of their adversaries. Ibn Taymiyya then cited the hadith that promised the revival of Islam in every century, creating an association between the estrangement of Islam and the parallel awakening and renewal. In other words, the symbolism of the rise and fall or the decline and renewal of Islam as a faith community was not absent from the historical narrative of Muslim thinkers themselves.

The tradition of renewal was connected to one of the central functions of prophecy: to share divine wisdom with humanity. Often the prophetic report about renewal of religion was connected to the traditions of learning and the discursive practices of Islam. Hence the learned of Islamdom were on par, in terms of function and service rendered, with the prophets of the children of Israel.

All commentaries on the centennial renewal report insisted that the primary function of the act of renewal was to ensure that the sunna displaced the heretical innovations (bid'a) that had superseded it in social practices and customs. Semantically, the concept of sunna was a continuation of the pre-Islamic sensibility or custom. After the advent of Islam, all customs pointed toward monotheism. Yet the sunna was a serious element of continuity in the Muslim community, for whatever was true and just was embodied in the sunna. As Ignaz Goldziher described the sunna in relation to the Arabs, "The sunna was their law and their sacra." Sunna could be understood as tradition, provided the latter also signified a strong sense of obligation. So when the sunna was tied to the person and identity of the Prophet Muhammad as the lawgiver and moral exemplar for Muslims, it also signified the completion of an ideal. As an ideal, the sunna represented how Muslims felt about the Prophet Muhammad. Imitating Muhammad was thus an essential part of proper Islamic living to simulate the representative feelings for the charismatic authority. Since the sunna became the accepted model of proper living, displacing the sunna was a sure sign of delinquency and signaled an intent to disavow the life practices ushered in by Islam.

Yet Muslim jurist-theologians quickly realized that idealizing the sunna as a cultural phenomenon was not practical. The sunna had to be sifted from the amalgam of reports gathered over time, then understood, rationalized, and turned into an interpretive logic as well as a charismatic reference point. One outcome was *fiqh*, literally the task of understanding the statements of the sunna and the Qur'an to constitute the core teachings of Muslim practice. Simultaneously, Islam's scriptural statements had to be understood in the light of changing times. This became one of the most challenging tasks for Muslims over the centuries and became especially acute in the rapidly changing historical period of modernity.

Reform in Modernity

It is now well accepted among scholars of Islam that tradition and modernity are not inherently opposed. Instead of approaching tradition as a field of discourses, types of knowledge, and norms that became irrelevant or outdated in the wake of modernity, it is more accurate to approach tradition as a continuing moral argument that has undergone particular shifts and transformations in new political and institutional conditions. Indeed, it might be most accurate to think of modernity also as a particular kind of tradition with its own expectations, sensibilities, and dreams of a good life. Some characteristics of modernity include the valorization of a "rational" subject unencumbered by the burden of myth and superstition, a renewed emphasis on the capacity of the individual to attain knowledge, and the articulation of a political theology that resists hierarchies and that champions the promise of a radically egalitarian ethos. Western colonialism transformed the discursive terrain in which Muslim actors and discourses could advance their projects of reform. Indeed, the career of the Muslim reform tradition also transformed in dramatic ways while it confronted the new conceptual and discursive terrain of Western colonial modernity. Most significantly, the modern episode in the tradition of Muslim reform took place in a postimperial context, when Muslim political power in various parts of the world, from the late 18th century onward, either had collapsed or was steadily dwindling. But ironically, this loss of political power served as a major catalyst for the intensification of intellectual activity among reform-minded Muslim scholars. Contrary to a rise-and-fall model of history that equated political loss to intellectual decline, the reformist tradition in Islam showcased a remarkable degree of intellectual fermentation during periods of political decline. Various reformist movements in such regions as Central Asia, the Middle East, and South Asia attest to this trend.

A hallmark of the Muslim reform tradition in the modern era was a renewed emphasis on protecting the absoluteness of divine sovereignty not only as an incontrovertible theological dogma but also as a moral imperative in everyday life. Several devotional practices, such as seeking the intercession of the Prophet and saints, visiting shrines of deceased saints in order to seek redemptive intercession, and attending birth and death ceremonies of charismatic pious figures, all emerged as objects of intense polemics and contestations. The legitimacy of these practices had been debated before the modern period: even in the premodern era, the problem of how a community should guard divine sovereignty from all potential human competitors produced much debate and many differences among Muslim scholars. The political and institutional conditions in which these battles were fought in modern times, however, had almost entirely changed. There were two main traditions or thought styles that most decisively shaped the contours of Muslim reformist thought in the modern era. Broadly conceived, these traditions can be called Muslim modernism and Muslim maximalism, or what is generally known as the Salafi tradition. Although the sources of knowledge that informed these two traditions were different, the recipe for religious and social reform offered by the custodians of these traditions shared certain key ingredients.

Perhaps most significantly, each placed a renewed emphasis on the Qur'an and the sunna as the only authentic sources of religious practice. They offered a scathing critique of devotional and popular practices that threatened divine sovereignty. There were perhaps two defining features of Muslim reformist thought in modernity. Remarkably, on these two foundational points, Muslim modernist and Salafi thinkers seem to be in total agreement. The famous 20th-century Indian poet-philosopher Muhammad Iqbal (d. 1939) was unambiguous in his chastisement of a worldview that placed antinomian mysticism above a commitment to treating the social and moral ills of this world. Iqbal reminded his readers in his classic *The Reconstruction of Religious Thought in Islam* that, after having received ultimate proximity with the divine during his famous ascension, the Prophet chose to return to this world. What the modern Muslim needed, Iqbal pleaded, was precisely this spirit of return to the world in order to address its challenges. Such a spirit was only possible, Iqbal argued, with an attitude that was inspired by the revolutionary ethos of the Qur'an. The reinvigoration of the self, the elevation of the self, required a renewed emphasis on the primacy of the Qur'an as the foundational source of Islamic practice. If such a project of reform required that certain nonessential rituals and customary conventions be jettisoned in order to serve moral and social change, then Iqbal was prepared to sacrifice them. "This one prostration which you consider to be a burden, relieves a person of a thousand other prostrations," Iqbal famously wrote. Iqbal's view, shared by several other Muslim modernists of his generation, emphasized transcendence articulated in a rationally grounded idiom. The way to confront the crisis of meaning caused by Western modernity, colonialism, and the larger processes of industrial capitalism was to recover that spirit of submission to a transcendent authority that had enabled Islam to emerge as a revolutionary ideological force at its beginnings.

Similarly, the famous 19th-century Egyptian reformer Muhammad 'Abduh's (d. 1905) conception of reform focused on retrieving an egalitarian ethos of a transcendent authority that for him had become corrupted by an overweening degree of dependence on hierarchies of human authority. As he stated most clearly in his well-known work *Risalat al-Tawhid* (The epistle on unity), his primary objective was "freeing the minds of Muslims from the chains of belief in authority because God has not created humankind in order to be led by a halter." 'Abduh's primary target was the principle of conforming to canonical authority (*taqlid*), which, in his view, had vitiated the capacity of the ordinary believer to apply his reason and intellect in interpreting the foundational sources of religion. Unlike Iqbal, 'Abduh was trained in the traditional canonical sources of law at the prestigious Azhar University in Cairo. Despite, or perhaps because of, his traditional training, however, 'Abduh was convinced that in order to challenge the looming threat of Westernization (*taghrib*) and colonialism with any integrity, it was imperative to reject any practice that did not value rational inquiry over dogmatic following, egalitarianism over submission to authority.

The Algerian thinker Malek Bennabi (d. 1973), building on the intellectual threads spun by Afghani, 'Abduh, and Iqbal, offered a critique of both Salafist and modernist reform projects. Bennabi lamented that the drive of Salafist reformism adopted a retrograde character, directing its intellectual energies to the past and providing imprints and templates that were "incompatible with the exigencies of the present and the future." The modernist reformers, he complained, uncritically adopted European ideas; they were obsessed with how they could be acquired but lacked the curiosity to know "how they were created." What Bennabi found lacking in all Muslim reformist thought was the absence of a doctrine of culture. Without developing a sense of culture, he believed that all "Iṣlāḥism [reformism] propagates a complacent symbolism that dreams of transforming the condition of life by communicating, above all, the taste for 'Muslim things' and Arab 'belles-lettres.'" The reformist movement did not know how to "transform the Muslim soul or to translate into reality the 'social function' of the religion." However, reformists were successful, he wrote, in making Muslims realize their position in the world, what he called the "secular drama." He argued that only by posing the problem of culture generally could the Islamic renaissance emerge from its embryonic state.

Apart from South Asia and the Middle East, a similar trajectory of Muslim modernist reform is found in Soviet Central Asia. In the 19th century, a small number of intellectual elites in such urban centers as Bukhara, Tashkent, and Samarqand established what came to be known as the Jadid (new) movement. At the heart of this movement was an attempt to establish the compatibility of scientific rationality and the foundational sources of Islam, mainly the Qur'an and sunna. Moreover, in ways similar to their modernist counterparts in South Asia and the Middle East, the Jadids sought to eradicate the influence of local customs, conventions, and rituals that in their view lacked a precedent in the Qur'an and sunna. Again, reform for them involved the separation of "local culture" from "authentic religion." The most crucial variable in enabling such a process of reform, for the Jadids, was education of both the religious and secular varieties. Therefore, prominent 19th- and 20th-century Jadid thinkers such as Munawwar Qari (d. 1933) and Mahmud Behbudi (d. 1919) were defiant in their call to adopt "new methods" of education in both secondary schools and institutions of higher learning. Their vision for Central Asian Muslims was unabashedly modern; the cultivation of a new civil society required discarding old myths, rituals, and superstitions and the need to embrace a rationally sound subjectivity. The enlightenment project of relegating older traditions to irrelevance seemed very real and possible to Jadid scholars like Qari and Behbudi. Their project of reform not only took place in the shadow of Soviet hegemony but also was heavily inspired by the Marxist-Communist narrative of progress and modernization in society. But they differed from the Soviet model in their belief that Islam was inherently compatible with scientific rationality. Hence they resisted the Soviet drive to completely eradicate religion from the public sphere.

Apart from these modernist discourses that emerged either as a response to or in the shadow of Western colonialism, another major trend of Muslim reform in the modern period was the maximalist or puritanical tradition, usually called Salafism. Literally, the term "Salafism" referred to the argument that only the body of norms that originated during the patristic community of the Prophet could be regarded as authoritative in Islam. In a move not all that different from Muslim modernist thinkers, puritanical reformers such as the well-known Muhammad b. 'Abd al-Wahhab (d. 1787) in Arabia and the lesser-known Shah Isma'il (d. 1831) in India also argued for a return to the Qur'an and the sunna as the exclusive reservoirs for an authentic religious normativity. What distinguished these puritanical reformers from their modernist counterparts was the degree to which they conceived of reform as equivalent to guarding the absoluteness of divine sovereignty. A mindset of constant rivalry between human and divine norms was central to their social imaginaries (norms regulating social existence), much more pronounced than in modernist thinkers like Iqbal or 'Abduh. A significant part of the reform project advanced by thinkers like Ibn 'Abd al-Wahhab and Shah Isma'il centered on such issues as the limits of prophetic intercession, the legitimacy of visiting shrines of dead saints, and the capacity of the Prophet to know the unknown, among other doctrines.

On each of these issues, their position was informed by a political theology that amplified divine sovereignty, even if that meant casting the humanity of the Prophet as a fallible subject. Theirs was a larger program to perpetuate social egalitarianism. They downplayed the Prophet's miraculous qualities and emphasized that his prophetic authority was enabled by the perfection of his humanity. Similarly, the authority of saints and other pious figures to perform such acts as interceding on behalf of sinners also had to be restrained in order to preserve a radical difference

between divine and human authority. The zeal of such thinkers to guard the absoluteness of divine sovereignty not only inspired a number of important movements
within Muslim reformist thought but also generated a great deal of controversy,
polemics, and a fair number of rebuttals.

One of the more interesting developments was the emergence of traditionalist reform-minded scholars who inhabited seemingly antithetical genealogies of Islamic thought. On the face of it, it appeared as certain reform-minded scholars were
bringing together new hybrid traditions and incommensurable discourses. Among
them is Ibrahim b. al-Hasan al-Kurani, but one can also include Shah Waliullah
of Delhi and also later Indian traditional scholars such as Anwar Shah Kashmiri,
among others, who were strong admirers of Ibn Taymiyya and also liberally drew
on, and defended, the teachings and insights of Ibn al-'Arabi. Ibn Taymiyya's salafist-
nominalism combined with Ibn al-'Arabi's dizzying immanentist metaphysics would
appear to be strange bedfellows. But some reform-minded scholars including the
Ghumari brothers ('Abdullah and Ahmad Ghumari) of North Africa combined
their reverence for the family of the Prophet (*ahl al-bayt*) with their Sunni traditionalism. All this suggests that multiple logics (heterologies) were at play in certain
reformist strains of thought that might be antithetical to more systematic thinkers
of reform. But it might well be that these contradictions are the product of a larger
modernist template in which things that appear to be antithetical can have perfect
synchrony in practice.

Contemporary Debates on Reform

In late 20th-century India, the rector of the Darul Uloom of Deoband, Qari Muhammad Tayyab (d. 1988), offered a narrative of revival and reform that represented
a traditional perspective of the 'ulama'. Tayyab argued that there were two means by
which the path of *din* was providentially protected. The first was through powerful
personalities who represented the preservation of *din*. The second was through the
inner spirit of *din*, which naturally shielded it from any subversive threat.

Tayyab argued that human mentality changed over the duration of a century
and that significant intergenerational changes had occurred. As a result, he wrote,
new modes of thinking and new experiences unfolded in a progressive manner. In
every generation, therefore, was a risk and a legitimate fear that the next generation
of the Muslim community might jettison the imprint of the previous generation.
The primary concern, Tayyab explained, was to prevent the original and traditional
imprint from becoming anachronistic for the new generation. For this reason the
teachings of the faith had to be continuously explained and interpreted in the light
of the new and altered mentality, and for this reason individuals were providentially
deputed to the world to serve as centennial renewers.

Anwar al-Jundi (d. 2002), a prominent Egyptian advocate of revival and reform
in the tradition of major reformers such as Ibn Hazm, Ghazali, Ibn Taymiyya, and

Ibn Khaldun, described each of these figures as "correctors of concepts and renewers of Islamic thought." Each one had made a specific methodological intervention to the intellectual tradition that gave integrity to the teachings of Islam in terms of the challenges of their respective times. Ibn Hazm, said Jundi, combated the distortion produced by the overuse of analogy and paved the way back to the straightforward and plain meaning of the Qur'an. The prevalent predisposition toward blind imitation of authority (*taqlīd*) was another distortion that Ibn Hazm opposed. Ghazali chose to work in the area of education and culture, Jundi explained, and brought the spiritual and legal into a meaningful integration. At the same time, Ghazali also combated the excessive claims of philosophy and the Muslim philosophers. Ibn Taymiyya, in turn, evaluated all Islamic thought on the touchstone of the truth of the Qur'an. Whatever could not sustain the scrutiny of the Qur'an and the sunna could be discarded, according to Jundi's reading of Ibn Taymiyya. Ibn Khaldun turned against the empty verbal polemics of his day that contributed to the lack of originality in Islamic thought. Ibn Khaldun's intervention was to give empirical observation a respectable place in the epistemological framework of religious thought, Jundi argued.

For Jundi and many advocates of reform in the modern period, the rebuttal of the idea of following ancient discursive authority of the law schools (*taqlīd*) was one of the most important rhetorical markers of the reform movement. Instead of following authority, they advocate *ijtihād*, or independent thinking. However, often *ijtihād* meant following a variety of legal opinions instead of one law school. And instead of following the canonical authority of a law school and its interpretations, in the sphere of moral teachings and ethics, the reformists sometimes resorted to plain readings derived from the Qur'an and sunna but more often fell back on the opinions of ancient schools.

The U.S./European wars in Afghanistan and Iraq against a range of Muslim groups from terrorists and militants to religious revivalists and pietists has had a major impact on the discourse of revival and reform. If certain Muslims in the 19th and 20th centuries were suspicious of the agenda of revivalism and reform as a vehicle for Westernization advanced by European colonizers, then in the early 21st century, discourses of revival and reform have become deeply politicized and polarizing within Muslim societies where some see revival and reform as a bridgehead for new crusades against Islam. For instance, after the U.S. invasion of Iraq in 2003, the Egyptian public intellectual Muhammad 'Imara wrote a pamphlet titled *Religious Discourse: Between Islamic Reform and American Subversion* (*al-Khitab al-Dini bayna al-Tajdid al-Islami wa-l-Tabdid al-Amrikani*), in which he identified himself as a protagonist of an Islamic reformist agenda. Renewal was not only a rational necessity, said 'Imara, but also a part of the "tradition (*sunna*), necessity (*ḍarūra*) and universal rule (*qānūn*)." He argued that without renewal, the chasm between "thought (*fikr*), ethics (*fiqh*), Islamic discourse (*al-khiṭāb al-Islāmī*)," which represent the shari'a on the one hand and the demands of societal change on the other, would only widen. 'Imara also argued that a unifying agenda of reform was impossible, and hence diversity would be a hallmark of any such project. However, he was highly skeptical of what he called the American-financed reform projects that supported Muslim secularists, Marxists, and mercenaries, whose purpose he viewed as the replacement of Muslim religious discourse with secularism. 'Imara's rhetoric, however exaggerated, has gained traction in contexts where conflict with the West has reached new levels of antagonism.

'Imara's focus was on the disagreement within Muslim circles over the rights to and limits of reform. But 'Imara chose a demonic rhetoric to describe his Muslim intellectual adversaries, similar to the way anthropologist Saba Mahmood charged certain Iranian and Arab Muslim thinkers of tailoring their reforms to American imperial designs. Among the targets of these critics were figures such as Nasr Hamid Abu Zayd (d. 2010), Hasan Hanafi, Khalil 'Abd al-Karim (d. 2002), and the pivotal Iranian reformist thinker Abdolkarim Soroush, who were engaged in fairly far-reaching criticisms of traditional Muslim discursive and interpretative paradigms. 'Imara invoked the authority of Afghani and 'Abduh in order to distinguish genuine reform from what he suspected was the bacillus of subversive reforms. This over-heated debate has echoes of early and mid-20th-century debates in Egypt, where such thinkers as Taha Husayn (d. 1973), 'Ali 'Abd al-Raziq (d. 1966), Qasim Amin (d. 1908), and Muhammad Ahmad Khalafallah (d. 1977) were demonized as hostile and subversive elements who attempted to undermine the authentic inherited narrative of Islamic thought. One of the perpetual challenges for Muslim reformers was to know where to draw the line in the realm of ideas.

Revival and reform also became the pretext for a largely sterile but earnest debate among academics in the Western academy during the 1980s over the larger political implications of revival and reform. Fazlur Rahman, the Pakistani scholar and émigré to the United States, observed a neo-Sufi revivalist tradition that in his view combined spirituality with activism, a move away from the passive, world-denouncing, ascetic Sufism of old. While some scholars, such as John Voll, agreed with him, others, including Rex O'Fahey, Bernard Radtke, Reinhard Schulze, and Ahmad Dallal, voiced alternative viewpoints. Their fundamental disagreement with the Fazlur Rahman and Voll thesis was that it tried to explain a range of revivalist Sufi practices under a singular rubric—neo-Sufism—whereas the actual story was much more complex. Rahman and Voll's detractors argued that Muslim intellectuals and social reform movements in the 18th century were generating revivals independent of European influences in creative and innovative ways that defied the charges of decline.

Conclusion

Revival and reform have been integral to Islam from its very beginnings. The idea of reform relates to mending a fractured present in order to generate something entirely new or to rehabilitate an original form. Whether reform seeks to renew or rehabilitate, it is always a creative and dynamic process that produces change and newness. The various projects of reform in the intellectual and social history of Islam both converged and diverged on important points. Almost all moments of reform engaged with certain authoritative discourses and bodies of knowledge such as the Qur'an, sunna, and traditions of canonical law. However, every moment of reform articulated varied points of emphasis on what reform entailed. For example, the conception of reform for premodern luminaries Ibn Khaldun and Shatibi was very different compared to later figures. Ibn Khaldun was captivated by the necessity of cultivating social solidarity, while Shatibi's concern was to synchronize the law with its fundamental objectives. Both of these thinkers engaged in what might be called reform, but the specific trajectories of reform differed significantly. Reform in Islam remains variegated, diverse, and unpredictable.

Fundamental to thinking about the question of reform in Islam is the role of memory and how that memory relates to the founder, the Prophet Muhammad, and the revelation, the Qur'an. The "body" of the Prophet, whether discursive, political, or mystical, remains a central reference point. In order for reform to be credible, however, reformers often strive to connect the memory of the past with the fractured and the always incomplete present. But a set of contentious and hotly debated questions remains. How much of the past should inform a project of reform and recovery? Can reimagining, reforming, and reviving political theology be constrained by boundaries and limits? How does the knowledge of the tradition relate and converse with modernity? Answers to these fundamental questions have varied significantly, depending on the individual agents of reform, as well as specific political, cultural, and material conditions. Therefore, in the modern period, developments such as colonialism and the eventual rise of the nation-state, the emergence of print, and the consolidation of such institutions of state building as the census all transformed the Muslim reform tradition in profound ways. These shifts in the political and institutional terrain enabled new trajectories of reform and brought into central view particular questions of authoritative debates (such as the humanity of the Prophet) with an unprecedented intensity and vigor. Like any other aspect of Islam, the Muslim reform tradition is neither monolithic nor predictable. Rather, reform in Islam is continually invested with and divested of particular meanings, knowledge, and aspirations at specific junctures in history.

Further Reading

Charles Adams, *Islam and Modernism in Egypt: A Study of the Modern Reform Movement Inaugurated by Muhammad 'Abduh*, 1968; M. Bennabi, *Islam in History and Society*, translated by A. Rashid, 1991; David Commins, *Islamic Reform: Politics and Social Change in Late Ottoman Syria*, 1990; A. Dallal, "The Origins and Objectives of Islamic Revivalist Thought, 1750–1850," *Journal of the American Oriental Society* 113 (1993): 341–59; Samira Haj, *Reconfiguring Islamic Tradition: Reform, Rationality, and Modernity*, 2009; B. Haykal, *Revival and Reform in Islam: The Legacy of Muhammad al-Shawkani*, 2003; N. Levtzion and J. O. Voll, ed., *Eighteenth-Century Renewal and Reform in Islam*, 1987; B. D. Metcalf, *Islamic Revival in India: Deoband, 1860–1900*, 1982; R. Peters, "Idjtihad and Taqlid in 18th and 19th Century Islam," in *Die Welt des Islams* (2000); Fazlur Rahman, *Revival and Reform in Islam: A Study in Islamic Fundamentalism*, edited by Ebrahim Moosa, 2000; J. O. Voll, "Foundations for Renewal and Reform," in *The Oxford History of Islam*, edited by J. Esposito, 1999.

Shari'a ◇◇◇

Devin J. Stewart

The shari'a (*sharī'a*) is the revealed, sacred law of Islam, though the primary term for law in the Qur'an is arguably *dīn*, ordinarily translated as "religion." Law is an essential feature of revealed religion in both the Qur'an and Islamic thought in general, and the term shari'a is used with reference not only to Islam but also to Judaism and Christianity, because all three are conceived as having a divinely given law. According to later jurists, 500 verses of the Qur'an, termed *āyāt al-aḥkām* (verses of rulings), treat legal subjects, including matters relating to prayer, fasting, alms, pilgrimage, permitted food, marriage, divorce, inheritance, slavery, and trade. This represents roughly one-thirteenth of the sacred text.

Fiqh (literally, "understanding") is the term for the human effort to work out God's law on particular issues. Like shari'a, with which it is often contrasted, it is translatable as law, but whereas shari'a refers primarily to God's regulation of human behavior, and thus the ideal, *fiqh* always stands for the human approximation of this ideal, the law as actually found in the books. Because it etymologically means "comprehension," *fiqh* is often translated as "jurisprudence" in English, but usually it corresponds to law, referring to the actual rules in the books. Jurisprudence, the science or methods of interpretation through which one determines the law, corresponds more closely to *uṣūl al-fiqh* (literally, "the roots of the law"), the science devoted to the hermeneutics of Islamic law.

For the vast majority of Muslims, law has determined—and still determines today—what Islam is. This distinguishes Islam from Christianity, which does not actually have a revealed law and in which theology is the queen of religious sciences; Judaism likewise stresses the importance and centrality of the law. The "clergy" of Islam, like the rabbis of Judaism, are jurists rather than theologians, and it is their study of the law and competence in addressing legal questions that gives them authority. Many other claimants to authority have coexisted with them in the course of history, but, for more than a millennium, jurists have been among the groups most successful in gaining acceptance for their claims.

The Law in the Books

Islamic law is not embodied in a single authoritative code but rather held to reside in the vast array of legal texts, based ultimately on legal responsa issued by recognized jurists over the course of history. A responsum (fatwa) is an opinion solicited from a legal authority on a specific legal question. In the early sources, opinions are often solicited by one jurist of another ("I asked so-and-so about the case of...") or by a student or a layperson; in later times, fatwas were typically issued in response to questions by laypersons. Not all opinions were considered equal: the most authoritative opinions were those issued by *mujtahid*s, jurists endowed with the ability acquired through intense legal study to derive independent legal rulings directly from the sources (*ijtihād*). Of the books recording these opinions, some were (and are) considered more important than others, but no one book gained the overriding authority of a work such as the *Shulchan Aruch* (The set table) of Joseph ben Ephraim Karo (d. 1575), which has served as the nearly exclusive basis for the elaboration of Jewish law over the past four centuries.

The law books divide their subject matter into set topical chapters that, already in the ninth century, followed a standard order, with some variations, that facilitated the location of particular legal topics in relatively large works without fixed pagination and often without indexes or tables of contents. The chapters fall into three large categories: *'ibādāt* (acts of worship); *mu'āmalāt* (transactions or contracts); and *qaḍāyā* (court cases). The *'ibādāt* sections start with ritual purity (*ṭahārah*), a prerequisite for ritual prayer and other acts of devotion, and proceed to discuss prayer itself, the first act of devotion since it is performed daily; this is followed by fasting, performed during at least one month of the year, the alms tax (zakat), which must be given once a year, and the pilgrimage, which must be performed once in a lifetime by those who are able to undertake it. The chapter order in the *mu'āmalāt* section is not as rigidly fixed, but it always appears after the *'ibādāt* section. Major topics include sales, marriage, divorce, inheritance, renting, pawning, sharecropping, partnerships, agents, slavery, deposits, found property, foundlings, endowments, and so on. The third section includes chapters on crimes, judicial procedure, and court cases. The crimes known as *ḥudūd* are those for which fixed punishments are sanctioned by the Qur'an, and they are generally held to be seven in number: apostasy, adultery, false accusation of adultery, burglary, highway robbery, sedition, and drinking alcohol.

The law books regulate many matters of ritual that one could scarcely hope to enforce. Muslims are not tried in court for failing to perform ablutions properly, even though the discussion of ritual purity is usually one of the longest sections in any given law book. Most actual court cases have to do with matters governed by contracts and agreements between individuals, such as business transactions of all types. In addition, the law does not simply regulate what is forbidden, obligatory, or permissible but rather seeks to rank all human acts in moral terms on a five-tiered scale: *ḥarām* (forbidden), *makrūh* (reprehensible, discouraged), *mubāḥ* (allowed), *mustaḥabb* (recommended), and *wājib* (obligatory).

The Sources of the Law

On what did the scholars base their responsa? The substance of their rules was often indebted to existing systems, both Arabian and Near Eastern (a conglomeration of systems of diverse origin, including Jewish, Byzantine, and Sassanian law), but this does not tell us on what basis the rules were counted as Islamic. Some will have been formulated by the caliphs, whose decisions seem initially to have been accepted as authoritative. In later times this was true only of those caliphs who were also Companions of the Prophet, notably 'Umar b. al-Khattab (r. 634–44), who is held to have made important contributions to the law. The laws relating to *dhimmī*s (non-Muslim communities under Muslim rule) must also have derived from caliphal decrees, even though the documents attributed to them are not always genuine. By most accounts, however, Islamic law was elaborated by thinkers who stood outside the government and were opposed to or at least stood aloof from it and who did not accept the decrees of the caliphs as a source of law. In the earliest material, their rules often rest on nothing but their considered opinion (*ra'y*); their decision is recorded, but their reasoning is not explained. Stringent principles for the derivation of law soon made their appearance, however.

The science of the *uṣūl al-fiqh* proposed that the law must be derived from an ordered series of sources, of which most Sunni jurists eventually accepted four: (1) the Qur'an; (2) the sunna (the customary way of the Prophet Muhammad), which was understood to be preserved in the hadith (recorded reports about the Prophet's words and deeds); (3) consensus (*ijmā'*); and (4) legal analogy (*qiyās*) or the exhaustive independent consideration of a legal question (*ijtihād*). The idea of an ordered list of sources originated in the eighth century and is seen in checklists presented in instructions for judges. The first extant work of *uṣūl al-fiqh*, the *Risala* of Shafi'i (d. 820), presents a sophisticated system of legal hermeneutics, but his system is based on the idea that there is only one source of the law: revelation. Revelation includes both the Qur'an and the corpus of prophetic hadith, but to Shafi'i they combined to form a coherent whole. This is quite a bit different from the later four-source theory. Jurists writing after Shafi'i interpreted his work anachronistically, in some cases even rearranging the text in order to bring it in line with the later conventions of the *uṣūl al-fiqh* genre. As the four-source theory gained ground, "considered opinion" as a basis of the law was eclipsed and suppressed in favor of a stricter reliance on texts; "opinion" came to be associated with whim or wild speculation. It survived in a disciplined form as *qiyās*, analogical reasoning from a known, determined case to a similar, undetermined case, but some jurists continued to oppose that too.

Consensus is usually negative and retroactive: the lack of dissenting opinions over the past generation is a sign that consensus exists. The body of acceptable opinion is thus made up of two parts, consensus and disputed points (*khilāf*), both within a particular legal school and between them, for variant opinions are allowed on those points of law for which a consensus does not exist. Lists of the requirements of a master jurist often stress that he must be aware of areas of consensus in the law—this is similar to a call for the necessity of examining relevant precedent before deciding a case.

Madhhabs and Madrasas

Two institutions that contributed to making the law central to Islamic societies and creating continuity over space and time are the *madhhab*, or the legal school (in the sense of a tradition of legal study based on a stable body of doctrine), and the madrasa, or college of law. The circles behind the legal schools organized and regularized the transmission of legal knowledge and interpretive authority, which have survived until the present day, and their activities represent a significant step in the professionalization of the jurists as a class. They solidified in the course of the ninth and tenth centuries, and four Sunni schools survive to this day: the Hanafi, named after Abu Hanifa (d. 767); the Maliki, named after Malik b. Anas (d. 795); the Shafi'i, named after Shafi'i (d. 820); and the Hanbali, named after Ahmad b. Hanbal (d. 855). But there were others as well, including the Dawudi *madhhab*, named after its founder Dawud b. 'Ali b. Khalaf al-Isfahani (d. 884), which was also called the Zahiri *madhhab* on account of the principle of reliance on the prima facie reading (*ẓāhir*) of revealed proof texts, and the Jariri, named after Muhammad b. Jarir al-Tabari (d. 923). In addition to these six, several non-Sunni legal schools arose. These included the Twelver Shi'i school, called the Imami *madhhab*, after their adherence to the teachings of their 12 imams, or Ja'fari, in reference to the sixth imam, Ja'far al-Sadiq (d. 765); the Zaydi Shi'i *madhhab*, named after the martyred rebel imam Zayd (d. 740); and the Ibadi Khariji school, named after 'Abdallah b. Ibad (d. 708), all of which were established by the 11th century, making nine in total. The Zahiri and Jariri schools had died out by the 12th century and were absorbed into the Shafi'i school, leaving the Imami, Zaydi, Ibadi, and the four well-known Sunni schools: Hanafi, Maliki, Shafi'i, and Hanbali. Isma'ili Shi'is developed their own legal tradition under the Fatimid caliphate (909–1171), chiefly in the work of the outstanding jurist Qadi al-Nu'man (d. 974), but their legal *madhhab* differs from the others in institutional terms because of continued access to and dependence on the teachings of an inspired imam. While the Shi'i and Khariji legal traditions preserved early doctrines that differed from those of the Sunni schools, such as the Twelver Shi'is' acceptance of *mut'a* or temporary marriage, the professionalization of the jurists as a class and the institution of the *madhhab* had the effect of making their systems of legal education and interpretation resemble those of the Sunnis more and more over time.

The main centers of formation of the schools were Fustat in Egypt and Baghdad in Iraq. The Hanafi school was supported by the Abbasid caliphs and associated with their rule until the late 12th century (when several caliphs adopted the Shafi'i school); later, it became the preferred school of all major Turkish dynasties, spreading in Central Asia, Anatolia, and India and in Syria and Egypt under the Ottomans. The Shafi'i school was strong in Iraq, Syria, Egypt, Arabia, and, later, Indonesia; that of the Malikis was strong in Egypt and dominant in North Africa, sub-Saharan Africa, and Andalus, where the Umayyad rulers supported it. The Hanbali school, more limited in scope, boasted adherents in some towns of Palestine, Syria, and Iraq. In modern times, it was chosen by adherents of the Wahhabi movement that grew in tandem with the Saudi state and through them became influential throughout the Islamic world. Iran was split between Hanafis and Shafi'is until the Safavids succeeded in converting most of the populace to Shi'i Islam. The remaining Sunnis—for the most part Kurds—are Shafi'is. The Twelver, Zaydi, and Khariji *madhhabs* developed primarily in Iraq and Baghdad in particular, gained ground during the Buyid period (945–1055), and spread to Iran and other areas from there. *Madhhab* allegiance has remained to this day a matter of region and has been influenced in many cases by political rule, illustrating the dictum that "people adopt the religion of their rulers."

The madrasa represents another milestone in the professionalization of the jurists. The madrasa originated in Khurasan—eastern Iran—in the tenth century and traveled west into Iraq, Syria, Egypt, North Africa and east into Central Asia, India, and beyond. It was an organization embodied in a physical building dedicated to legal education through the establishment of an endowment. Agricultural land or rental properties that produced an annual income were placed in a charitable endowment in perpetuity, and the funds were used to pay for the maintenance and upkeep of the building, for the salary of a law professor (*mudarris*), and for monthly stipends for law students. Like the European universities, such as that of Bologna, it grew out of the needs of out-of-town law students. Previously, many prominent jurists had taught their lessons in a mosque, and an adjacent inn provided convenient lodging for students who were not local. This often continued to be the case, but the madrasa combined these two functions: a typical madrasa was a two-story building with an open courtyard. Lessons would be held on the ground floor in alcoves designed for teaching purposes, and the upper floor served as a dormitory for the stipendiary students and sometimes the *mudarris*. By the late 11th century, a number of madrasas had been founded in Baghdad; the most impressive of them was the Nizamiyya, one of a series of such institutions founded by the famous Seljuq vizier Nizam al-Mulk. The Zengids and Ayyubids made the madrasa a prominent feature of the major cities of Syria and Egypt, where they spread its influence in the 12th century. It continued moving west, and the Marinids established numerous madrasas in Morocco in the 14th century. At the same time, madrasas also spread into Anatolia, Central Asia, India, and beyond.

The spread of the madrasa did not initially change the nature of legal study, for the curriculum, stages of study, and methods of teaching apparently remained the same. They did, however, serve visibly to increase the power and prestige of jurists by raising the status of the *mudarris*, and they increased societal support for legal education as a whole, especially on account of the stipends accorded to law students. In addition, they bolstered the institution of the legal school, since each madrasa was devoted to the teaching of the law according to a single school, with one law professor teaching stipendiary students belonging to the same school. Over time, the madrasa came to dominate legal education, and access to the judiciary came to be controlled primarily by the law professors, who would recommend their students to the chief judge of the district for patents of probity—essentially, a document from the local judge attesting that a student was of good character and had a clean moral record and was thus not barred from holding positions of legal responsibility—and then, probably, for the certificate of permission to teach law and grant legal opinions.

Legal Education and Careers

The study of the law in the 10th to 14th centuries was divided into three stages: preparatory studies, including Arabic grammar, rhetoric, and logic; the legal doctrine of the particular school to which one belonged, studied in epitomes; and the disputed points of the law, legal hermeneutics, and dialectic—the rules of legal debate. Advanced students often became the disciples of a master jurist, studying with him for many years and eventually composing a commentary called a *ta'liqa*, based on the lectures of the professor. In recognition that a student had completed his legal education, the master jurist conferred on him a diploma termed *ijāzat al-tadrīs wa-l-iftā'* (certificate to teach law and grant legal opinions). This diploma established the student's qualifications as a jurist or *faqīh* able to analyze legal questions, as a mufti or jurisconsult entitled to answer legal questions from the lay public, and as a scholar of law able to teach law students of his own.

One of the functions of the system of legal education was to provide legal experts to serve in the judiciary. At a low level, a scholar who had a good basic knowledge of the law and a patent of probity could obtain work as a private notary who drew up documents such as marriage, divorce, sales, and other contracts or as an official witness, notary, or clerk attached to a judge's court. A more experienced jurist could serve as a deputy judge and eventually as a judge in his own right. After the 11th century, more and more salaried positions as law professors (*mudarris*) or repetitors (*mu'īd*, essentially an assistant professor) became available. Jurists who had a good knowledge of mathematics could also make a living as inheritance law experts (*faraḍī*), who, like notaries for marriage and divorce contracts, were often in high demand.

The relative ranking of the jurists within a given legal school in a city was generally known, though it was not official. A pecking order was established not only by debate, authorship, teaching, and serving as judges but also by the public activity of granting fatwas and endorsing, revising, correcting, or denouncing the fatwas of other jurists. The top living jurist within a given *madhhab* was termed *ra'is* (chief) or foremost jurist. The hierarchy was theoretically independent of specific offices such as that of chief judge, but rank and office often tended to go together. The endowment deeds of a number of madrasas specified that the law professor at the madrasa should be the top Shafi'i legal scholar of the time. Related to this juristic hierarchy was the controversy over *ijtihād*. Theorists such as Yahya b. Sharaf Nawawi (d. 1277) wrote that the jurists were to be ranked according to various levels of *ijtihād*, often with one or more of the top ranks empty. While the texts of jurisprudence present this as a theoretical exercise about past jurists, it also reflects an understanding that contemporary jurists form a hierarchy of authority.

Rival Authorities

The legal schools served not only to establish regular methods of textual transmission and legal education but also to exclude other groups from participation in the elaboration of law. In the ninth and tenth centuries, the main contenders for religious authority among the scholars were the theologians (*mutakallim*s). The jurists took the view that every believer should know a basic catechism: there is one God, the Prophet Muhammad is the messenger of God, the Qur'an is God's word, and so on. Beyond that, theology was necessary only to defend Islam from heretics, and an advanced knowledge of theology was not required for the populace at large or important for their daily lives and worship. The theologians, by contrast, held that the law merely treated details whereas theology dealt with the large, important questions. Mu'tazili theologians explicitly stated that the study of hadith and law were subordinate to the study of theology.

The conflict between the two groups, jurists and theologians, is nowhere more evident than in the *miḥna* (literally, trial, tribulation, often called "inquisition") of the mid-ninth century, in which the theologians in cooperation with the caliph Ma'mun and his successors sought to impose the doctrine that the Qur'an was created by God at a particular point in historical time (rather than being eternal) on the officials and prominent scholars of the empire. The theologians lost this battle, but they regained ground through the patronage of later rulers. By the tenth century, however, the legal schools had grown so powerful that the theologians had to declare allegiance to one of them in order to legitimate their scholarship. In general, the Mu'tazilis chose the Hanafi school, while the Ash'aris chose that of Shafi'i. A tenth-century Mu'tazili is said to have encouraged his students to join different schools in order to populate them all with proponents of Mu'tazilism. The Mu'tazili school of theology waned in the 11th and 12th centuries, and with it, the authority of theologians in general. It lived on in part in the Twelver and Zaydi Shi'i traditions, whose leading scholars were profoundly influenced by Mu'tazili theology between the 9th and 11th centuries, but in those traditions as well, religious authority came to be based on the study of law rather than theology. While theology continued to be an important Islamic science, it was relegated to a subordinate and ancillary position.

There was also some conflict between jurists and hadith experts. The *ahl al-ḥadīth* were scholars of reports concerning the words and deeds of the Prophet Muhammad, which they examined in order to determine his exemplary or normative behavior, or sunna. They believed that these rules determined the law for contemporary Muslims. They rejected the use of rational inquiry independent of such texts for the elaboration of the law, and they were able to maintain a distinct authority in the ninth and tenth centuries, compiling many legal works termed *Sunan*, which arranged hadith reports by legal chapter. Jurists who were more inclined to rational inquiry decried the *ahl al-ḥadīth* as uncritical, simple-minded collectors who were incapable of understanding the implications of the texts they transmitted. By the end of the 11th century, the hadith scholars had lost much of their former authority and came to be subsumed under the legal scholars. Signs of this development include statements that the fully qualified jurist need not have memorized hadith reports but should know where to look them up in standard reference works.

Other rivals of the jurists were the philosophers and Sufi masters (who were rivals themselves). Both groups tended to see themselves as elites, holding that their understanding of the world was only accessible to a few; those who were not adept at rational analysis (according to the philosophers) or not sensitive to the spiritual world of the unseen (according to the Sufis) could make do with following the dictates of the jurists and simply performing their religious obligations in the ordinary fashion. This identified the jurists as low-level leaders, somewhat like school teachers in relation to professors. The jurists responded by often denouncing the philosophers as unbelievers, but the Sufis were a more prevalent and persistent threat. Their claim to access to divine knowledge through paths other than study of the law threatened to undermine the jurists' authority, leading one 16th-century scholar to remark to a Sufi friend that the jurists and the Sufis were mentioned right next to each other in the Qur'an, in the verse that reads, "Are the two equal: those who know and those who do not know?" (Q. 39:9); he obviously took "those who know" to mean the legal scholars. The jurists did come to terms with Sufis who adhered to the law, and they often joined them, too, but they vigorously condemned those who claimed that the ordinary rules concerning religious obligations did not apply to them because they were in direct communion with the divine, often charging them with antinomianism—categorical disregard for the law—and belief in reincarnation and divine immanence. They also accused Sufis of vices such as laziness, excessive dependence on others, dancing and singing, and pederasty and tended to react adversely to their apparently blasphemous ecstatic statements. Fierce debates raged over the mystical poetry of Ibn al-Farid (d. 1235), which many jurists declared heretical. Defenders of the poetry, who also included jurists, insisted that one could not interpret the ecstatic and inspired statements of the Sufis literally, for the true meaning was incomprehensible to the uninitiated. Sufism has continued to be extremely influential in many areas in the Muslim world, and Sufi groups continue to risk conflicts with representatives of juristic authority, such as in Pakistan, where their shrines have been bombed by Salafi zealots, or in Iran, where the Islamic Republican government has disbanded several Sufi orders in the last decade.

Caliphs

The jurists' most important rivals in the first centuries were the caliphs, who claimed religious authority in legal and theological matters alike. The rivalry between them came to a head in the "inquisition" of the mid-ninth century, a battle that the caliphs lost along with the theologians. Nonetheless, they never lost their religious authority completely. They retained some room for maneuver through their control of the judiciary, the main institution that applied the law; the chief judges (*qāḍī al-quḍāt*) they appointed were prominent ideologues with authority throughout the empire and had tremendous influence on legal doctrine and practice. In the late 10th and early 11th centuries, the caliph Qadir (991–1031) made a number of attempts to enhance his religious authority and was particularly active in denouncing the public presence of Mu'tazili theology and Twelver and Isma'ili Shi'ism. In league with Hanbali and other conservative Sunni theologians, he repeatedly and publicly promulgated, in 1018 and subsequent years, the Qadiri Creed, a document that declared Mu'tazili and Shi'i theology heretical and prohibited debate with their scholars. His policy was continued by Qa'im, his son and successor. Even until the late Abbasid period, dynasts throughout the central Islamic lands regularly sought the caliph's recognition of their position and even his sanction for their military campaigns against the Byzantines and others. The idiosyncratic caliph Nasir (r. 1180–1225), who endeavored to revive the glory of the early Abbasid caliphate by placing himself at the pinnacle of all societal structures of authority, wrote four *ijāzah*s or certificates authorizing the activities of the four Sunni schools, granting one to the leading jurist of each one of them. Much later, in the Treaty of Kuchuk-Kainardja, signed in July 1774 between the Ottoman sultan Abdülhamid I (1774–89) and the Russian empress Catherine the Great (1762–96), the Ottomans recognized the independence of Crimea but insisted that the sultan remained the spiritual leader of the Tartars on the grounds that he was the caliph of the Muslims. This may be seen as a move to counter Russian and French claims to represent the cause of Christian minorities within the Ottoman Empire, similarly claiming jurisdiction over Muslims outside the official boundaries of Islamdom. Whatever the reasoning behind it, the condition nevertheless indicates a strong claim to religious authority on the part of the caliph many centuries after the heyday of the Abbasids.

As far as the caliph's relations with the jurists are concerned, it could be said that a compromise was reached whereby the jurists claimed direct jurisdiction over private law while recognizing the caliphs' (and eventually other rulers') control over public law; the jurists publicly supported the legitimacy of the government, while the rulers supported the jurists as a class. This was possible because the shari'a leaves large parts of the law relatively undeveloped, particularly public law (except for taxation, a constant bone of contention). Rulers thus had some freedom to act, and they imposed a wide variety of systems of civil, criminal, and even tax law throughout Islamic history. The most famous is the *Qanun* of the Ottoman sultans. Collected by Mehmed the Conqueror in the mid-15th century, this code was revised in 1501 and again in the mid-16th century by Sultan Süleiman; it dealt primarily with the organization of government and the military, taxation, and treatment of the peasantry.

Jurists periodically attempted to assert broader control, arguing that the ruler, even when acting on his own, was required to adhere closely to the dictates of the shari'a. They made such arguments in works under the generic rubric of *siyāsa shar'iyya* (public policy that conforms to the shari'a), including such works as *al-Siyasa al-Shar'iyya* (The book of governance according to the shari'a) by Ibn Taymiyya and *al-Turuq al-Hukmiyya* (Methods of rule) by Ibn Qayyim al-Jawziyya. Such works stressed the authority of the jurists as a professional class and the obligation of the caliph or ruler to heed their advice and carry out their dictates. They occasionally admitted that the caliph could decide legal questions on his own, but only if he were himself a qualified jurist.

Similarly, many premodern reform movements emphasized the importance of adherence to the law on the part of the ruler and/or the populace in general, or the necessity of ridding society of beliefs and practices that were inauthentic accretions contradicting the law in its pure form. Such movements included the Almohad movement that held sway in North Africa in the 12th and 13th centuries, the Wahhabi movement founded in central Arabia by Muhammad b. 'Abd al-Wahhab (d. 1792), the Sanusi movement in 19th-century Libya, the thought of Indian Muslim reformers such as Shaykh Ahmad Sirhindi (d. 1624) and Shah Waliullah (d. 1762), and so on. The same logic led to public expressions of repentance and atonement on the part of rulers who promised to turn over a new leaf, giving up wine drinking, dancing girls, illegal taxes, and other un-Islamic practices. One dramatic example of this was the Edict of Sincere Repentance promulgated by the Safavid monarch Shah Tahmasp in 1556, in which he forswore not only alcohol and other vices but also the patronage of painting and other secular arts.

Judges and Muftis

Judges (qadis) theoretically arrived at their verdicts independently of outside interference, but they were appointed directly by the ruler, and thus in a sense they were his representatives and beholden to him. The position of judge was considered morally dangerous by many, not least of whom were the jurists themselves. A judge was often under considerable pressure to violate the law in order to enforce the ruler's will or justify his actions or those actions of influential and powerful viziers or army commanders, and stories abound of prominent scholars refusing the office in order to avoid such a predicament. Many jurists were also reluctant to accept a salary that could have been acquired through illegal taxes or through seizure or extortion. In addition, the office presented many opportunities for increasing one's income in less than honest ways. The judge and other court officials often lined their pockets by charging various fees for hearing cases and processing documents, not to mention by accepting gifts and bribes to influence the outcome of cases. A judge was often in charge of the property of orphans and other individuals who were wards of the court, lost property, unclaimed estates, and so forth and could divert funds for his own benefit or that of his accomplices. He often became the trustee of endowments, a position that usually paid 10 percent of the annual endowment income, or he could appoint relatives or friends as trustees or sell these positions for bribes or kickbacks. The same was true of various salaried positions funded by endowment income, such as professorships at madrasas and positions as Qur'an readers and imams at mosques. Many judges accumulated a large number of such endowed positions in the course of their career and had deputies carry out the duties associated with them. Perhaps the largest income, though, came from selling deputy judgeships for the various subdistricts within his territory. Aspiring judges were often ready to pay large sums for such deputyships because they knew they would be able to recoup their investment in a short time. In short, if they could stay in office for a considerable period, chief judges could accumulate vast fortunes, and it is likely that many appointees paid a huge fee or bribe to the ruler for the office. Indeed, the sums involved were so significant that the later Fatimid caliphs' urgent need for funds was provided, to a large extent by the payments involved in a rapid succession of appointments to the position of chief judge. A judge who remained unsullied by venality was deserving of comment.

Judges adjudicated cases that appeared before them but did not investigate and bring cases to trial unless a private citizen filed a suit. Another legal arm of the government was the *muhtasib* or "market inspector," who was in charge of inspecting weights and measures, preventing fraud in economic transactions, setting prices, and preventing hoarding and price gouging for basic commodities. He was also in charge of public morality and was responsible for closing down wine taverns and houses of ill repute. Also important were the *shurṭa* or police, who actively sought to prevent crime, investigate incidents of crime, and bring criminals to justice. Grievance courts were a standard feature of Islamic governments and were intended to be an avenue for the redress of wrongs committed by government officials and the like. This court was ideally presided over by the ruler himself, but a specific judge was often appointed to represent him. While the official appointed as judge of the grievance court was often a qualified jurist, he was not required to apply Islamic legal rules in a strict fashion and often had wide discretion to resolve disputes as he saw fit.

Jurisconsults (muftis) remained relatively freer of government control than judges, but eventually they too became government-appointed officials. Muftis were (and are) supposed to grant fatwas to lay Muslims on legal questions having to do with personal devotion, ritual practice, marital issues, commercial disputes, or other issues. Since such consultation should ideally be free of charge and accessible to all, Mirrors for Princes regularly suggest that the ruler should pay stipends to muftis so that they could carry out their service without asking for payment; from the 12th century onward, the Zengid, Ayyubid, and Mamluk rulers of Syria and Egypt provided state-appointed muftis to answer the legal questions of the public at large.

In tenth-century Khurasan, prominent jurists began to be recognized as the leading muftis of their cities, each one of them under the title of shaykh al-Islam (master of Islam). At first an informal position, it became an official government appointment in later centuries and spread throughout Iran, Central Asia, India, Anatolia, and then to Syria and Egypt. The shaykh al-Islam of the capital city came to wield enormous power and was viewed as the highest legal authority in the realm under such dynasties as the Ottomans, Safavids, Uzbeks, and Mughals. He not only answered thousands of petitions from the laity but also oversaw all the shaykhs al-Islam in the cities of the empire and sanctioned the policies and actions of the ruler. In the 16th century, the position of the Ottoman shaykh al-Islam was integrated fully into the government bureaucracy, and along with him the entire network of shaykhs al-Islam in provincial cities. Many Muslim states such as Egypt and Pakistan continue to appoint grand muftis who are responsible for answering questions of public import.

In the Twelver Shi'i system, the jurists successfully maintained more independence from the government, in part because they were less dependent on the income of endowments, which could more easily by confiscated or controlled by the government. Instead, the Shi'i scholarly establishment was supported by the payment of the *khums* (literally, "fifth"), an income tax paid by lay believers directly to the leading Shi'i scholars, which often crossed borders and remained inaccessible to rulers. Even though religious authority is understood to reside in the imam, the authority of Twelver jurists has grown steadily since the tenth century, when the Twelfth Imam was said to have gone into occultation. In 874 the 11th imam died in Samarra, Iraq. A series of four representatives maintained contact with his son, the Twelfth Imam, who remained in hiding, during a period known as the Lesser Occultation. In 941 the last of the four representatives died without designating a successor, and it was held that the Twelfth Imam was now in Greater Occultation: ordinary communication with the Twelfth Imam was cut off, as he circulated incognito among the believers. Since then, Twelver jurists gradually arrogated to themselves many of the prerogatives of the Twelfth Imam, making ever-stronger claims concerning their own religious authority. In the 13th century, they accepted the concept of *ijtihād*, claiming the exclusive right to determine the correct rulings on legal questions through legal study and investigation. In the 16th century, the theory developed that the leading jurists' authority derived from the fact that they had been designated the general representatives of the Hidden Imam. A hierarchy was established among the jurists in which the top rank is occupied by a *marja' al-taqlid* (reference for adoption of opinions), who serves as an authority for lay believers and is now termed *āyat allāh 'uẓmā* (a greater sign of God). This process culminates in Ayatollah Khomeini's theory of the comprehensive authority of the jurist (*wilāyat al-faqīh*), according to which the leading jurist is actually responsible for political rule, which goes against the theories of many earlier Shi'i legal thinkers, who argue that certain prerogatives of the Hidden Imam, such as direct political rule, the conduct of jihad, taxation, and the establishment of Friday prayer, are in abeyance until he reveals himself.

The Law and the Family

Unsurprisingly, the shari'a assumes a patriarchal system in which the head of the family is male. Paternity determines what family one belongs to, and in Sunni law a person's male agnatic relatives form part of the extended family. The law of inheritance grants them the remnant of the estate when it is not exhausted by the fixed shares (a rule rejected in Shi'i law), and they are also responsible for paying blood money for injury or death (except in Hanafi law). Laws regarding child custody are based on the premise that the natural allegiance of a child is to the father's side of his or her family, and custody always reverts to the father even though very young children may remain with their mothers temporarily.

Men are generally dominant over women. While men and women are held to believe in the same way and to have roughly equal religious obligations, one may argue that in a blunt, practical sense, a woman's value is half that of a man of similar status. According to the traditional system of blood money payments, which likely goes back to pre-Islamic customs in pagan Arabia, a free Muslim woman is worth 50 camels, exactly one-half the price of a free Muslim man and equal in value to a Jewish or Christian male or a male slave. Similarly, a daughter's share of inheritance from her parents is half that of a son, and the testimony of a woman in court is worth one-half of the testimony of a man. Nevertheless, women have many rights under Islamic law, including the right to own and dispose of property without the interference of their husbands, something that women in Western societies did not have until quite recently. Husbands are required to pay for the food, shelter, clothing, and upkeep of their wives and children, while wives are not required to use any of their own property or income, even if it is vast, to support the family.

Slavery is accepted as a legitimate institution, though there are rules for the humane treatment of slaves, and slaves are not merely property but also individual agents. They can be Muslims and have the same religious obligations as other Muslims, such as fasting and regular prayer. They may marry and they may own property, though, technically, until they gain their freedom, their property belongs to their master. Many apologists claim that Islam set out to abolish slavery gradually, basing this idea on the Qur'anic verses that urge emancipation of slaves as a means to atone for infractions of religious obligations.

All free men are generally awarded the same rights and duties, but there are a few exceptions. The law of marriage equality (*kafā'a*, literally, "suitability") stated that a man had to be of appropriate status to marry a woman of high status and could be used to annul the marriage of an heiress who ran off with a servant or the local butcher. Some held that a non-Arab was not a suitable partner for an Arab woman, nor an ordinary man for a woman descended from the Prophet. The descendants of the Prophet (termed *sayyids* or sharifs) are also distinguished from other Muslims in some other respects, but the vast respect they enjoyed in medieval Muslim society had little to do with the law.

Modernity

During the 19th and 20th centuries, most of the Islamic world came under the direct rule of colonial powers, especially France and Britain but also Holland, Italy, Portugal, and Russia (later the Soviet Union). Colonial rule and the modern nation-states that followed in the mid-20th century had far-reaching effects on the law enforced in those areas. From 1850 onward the traditional legal system was increasingly replaced by codes based on European models, and traditional Islamic law was largely restricted to ritual, family, and inheritance law. With the new codes came a system of law depending on constitutions, codes, and statutes, together with a new system of secular legal education and a new class of legal professionals; Saudi Arabia was the only country to have a shari'a court system in 2011. The jurists in the traditional system lost their monopoly on organized education and saw their social power and status plummet. In nearly every nation in the Muslim world, the endowment properties that had funded most of the institutions of Islamic legal education were confiscated by the colonial powers and then the modern nation-state. Most members of the class of jurists, including the top religious authorities, became government employees.

In colonial India, the British sought to apply the law of the various religious communities to their members and thereby prevent the unfair imposition of Hindu law on Muslims, so that they created "Anglo-Muhammadan law" for the Muslims. In so doing, they inadvertently turned Islamic law into code law, for they chose the Hanafi work *al-Hidaya* by Burhan al-Din al-Marghinani (d. 1197) for the administration of Hanafi Muslims in India, translated it into English, and used it as the nearly exclusive reference for Islamic law. Similar developments occurred in Dutch Indonesia and elsewhere.

The modern period witnessed many attempts to change Islamic law and debates about how it could be done. Muslim reformers such as Muhammad 'Abduh (d. 1905) and Rashid Rida (d. 1935) argued for modern jurists' freedom to adapt rules from other legal schools to those of their own, a process called *talfiq* (piecing together). A prominent example of *talfiq* put into practice was the use of principles borrowed from Maliki law to reform the Hanafi law of divorce in the Anglo-Muhammadan legal system. Another method was *takhayyur*, granting jurists the freedom to choose from all the opinions found in the traditional corpus, including those of other schools and minority views within one's own. This generated the new field of *fiqh muqāran* (comparative law), the study of similar issues across the different schools.

Others argued for a rethinking of the hermeneutics of Islamic law, generally presented as a form of *ijtihād*, which takes on here a new sense allowing traditional rules to be set aside and permitting those with secular education to participate. Muhammad 'Abduh argued that laws should change with the times and the conditions of the societies to which they apply; since reason and revelation are intended to be in harmony, independent rational inquiry should be used to revise and reform the law as needed. Many liberal proposals have involved the rejection or limitation of one or more of the "sources" on which law was based. 'Ali 'Abd al-Raziq (d. 1966) and others argued for the rejection or limitation of consensus; some, such as the Shi'i thinker Murtada Mutahhari (d. 1979), denounced *qiyās*; Ahmed Mansour, leader of the contemporary Ahl al-Qur'an movement in Egypt, has argued for the rejection of hadith, seeking the law in the Qur'an alone; and some would even limit the sources to the suras, or chapters of the Qur'an, revealed at Mecca (which would yield almost complete freedom, since they contain practically no legislation). Radical proposals of this sort have met with limited success and have often been vehemently rejected.

Strategies for reform that do not throw out any of the traditional bases of the law but rather urge an emphasis on lesser-known aspects of medieval Islamic legal hermeneutics have met with better acceptance from traditional legal authorities. Proponents of these strategies have championed a more expansive and aggressive use of the concepts of public interest (*maṣlaḥa*) or "the objectives of the law" (*maqāṣid al-sharī'a*). Frequent recourse is also had to the traditional principle of *al-barā'a al-aṣlīyya* (original permissibility), according to which something is considered permissible unless a text states that it is not.

Political Islam

The late 20th century has called for the application rather than change of the shari'a that multiplied throughout the Muslim world, becoming the basis for myriad political campaigns, resistance movements, and even revolutions. This is usually seen as a response to the failure of secular nation-states to keep up with the economic aspirations of Muslim populations, and it was also seen as an attempt to return to culturally authentic forms of government, social organization, and regulation of public behavior in the face of a perceived cultural invasion from the West. Drawing on leftist anticolonialist thinkers from Europe, the new leaders couched their push for the application of the shari'a in terms of a resistance struggle, believing that the shari'a would guarantee social and economic justice by replacing despotic, self-interested rulers with pious officials reined in by the revealed law. Khomeini and many other activists stressed the corruption and predatory nature of the secular rulers in the Islamic world, who were enriching themselves at the expense of the Muslim populace and not using oil wealth and other resources to improve the lot of the common people, something they claimed a return to Islamic law would change. Modern reformers and activists claim that Islamic law provides an answer to all possible questions, an idea captured in the common slogan *al-Islām huwa al-ḥall* (Islam is the solution).

In a number of ways, these calls for the implementation of shari'a are quite different from the periodic insistence of premodern reform movements that the ruler should adhere strictly to the sacred law; they cannot be interpreted as pure traditionalism, for the Muslim world has irrevocably changed. The modern, bureaucratic nation-state exerts a level of invasive control over the populace that its premodern precursors never had; modern education and administration have depersonalized the context in which the law used to be studied and applied. Just as the veils required for women in Iran do not resemble those worn by their precolonial counterparts, so the Islamic regime imposed on them differs starkly from a traditional Islamic state. Similarly, when Zia-ul-Haq (d. 1988) undertook a series of Islamizing reforms to appease Islamists in Pakistan, including a new law that required banks to deduct zakat automatically, this was something unprecedented in Islamic history. In addition, Western concept categories and modes of thought have indelibly affected those of Muslims, who are reacting to this "colonization of their minds" by seeking their identity in Islam. Jihad, traditionally a duty to expand and defend the borders of the Islamic world, is now understood as part of a broader defense of Muslims against cultural imperialism.

The urge to find culturally authentic forms is prominent in the continuing attempts to apply Islamic law to modern economic institutions, including corporations, bank accounts, mortgages, stock exchanges, and insurance of all kinds, throughout the Islamic world. These present a challenge for several reasons. The corporation, an economic entity that can act as a fictional person, does not exist in Islamic law, which assumes that all economic actors are individuals, partnerships, or agents for individuals or partners. Islamic law traditionally forbids both the taking and payment of interest, termed *ribā*. It forbids the unequal assumption of risk, such as the buying or selling of something the value of which is unknown because of contingency for a fixed price, as this is akin to gambling. It is understood in medieval legal texts that one lends money as a favor or act of piety in order to help a fellow believer and should expect no profit in return. This created, and continues to create, an economic problem, as the use of loans is a necessary part of any economic system. One avenue of reinterpretation of the traditional laws is to argue that *ribā* in the Qur'an and hadith did not refer to all interest but rather to exorbitant interest or usury, so that reasonable interest is excluded from the prohibition. For bank accounts, theorists have often resorted to the concept of *muḍāraba*, a type of sleeping or limited partnership, whereby the account holder essentially shares in the profit of the bank's investments. Of course, this arrangement is often understood to require, though, that the interest rate not be fixed and that the account holder lose money if the bank's investments are not profitable. Similar shari'a-compliant banking and financial instruments have become a major area of investigation and legal innovation and interpretation, and economic globalization is having an enormous effect on traditional business structures, from halal pizza chains to banking conglomerates and multinational corporations.

The calls for the application of shari'a have had major political effects starting in the 1970s, when the Egyptian and Syrian Constitutions were amended to name Islamic law as their basis. The Iranian Revolution of 1979 and the subsequent establishment of the Islamic Republic was a watershed, for they proved that it was possible to topple a secular regime and replace it with a theocratic Islamic one. It was also in 1979 that Zia-ul-Haq began his Islamicizing reforms, establishing benches charged with delivering verdicts in accordance with Islamic law, reviving the amputation of the hand for theft; the stoning of married adulterers; the flogging of unmarried fornicators; and a fine of 5,000 rupees or imprisonment, or both, for Muslims who sold or drank alcohol. He also instituted a blasphemy law prohibiting disparagement of the Prophet, his family, his Companions, and other prominent symbols of Islam; forbade the Ahmadis to call themselves Muslims or use Islamic rituals; and prosecuted Shi'is and Pakistani Christians under the blasphemy law. These laws remain on the books.

Forms of the shari'a have likewise been instituted in Saudi Arabia, Iran, Sudan, northern Nigeria, and Afghanistan, where Mulla Muhammad 'Umar, the leader of the Taliban movement, became de facto head of state during Taliban rule (1996–2001), styling himself Commander of the Faithful. All these cases of Islamization of the law are primarily symbolic, focusing on visible issues associated with Muslim identity and morality such as women's clothing in public and the enforcement of *ḥudūd* punishments. Entire new codes of law have not been introduced. Even in Iran, where an ideologically based theocratic regime is in place and new legislation is checked for violation of the shari'a by the Council of Experts, the laws already on the books remain unchanged until they are challenged for some other reason.

Calls to implement the shari'a meet with resistance from various quarters, including women's organizations and advocates of human rights and religious freedom. Muslim minorities such as Shi'is in Afghanistan and Pakistan or Baluchi and Kurdish Sunnis in Iran have in fact been subject to regular abuse by regimes intent on applying shari'a law, and Coptic Christians look upon the application of shari'a in Egypt with some trepidation, since it threatens to strip them of gains they made under colonial regimes and later nation-states in favor of the restrictions associated with *dhimmī* status. Indeed, their perception is that their Muslim compatriots are already treating them according to many of the medieval rules associated with *dhimmī* status, even though this contradicts the Egyptian Constitution and other laws.

Discussions of the merits or flaws of Islamic law often suffer from a failure to distinguish between several levels of what may be held to represent "Islam" or Islamic legal rules, conflating (1) what is stated in the Qur'an, (2) what is stated in the legal works of one or more legal schools, (3) the idealized or exemplary behavior of Muslims, (4) the actual or nonexemplary behavior of Muslims, and (5) local customs in a particular area inhabited by Muslims, which often diverge from Islamic law. In some cases, the problems do not arise from the law itself but rather from the way it functions. For example, Islamic law provides a wife with a right to her entire dower (*mahr*), including any deferred amount, in case of a divorce initiated by the husband. Requiring a large deferred dower in the contract is a way for a bride's family to provide a sort of divorce insurance for her or to provide for her significant wealth to support herself in case divorce actually occurs. In practice, though, a husband who decides to divorce his wife but does not wish to pay an enormous deferred *mahr* to her may simply mistreat her until she promises to relinquish her claim to the *mahr* in exchange for being released from the marriage. Ensuring that the law function as it should is a problem whatever the legal system may be.

Throughout Islamic history, the shari'a has played a crucial role in defining Islam, determining the boundaries of Islamic orthodoxy and shaping societal institutions, including political rule. Its hegemony has not been total, however, and it has had to contend with and adapt to other systems of thought and social and political organization. The impact of colonialism and the rise of the secular nation-state in the Islamic world did much to limit the purview of the shari'a, and some observers in the 20th century imagined that its influence, along with that of religion in general, would steadily decline. However, the failure of secular nationalisms to support steady material progress and to keep up with the expectations of the populace led to a turn toward religion, and adherence to the shari'a became a key component of identity politics in the modern Muslim world. It is bound to remain an important feature of political movements in Muslim nations that stress cultural authenticity and independence in the face of Western political, economic, and cultural dominance. The shari'a, though, is not a monolithic and static category: governments are defining and applying it in diverse ways, and modern thinkers are revising and formulating its concrete rules and its hermeneutic methods, drawing both on the rich historical legacy of Islamic legal thought and on Western theories and legal models.

Further Reading

Khaled Abou El Fadl, *Speaking in God's Name: Islamic Law, Authority and Women*, 2001; Norman Calder, "Al-Nawawī's Typology of Muftis and Its Significance for a General Theory of Islamic Law," *Islamic Law and Society* 3, no. 2 (1996): 137–64; Wael B. Hallaq, *A History of Islamic Legal Theories: An Introduction to Sunni Uṣūl al-Fiqh*, 1997; Idem, *An Introduction to Islamic Law*, 2009; Idem, *The Origins and Evolution of Islamic Law*, 2005; Idem, *Sharīʿa: Theory, Practice, Transformations*, 2009; Colin Imber, *Ebu's-Suʿud: The Islamic Legal Tradition*, 1997; George Makdisi, *The Rise of Colleges*, 1981; Muhammad Khalid Masud, Brinkley Messick, and David S. Powers, eds., *Islamic Legal Interpretation: Muftis and their Fatwas*, 2005; Christopher Melchert, *The Formation of the Sunni*

Schools of Law, 9th–10th Centuries, 1999; Joseph Schacht, *An Introduction to Islamic Law*, 1964; Idem, *Origins of Muhammadan Jurisprudence*, 1950; Devin J. Stewart, *Islamic Legal Orthodoxy: Twelver Shiite Responses to the Sunni Legal System*, 1998; Knut S. Vikør, *Between God and Sultan: A History of Islamic Law*, 2005; Bernard Weiss, *The Spirit of Islamic Law*, 1998; Roland Knyvet Wilson, *A Digest of Anglo-Muhammadan Law*, 1895.

Traditional Political Thought ◇◇◇◇◇◇◇◇◇◇◇◇

Patricia Crone

In terms of political thought, as in so many other respects, Muslims today could be said to be bilingual. On the one hand, they speak the global political language of Western derivation marked by key concepts such as democracy, freedom, human rights, and gender equality; on the other hand, they still have their traditional political idiom, formed over 1,400 years of Islamic history and marked by concepts such as prophecy, imamate, and commanding right and forbidding wrong. The Islamic tradition is alien to most Western readers. What follows is an attempt to familiarize them with it to make it easier for them to follow the other entries in this volume.

The single most important difference between contemporary Western political thinking and the Islamic tradition is that contemporary thought focuses on freedom and rights whereas the Islamic tradition focuses on authority and duties. This separates contemporary political thought from that of all premodern societies, not just that of the Islamic world. Premodern political thought centered on authority and duties because government, law and order, and the agreeable forms of life that they make possible were precious goods that could not be taken for granted. How to maintain political unity, social stability, and collective welfare were more urgent problems than protecting the interests of minorities and individuals.

Islamic political thought is based on the assumption that humans are fundamentally antisocial animals constrained by their own needs to live in societies. By nature, it was said, human beings are given to the ruthless pursuit of their own interests at the cost of everyone else; without government the strong would eat the weak, and the social bonds required for reproduction and coexistence would unravel. In the European tradition this view is represented by Thomas Hobbes (d. 1679), who, writing at the time of the English Civil War, famously said that life in a state of nature would be "solitary, poor, nasty, brutish and short." Yet man was also a social (or political) animal, the Muslims said, using Aristotle's no less famous phrase. What they meant was that humans had to come together and collaborate so that they could engage in division of labor and satisfy their many diverse needs. Even to produce a loaf of bread required cooperation; nobody could satisfy all his or her needs on his or her own, and without communal life, nobody would be free to pursue higher aims. How then was it possible for political society to be established? According to Hobbes, the creation of political society required an agreement whereby people surrendered their sovereignty to a single individual, the king. This was also the Muslim view. But whereas Hobbes envisaged people as signing away their freedom to a human king, the Muslims held them to sign it away to God, the king of the universe. In other words, God solved the problem by sending a prophet bearing a divine law; those who accepted this law would form a community together, ruled by God as represented by the Prophet and his successors. God, an infinitely superior and impartial party, defined the rules of communal life. Vis-à-vis God humans had no freedom at all, but by following God's law, they were freed from the tyranny of other human beings.

Prophets

To the Muslims, the answer to the question of how authority was to be created thus lay in divine revelation. Religion was the key to the creation of political society, not in the sense that it should legitimate an existing power structure but rather in the sense that it could supply such a structure. This reflected their own historical experience, for the Muslim community had in fact been created by a prophet, Muhammad, who had preached to the Arabs and freed them from tribal anarchy by uniting them in allegiance to God and His law. It also reflected an ancient tradition in the Near East, well known to Westerners from the case of Moses, who led his people out of Egypt at the command of God and founded the polity that was eventually to become the Davidic monarchy that lies at the heart of the Jewish political tradition.

More than anything else, it is probably this fusion of the religious and the political that makes Islamic political thought a closed book to modern Westerners, accustomed as they are to thinking of religion and politics as belonging in separate compartments. Their thinking also has long historical roots. Christianity grew up inside the Roman Empire as a religion that transcended ethnic, social, and political divisions. The Christians abandoned the Jewish political tradition, remembering Jesus as having said that His kingdom was not of this world; and as subjects of the Roman Empire they left government to Caesar. Later they converted Caesar to Christianity, took over the empire, and Christianized it: this was the closest they could get to fusing religion and politics. But the empire was still a structure originating outside Christianity, with a history stretching back into pagan times, and however entangled their jurisdictions became, state and church always remained distinct. This is what allowed for their gradual separation in modern times, and it is thanks to this separation that modern Westerners find it difficult to envisage politics as intrinsically religious: they always react by trying to separate the two, wondering whether this or that is *really* religious or *really* political or seeing the religious element as mere wrapping for secular aims. But Islam shares with secular belief systems such as nationalism or communism the feature that it can *define* political aims, not just legitimate them (though of course it can do that, too).

Religion serves to create authority because people defer to the divine. They throw themselves to the ground in fear and awe in encounters with God or angels; they go down on their knees and kiss the hands or feet of religious leaders such as the Pope or ayatollahs. A man of God can gather people around him without any need for armies and police; people come to him of their own accord, attracted by his sanctity, and directed by him, they can take political action. The reader who still finds it hard to envisage a prophet as a political leader could do worse than read Naguib Mahfouz's *Children of Gebelawi*, an allegorical novel about human history from the expulsion from paradise to the modern age set in the slums of Cairo. It brilliantly captures the prophets as political activists in the portraits of Moses and Muhammad, both very vivid, whereas that of Jesus is flat and lifeless: he was only a spiritual leader. Needless to say, the Muslims saw the prophets as spiritual figures, too; Muhammad, the object of immense devotion, was eventually to be elevated to a quasi-divine position in Sufism. But this was not meant as a denial of his political role. In the period after the Mongol invasions, holy men and leaders of Sufi orders also came to found states in the Middle East and North Africa; it is thanks to the leader of a Sufi order that Iran is a Shi'i country today. Holy men led the resistance to Western colonialism in several parts of the Muslim world as well.

Like everyone else, medieval Muslims took their own historical experience to be paradigmatic and so assumed that polities were normally founded by prophets bringing revealed law. (There had also been prophets of other kinds, but we can ignore them here.) When Plato and Aristotle were translated into Arabic, their Muslim readers understood their accounts of Greek lawgivers as descriptions of prophets. They thereby inaugurated a philosophical tradition of political thought that became highly influential in the Middle East among Muslims, Christians, and Jews alike and also came to play a role in medieval Europe via Jewish intermediaries. Muslim philosophers subscribed to the idea that all polities rested on religious law brought by a prophet. In the 14th century, two thinkers (Ibn Taymiyya and Ibn Khaldun) noted that they were wrong: it was perfectly possible to base a polity on man-made rather than revealed law, and many people had in fact done so, they observed. Eventually, this was to become all too well known, for the peoples in question included the Europeans, and it was when they rose to world dominance that the idea of a purely man-made law and political order had to be taken seriously. From a traditional Muslim point of view, it looked like a recipe for anarchy and oppression.

Caliphs and Imams

Having created authority by recourse to the concept of prophets, the Muslims faced the problem of how to maintain it when Muhammad died in Medina in 632. They reacted by establishing the caliphate or imamate. A caliph was a "deputy of God" (*khalīfat Allāh*), another direct representative of God on Earth; just as God and his subordinates, the angels, rule the created world, so the deputy and his subordinates, his governors, rule the part of humanity that has submitted to God. An imam is somebody whose example is to be followed in religious and moral matters; a prayer leader is an imam, for instance. Applied to the head of state, the term stressed his presumed moral perfection, the quality that caused others to follow him and entitled him to high office; in principle he was the most meritorious Muslim of his time (*al-afḍal*). Most Muslims held that the first caliphs in Medina had been such paragons of virtue. Having embarked on conquests, however, the caliphs came to preside over a huge empire that rapidly gave them political interests and personal tastes at variance with those of their subjects, and they were soon deemed undeserving of their office. The problems posed by morally flawed and increasingly tyrannical occupants of the caliphal office generated three civil wars between 656 and 750 and led to the emergence of the three main groups into which the Muslims are still divided: the Kharijis (now an insignificant minority represented only by the Ibadis); the Shi'is (Zaydis, Imamis, Isma'ilis and others, perhaps 10 percent of Muslims today); and the Sunnis (around 90 percent of Muslims today), a residual category formed around the scholars who called themselves *ahl al-sunna wa-l-jamā'a* and whom Western scholars usually call Traditionalists.

The First Civil War (656–61) was won by the Umayyads, who moved the capital from Medina to Syria. Both the Kharijis and the Shi'is regarded the Umayyads as usurpers, but they fully accepted that the legitimate head of the community would be a caliph in the sense of deputy of God and imam, a moral exemplar endowed with overriding religious authority. They differed radically about everything else about him. According to the Kharijis, moral perfection was assessed by the community. Any free Muslim man might be deemed to possess it and so qualify for the highest office, but he had to be deposed if he lost his superior merit. It obviously would not be possible to run an empire on this basis. The Shi'is, on the other hand, took the view that moral perfection was to be found only in the Prophet's family, and the Imami Shi'is limited the pool of candidates to one particular line in which the imamate passed from father to son so that the identity of the true leader of the community was always known. This man was the true caliph in the here and now, endowed with overriding, indeed infallible, authority in matters of law and doctrine. He was never put to the test of actually having to govern, however, and in 874 the 12th of the line was deemed to have gone into hiding, from which he would not emerge until the end of times. To the Imami Shi'is, the imams had become more important as religious than as political figures. The imams kept their political role in Zaydi Shi'ism, but here as in Kharijism, they did so in a form incompatible with stable government. It was only on the tribal fringes that the Kharijis and the Zaydis enjoyed a measure of political success.

In effect, then, both the Kharijis and the Shi'is retained the ideal of morally perfect government by divorcing it from political reality. By contrast, the Traditionalists, eventually followed by the vast majority of Muslim thinkers, accepted that the head of state could not be morally perfect and that one had to look elsewhere for imams in the sense of paragons of virtue. Their solution was to redefine the nature of the caliphal office so as to detach religious guidance from it. God was still the ultimate source of all authority, but He had no direct representatives on Earth any more, they said; Muhammad was the last, and all authority now came from him, not directly from above. In their opinion the caliphal title stood for "successor of the messenger of God" (*khalīfat rasūl Allāh*), and this, they said, was the form in which the first caliph had adopted it. (In practice, the only caliphs to have used this version seem to be the early Abbasids, who adopted it along with the title of imams, not instead of it.) When Muhammad died, his political position had passed to the caliphs and his religious leadership to his Companions, the Traditionalists said; the latter had passed on their knowledge of what Muhammad had said and done to the religious scholars ('ulama').

A religious scholar was a person who had acquired knowledge (*'ilm*) of the Qur'an and the hadith, in other words, the reports of what Muhammad said or did on particular occasions. These were the primary sources of Islamic law and doctrine. The law (shari'a) on which the Muslim community was based was divine, not only in the sense of being in accordance with God's will but also in the sense of being actually given by Him. God had revealed His will in the Qur'an, His own words. But the Qur'an needed both interpretation and supplementation, and the question was who was authorized to provide it. The early caliphs apparently thought that they were, but they were overruled by the scholars, who held the key supplement to the Qur'an to be the hadith as expounded by themselves. With the victory of the scholars, Islamic law came to be a law elaborated by private scholars rather than the government, like Jewish law. The shari'a seeks to establish what is obligatory, allowed, and forbidden in the eyes of God and also what is morally preferable or disapproved within the category of the allowed. This is an endeavor full of uncertainty and disagreement, for although God's will is eternal and unchanging, every scholar is just a fallible human being, and scholarly interpretations differ. Some scholars are more learned and authoritative than others, but nobody can settle controversial questions on behalf of all. Every juristic decision is uncertain and provisional until it has been accepted by so many for so long that it counts as validated by consensus. Consensus is the ultimate authority, for although every scholar is individually fallible, collectively they cannot go wrong: "My community will never agree on an error," as the Prophet is believed to have said.

Where the Imami Shi'is concentrated religious authority in the imam, the Sunnis thus dispersed it in the community. When the Twelfth Imam went into hiding, much the same pattern came to prevail in Imami Shi'ism. The caliph was only the executor of the law; his legitimacy no longer rested on moral superiority but rather on his ability to cooperate with the scholars. Though he was to be replaced by rulers of other types and new religious leaders were to appear in the form of Sufis, this was essentially the division of labor that prevailed in the Sunni world until modern times.

Islamic history is punctuated by the periodic appearance of religious leaders who tried to concentrate religious authority in their persons again in order to introduce radical religiopolitical change. Most commonly, they would claim to be the Mahdi, the savior expected to appear at the end of times, but they might also cast themselves as the "renewer" (*mujaddid*) expected to appear in every century or claim a special relationship with God as Sufis; some even claimed prophetic status or divinity, though this put them beyond the pale. There were also attempts by political rulers to organize the religious scholars within their realm on a hierarchical basis, notably in the Ottoman Empire. Something in the nature of a hierarchy also developed in Shi'i Iran. But the dispersed pattern was the default mode, and in the Sunni world it still prevails.

Amirs, Kings, and Sultans

In 750 the Umayyad caliphs were replaced by the Abbasids, who were members of the Prophet's family (though not 'Alids) and who moved the capital from Syria to Iraq, where their dynasty survived until 1258. In practice, their power began to disintegrate already in the ninth century, when autonomous rulers took over the provinces and they themselves were reduced to mere puppets at the center. The new rulers used secular titles such as king, amir (governor), or sultan (power, authority), and since there were no provisions in the religious law for wielders of power other than the caliph and his delegates, most of the new rulers tried to legitimate their position by seeking a letter of appointment from the caliph, acknowledging that all legitimate power came from him. In 1258, however, the Mongols conquered Baghdad and put the caliph to death without setting up another in his place. The succession of men who were both relatives of the Prophet and rulers of the community (*umma*) that the Prophet had founded thus came to an end. The Muslim world had long ceased to be a single political unit by then, but now it did not even have a single figurehead any more. For all that, the Muslims continued to feel that they lived in a single Muslim society.

In fact, a caliphate of sorts did survive, for the sultans of Mamluk Egypt (1250–1517) enthroned an Abbasid as caliph in Cairo, but this caliphate was both politically impotent and devoid of general recognition. Its significance lies mainly in the fact that when the Ottomans conquered Egypt in 1517, they claimed the caliphal title for themselves. By then the title was devalued currency, for many others had claimed it, too, often without fulfilling the legal requirement that the caliph must be a member of Muhammad's tribe (Quraysh). But though the Ottomans did not fulfill this requirement either, they came close to reuniting the Muslim world, and this, as well as their control of the holy cities of Mecca and Medina, made their claim to caliphal status meaningful. It came as a shock to many when Atatürk abolished the Ottoman caliphate in 1924. All rulers of the Islamic world today are either kings, amirs, sultans, or presidents, with the partial exception of Iran; there the head of state, ranking above the president, is simply called leader (*rahbar*), popularly "supreme leader," a new title coined in the Iranian Revolution of 1979. There are, however, still Muslims who dream of reestablishing the caliphate, associated as it is with the heyday of Islamic power.

Political Freedom

The early Muslims had a strong sense that Islam had arrived to free mankind not only from tribal anarchy but also from kings, meaning those who ruled in accordance with their own whims rather than God's dictates. ("King" was a term of abuse when contrasted with caliph or imam, though not otherwise.) When the conquests endowed the caliphs with imperial power, the Muslims accused them of "turning the caliphate into kingship" and vigorously resisted what they perceived as despotic rule. But three civil wars over less than a hundred years deprived most of them of their taste for activism. All rulers turned into kings, as some observed; fighting to replace one with another was too costly in terms of lives, general security, and Muslim solidarity to be worth it. What then were the alternatives? A rebel in eastern Iran in the 730s experimented with ideas of setting up an institution to control the local governor, a few thinkers around 800 held that it might be possible to do without a ruler altogether, and the Mu'tazili theologian Nazzam (d. ca. 845) thought that it might be best to replace the caliph with a federation of locally elected rulers. But nothing came of these ideas.

The Traditionalists around whom the Sunnis were formed held that it was best simply to tolerate tyranny while at the same time withdrawing as much of communal life as possible from the caliph's control. In their view even a morally flawed and oppressive ruler had to be obeyed as long as it did not entail a violation of God's command. The ruler's moral status did not affect the law, they said (in disagreement with the Shi'is). Even a sinful ruler could lead the prayer or conduct holy war, and participation carried the same divine rewards as when they were led by a righteous imam. One was not to rebel, since the rightly guided nature of the community did not depend on the head of state, and keeping the community together was all important. The only remedies against oppressive rulers were hellfire sermons and books of advice designed to inculcate virtue. A great many of such were produced, but needless to say their effectiveness was limited.

The jurists writing in the 11th and 12th centuries did hold that a wrongful caliph could be deposed. There were even some who held that it was a religious duty to do so. But they did not specify who should determine when or on what grounds a caliph merited deposition or how his removal was to be effected. Those who had chosen him should remove him, they said, but this simply delegated the task to whoever wielded power and influence at the center at any given time. It was never suggested that the courts should play a role in the proceedings, and there were no other formal institutions, such as a privy council or parliament, to which the task could be assigned. When the caliph lost his power to upstart rulers, even the principle that the head of state could be deposed was abandoned. God raised them up, it was said, and God would raise up others in their stead if they sinned. There is nonetheless an interesting example of a local ruler by the name of Ahmad Khan being taken to court, deposed, and executed in Samarqand (now Uzbekistan) in 1095. The charge was a heresy so grave that it amounted to apostasy. Of this he was probably innocent, but he had been a terrible oppressor, and a conviction of apostasy was an effective way of securing his removal. Why the military leaders who formed part of the coalition against him did not simply assassinate him, the normal solution, is not clear, but it did not set a precedent.

Tyranny was bearable because large parts of life were not affected by the state at all. The main way in which the government made its presence felt was through taxation, here as elsewhere a heavy burden on the peasantry. It was also a constant bone of contention between rulers and scholars, for the scholars had elaborated the fiscal law of the shari'a in such a way that did not allow enough resources for the state so that rulers were forced to impose additional taxes, which the scholars denounced as uncanonical (*maks*). The taxes went to finance the state apparatus, war, building projects, and cultural life, especially at the court. But schooling, educational training, funding, loans, health care, and the running of local affairs—all these and many other things now taken over or supervised by the state—were then in the hands of family, neighbors, friends, religious scholars, and local notables, with only intermittent attention by the government at best and often none at all. The closer one came to the center of power, the more dangerous life became (while at the same time becoming vastly much more rewarding in material terms); a great many of those who rose to powerful positions came to a violent end. But though others certainly suffered from time to time, the main problem posed by government was not usually that it was oppressive but rather that it was arbitrary and inefficient. General insecurity and local oppressors were probably more of a problem to most than the tyranny of kings, though these factors are not easily separated.

The modern state brought higher levels of security, but it also assumed a far greater role in people's lives than was formerly the case, and in combination with modern means of communication and surveillance, this transformed the old-style tyrants into dictators of a new and more totalitarian kind.

Religious Freedom

In a society based on religious law, there evidently cannot be religious freedom in the modern sense that anybody is free to choose whatever religion (if any) that he or she prefers. What Muhammad had founded was a community of believers, not a territorial state, and a community of believers it remained, even though it was eventually divided into many states. There was no room in it for unbelievers.

It is nonetheless possible to speak of religious freedom in the Islamic world. The Muslims themselves never used the expression "religious freedom" until they learned it from the West; indeed, it has an offensive ring to it from a traditional point of view, suggesting as it does that people have no obligations to their creator. But there were in fact mechanisms whereby adherents of divergent beliefs, whether infidel or just heretical, could be accommodated. As regards the former, unbelievers could be accepted as protected peoples (*dhimmī*s), at least if they were Jews, Christians, or Zoroastrians; even pagans qualified according to some legal schools. *Dhimmī*s were entitled to practice their ancestral religion and manage their own internal affairs under Muslim sovereignty, though they were subject to certain conditions, including payment of a special tax that was meant as a mark of humiliation. This was a right granted to communities, not to individuals, and individuals retained it only as long as they retained their ancestral faith. If they wished to convert, they could in principle do so only to Islam. Entrance into the Muslim community was open to all, but the exit was closed, so that once people had become Muslims, they were not allowed to convert to another religion at all. Apostasy was a betrayal of the community and punishable by death. A Muslim who converted to another religion would be safe only if he left the Islamic world for a country professing the religion for which he had betrayed his own.

Regarding fellow Muslims, the schisms between Kharijis, Shiʿis, and the majority Muslims were deeply regretted by all involved, but the majority rarely tried to impose their own views on the minorities, except in the sense that the latter risked harassment when they ventured out of their own quarters (adherents of different beliefs tended to segregate physically). Local fighting between Sunni and Shiʿi quarters was common at times, but the government took military action against dissident communities only when the latter took to arms themselves. Virulent though their polemics were, the three branches of Islam in effect accepted one another as legitimate in the sense that nobody had the right to eradicate the others by force. The habit of toleration inculcated by the recognition of non-Muslim communities may have made it easier to accept the presence of sectarian communities as well. It was only when religious leaders set out to seize political power and reform the world that the pattern of toleration was broken, usually because all normal political and social relations were thrown into turmoil, not because the leaders saw themselves as called upon to eliminate other religious groups. The only major exception is the Safavids (1501–1732), who imposed Shiʿism on Iran and engaged in the forcible conversion of Christians and Jews as well.

The fundamental schisms apart, Muslims tolerated divergent beliefs by distinguishing between external observance and inner conviction and insisting on the former alone for purposes of membership. All Muslims were expected to observe the rules relating to food, marriage, divorce, inheritance, purity, and ritual, meaning the five daily prayers (which can be performed anywhere), the weekly Friday prayer (a public ritual that men must perform in a *jāmiʿ* or "cathedral mosque"; whether women can or must is disputed), the annual fast (observed by all healthy adults), the pilgrimage to Mecca once in a lifetime for those who had the means to undertake it, and the annual payment of alms. These rituals served visibly to mark out the community from others. Their neglect might be tolerated as long as it was intermittent rather than systematic, but principled denial of their validity amounted to apostasy.

Most Muslims, however, soon came to supplement this "external" religion, as some called it, with religion of a more personal kind, such as philosophy, mysticism, or esotericism, which established a direct relationship between the individual and God. (Philosophy was not a secular pursuit directed against religion but rather a rival form of it.) Only the Traditionalists did their best to live by the Qur'an and hadith, and even they were gradually sucked into Sufism, all dominant in the post-Mongol world. Since the new forms of religion were pursued by individuals in search of their own private salvation, they often brought their adherents into conflict with the law. All downplayed the importance of the law one way or the other by holding salvation to lie in spirituality or human reason or in the mixture of the two known as theosophy. The law was deemed to be no more than a first step on the ladder to the truth, or just a metaphorical version of the absolute truth for those unable to understand higher things. In some cases, the law was not even deemed a metaphorical version of the truth but simply a utilitarian institution required for social life or even chains and fetters that had to be cast off by those in search of salvation. There were also those who accepted the law as a genuine but temporary form of religion that would be swept away when the Mahdi came to transfigure the world, so that all would be able to experience the truth directly and worship God of their own accord without the need for all the paraphernalia of institutionalized religion. Such views were widely perceived as attacks on the very foundations of Muslim society, but most of them could be tolerated as long as the "external" religion was respected and the private convictions were handled with discretion.

Freethinkers could discuss their views with like-minded individuals in private salons, in learned gatherings at the court, and to some extent in books and even more so in poetry, where things could be put ambivalently. One could also debate radical propositions as if for the sake of argument alone or voice them as part of *mujūn*. *Mujūn* was playful behavior or writing that violated the normal rules of propriety, an accepted part of the high culture which allowed people to say things that bordered on the blasphemous, the scurrilous, or the pornographic as long as they did so with literary elegance and wit and had a good sense of where to stop. There was no institutionalized confession of sins, no inquisition, and no prying into people's hearts. The authorities were responsible for the maintenance of the society in which Muslim law was practiced and without which there could be no salvation, but they were not responsible for the salvation of individuals, and what people concealed in their innermost consciences was between them and God.

In short, freedom lay essentially in privacy. The public sphere was where public norms had to be maintained, where there might be censors or private persons fulfilling the duty of "commanding right and forbidding wrong" who would break musical instruments, pour out wine, and separate couples who were neither married nor closely related. But their right to intrude into private homes was strictly limited. Here the veils came off. What went on privately was not meant to become public knowledge, and those who knew one's private life should not reveal it. Casting a veil over other people's faults was as virtuous as covering one's own; one certainly should not wash dirty linen in public. A sin that was kept secret only harmed the person who had committed it, as it was said, whereas once it was revealed, it had to be denounced lest everyone be harmed by it (in that it would weaken public norms). For the same reason, it was wrong to give clear accounts of heretical views. All these attitudes were deeply ingrained in the Near East and by no means limited to Muslims.

Again, the modern state ruined the traditional pattern. It imposes its law directly on all inhabitants of a particular territory regardless of faith and awards citizenship on the basis of criteria of secular origin, in principle awarding all citizens the same rights and duties, so that Muslims, non-Muslims, Sunnis, and Shi'is were brought out of their separate communities as members of the same national state. The national and the religious principle now coexist uneasily in the Muslim world. At the same time nationalism highlighted ethnic cleavages hitherto masked by religious fellowship. Tensions formerly defused by segregation and hierarchical ordering (with the Muslims on top) thus became difficult to contain. In addition, the home ceased to be a castle shielding the family from external intrusion. The faces and voices of the outside world, including the government, came to be seen and heard on radio, television, cassettes, and so on, and the old respect for boundaries was eroded. After the Iranian Revolution, the religious police would routinely raid private homes. Thanks to the modern economy, even the family itself is changing, as women are entering the work force and rebelling against their traditional subordination, while a growing number of the young are escaping parental supervision in cyberspace, which offers instant access to both peers and the rest of the world. All this is inevitably affecting political thought.

Outsiders

Like many other peoples, the premodern Muslims conceived of the world in which their own norms prevailed as a haven of peace and safety surrounded by threatening outsiders lacking in civilized standards; they called the former "the abode of Islam" and the latter "the abode of war." Again like many, they saw themselves as called upon to expand their haven of peace and moral rectitude so that others, too, could enjoy its benefits. Unlike the Greeks, Romans, Chinese, French, British, and others who have entertained comparable ideas but like the Spanish, the Muslims saw themselves as bringing not only benefits in this world but also salvation in the next, obedience to God being the key to both. Expanding the sovereignty of God was the aim of jihad, the Muslim form of holy war. Once brought under Muslim law, non-Muslim populations could retain their religion as *dhimmi*s, but it was hoped that they would convert, and many invariably did with the passing of time. The jurists identified jihad primarily as missionary warfare.

To the Christians, jihad has always been a stumbling block. Jesus did not use force to establish, or even to defend, himself but rather died as the victim of coercive power; the early Christians also preferred martyrdom to the use of arms. By contrast, Muhammad waged war to establish his message and died as the leader of a polity, whereupon his followers set out to conquer the world. This contrast has figured in Christian polemics against Islam for over a thousand years, often in a manner suggesting that holy war is the opposite of no war, whereas in fact it is merely the opposite of secular war (i.e., war lying outside the religious domain). The Muslims elevated one type of war to religious status, whereas their Christian counterparts assigned all war along with politics to a compartment separate from that of religion. But this does not mean that the Christians stopped fighting wars of expansion or even that they refrained from doing so in the name of religion.

The Muslim jurists identified jihad as a duty imposed on the community rather than the individual, except when it was conducted for the defense of Islam rather than its expansion, and it was typically discharged by the ruler and his troops. Volunteering was highly meritorious, however, and jihad was lawful even without official direction or authorization. Self-help was also authorized against other Muslims when they were deemed to be apostates. If a religious scholar declared a certain person to be an infidel, any Muslim could kill him with impunity. (A person found guilty of unbelief by a court would normally be executed by the authorities.) Muslims frequently declared one another to be infidels, often, it would seem, without anything happening, presumably because the declarations were confined to books. If they were widely publicized, however, the alleged infidel might be no better off than the outlaw in medieval European society. Self-help was likewise authorized in the maintenance of public morality. Any Muslim could, indeed should, command right and forbid wrong by counseling people if he saw them acting contrary to what he knew to be the law or even by using force, though this was a contentious issue.

The early jurists who divided the world into an abode of Islam and an abode of war took it for granted that a Muslim could not live permanently outside the Islamic abode. To be a Muslim was to live under the sovereignty of God as represented by a Muslim ruler upholding Islamic law. In practice, however, Muslims soon came to live as (usually commercial) minorities in other countries, while conversely parts of the Muslim world eventually came to be ruled by non-Muslims in the form of Crusaders, Mongols, and Europeans, so the abode of Islam came to be understood as anywhere that Islam could be openly practiced; political sovereignty was not required. Today a full third of all Muslims live as minorities under non-Muslim sovereignty.

These developments have put an end to jihad of the traditional type. In the later 19th century, the Muslims of British India began to reinterpret the duty as purely defensive, and this has become the prevalent view today; many Muslims even deny that it has ever meant expansionist war, dismissing the traditional concept of jihad as an Orientalist invention. Instead, a new type of global jihad has appeared.

That, too, is cast as defensive and thus defined as as an individual duty, not simply a communal one that can be discharged by some on behalf of all. Conducted by way of self-help without government direction, it is distinguished by systematic disregard of traditional boundaries. The same is true of self-help against apostates. When the Shi'i Ayatollah Khomeini declared the novelist Salman Rushdie to be as an apostate, many tried to kill him, even though Rushdie lived in England rather than a Muslim state (and had never been Shi'i). Similarly, offensive Westerners such as the Dutch filmmaker Theo van Gogh or the Danish cartoonists who drew mocking images of Muhammad were treated as if they were *dhimmī*s under Muslim rule. All these cases are exceptional, but they illustrate the flux into which traditional concepts have been thrown by modern changes.

Overview

Religion in the broad sense of appeals to the supernatural has played a major role in all political thought wherever it is found, but there is no denying that it is particularly prominent in Islam. In line with this, Muslim thinkers display strong awareness of the degree to which reality is shaped by constructions put on it and of the power to be derived from working people's minds. In that sense they could be said to be the true heirs of the Christians, who succeeded in taking over the Roman Empire armed with nothing but the power of their convictions. Islamic political thought is also unusual in the degree to which it endorses self-help, as opposed to reliance on political or ecclesiastical authorities, and not just in matters involving the use of force. The standard example is the lunar calendar. Even illiterates can handle it because the beginning and end of each month is established on the basis of a sighting of the new moon rather than astronomical calculation (though scientists liked to engage in that, too). The religion is institutionally lightweight; indeed, there is a vision in some juristic writings of every Muslim as personally responsible for the maintenance of Muslim norms for himself and his neighbors—a view often in a state of tension with authoritarian respect for social and political hierarchies.

The historical roots of this vision lie partly in the tribal heritage of Arab conquerors who founded Muslim society in the Middle East and partly in the colonial past of the provinces in which they established their first capitals. As tribesmen from a stateless society, the Arabs were used to managing their own affairs without recourse to political and ecclesiastic hierarchies, and having been ruled by Greeks and Persians for close to a thousand years, the inhabitants of Syria and Iraq, as well as Egypt, had a long tradition of living communal lives separate from those of their imperial masters without renouncing obedience to them. When the Muslims discovered that their own caliphs kept turning into kings, most of them in effect opted for the same solution: what mattered was communal life, not the state, which they saw as a mere protective envelope; certainly, this envelope had to be maintained, but in terms of the morally significant domains of life, the believers took charge of themselves. This gave Islamic political thought a very different character from that of Western Christendom, where an immense amount of attention was devoted to a hierarchical institution, the church.

Further Reading

Patricia Crone, *Medieval Islamic Political Thought*, 2005.

'Ulama' ◇◇

Muhammad Qasim Zaman

The Arabic term *'ulamā'* (sing., *'ālim*) refers to Muslim scholars specializing in the Islamic religious sciences. A number of other terms are often used to characterize the particular focus of a scholar's work, among them *muḥaddith* (concerned with the study of the hadith reports attributed to the Prophet Muhammad), *mufassir* (an exegete of the Qur'an), and *faqīh* and mufti (a scholar of Islamic law and a jurisconsult, respectively). The term "'ulama'" usually is understood to encompass these somewhat narrower categories. The boundaries between "religious" and "secular" learning were less clearly delineated in premodern Islam than they have been in the modern world, and those recognized as 'ulama' sometimes made significant contributions to fields of knowledge lying well beyond the aforementioned areas. Further, the same person might well be a scholar of Islamic law, a theologian, a philosopher, and a Sufi. In modern times some "new religious intellectuals"—that is, people who are educated not at institutions of traditional Islamic learning but rather at Western or Westernized colleges and universities and who are active contributors to religious discourse—have sometimes claimed that they, too, should be considered as 'ulama'. As the Sudanese Islamist Hasan al-Turabi (b. 1932), who received a doctorate in law from the Sorbonne, put it, "Because all knowledge is divine and religious, a chemist, an engineer, an economist, or a jurist are all ulama." Despite occasionally blurred boundaries, the term "'ulama'" is usually understood as those who claim religious authority on the basis of their grounding in the Islamic religious sciences. This chapter focuses on such traditionally educated religious scholars.

The 'Ulama' in Medieval History

The origins of the 'ulama' are to be traced to those figures of the first generations of Islam who had come to be seen by their contemporaries and successors as especially knowledgeable in matters relating to the Qur'an, as sources of information on the life and teachings of the Prophet Muhammad, and as jurists. By the early eighth century, scholarly circles had begun to emerge in several major Islamic towns in Arabia, Syria, Iraq, and elsewhere. Statements attributed to the Prophet and to his

Companions also began to be collected with much vigor during the second century of Islam (roughly the eighth century), though it would take many generations of scholarly contestation before the authority of hadith reports attributed to the Prophet Muhammad (as distinguished from statements ascribed to his Companions and other early Muslims or the evolving juridical discourses of particular scholarly circles) would be recognized as a source of legal norms second to the Qur'an.

Many prominent scholars of early Islam worked under the patronage of the rulers. One notable example is Muhammad b. Shihab al-Zuhri (d. 742), who served several Umayyad caliphs and was instructed by the caliph 'Umar b. 'Abd al-'Aziz (r. 717–20) to collect normative traditions (*sunan*, best understood here, as Wael Hallaq has observed, as reports relating to the teachings and practices not just of the Prophet but also of other early figures). Another example is Muhammad b. Ishaq (d. 767), the author of an early biography of the Prophet, which he composed at the behest of the second Abbasid caliph Mansur (r. 754–75) as part of a larger history of the world. Abu Yusuf (d. 798), a founding figure in the history of the Hanafi *madhhab*, or school of law (named after his teacher, Abu Hanifa [d. 767]), served as an influential judge in Baghdad and wrote a treatise on taxation for the Abbasid caliph Harun al-Rashid (r. 786–809). Medieval biographical dictionaries are replete with instances of scholars visiting caliphs and other notables, receiving their gifts, and benefiting in sundry other ways from royal patronage.

Yet the emergence of religious scholars also represented a multifaceted challenge to the ruling elite. For one thing, many scholars were willing to lend their support to trends and movements hostile to the political establishment. This was the case especially with those who came to be allied with various Shi'i groups in the late Umayyad and early Abbasid period. But even those not so allied were sometimes opposed to particular policies adopted by the caliphs and their officials, from unjust taxation to the failure to conform to the ideals and norms as they were being articulated in these scholarly circles. Quite apart from specific instances of scholarly disaffection, the fact that the scholars had come to represent an increasingly independent locus of authority in Muslim society was a cause of much apprehension on the part of the ruling elite. It was independent in the sense that, unlike the judges appointed by the state, the scholars did not need authorization from the caliph to do their work, for example, responding to people's queries on matters of law, interpreting the Qur'an, collecting hadith reports, and engaging in theological debates. From the mid-eighth century onward, the scholars also began defining the position of the caliph in such a way that it lacked any privileged authority in religious as opposed to political matters.

The most serious challenge to the increasing influence of the 'ulama', as represented by the scholars of hadith, came from the Abbasid caliph Ma'mun (r. 813–33). Toward the end of his reign he instituted an "inquisition" (the *mihna*) requiring the scholars to affirm the "createdness" of the Qur'an. Though ostensibly intended to guard the cardinal Islamic doctrine of the oneness of God against any coeternal competitors, hence the caliph's insistence that the Qur'an be regarded as the created rather than uncreated (and, by implication, eternal) word of God, this ingenious test is better seen as an effort to put the increasingly assertive scholars in their place by affirming the caliph's prerogative to articulate correct beliefs. The *miḥna* eventually was terminated during the reign of caliph Mutawakkil (r. 847–61), its end signaling caliphal recognition of the 'ulama' collectively as the authoritative guardians of the evolving religious tradition. The caliph was scarcely divested of "religious" functions with the end of the *miḥna*, however. One of the primary functions, and justifications, of government was, after all, the upholding of the shari'a; several influential jurists writing on government stipulated that the caliph should be knowledgeable in matters of the law to the rank of a scholar capable of arriving at independent legal opinions (*ijtihād*). Irrespective of whether these jurists seriously expected the caliphs to have such legal expertise, stipulations of this sort suggest the degree to which the scholars had come to define what constituted legitimate political authority as well as the centrality of their own vocation to all Islamic matters.

The 'ulama' also wrote themselves into medieval constitutional theory by stipulating that they were the people responsible, either exclusively or together with other notables, for choosing the ruler. In practice, of course, the 'ulama' had little say in who ruled the polity and, in keeping with their generally quietist politics, the jurists studiously avoided discussing the mechanisms through which a corrupt, incompetent, or irreligious ruler should be removed from office. Yet this quietism did not quite extend to the degree where the ruler could necessarily take the 'ulama' for granted. The ruling elite needed political legitimacy, which came not from popular will or good governance but rather, in considerable measure, from the allegiance of the religious scholars. Moreover, as observed by Jonathan Berkey, given the fact that the medieval political and military ruling classes often had shallow roots in the societies over which they ruled, the 'ulama', with much deeper local roots, could serve as a constraint of sorts on the arbitrary exercise of power even as they helped mediate between the ruling elite and their subjects. Nor, by the same token, did the scholars' concern with political stability mean that they were necessarily wedded to a particular ruler: a successful challenger to an existing regime could very well receive the same endorsement from the scholars as had his predecessor. As Khaled Abou El Fadl has shown, many medieval jurists also argued that while it was wrong to rebel against constituted political authority, Muslim rebels did nonetheless have political rights. They were not to be treated by the rulers in the manner of mere brigands but rather as people with an "interpretation," albeit an incorrect one, that had led them to adopt a particular course of action. Such reasoning was not merely an effort to distinguish wrongheaded Muslim rebels from either the brigands or the non-Muslim foes; it was also an implicit warning to the rulers that the jurists' quietist worldview could nonetheless countenance an alternative to the existing political dispensation.

Inasmuch as they sought to exercise some degree of restraint on the political elite, the jurists, and the 'ulama' in general, remained vulnerable to political pressure and influence. This made for an often tense relationship between the religious and the political elite. The social institutions and the scholarly culture of the 'ulama' do nonetheless seem to have served them well in trying to safeguard the space they had been carving out for themselves since the ninth century. For instance, the institution of the waqf, or the charitable endowment, was understood as existing in perpetuity, so that, even when established by members of the ruling elite, it was expected to be rather more resistant to political interference than might have been the case otherwise. It was such waqf endowments that helped sustain Islamic institutions of learning, the madrasas, which had begun to appear in Muslim societies in the late 11th century.

Religious scholarship also made for a remarkable cosmopolitanism in the world of the 'ulama': for all their local roots, many among the 'ulama' traveled widely and, despite the limitations of a manuscript culture, their work could enjoy broad recognition. Among other things, this cosmopolitanism served again to limit the degree to which the ruling elite could regulate, even when so inclined, the activities and discourses of the 'ulama'. The very nature of the scholarly tradition of the 'ulama' was, furthermore, resistant to political encroachment. With the veritable canonization of particular collections of hadith reports and with the crystallization of their schools of law, complete with their agreed-upon methods and their authoritative norms, the scholars were keen not to leave the door ajar for political manipulation of their tradition. Contrary to how Muslim modernists as well as an earlier generation of Western observers viewed the medieval Islamic scholarly tradition, mechanisms for rethinking legal norms and adapting them to changing needs did continue to exist. For their part, the rulers were seldom at a loss in finding pliant scholars who would endorse this or that measure. Nonetheless, in constructing an elaborate scholarly tradition and anchoring their identity and authority in it, the 'ulama' sought to guard it from political and other vicissitudes. To the extent that the 'ulama' can be seen as a key component of a public sphere in medieval Islamic societies, their scholarly tradition and attendant socioreligious roles were crucial to it.

A significant exception to the pattern of 'ulama'-state relations discussed here is represented by their position in the Ottoman Empire. The Ottoman 'ulama' comprised a veritable religious establishment that was headed by the shaykh al-Islam (the grand mufti) who belonged, as did the sultans, to the Hanafi school of law. The close identification of the 'ulama' with the state carried important dividends: their leading madrasas were richly endowed, the Hanafis were the dominant school even in regions whose Muslim inhabitants belonged to other schools of law, and the shaykh al-Islam was one of the most powerful officials in the empire. The close relationship with the political elite also had very considerable costs, however: in the 17th and early 18th centuries, as Madeline Zilfi has noted, no fewer than three shaykhs al-Islam were executed, and others came close to that fate. And the demise of the Ottoman Empire in the early 20th century meant that the fate of the Ottoman religious establishment, too, was sealed.

The 'Ulama' in the Modern World

The 'ulama' have faced major challenges in all Muslim societies since the 19th century. Among the most significant was the onset of European colonial rule, which, in many cases, spelled the end of Muslim political authority. While many among the 'ulama' had maintained their distance from the governing elite, they depended on the government for the upholding of Islamic law. The sultan did not need to be virtuous for the 'ulama' to serve as judges in his administration or to attend to various aspects of intellectual and religious life in society. The advent of colonial rule jeopardized the practice of Islamic law as never before, however. With the establishment of British colonial rule in India, for instance, the scope of Islamic law was gradually reduced to matters of personal status (e.g., marriage, divorce, and inheritance), which is what the "shari'a" came to mean in British India. But even this limited body of Islamic law was administered by judges who were usually non-Muslim. The judges based their decisions on a small set of "authoritative" Islamic legal texts, but they did so while being guided by norms of English common law. The 'ulama' tended to see the resulting jurisprudence—the "Anglo-Muhammadan law"—as nothing but a travesty of the shari'a. Many among them considered it illegitimate for people to have recourse to colonial courts even for such routine matters as the dissolution of a marriage, which meant further restrictions on the practice of Islamic law even in areas that the colonial administration had officially recognized.

Colonialism brought new institutions not just in the judicial realm but also, among others, in that of education. Even as many madrasas and related institutions declined with the drying up of earlier forms of financial patronage, not the least the disintegration of what had once been substantial waqf endowments, a new generation of Muslims began to be educated in modern institutions of Western learning. Such institutions had only limited space for Islamic learning. In part, this was because their raison d'être was to provide Muslims with the sort of education that would help them succeed in the colonial economy, and in part, it had to do with the highly critical stance the founders of such institutions adopted toward the traditionalist 'ulama', holding them responsible for the cultural and intellectual decline of Islam. But it also had to do with the 'ulama''s own suspicion of such modern institutions, which they saw not merely as trespassing on their territory—in this instance, education—but as yet another instrument of a colonial enterprise bent on the very destruction of Islam.

Despite the lack of any sustained formal training in the Islamic sciences, those educated in such modern institutions have had a keen interest in Islamic matters. But their engagement with Islam—as Muslim modernists, Islamists, and other new religious intellectuals—has been of a decidedly different sort than the manner in which the 'ulama' have tended to understand and interpret their religious tradition. By the same token, the products of these modern institutions of learning have often taken a dim view of the intellectual tradition of the 'ulama' and of their relevance, thus representing a serious challenge to the authority and social influence of the 'ulama'.

A related challenge has come from the fact that print and information technologies, in tandem with the impact of mass education, have made the sources of religious knowledge far more accessible to larger groups of people than had ever been the case before the early 20th century. The 'ulama' have never been a cohesive social or religious group and, despite considerable overlaps between "religious" and other forms of learning in medieval Islam, their claims to authority were sometimes vigorously contested by the philosophers, the Sufis, members of the urban cultural elite, and popular preachers, just as scholars of hadith and law might contest the claims of, say, the theologians. The degree to which modern Islam has seen what Dale Eickelman and James Piscatori have characterized as the "fragmentation" of religious authority is nonetheless unparalleled. Also unprecedented is the power and reach of the modern state, which has been far less willing to allow the 'ulama' to have the sort of social and religious autonomy that they had so jealously guarded in many premodern Muslim societies.

It was common for observers of Muslim societies in the mid- and late 20th century to assume that the 'ulama' had fared altogether badly in the face of such challenges. Adherents of modernization and secularization theories had little doubt that the 'ulama' and their institutions were mere relics of the past waiting to be swept aside by the forces of Westernization. They were not entirely wrong in this view. In Turkey under Atatürk, the institution of the shaykh al-Islam had been abolished, as noted earlier, and the madrasas and Sufi orders were closed down. In Morocco and Tunisia, long-established madrasas such as the Qarawiyyin in Fez and the Zaytuna in Tunis underwent radical transformations at the behest of the ruling elite. So did Azhar University in Egypt: the reforms of 1961, representing a culmination of decades of governmental effort at regulation, sought simultaneously to transform this venerable seat of Sunni learning into a modern university (with faculties of Arabic and Islamic studies now part of a much broader educational mandate) *and* to make it more fully subservient to the government. Even in Iran, where the 'ulama' and their madrasas were considerably freer of state regulation than they were in many Sunni countries because of structures of religious authority peculiar to Shi'ism, the 'ulama''s institutions saw sharp decline under the Pahlavi dynasty.

The Iranian Revolution (1978–79) was a major corrective to conventional wisdom. A seemingly strong and Westernized regime was overthrown by a massive movement that was not merely suffused with a religious idiom but also led by traditionally educated religious scholars, who then proceeded to occupy a prominent place in the Islamic Republic. Together with developments in Pakistan, Saudi Arabia, Afghanistan, Egypt, and elsewhere in the Muslim world, the Iranian Revolution helped draw the attention of scholars, policy analysts, and other observers to Islamism. Yet given that Sunni Islamists have tended to be drawn not from the ranks of the 'ulama' but rather from those of the college- and university-educated, a recognition of the limits of modernization theories did not immediately translate into attention to the 'ulama' and their institutions in Sunni societies. It has come to be increasingly recognized, however, that Sunni 'ulama'—and the 'ulama' in general—continue to be an important facet of Muslim politics and the public sphere and that it is difficult to understand contemporary Islam in all its complexity without serious attention to them.

Some of the very forces that posed severe challenges to the 'ulama' and, in many cases, marginalized them have, paradoxically, served to bring them back into prominence. The onset of colonial rule in India goaded the establishment not only of the Westernizing Muhammadan Anglo-Oriental College (later Aligarh Muslim University) in 1875 but also, a few years earlier, of a new madrasa in the North Indian town of Deoband. While the founders of the Aligarh college wanted Muslims to effectively compete with their Hindu compatriots by learning the language and the ways of the new rulers, those of the Deoband madrasa sought to defend Muslim identity through a renewed focus on Islamic learning. Unlike earlier institutions of Islamic learning in India and elsewhere, the Deoband madrasa was sustained not by the support of rich and powerful patrons but rather by the donations of ordinary people. Though admitting of different permutations, this pattern was followed by other institutions throughout South Asia and beyond. "Deobandi" madrasas—so called because they adhere to a shared approach to Islam anchored in the study of hadith and Hanafi law—now number in the tens of thousands, though significant numbers of madrasas belonging to other doctrinal orientations also dot the religious landscape in South Asia.

While mass education and print and information technologies have made it possible for people to access normative religious texts on their own, unaided by the 'ulama', and to compete with the 'ulama' in the production of religious discourse, the very same developments have also enabled the 'ulama' to disseminate their writings in new ways and to reach new audiences. Though many among the 'ulama' have resisted governmental efforts to open up their madrasas and related institutions to modern, secular learning, they have come to benefit from such learning as well. At Azhar University in Cairo, as Malika Zeghal has shown, the opening of new faculties devoted to the modern sciences has contributed to the ability of at least some 'ulama' to interact with greater facility with college- and university-educated Islamists than would otherwise have been the case. Some of the most influential of the contemporary 'ulama'—for example, Muhammad Taqi 'Uthmani (b. 1943) of Pakistan and the Egyptian religious scholar Yusuf al-Qaradawi (b. 1926), who moved to the oil-rich Persian Gulf emirate of Qatar in the early 1960s—have come to base their authority not only on a demonstrated mastery of the Islamic tradition but also on their putative ability to make it relevant to contemporary circumstances, which, in turn, is recognized as depending on their understanding of the modern world. The prominence Qaradawi enjoyed in the early years of the 21st century had to do, in considerable measure, with his dexterous use of the Internet and satellite television, together with the opportunities made available long ago by print, to reach multiple audiences well beyond the Arab Middle East.

Notwithstanding the challenges posed by the modern state to the autonomy of the 'ulama', the ability of individual governments to regulate their institutions has also varied significantly. There is a marked contrast, for instance, between successful governmental efforts toward integrating Islamic institutions of learning into the educational mainstream in Indonesia and the halting and far from effective attempts of successive Pakistani governments to do the same. In Egypt, for its part, the ability of an authoritarian regime to make Azhar University amenable to its will has come at the cost of having to cede oversight of the religious public sphere to it, sometimes at considerable international embarrassment to a regime keen to project a "liberal" image.

Fragmentation and Rearticulations of Authority

The discourses and practices of the 'ulama' have been subject to significant counter-vailing pressures in modern Islam, revealing—as might be expected for a still-active scholarly community with deep roots in history—elements of both continuity and change. In many cases, the most distinctive of their institutions, the *madhhab*, has tended to decline in terms of the authority it carries over the lives of the people, even as new institutions and practices have continued to emerge in efforts to stan-dardize belief and practice in new ways. For a millennium since their beginnings in the ninth century, the *madhhab*s have provided the normative legal framework in which the Sunnis (and Shi'is) have led their lives. Since the late 19th century, the 'ulama' tied to particular schools of law have been fiercely challenged by those who seek to base all belief and practice squarely on the foundational texts—the Qur'an and the normative example of the Prophet—as well as the practices of Islam's first generations (the *salaf*), rather than on the agreed-upon doctrines of the medieval schools. The Salafis, as these putative adherents of the forebears style themselves, have differed much among themselves. They include those who have sought to rethink particular norms in the conviction that "true" Islam, as enshrined in the Qur'an and the practices of the first Muslims, can be shown to be in much greater accord with modern liberal sensibilities than it is with traditional religious practices. But the Salafis also include those who reject a good deal of the ideas, practices, and institutions characteristic of the modern world on grounds of their perceived in-compatibility with the foundational texts. Either way, the Salafi view that Muslims should follow the unalloyed teachings of the foundational texts and the example of the pious forebears rather than the doctrines and hermeneutical approaches of the medieval schools of law has had considerable resonance in many Muslim circles, and it has done much to undermine the authority of the *madhhab*. So have the legislative initiatives of the modern state, given that modern Islamic legislation and codifications of the law have tended to draw on the resources of the schools of law as a whole rather than those limited to any particular *madhhab*.

It would nonetheless be an exaggeration to conclude that the schools of law have ceased to matter much in contemporary Islam. In some regions, notably South Asia, most Muslims still identify themselves as Hanafis—that is, as adherents of the Hanafi school of law; it is as Hanafi scholars that Deobandis, and many other Sunni scholars, articulate their claims to authority in this region. Even in contem-porary Saudi Arabia, a Salafi orientation toward the foundational texts tends to be combined with a continuing reliance on the norms of the Hanbali school of law. Yet the schools of law carry less overarching authority than they did a century ago, even in regions whose inhabitants continue to adhere to them, with the result that the 'ulama', whose authority was long tied to the *madhhab*, have had to look for alternative loci of authority.

These alternatives have assumed many forms, but common to them is the tendency toward a new institutionalization of authority. Building on previous juridical hierarchies, the Dar al-Ifta' al-Misriyya (the Egyptian Organization for Granting Legal Opinions) was established in Egypt in 1895 as a way of both standardizing the issuing of juridical opinions and giving them an official imprimatur. In India, the Deoband madrasa had established its own Dar al-Ifta' two years prior to the Egyptian namesake. In more recent decades, a number of "*fiqh* academies" have been established to provide forums for collective deliberation on matters of Islamic law (*fiqh*). Some, notably the International Islamic Fiqh Academy in Jeddah, Saudi Arabia (established in 1983 under the auspices of the Organization of the Islamic Conference), brings together scholars from the Muslim world at large. Others, such as India's Islamic Fiqh Academy (founded in 1989), are limited to one country, though it, too, seeks to foster ties with scholars elsewhere. More recent institutional ventures include the European Council for Fatwa and Research, founded in 1997 under the leadership of Qaradawi with a view to providing legal guidance to increasingly substantial numbers of Muslims living in Europe, as well as the International Union of Muslim Scholars, founded in 2004 with Qaradawi again as its founding president.

Though such institutions do not necessarily seek to supplant the *madhhab*—the Dar al-Ifta' of Deoband is the juridical arm of the Hanafi madrasa, and even members of transnational *fiqh* academies are not required to relinquish their legal affiliations—they do occupy some of the space that the school of law would have inhabited, and often still does, for its adherents. They are equally a facet of the increasing standardization of religious norms and practices that have been witnessed not just in Islam but also, as C. A. Bayly has observed, in many other religious traditions in the modern world. In medieval Islam the *madhhab*—and the expectation that all but the most distinguished jurists would adhere strictly to its established norms and methods (a practice known as *taqlīd*)—had itself represented efforts toward standardization of doctrine. While standardization and institutionalization are not new to the culture of the 'ulama', they have come to assume distinctive forms in the modern world.

Another expression of this standardization is an increasing interest in the idea of collective fatwas and, indeed, of "collective *ijtihād*." While *ijtihād* has long been viewed as the exercise of an individual jurist's mental faculties and legal acumen to arrive at new rulings on matters not hitherto regulated by the foundational texts, the 20th century has seen increasing initiatives toward making this a collective venture. In part, this is an effort to answer rhetorical objections of those among the 'ulama' who have long opposed *ijtihād* on the grounds both that their abilities did not match those of their incomparably more learned predecessors and that encouraging possibilities of *ijtihād* would open the door to willful manipulation of the sacred law in an age of rampant intellectual and moral decline. Against such objections, still not without resonance in particular circles, collective *ijtihād* offers the possibility of pooling together the resources of scholars who would supposedly be inadequate on their own but are more credible as a collective. By the same token, it is also a very visible effort to bring together traditionally educated religious scholars and "experts" in modern, secular domains, underscoring the oft-repeated claim that Islam can provide guidance on all matters, including those that go well beyond the traditional religious expertise of the 'ulama'. In recent years, particular regimes have also sought to encourage collective, quasi-official venues of fatwas as a means of reining in the diverse voices in the public sphere and, increasingly, in cyberspace.

Yet modern initiatives toward standardization and institutionalization— sometimes as a way of facilitating state regulation of Islam and sometimes as a way of resisting it—often exist side by side with an increasing fragmentation of authority, with the 'ulama''s assertions and interpretations being questioned by ever-increasing numbers of educated men and women in light of their own access to the foundational texts and their diverse bodies of knowledge. The 'ulama' themselves are to be found on both sides, sometimes simultaneously. Thus even as many jurists among them are part of institutional forums of collective *ijtihād* and of collective fatwas, some of the very same scholars continue to issue fatwas on their own individual authority as well. Standardization and institutionalization, on the one hand, and individualization and fragmentation, on the other, have continued to shape the discourses, practices, and institutions of the 'ulama' as well as their claims to authority. As much as they would have liked it to be the case, the 'ulama' of medieval Muslim societies were scarcely unchallenged in their claims to authority. Such challenges have only grown in range and intensity in modern and contemporary Islam. Yet they have not necessarily marginalized the 'ulama', and, in local, regional, and global contexts, many among them have continued to lay claim to, and not unsuccessfully compete with others for, authority and influence within and outside the religious sphere.

Further Reading

Khaled Abou El Fadl, *Rebellion and Violence in Islamic Law*, 2001; Aziz Ahmad, "The Role of Ulema in Indo-Muslim History," *Studia Islamica* 31 (1970); C. A. Bayly, *The Birth of the Modern World, 1780–1914*, 2004; Peri Bearman et al., eds., *The Islamic School of Law*, 2005; Jonathan Berkey, *The Formation of Islam*, 2003; Michael Cook, *Commanding Right and Forbidding Wrong in Islamic Thought*, 2000; Patricia Crone, *God's Rule: Government and Islam*, 2004; Patricia Crone and Martin Hinds, *God's Caliph: Religious Authority in the First Centuries of Islam*, 1986; Dale F. Eickelman and James Piscatori, *Muslim Politics*, 1996; Wael B. Hallaq, *The Origins and Evolution of Islamic Law*, 2005; Sherman Jackson, *Islamic Law and the State: The Constitutional Jurisprudence of Shihab al-din al-Qarafi*, 1996; George Makdisi, *The Rise of Colleges*, 1981; Barbara D. Metcalf, *Islamic Revival in British India: Deoband, 1860–1900*, 1982; Stefan Reichmuth, *The World of Murtada al-Zabidi (1732–91): Life, Networks and Writings*, 2009; Jakob Skovgaard-Petersen,

Defining Islam for the Egyptian State: Muftis and Fatwas of the Dār al-Iftā, 1997; Muhammad Qasim Zaman, "The Ulama and Contestations on Religious Authority," in *Islam and Modernity: Key Issues and Debates*, edited by M. K. Masud et al., 2009; Idem, *The Ulama in Contemporary Islam: Custodians of Change*, 2002; Malika Zeghal, *Gardiens de l'Islam: Les ulama d'al-Azhar dans l'Egypte contemporaine*, 1995; Madeline C. Zilfi, *The Politics of Piety: The Ottoman Ulema in the Post-Classical Age (1600–1800)*, 1988.

Women ◇◇

Ayesha S. Chaudhry

A look at Muslim historical sources illustrates that the role of gender in Islamic political thought has been varied and complicated. The complex relationship between gender and Islamic political thought will be considered here through a few snapshots: the Qur'an, female contemporaries of Muhammad, medieval Islamic scholarship, and modern Muslim women.

Women in the Qur'an

Several women are mentioned in the Qur'an, some of whom demonstrate a strong independent spirit. They are held responsible for their own salvation, apart from their husbands or male relatives. The stories of these women trump the patriarchal gender norms of a seventh-century Arabian context in which the Qur'an was purportedly revealed. Such women include Eve (Q. 20:117–23); the wives of Noah, Lot, and Pharaoh (Q. 66:10–12); Sarah, the wife of Abraham (Q. 11:71–73; 51:29–30); Moses's mother (Q. 28:7, 13) and sister (28:10–11); Potiphar's wife (Q. 12:23–32); and Mary, the mother of Jesus (Q. 19). All references to these women are made through their relations to the central male figures in their lives, be they husbands, fathers, sons, or brothers. Mary is the only woman who is mentioned by name in the Qur'an and has a chapter named after her.

The story of the Queen of Sheba is especially noteworthy, since she represents the only positive, nonmonotheistic model of political leadership in the Qur'an (27:15–44). Although the Queen of Sheba is never mentioned by name in the Qur'an, she is identified by her political role as a ruler whose power rivaled that of the prophet and king Solomon. She was the queen of a people called "Saba" (Sheba), a prosperous nation of sun worshipers. All descriptions of the Queen in the Qur'an are salutary; her wisdom and power are highlighted in the story through her pragmatic, diplomatic, and consultative leadership. In the Qur'anic story, the queen's encounter with Solomon occurs in the context of an aggressive unilateral threat delivered by Solomon's avian emissary, named Hudhud. In the missive, Solomon announced the oneness of God and called the queen to submit through Solomon to this God ("Do not exalt yourselves against me and come to me in submission," Q. 27:31). Contrary to her chieftains' counsel favoring military confrontation, the queen opted to pursue diplomatic negotiations with Solomon by offering him gifts. When Solomon rejected these gifts, seeing them as an insult, and then threatened war, the queen visited Solomon personally. After a series of interactions, in which she passed a test devised by Solomon, she successfully avoided war by submitting, not *to* Solomon as he had suggested, but *with* him, to the "Lord of the worlds" (Q. 27:44). While the story of the Queen of Sheba is powerful and meaningful for modern Muslim political thought, its meaning and significance were contested in medieval Qur'anic exegesis.

Although the Qur'an can be seen as challenging patriarchal gender norms through the example of the earlier-mentioned women, it also can be seen as confirming these norms through other stories (e.g., Q. 60) and through its legal dictates. Qur'anic legal verses dealing with marital discord (Q. 4:34), polygamy (Q. 4:3), the higher rank of men over women (Q. 2:228), and women's testimony (Q. 2:282) establish an asymmetrical relationship between men and women in both private and public spheres. Premodern Muslim scholars regularly cited such verses to limit women's participation in the public sphere and the political process. At the same time, the Qur'an speaks of the spiritual equality of believing men and women (Q. 33:35), promising them similar rewards in the hereafter. While some verses suggest that women become polluted during menstruation (Q. 2:222), other verses warn against devaluing the birth of a daughter over that of a son (Q. 16:58–59) and condemn female infanticide (Q. 81:8–9).

Another complex set of verses, which have become highly politicized in contemporary Muslim thought, revolve around the seclusion of women and the appropriate attire when they are in public spaces. One verse in the Qur'an commands Muhammad's wives to "stay in [their] homes" and not to make a "dazzling display" of themselves, a practice that the verse associates with the pre-Islamic "time of ignorance" (*jāhiliyya*; Q. 33:33). The believers are further instructed to speak to Muhammad's wives from behind a screen (*ḥijāb*; Q. 33:53). Muhammad's wives, daughters, and "believing women" are also instructed to "draw their outer garments [sing. *jilbāb*] over their person" when in public in order to be both "recognized" and to avoid being molested (Q. 33:59). The Qur'anic text also exhorts both men and women to observe modesty but further specifies that believing women should "draw their veils [sing. *khimār*] over their bosoms" and "not display their beauty except that which is apparent" (Q. 24:30–31). Although these verses do not provide specific instructions about what Muslim women should wear, or which parts of their body they should cover, medieval Muslim exegetes and jurists concluded that it was obligatory for a Muslim woman to cover her entire body, including, in most cases, her face. In practice, however, the dress code of Muslim women has varied significantly in different social, cultural, and historic moments, where social and economic factors have played a significant role in the determination of women's public attire.

Muhammad's Contemporaries: Wives and Companions

The independent personalities of women who appear in the Qur'an are reflected in the stories of early Muslim women as recorded in Islamic history. Muhammad's wives played key political roles during the lifetime of Muhammad and the early generations of Islam. His first wife, Khadija, was the first convert to Islam and helped launch his prophetic career through tangible social, economic, and political support. Muhammad was monogamous during his marriage to Khadija, though he was continuously polygamous after her death. Muhammad regularly consulted his wives about political affairs, most famously taking the advice of Umm Salama (d. ca. 680) about how to lead his community after concluding the treaty of Hudaybiyya (628). Muhammad's youngest wife, 'A'isha (d. 678), became intellectually and politically active after his death. She is responsible for the transmission of the second largest number of prophetic traditions in Sunni hadith literature. She publicly condemned the policies and person of the third caliph, 'Uthman b. 'Affan (ca. 579–656), and fought against his successor, 'Ali b. Abi Talib (d. 661). 'A'isha personally led an army of 3,000 against 'Ali but lost to him in the Battle of the Camel (656). She had a contentious relationship with Muhammad's daughter Fatima (d. 633), who was married to 'Ali. Fatima, the mother of Muhammad's grandsons Hasan (d. 669) and Husayn (d. 680), is highly venerated by both Sunnis and Shi'is, although Shi'is have a special reverence for her.

'A'isha's leadership of a military campaign was unique, though women were regularly present on the battlefield. Several female Companions of Muhammad fought alongside men, including Nusayba bt. Ka'b, who is credited with saving Muhammad's life several times during the Battle of Uhud (625). Women also played key roles in the transmission of the Qur'an. Hafsa (d. 665), Muhammad's widow and the daughter of the second caliph, 'Umar b. al-Khattab (ca. 580–644), was instrumental in the transmission of the text of the Qur'an. The Qur'anic text itself formalized the inclusion of women into the religious-political community of early Muslims by citing the specific words that women spoke when taking an oath of allegiance (*bay'a*) to Muhammad (Q. 60:12). Even though the words of the oath highlight the gendered responsibilities of women, focusing on the control of sexuality ("You will not commit adultery or kill your children"), it is nevertheless significant that women were required to state their independent fealty to Muhammad and the community of believers.

The role of women in the mosque was contested in the early Muslim community and reflected the tension surrounding women's political leadership. The mosque in the early Muslim community was more than a religious center. It was also a center of communal life, political administration, and adjudication. The fact that Muhammad appointed Abu Bakr to lead the prayer in the mosque as Muhammad lay on his deathbed was used by Abu Bakr's supporters to legitimate his political succession to Muhammad and reign as the first caliph. By the same token, it is significant that Muhammad appointed a person to chant the call for prayer (*mu'adhdhin*) for the household of Umm Waraqa, who, for her part, led her household in prayer. In the contemporary period, much has been made of whether this represents Muhammad's approval of women-led prayer. At the heart of the debate is whether Umm Waraqa was given a special dispensation to lead her specific mixed-gender household or if her example points to a general permission for women to lead men in prayer.

The debate in the early community about women's political participation was reflected in the imposition and removal of a physical gender barrier in the mosque. 'Umar instituted a gender-segregating barrier in the mosque in Medina and reportedly discouraged women from regularly attending the mosque for prayers. 'Uthman removed the barrier upon assuming power. Despite 'Umar's general attitude of discouraging women from participating in the mosque, women still played a public and political role during his reign. For instance, while delivering a Friday sermon, 'Umar proposed limiting the acceptable dower (*mahr*) that could be offered to wives in marriage, and a woman stood up to interrupt him. She challenged his proposition by citing a verse in the Qur'an that makes it acceptable to offer wives a "heap of gold" (Q. 4:20) as *mahr*. 'Umar responded to this by saying, "The woman is right and 'Umar is wrong." Despite 'Umar's strong desire for gender segregation, during his rule a woman was able to challenge and prevail against the caliph's proposition.

In modern conversations about women's political leadership, a particular tradition attributed to Muhammad has become especially controversial. Muhammad is reported to have said, "Never shall a folk prosper who delegate their affairs to a woman." Although this report seems to contradict the Qur'anic story of the Queen of Sheba, whose people were prosperous, it has been used in multiple ways to argue against women's political and religious leadership. It has also been used to caution against the use of overtly misogynistic prophetic reports when determining the role of women in contemporary Muslim society. The feminist scholar Fatima Mernissi used this prophetic report to advocate for increased text criticism of prophetic reports, while Mohammad Fadel, a professor at the University of Toronto, used this same report to promote "hermeneutical historicism" as the primary approach to deal with traditional texts that appear ethically problematic at first glance.

Women in Medieval Islam

Women's political and religious authority was restricted in the medieval period, especially as compared to their role in early Islam. Leila Ahmed, a pioneer in the field of gender studies in Islamic studies, has shown that scholars in the medieval period were almost entirely male and were products of their sociohistorical context. They produced Qur'anic exegesis and Islamic legal works that reinstituted existing patriarchal norms and, in many cases, expanded the patriarchy of the Qur'anic text to map onto their own patriarchal contexts. Consequently, discussions of female political authority assumed that women should not hold political positions due to what were seen as their physical and intellectual deficiencies. The discussion of essential gender differences often echoed and borrowed from the thought of Hellenistic philosophers and sometimes reflected Aristotelian understandings of gender as differentiated by temperatures of "hot" and "cold."

Women's position in the medieval public sphere was challenged in several ways. Their access to political leadership was disputed through the hadith, which warned against delegating the affairs of the community to a woman. The potential for women to serve as caliph was uniformly denied in Islamic law, though their role as judges was more contested. Karen Bauer's work on the debate regarding female judges illustrates the predominant thought on women's leadership in the medieval period. Most Sunni jurists prohibited women from being judges, although some Hanafi and Maliki jurists allowed women to adjudicate in civil cases. The opposition against female judges was based on four broad arguments. Two of the arguments were based on Qur'anic texts, one on a prophetic tradition, and one on a social argument. The Qur'anic text arguments used 4:34's assertion that "men are in authority (*qawwāmūn*) over women because God has preferred (*faḍḍala*) some over others" to argue that women could not be in a position of authority over men because God preferred men to women and gave them authority over women. The second Qur'anic text used in these discussions was 2:282, which states that the testimony of one male is equivalent to that of two women, particularly in financial transactions. The text was interpreted to mean that because the testimony of two women was equivalent to the testimony of one man, women could not adequately judge the testimony of men. The prophetic report used to limit women's authority was the one warning against a woman leading a community. Finally, the social argument against female judges was that being a judge would allow women to interact with men, which could only result in social and sexual chaos.

These scholarly debates aside, there are some examples of female judges in the medieval period. One of them was the mother of the Abbasid caliph Muqtadir (d. 932), who held a weekly court in the tenth century. There are also some examples of female rulers of Muslim empires, such as Razia Sultana (d. 1240), ruler of the sultanate of Delhi in India, and the Mamluk queen Shajarat al-Durr (d. 1259) in Egypt. Additionally, despite the arguments regarding women's intellectual weaknesses, several Muslim women gained prominence as religious teachers and scholars in Muslim history. Some of them reached the highest level of spiritual authority, such as Rabi'a al-Basri and Ibn al-'Arabi's (d. 1240) female teacher Fatima bt. al-Muthanna. In the traditional sciences, Umm Hani (d. 1466) is an example of an acclaimed teacher who taught men multiple subjects including grammar, history, and hadith studies. Recent studies have detailed the lives of such female figures who appear in the written works of male scholars. One fecund genre for such study is biographical literature, where female figures appear as noteworthy scholarly figures. Research conducted by Ruth Roded, Marilyn Booth, and Devin J. Stewart shows that even though the number of these women is small, especially in comparison to the male scholars cited in the biographical literature, it is nevertheless important that female scholars were able to attain scholarly prominence in patriarchal contexts, where the education of women was not the norm.

Modern Muslim Women

The relationship between women and political authority in the modern period is embedded in the discourse of colonialism. Since the encounter of much of the Muslim world with modernity coincided with the economic and political project of Western colonialism, the two have become intertwined in popular Muslim imagination. To compound the issue, a major moral argument in support of colonialism was the emancipation of Muslim women from the oppression of Muslim men. Colonists such as Lord Cromer (d. 1917) in Egypt championed the cause of Muslim women by encouraging unveiling, while at the same time restricting their participation in the public sphere to roles he considered especially suited for women, such as midwifery as opposed to medicine. Such disingenuous rhetoric for female emancipation on the part of the colonists (Cromer having also headed the antisuffragist movement in Britain) tended to tie the feminist movement to the colonial enterprise such that advocating for feminist causes became tantamount to supporting colonialism. As a result, women's public and political participation in the modern world is fraught with postcolonial trauma.

Still, the 20th and 21st centuries have witnessed several feminist movements in the Muslim world. In Egypt women have been increasingly active members of society and politics; they played key roles in anticolonialist movements and participated in the public discourse regarding the creation of a postcolonial nationalist identity. Women began working in and contributing to newspapers in the late 19th century, and by the early 20th century, women's journals, such as *Al-'Afaf* (Honor) and *Fatat al-Sharq* (Women of the east), began to appear alongside feminist organizations such as the Society for the Advancement of Women, the Intellectual Association of Egyptian Women, and the Egyptian Feminist Union. Women collaborated with male politicians, and they participated in demonstrations and riots alongside men, though Egyptian women were not given the vote until 1957 when Rawya 'Atiya (d. 1997), the first female member of parliament in the Arab world, was elected. Egyptian political and feminist movements were sometimes spearheaded by secular feminists such as Huda Sha'rawi (d. 1947) and Saiza Nabarawi (d. 1985), who were comfortable using both Egyptian and Western ideas to fight for Egyptian women's rights. Other, more conservative feminists also emerged, such as Malak Hifni Nassef (d. 1918) and Zainab al-Ghazali (d. 2005), who were more interested in developing an Egyptian Islamic feminism that was independent of Western influence. 'A'isha 'Abd al-Rahman (d. 1996), who wrote under the pen name Bint Shati', became the first female to write a commentary on the Qur'an.

In the modern period, "Muslim women" as an abstract, essentialized entity has become a measuring stick for "progress" as well as an embodiment of "authentic"

Islamic values. Western political rhetoric often cites the treatment of Muslim women to argue for the "progress" or "backwardness" of Muslim-majority countries. The view that Afghan women were oppressed and in need of saving played an important role in the moral rationale for the American invasion of Afghanistan in 2001. Muslim political movements and governments likewise use the concept of the "ideal" Muslim woman to evaluate the influence of either "Westernization" or "authentic" Islamic values. In Afghanistan, the Taliban used their treatment of Afghan women as the physical embodiment of their version of "authentic" Islam. In this way, Afghan women were used by both the Taliban and the U.S. government to project varied images of themselves; the Taliban used women's bodies to demonstrate their commitment to a pure, unadulterated Islam, while the U.S. government used the image of these same women to establish their commitment to human rights.

Simplified constructions of "the veil" offer a useful example of the politicization of Muslim women. Many governments have used the veil to demonstrate their own commitment to either Islamic piety or secular values. In Saudi Arabia, for instance, Islamic law is interpreted as requiring women in public to cover their entire bodies with a loose robe (*'abāya*), and women are usually expected to cover their faces by wearing a face veil (*niqāb*). In Iran, women must similarly cover their entire bodies, but the *niqāb* is not required. Whereas women are required to dress in a concealing manner in Saudi Arabia and Iran as a sign of the country's fidelity to Islamic law, France prohibits women from dressing in this manner, making the face veil a punishable offense, as a sign of that country's commitment to secular values. A similar debate took place in Canada's province of Quebec, where Bill 94 proposed to deny women who chose to wear the *niqāb* access to public services. In both cases, a key argument was that the *niqāb*, even when worn by choice, subjugated Muslim women, who needed to demonstrate their belief in gender equity, assimilation, and liberal democracy by renouncing certain types of dress. In Turkey the head scarf is officially banned in public settings, though the ban is not strictly enforced, and the head scarf is seen as a litmus test for one's religiosity and commitment to secularism. The method of gauging women's freedom and independence as directly proportional to how much they are covered was called into question by the mass demonstrations in 2011 in Egypt, Libya, Bahrain, and Yemen, wherein veiled and nonveiled women have played and continue to play key public roles.

Stereotypical images of women and gender in Muslim societies do little to capture their complexity or shed light on the meaning of women's increasing visibility in the public spheres for evolving understandings of Islam. Some Muslim women have become highly visible in the politics of postcolonial nation-states. The Muslim-majority countries of Indonesia, Pakistan, Bangladesh, and Turkey have democratically elected female presidents and prime ministers in the past three decades. Muslim women are also active in other political and public offices in many Muslim-majority countries. Some Muslim countries have designated a specific number of seats for women in their houses of parliament. Such countries include Afghanistan, Bangladesh, Egypt, Iraq, Jordan, Morocco, Pakistan, and Syria.

Yet important as they are, such examples do not necessarily reflect an egalitarian shift in modern Islamic discourse. Just as patriarchal norms did not necessarily translate into the obliteration of the possibility of female leadership, observed female political and religious authority does not translate into egalitarian religious norms. However, the contrast between normative texts and social values in the modern period has led to a contestation of religious authority. In the case of gender, egalitarian social and political Muslim values are fundamentally at odds with inherited patriarchal norms. This discord gives rise to what can be called the egalitarian-authoritarian paradox. The paradox is that religious authority is gained by connecting oneself to the inherited tradition. This means that those who support a gender-egalitarian vision of Islam compromise their religious legitimacy if they break from the patriarchal tradition. However, if they root themselves in the inherited patriarchal tradition, they must compromise their commitment to gender egalitarianism and opt for the gender complementarity model at the expense of gender equality.

Muslim women are beginning to reclaim religious authority amid this dilemma by both breaking from the patriarchal tradition and simultaneously insisting on their religious legitimacy. An example of this was the 2005 mixed-gender Friday prayer led by Amina Wadud in New York City. Recognizing that leading men and women in prayer represents religious, political, and social authority, Wadud attempted to reclaim women's authority in Islam by leading men and women in ritual prayer. Although females had led the Friday prayer before, most notably in South Africa, the New York City prayer elicited responses from scholars and leaders across the globe. Most condemned the prayer, while others, such as Khaled Abou El Fadl and Abdennur Prado of the Catalonian Islamic Board, issued opinions of wholehearted support. Shaykh 'Ali Goma'a of Azhar University in Cairo issued a fatwa that appeared to support the prayer, but he later clarified that he was only recounting the positions of some historical scholars who approved of female-led prayer and that none sanctioned a woman leading the Friday prayer. Whatever the particular reactions to the prayer, the event changed the discourse of gender in Islam by forcing a conversation in liberal and conservative circles alike about female religious and political authority. Issues of women's leadership are at the heart of modern Muslim discourse in the contemporary period and will help determine the future direction of Muslim communities.

Further Reading

N. Abbott, *Two Queens of Baghdad: Mother and Wife of Harun al-Rashid*, 1946; L. Ahmed, *Women and Gender in Islam*, 1992; K. Ali, *Sexual Ethics and Islam*, 2006; K. Bauer, "Debates on Women's Status as Judges and Witnesses in Post-formative Islamic Law," *Journal of the American Oriental Society* 130, no. 1 (2010): 1–21; J. P. Berkey, *The Transmission of Knowledge in Medieval Cairo: A Social History of Islamic Education*, 1992; M. Booth, *May Her Likes Be Multiplied: Biography and Gender Politics in Egypt*, 2001; A. Chaudhry,

"The Ethics of Marital Discipline in Pre-Modern Qur'anic Exegesis," *Journal of the Society of Christian Ethics* 30, no. 2 (2010): 123–30; M. Fadel, "Is Historicism a Valid Strategy for Islamic Law Reform? The Case of 'Never Shall a Folk Prosper Who Have Appointed a Woman to Rule Them,'" *Islamic Law and Society* 18 (2011): 131–76; F. Malti-Douglas, *Woman's Body, Woman's Word*, 1991; F. Mernissi, *Beyond the Veil: Male-Female Dynamics in Modern Muslim Society*, 1987; Idem, *The Forgotten Queens of Islam*, 1993; R. Roded, *Women and Islam in the Middle East*, 2008; D. Stewart, "Women's Biographies in Islamic Societies: Mirza Abd Allah al-Isfahani's Riyad al-Ulama," in *Biography in the Middle East*, edited by Louise Marlowe, forthcoming; A. Wadud, *Inside the Gender Jihad: Women's Reform in Islam*, 2006.

Contributors ◇◇◇

Gerhard Bowering
Professor of Religious Studies and Islamic Studies, Yale University

Ayesha S. Chaudhry
Assistant Professor of Islamic Studies and Gender Studies, University of
British Columbia

Patricia Crone
Andrew W. Mellon Professor, Institute for Advanced Study (Princeton, NJ)

Roxanne Euben
Ralph Emerson and Alice Freeman Palmer Professor of Political Science,
Wellesley College

Yohanan Friedmann
Max Schloessinger Professor Emeritus of Islamic Studies, Hebrew University
of Jerusalem

Paul L. Heck
Associate Professor of Islamic Studies, Georgetown University

Roy Jackson
Course Leader in Religion, Philosophy, and Ethics, University of
Gloucestershire (England)

Wadad Kadi
Avalon Foundation Distinguished Service Professor of Islamic Studies,
University of Chicago

John Kelsay
Richard L. Rubenstein Professor of Religion and Bristol Distinguished
Professor of Ethics, Florida State University

Gudrun Krämer
Director of the Institute of Islamic Studies, Free University of Berlin
(Germany)

Ebrahim Moosa
Professor of Religious and Islamic Studies, Duke University

Armando Salvatore
Associate Professor of Sociology of Culture and Communciation, University
of Naples–L'Orientale (Italy)

Aram A. Shahin
James Madison University

Emad El-Din Shahin
Professor of Public Policy and Administration, American University in Cairo

Devin J. Stewart
Associate Professor of Arabic and Islamic Studies, Emory University

SherAli Tareen
Franklin and Marshall College

Muhammad Qasim Zaman
Robert H. Niehaus '77 Professor of Near Eastern Studies and Religion,
Princeton University

Index